# The Mortgage Encyclopedia

# The Mortgage Encyclopedia

## An Authoritative Guide to Mortgage Programs, Practices, Prices, and Pitfalls

## Jack Guttentag
### "The Mortgage Professor"

**McGraw-Hill**
New York  Chicago  San Francisco  Lisbon
London  Madrid  Mexico City  Milan  New Delhi
San Juan  Seoul  Singapore  Sydney  Toronto

The *McGraw·Hill* Companies

2 3 4 5 6 7 8 9 0 DOC/DOC 0 9 8 7 6 5 4

ISBN 0-07-142165-3

Editorial and production services provided by CWL Publishing Enterprises, Inc., Madison, Wisconsin, www.cwlpub.com.

This publication is designed to provide accurate and authoritative information in regard to the subject matter covered. It is sold with the understanding that neither the author nor the publisher is engaged in rendering legal, accounting, or other professional service. If legal advice or other expert assistance is required, the services of a competent professional person should be sought.
—*From a Declaration of Principles jointly adopted by a Committee of the American Bar Association and a Committee of Publishers*

McGraw-Hill books are available at special quantity discounts to use as premiums and sales promotions, or for use in corporate training programs. For more information, please write to the Director of Special Sales, McGraw-Hill, 2 Penn Plaza, New York, NY 10121-2298. Or contact your local bookstore.

 This book is printed on recycled, acid-free paper containing a minimum of 50% recycled de-inked fiber.

# Topics

## O

## P

# Introduction

For all practical purposes, I began writing this book in 1998 when I started writing a weekly newspaper column on mortgages that was syndicated by Inman. In 1999, I started www.mtgprofessor.com, which pulled the columns together, and added calculators, spreadsheets, and other materials including a way for readers to send me questions. I spent a lot of time organizing these materials into a coherent structure, and my thinking about a book version posited a similar organization.

For that reason, when Richard Narramore of McGraw-Hill approached me about preparing a book organized in an encyclopedia format, I resisted. But Richard was persistent, and I began to reconsider. Although I liked the organization on my Web site, I was forced to admit that my readers had a lot of trouble with it. About a third of my replies to those who wrote me consisted of referrals to the Web pages where the answer to their questions would be found.

Many of the questions I receive from consumers reflect what they have been told by loan officers and mortgage brokers, who don't think about mortgages the way I do. As one example, a mortgage contract may have a provision that allows the borrower to pay only the interest for some period—"interest-only." Any mortgage, whether it is fixed rate or adjustable rate, can have such a provision. It is an option. But that is not the way it is marketed. Loan officers and mortgage brokers sell it as a special kind of mortgage, as if there were fixed-rate, adjustable rate, and interest-only mortgages. Then their customers may write me to ask about the advantages and disadvantages of interest-only mortgages compared to those other types. While this question makes no sense, those who ask it need to learn, with the least expenditure of time and effort, why it makes no sense.

The encyclopedia A to Z format turns out to be an efficient way to convey this information, avoiding conflict between the way I perceive a problem and the way many readers perceive it. I see interest-only as an option, many readers see it as a type of mortgage, but we can both agree that in an encyclopedia it appears under "I."

I'm known as "The Mortgage Professor." Often in this book I refer to my Web site, **www.mtgprofessor.com**, where you'll find backup information, mortgage calculators, and more to help you make the best decisions about financing or refinancing your real estate.

# Acknowledgments

Much of what I know about the home mortgage market I learned from the 25,000 or so borrowers who have e-mailed questions and comments to me over the last six years. A number of loan officers and mortgage brokers have also contributed to my education, often by being combative, occasionally for good reason. Catherine Coy, who brokers in Los Angeles, has been particularly helpful in improving my understanding of what goes on in the mortgage trenches. My wife Doris has been quietly supportive, as she has been throughout the best years of my life.

—Jack Guttentag

# The Mortgage Encyclopedia

**A-Credit**  *A borrower with the best credit rating, deserving of the lowest prices that lenders offer.*

Most lenders require a FICO score above 720. *See **Credit Score/Use of FICO Scores by Lenders***. There is seldom any payoff for being above the A-credit threshold, but you pay a penalty for being below it.

---

**Acceleration Clause**  *A contractual provision that gives the lender the right to demand repayment of the entire loan balance in the event that the borrower violates one or more clauses in the note.*

Such clauses may include sale of the property, failure to make timely payments, or provision of false information.

I have never seen a note that did not have such a clause. Borrowers need not concern themselves with it except where the lender has discretion to exercise it without conditions. This would be referred to as a "demand feature," and it would be flagged on the Truth in Lending Disclosure Statement. If that statement shows "This loan has a Demand Feature...," the note should be read with care. *See **Demand Clause***.

---

**Accrued Interest**  *Interest that is earned but not paid, adding to the amount owed.*

For example, if the monthly interest due on a loan is $600 and the borrower pays only $500, $100 is added to the amount owed by the borrower. The $100 is the accrued interest. On a mortgage, accrued interest is usually referred to as **Negative Amortization**.

---

**Adjustable Rate Mortgage (ARM)**  *A mortgage on which the interest rate can be changed by the lender.*

While ARM contracts in many countries abroad allow rate changes at the lender's discretion (**Discretionary ARMs**), in the U.S. rate changes on ARMs are mechanical. They are based on changes in an interest rate index over which the lender has no control. Henceforth, all references are to such **Indexed ARMs**.

***Reasons for Selecting an ARM:*** Borrowers may select an ARM in preference to a fixed rate mortgage (FRM) for three reasons:

- To qualify: they need an ARM to qualify for the loan they want.
- To take advantage of low initial rates on ARMs and their own short time horizon: they expect to be out of their house before the initial rate period ends.
- To gamble on future interest rates: they expect that they will pay less on the ARM over the life of the loan and are prepared to take the risk that rising interest rates will cause them to pay more.

I will return to these reasons later.

***How the Interest Rate on an ARM Is Determined:*** There are two phases in the life of an ARM. During the first phase, the interest rate is fixed, just as it is on an FRM. The difference is that on an FRM the rate is fixed for the term of the loan, whereas on an ARM it is fixed for a shorter period. The period ranges from one month to 10 years.

At the end of the initial rate period, the ARM rate is adjusted. The adjustment rule is that the new rate will equal the most recent value of a specified interest rate index, plus a margin. For example, if the index is 5% when the initial rate period ends, and the margin is 2.75%, the new rate will be 7.75%. The rule, however, is subject to two conditions.

The first condition is that the increase from the previous rate cannot exceed any rate adjustment cap specified in the ARM contract. An adjustment cap, usually 1% or 2% but ranging in some cases up to 5%, limits the size of any interest rate change.

The second condition is that the new rate cannot exceed the contractual maximum rate. Maximum rates are usually five or six percentage points above the initial rate.

During the second phase of an ARM's life, the interest rate is adjusted periodically. This period may or may not be the same as the initial rate period. For example, an ARM with an initial rate period of five years might adjust annually or monthly after the five-year period ends.

***The Quoted Interest Rate:*** The rate that is quoted on an ARM, by the media and by loan providers, is the initial rate—regardless of how long that rate lasts. When the initial rate period is short, the quoted rate is a poor indication of interest cost to the borrower. The only significance of the initial rate on a monthly ARM, for example, is that this rate may be used to calculate the initial payment. *See **How the Monthly Payment on an ARM Is Determined***.

***The Fully Indexed Rate:*** The index plus margin is called the "fully indexed rate," or FIR. The FIR based on the most recent value of the index at the time the loan is taken out indicates where the ARM rate may go when the initial rate period ends. If the index rate does not change, the FIR will become the ARM rate.

For example, assume the initial rate is 4% for one year, the fully indexed rate is 7%, and the rate adjusts every year subject to a 1% rate increase cap. If the index value remains the same, the 7% FIR will be reached at the end of the third year.

The FIR is thus an important piece of information, the more so the shorter the initial rate period. Nevertheless, it is not a mandated disclosure and loan officers may not have it. They will know the margin and the specific index, however, and the most recent value of the index can be found on the Internet, as explained below.

***ARM Rate Indexes:*** Every ARM is tied to an interest rate index. An index has three relevant features:

- Availability
- Level
- Volatility

All the common ARM indexes are readily available from a published source, with the exception of one called the *Cost of Savings Index, or COSI.* I would avoid it.

In principle, a lower index is better for a borrower than a higher one. However, lenders take account of different index levels in setting the margin. A 3% index with a 2% margin provides the same FIR as a 2% index with a 3% margin. Assuming volatility is the same, there is nothing to choose between them.

An index that is relatively stable is better for the borrower than one that is volatile. The stable index will increase less in a rising rate environment. While it will also decline less in a declining rate environment, borrowers can take advantage of declining rates by refinancing.

The most stable of the more widely-used rate indexes is the 11th District Cost of Funds Index, referred to as COFI (not "coffee"). Most of the others are significantly more volatile. These include the Treasury series of constant (one-, two-, or three-year) maturity, one-month and six-month Libor, six-month CDs and the Prime Rate.

Another series known as MTA is a 12-month moving average of the one-year Treasury constant maturity series. MTA is a little more volatile than COFI but less volatile than the other series.

An ARM should never be selected based on the index alone. That would be like buying a car based on the tires. But if an overall evaluation (see below) indicates that two ARMs are very close, preference could be given to the one with the more stable index.

Current and historical values of major ARM indexes can be found on the following Web sites: mortgage-x.com, bankrate.com, nfsn.com, and hsh.com.

**How the Monthly Payment on an ARM Is Determined:** ARMs fall into two major groups that differ in the way in which the monthly payment of principal and interest is determined: fully amortizing ARMs and negative amortization ARMs.

*Fully Amortizing ARMs* adjust the monthly payment to be fully amortizing whenever the interest rate changes. The new payment will pay off the loan over the period remaining to term if the interest rate stays the same.

For example, a $100,000 30-year ARM has an initial rate of 5%, which holds for five years, after which the rate is adjusted every year. (This is referred to as a "5/1 ARM.") The payment of $536.83 for the first five years would pay off the loan if the rate stayed at 5%. In month 61, the rate might increase to, say, 7%. A new payment of $649.03 is then calculated, at 7% and 25 years, which would pay off the loan if the rate stayed at 7%. As the rate changes each year thereafter, a new payment is calculated that would pay off the loan over the remaining period if that rate continued.

*Negative Amortization ARMs* allow payments that don't fully cover the interest. They have one or more of the following features:

- **Payment Rate Below the Interest Rate:** The payment rate, which is the interest rate used to calculate the payment, may be below the actual interest rate. If the payment rate is so low that the initial payment does not cover the interest, the result will be negative amortization.

- **More Frequent Rate Adjustments than Payment Adjustments:** If, e.g., the rate adjusts every month but the payment adjusts every year, a large rate increase within the year will lead to negative amortization.

- **Payment Adjustment Caps:** If a rate change is large and a payment adjustment cap limits the size of a change in payment, the result will be negative amortization.

Virtually all ARMs are designed to fully amortize over their term. This means that negative amortization can only be temporary and at some point or points in the ARM's life history the monthly payment must become fully amortizing.

Two contract provisions are used to assure that negative amortization ARMs pay off at term.

- A recast clause requires that periodically, usually every five years, the payment must be adjusted to the fully amortizing level.

- A negative amortization cap is a maximum ratio of loan balance to original loan amount, for example, 110%. If that maximum is reached, the payment is immediately adjusted to the fully amortizing level, overriding any payment adjustment cap. In a worse case scenario, the required payment increase may be very large.

**Identifying ARMs:** There are no industry standards for identifying ARMs and practices vary across lenders. Some identify their ARMs by the index used, e.g., "COFI ARM" or "six-month Libor ARM."

Some identify their ARMs by the rate adjustment periods, e.g., "5/1" or "3/3."

None of these shorthand descriptions are of much use to borrowers because there are so many differences within each. Indeed, even if the features of each were standardized, to compare one type of ARM with another, one needs to know exactly what those features are.

***Selecting an ARM to Qualify:*** It is easier to qualify with an ARM than with an FRM. In deciding whether an applicant has enough income to meet the monthly payment obligation, lenders usually use the initial interest rate on an ARM to calculate the payment, even though the rate may rise at the end of the initial rate period.

That's why, when market interest rates increase, ARMs become more common and FRMs less common. Some borrowers who could have qualified with an FRM at the lower rates, now require an ARM to qualify.

However, many borrowers who appear to require an ARM to qualify in fact could qualify with an FRM. It just takes a little more work. *See* **Qualification/*Meeting Income Requirements*/Is an ARM Need to Qualify?**

***Taking Advantage of Low Initial Rates:*** Borrowers with short time horizons can take advantage of the initial interest rates that are lower on ARMs than on FRMs. For example, at a time when a borrower is quoted 6.5% on a 30-year FRM, the quoted initial rates on 3/1, 5/1, 7/1, and 10/1 ARMs might be 6%, 6.125%, 6.25%, and 6.375%, respectively.

The correct choice depends on how long the borrower expects to have the loan and on the borrower's attitude to risk. For example, a borrower who expects to hold the mortgage for six years might play it safe by selecting a 7/1. Or, he might take the 5/1 on the grounds that the savings over five years justifies taking the risk of having to pay a higher rate in year six.

Borrowers who take this risk, whether deliberately as in the example above, or inadvertently because they aren't sure how long they will hold the loan, should consider what can happen at the end of the initial rate period. Suppose the borrower deciding between the 5/1 and 7/1, for example, finds that the indexes, margins, and maximum rates are the same, but the rate adjustment caps are 2% on the

5/1 and 5% on the 7/1. This could tilt the decision toward the 5/1.

If the ARMs being compared differ in a number of ways, however, comparing one with another (or with an FRM) can be very confusing. In this situation, borrowers with short time horizons seeking to take advantage of low initial rates on ARMs are no different than borrowers with longer horizons who seek to pay less on the ARM over the life of the loan and are prepared to take the risk that they will pay more. Both should analyze the potential benefits and risks with calculators, as explained below.

***Gambling on Future Interest Rates:*** Taking an ARM (when an FRM is an option) is a gamble, and the question is whether it is a good gamble in any particular case. A good gamble is one where the borrower can reasonably expect that the **Interest Cost** (IC) will be lower on the ARM than on a comparable FRM over the period the mortgage is held; and where the borrower won't face extreme hardship if interest rates explode.

There are four calculators on my Web site designed to deal with these issues. Two of them, 9a) and 9b), show IC over periods specified by the user. Two others, 7c) and 7d), show mortgage payments month by month. For both IC and payments, one calculator is for ARMs that allow negative amortization and one is for ARMs that don't.

***Information Needed:*** All the calculators require the following information about each ARM:

**Basic Loan Information**

- New loan amount or existing loan balance (e.g., 100,000)
- Initial interest rate on new loan or current rate on existing loan (e.g., 7.50)
- New loan term or remaining term on existing loan, in months (e.g., 360)

**Interest Rate Index**

- Selected index, e.g., 11th district cost of funds or "COFI"
- Margin that is added to interest rate index (e.g., 2.75)

7

## First Rate Adjustment

- Number of months to first rate adjustment (e.g,. 36)
- Maximum interest rate change on first rate adjustment (e.g., 5.0)

## Subsequent Rate Adjustments

- Duration, in months, between subsequent rate adjustments (e.g., 12)
- Maximum interest rate change on subsequent rate adjustments (e.g., 2.0)

## Maximum/Minimum Rates

- Maximum interest rate over life of mortgage (e.g., 12.5)
- Minimum interest rate over life of mortgage (e.g., 4.5)

On negative amortization ARMs, the following is also needed:

## Payment Information

- Initial monthly payment of principal and interest (e.g., 753.45)
- Payment adjustment period, in months (e.g., 12)
- Payment adjustment cap, in percent (e.g., 7.5)
- Payment recast period, in years (e.g., 5)
- Negative amortization cap, in percent (e.g., 110)

The calculators directed to IC will ask for additional information needed to calculate IC. This includes the user's tax bracket, down payment, points, and other upfront fees.

## Assumptions About Future Interest Rates

- Stable index: interest rate index stays unchanged for the life of the mortgage
- Worst case: ARM rate rises to the maximum extent permitted by the loan contract

|  | Number of years | Percent per year |
|---|---|---|
| - Rising trend: interest rate index rises: | 5 | 1 |
| - Declining trend: interest rate index falls: | 3 | 0.5 |

|  | Years between direction changes | Percent per year |
|---|---|---|
| • Volatile: interest rate index rises/falls: | 2 | 1 |
| • Volatile: interest rate index falls/rises: | 2 | 1 |

**Note:** the above numbers are illustrative.

The stable index or "no-change" scenario provides the closest approximation to an "expected" result and is an excellent benchmark. The worst case is exactly that—the ARM rate rises as far and as fast as the loan contract permits. The worst case is so improbable that borrowers may want to design something less extreme, such as the rising trend scenario used below where the index rises by 1% a year for five years.

**An illustration:** On July 25, 2002, I used the calculators to compare the six-month fully amortizing ARM and the FRM shown below.

| Mortgage Features | FRM | ARM |
|---|---|---|
| Term | 30 Years | 30 Years |
| Initial Interest Rate | 6.375% | 3.5% |
| Points | 0.5 | 1.5 |
| Index Value | | 1.81% |
| Rate Adjustment Period | | 6 months |
| Rate Adjustment Cap | | 1% |
| Margin | | 1.625% |
| Maximum Rate | | 11% |

Using the interest cost calculator for fully amortizing ARMs (9a), I developed the following table.

| Interest Cost on ARM and FRM, July 25, 2002 | | | | |
|---|---|---|---|---|
| | FRM | 6-Month Libor ARM | | |
| Period | | Stable Rates | Rising Trend | Worst Case |
| 3 Years | 6.56% | 3.99% | 5.20% | 6.45% |
| 5 Years | 6.50 | 3.79 | 5.90 | 7.84 |
| 7 Years | 6.47 | 3.70 | 6.48 | 8.53 |
| 12 Years | 6.44 | 3.61 | 7.06 | 9.20 |
| 30 Years | 6.42 | 3.56 | 7.39 | 9.57 |

The appeal of the ARM at that time is evident. In a stable rate environment, the borrower would save more than 2.5% relative to the FRM. In a rising trend environment, the ARM would cost less than the FRM if the borrower is out in five years, and even in a worst case the ARM is better if the borrower is out in three years.

For many consumers, the bottom line is what might happen to the payment. Using the payment calculator for fully amortizing ARMs (7b), I developed the table below. The scenarios are the same and the loan is assumed to be $300,000.

| Mortgage Payment on a $300,000 ARM and FRM | | | | |
|---|---|---|---|---|
| | FRM | 6-Month Libor ARM | | |
| Months | | Stable Rates | Rising Trend | Worst Case |
| 1-6 | $1,872 | $1,347 | $1,347 | $1,347 |
| 7-12 | | 1,336 | 1,420 | 1,518 |
| 13-18 | | | 1,505 | 1,696 |
| 19-24 | | | 1,592 | 1,882 |
| 25-30 | | | 1,679 | 2,073 |
| 31-36 | | | 1,768 | 2,270 |
| 37-42 | | | 1,858 | 2,471 |
| 43-48 | | | 1,949 | 2,676 |
| 49-54 | | | 2,040 | 2,780 |
| 55-60 | | | 2,132 | |
| 61-66 | | | 2,224 | |
| 67-360 | | | | |

The payment increases on the six-month Libor ARM under a worst-case scenario are substantial but spread out over four years. None of the increases exceed 13%. There are other ARMs in which the payment under a worst case can jump 50% or more at one adjustment. This is sometimes referred to as "payment shock."

***Mandatory Disclosures:*** The theory underlying the Federal Reserve's disclosure rules for ARMs is that consumers should first receive a general education on ARMs and then should receive specific information about any ARM program in which they might be interested. This is a reasonable approach.

The general education is provided by a *Consumer Handbook on Adjustable Rate Mortgages*, sometimes referred to as the "Charm Booklet." The booklet is a passable effort, but it is too long so few people read it.

The second part of ARM disclosure is a list of ARM features that must be disclosed and an explanation of, "each variable-rate program in which the consumer expresses an interest." This is where the process breaks down. The list of ARM features is too long and includes all kinds of pap.

Overwhelming borrowers with more information than they can handle is counter-productive. Disclosing everything is much the same as disclosing nothing, it just takes longer.

Government agencies with responsibility for disclosure are extremely reluctant to recognize this. If they did, they would be obliged to determine what was truly important. They could no longer compromise divergent views about what to include by including everything. Even worse, they could no longer ignore mandated disclosures from other agencies that hit the borrower at about the same time.

Lenders don't make this mistake. They know they can't sell an ARM (or anything else) by overwhelming the customer. They tend to focus on a single theme or hook—an easy to understand ARM feature that is appealing. For example, in 2003 they sold COFI ARMs based on the stability of the COFI index and Libor ARMs based on a very low initial rate index.

ARM disclosures would be a useful counterweight to lender sales pitches if they were limited to critically important information and presented clearly. The most critical information for most borrowers is 1) What would happen to the interest cost on the loan and the monthly payment per $100,000 of loan amount, if the interest rate index doesn't change; and 2) What would happen if the loan rate rises to the maximum permitted by the loan contract? Simple and easy to understand tables for displaying this information were shown above.

Instead, borrowers are presented with a list of ARM features, including those needed to derive useful tables, provided that the borrower knows a) which items are relevant and b) how to derive the tables from them. But such borrowers don't need mandatory disclosure; they can get the information they want by asking for it. Mandatory disclosure is for borrowers who don't know what they need and, therefore, don't know what to look for in voluminous disclosures.

In addition to the list of ARM features, lenders are required to describe each program, but there is no requirement for clarity. So long as the mandated items are included, it seemingly doesn't matter whether the descriptions are comprehensible. I have seen a few that are pretty good, but most are unreadable.

**Convertible ARMs:** Some ARMs have an option to convert to an FRM after some period, at a market rate. The advantage, relative to a refinance, is that the conversion avoids settlement costs. The disadvantage is that the borrower loses the flexibility to shop the market.

The conversion interest rate on the FRM is usually defined in terms of the value of a rate index at the time of conversion, plus a margin. To determine whether the conversion option has value, assume you can convert immediately. Find the current index value, add the margin and compare it to the best FRM rate you can obtain in the market. If the second rate is lower, which is likely to be the case, the conversion option has little value.

Market conditions do change and it is possible that the option could have value in the years ahead. But don't give up anything important for it.

*Also see*: **Points/*Paying Points on an ARM*, Partial Prepayments/ *Effect of Early Payment on Monthly Payments*/ARMs, Qualification/ Meeting Income Requirements/Is an ARM Needed to Qualify?, Interest-Only Mortgage/*Interest-Only ARMs*, Second Mortgages/ *Negative Amortization ARM May Prevent a Second Mortgage*.**

---

**Adjustment Interval**  *On an ARM, the time between changes in the interest rate or monthly payment.*

These are the same on a fully amortizing ARM, but may not be on a negative amortization ARM. *See* **Adjustable Rate Mortgage**.

---

**Affordability** *A consumer's capacity to afford a house.*

Affordability is usually expressed in terms of the maximum price the consumer could pay for a house and be approved for the mortgage required to pay that amount.

***Calculating the Maximum Affordable Sale Price:*** The affordability calculation is fairly complex when done correctly, and some approaches oversimplify it. The calculation also involves a number of assumptions that affect the answer.

To do it properly, affordability must be calculated three times using an "income rule," a "debt rule," and a "cash rule." The final figure is the lowest of the three. When affordability is measured on the back of an envelope, usually it is based on the income rule alone, ignoring the other two. This can result in error.

*The income rule* says that the borrower's monthly housing expense (MHE), which is the sum of the mortgage payment, property taxes and homeowner insurance premium, cannot exceed a percentage of the borrower's income specified by the lender. If this maximum is 28%, for example, and John Smith's income is $4,000, MHE cannot exceed $1,120. If taxes and insurance are $200, the maximum mortgage payment is $920. At 7% and 30 years, this payment will support a loan of $138,282. Assuming a 5% down payment, this implies a sale price of $145,561. This is the maximum sale price for Smith using the income rule.

*The debt rule* says that the borrower's total housing expense (THE), which is the sum of the MHE plus monthly payments on existing debt, cannot exceed a percentage of the borrower's income specified by the lender. If this maximum is 36%, for example, the THE for Smith cannot exceed $1,440. If taxes and insurance are $200 while existing debt service is $240, the maximum mortgage payment is $1,000. At 7% and 30 years, this payment will support a loan of $150,308. Assuming a 5% down payment, this implies a sale price of $158,218. This is the maximum sale price for Smith using the debt rule.

*The required cash rule* says that the borrower must have cash sufficient to meet the down payment requirement plus other settlement costs. If Smith has $12,000 and the sum of the down payment requirement and other settlement costs are 10% of sale price, then the maximum sale price using the cash rule is $120,000. Since this is the lowest of the three maximums, it is the affordability estimate for Smith.

When the cash rule sets the limit on the maximum sale price, as in the case above, the borrower is said to be cash constrained. Affordability of a cash-constrained borrower can be raised by a reduction in the down payment requirement, a reduction in settlement costs, or access to an additional source of down payment—a parent, for example.

When the income rule sets the limit on the maximum sale price, the borrower is said to be income constrained. Affordability of an income-constrained borrower can be raised by a reduction in the maximum MHE ratio, or access to additional income—sending a spouse out to work, for example.

When the debt rule sets the limit on the maximum sale price, the borrower is said to be debt constrained. The affordability of a debt-constrained borrower (but not that of a cash-constrained or income-constrained borrower) can be increased by repaying debt.

Affordability will be affected by changes in the assumed maximum MHE and THE ratios, which vary from loan program to program and can also vary with other characteristics of the loan such as the down payment. Affordability may also be affected by changes in the assumptions made regarding settlement costs, taxes and insurance, interest rate and term.

**Some Estimates:** The table below provides some ballpark estimates of how much house a borrower can afford with a 7.5% two point mortgage for 30 years. For each of seven sale prices, the table shows the total cash required to meet down payment requirements and settlement costs, the total monthly housing expense, the minimum income required to cover housing expenses and the maximum amount of debt service allowable on the minimum income.

These numbers were calculated from the Housing Affordability calculator (5a) on my Web site. The assumptions used are not likely to apply exactly to any individual situation. However, readers can use the calculator to change any of the assumptions as they please.

The table assumes that the borrower pushes buying power to the limit. In particular, the table assumes that the down payment is the lowest lenders are willing to accept, which requires mortgage insurance that increases borrowing cost. This may not be prudent. *See* **Housing Investment**.

| How Much House Can You Afford with a 7%/2-Point /30-Year Mortgage? | | | | | | |
|---|---|---|---|---|---|---|
| To Spend This Amount on a House | You Need at Least This Gross Monthly Income | To Cover This Monthly Housing Expense | Other Monthly Debt Payments Should Not Exceed | And You Need at Least This Much Cash | For the Down Payment Lenders Are Most Likely to Require | And the Closing Costs |
| $400,000 | $11,290 | $3,160 | $903 | $59,200 | $40,000 | $19,200 |
| 350,000 | 10,260 | 2,871 | 820 | 51,800 | 35,000 | 16,800 |
| 300,000 | 8,790 | 2,461 | 703 | 44,400 | 30,000 | 14,400 |
| 250,000 | 7,330 | 2,051 | 586 | 37,000 | 25,000 | 12,000 |
| 200,000 | 6,280 | 1,756 | 502 | 19,800 | 10,000 | 9,800 |
| 150,000 | 4,710 | 1,317 | 376 | 14,850 | 7,500 | 7,359 |
| 100,000 | 3,230 | 903 | 258 | 7,940 | 3,000 | 4,940 |

**Notes:** Minimum monthly income is based on a ratio of monthly housing expense to income of 28%. Closing costs excluding points are assumed to total 3% of the sale price. The maximum monthly debt service payment is assumed to be 8% of minimum monthly income. Monthly housing expense includes principal and interest, mortgage insurance, taxes and hazard insurance. Taxes and hazard insurance are assumed to be 1.825% of sale price. The down payment requirement is assumed to be 10% on prices of $250,000-400,000, 5% on $150,000-200,000, and 3% on $100,000. Mortgage insurance premium rates are .9% with 3% down, .78% with 5% down, and .52% with 10% down.

---

**Agreement of Sale**   *A contract signed by buyer and seller stating the terms and conditions under which a property will be sold.*

---

**Alternative Documentation**   *Expedited and simpler documentation requirements designed to speed up the loan approval process.*

Instead of verifying employment with the applicant's employer and bank deposits with the applicant's bank, the lender will accept paycheck stubs, W-2s, and the borrower's original bank statements. Alternative documentation remains "full documentation," as opposed to the other documentation options. *See* **Documentation Requirements/*Full Documentation***.

---

**Amortization**   *The repayment of principal from scheduled mortgage payments that exceed the interest due.*

The scheduled payment is the payment the borrower is obliged to make under the note. The scheduled payment less the interest equals amortization. The loan balance declines by the amount of the amortization, plus the amount of any extra payment. If such payment is less than the interest due, the balance rises, which is negative amortization.

***The Fully Amortizing Payment:*** The monthly mortgage payment that will pay off the loan at term is called the fully amortizing payment. On an FRM, the fully amortizing payment is calculated at the outset and does not change over the life of the loan. For example, on a FRM for $100,000 at 6% for 30 years, the fully amortizing payment is $599.56. If the borrower makes that payment every month, the balance will be extinguished with the 360th payment.

On an ARM, the fully amortizing payment is constant only so long as the interest rate remains unchanged. When the rate changes, the fully amortizing payment also changes. For example, an ARM for $100,000 at 6% for 30 years would have a fully amortizing payment of $599.55 at the outset. But if the rate rose to 7% after five years, the fully amortizing payment would jump to $657.69.

***Amortization on Standard Loans:*** Except for simple interest loans, which are discussed below, the accounting for amortized home loans assumes that there are only 12 days in a year, consisting of the first day of each month. The account begins on the first day of the month following the day the loan closes. The borrower pays "per diem interest" for the period between the closing day and the day the record begins. The first monthly payment is due on the first day of the month after that.

For example, if a 6% 30-year $100,000 loan closes on March 15, the borrower pays interest at closing for the period March 15-April 1, and the first payment of $599.56 is due May 1.

The payment is allocated between interest and reduction in the loan balance. The interest payment is calculated by multiplying 1/12 of the interest rate times the loan balance in the previous month. 1/12 of .06 is .005. The interest due May 1, therefore, is .005 times $100,000 or $500. The remaining $99.56 is used to reduce the balance to $99,900.44.

The process repeats each month, but the portion of the payment allocated to interest gradually declines while the portion used to reduce the loan balance gradually rises. On June 1, the interest due is .005 times $99,900.44, or $499.51. The amount available for reducing the balance rises to $100.06. See the chart below.

While the payment is due on the first day of each month, lenders allow borrowers a "grace period," which is usually 15 days. A payment received on the 15th is treated exactly in the same way as a payment received on the 1st. A payment received after the 15th, however, is assessed a late charge equal to 4 or 5% of the payment.

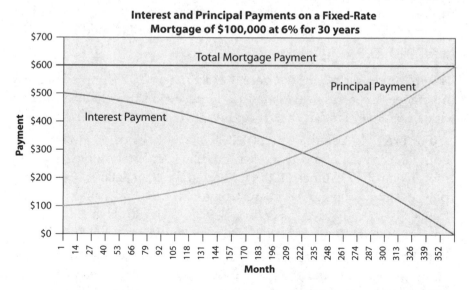

**Interest and Principal Payments on a Fixed-Rate Mortgage of $100,000 at 6% for 30 years**

***Amortization Schedule:*** This is a table that shows the mortgage payment, broken down by interest and amortization and the loan balance. Schedules prepared by lenders will also show tax and insurance payments if made by the lender and the balance of the tax/insurance escrow account.

Readers are encouraged to develop an actual amortization schedule, which will allow them to see exactly how they work. They can do that using one of my calculators. For straight amortization without extra payments, use calculator 8a. To see how amortization is impacted by extra payments, use calculator 2a.

Readers who want to maintain a continuing record of their mortgage under their own control can do this by downloading one of two spreadsheets from my Web site. These are "Extra Payments on Monthly Payment Fixed-Rate Mortgages" and "Extra Payments on ARMs." As the titles indicate, the spreadsheets will allow you to take account of extra payments in addition to regular payments.

*Payment Rigidity:* The payment requirement of the standard mortgage is absolutely rigid. Skip a single payment and you accumulate late charges until you make it up. If you skip May, for example, you make it up with two payments in June plus one late charge, and you record a 30-day delinquency in your credit file. If you can't make it up until July, the price is three payments plus two late charges plus a 60-day delinquency report in your credit file. Falling behind can be a slippery slope.

*Amortization on a Simple Interest Mortgage:* On a simple interest mortgage, interest is calculated daily based on the balance on the day of payment, rather than monthly, as on the standard mortgage.

For example, using a rate of 7.25% and a balance of $100,000 on both, the standard mortgage would have an interest payment in month one of .0725 times $100,000 divided by 12, or $604.17. On a simple interest mortgage, the interest payment per day would be .0725 times $100,000 divided by 365 or $19.86. Over 30 days this would amount to $589.89 while over 31 days it would amount to $615.75.

A borrower who pays on the first day of every month in both cases would come out the same over the course of a year. But borrowers who pay late while staying within the usual 15-day grace period provided on the standard mortgage, do better with that mortgage. If they pay on the 10th day of the month, for example, they get

10 days free of interest on the standard mortgage whereas on the simple interest mortgage, interest accumulates over the 10 days.

Similarly, borrowers who make extra payments of principal do better with the standard mortgage. For example, if they make an extra payment of $1,000 on the 15th of the month, they pay 15 days of interest on the $1,000 on the simple interest mortgage, which they would save on a standard mortgage.

The only borrowers who will do better with the simple interest mortgage are those in the habit of making their monthly payments early. If you make your payment 10 days before it is due, you will receive immediate credit with the simple interest mortgage, saving the interest on the portion of the payment that goes to principal reduction for the 10 days. With the standard mortgage, a payment received 10 days early is credited on the due date, just like a payment that is received 10 days late.

---

**Annual Percentage Rate (APR)**   *A measure of the cost of credit that must be reported by lenders under Truth in Lending regulations.*

The APR takes account of the interest rate and upfront charges paid by the borrower, whether expressed as a percent of the loan or in dollars. It is usually higher than the interest rate because of upfront charges. The APR is adjusted for the time value of money, so that dollars paid by the borrower upfront carry a heavier weight than dollars paid in later years. For the algebraic expression *see* **Mortgage Formulas/*Annual Percentage Rate***.

*Incomplete Fee Coverage:* In principle, the APR should include all charges that would not arise in an all-cash transaction. In fact, only charges paid to lenders and mortgage brokers are included, and not all of those. No charges paid to third parties are included. Examples are title insurance and other title-related charges, appraisal, credit report, and pest inspection fees.

Incomplete fee coverage means that the APR understates the true credit cost. If the understatement was consistent, this would not be a major problem, but it is not consistent. Fees that are not included in the APR are sometimes paid by the lender, in exchange for a higher interest rate. The APR in such cases indirectly includes fees that are excluded when paid by the borrower. Mortgage shoppers should not use the APR to compare loans where they pay settlement costs with loans where the lender pays the settlement costs.

**Assumption That Loans Run to Term:** A second major shortcoming of the APR is that it assumes that all loans run to term, when in fact more than 90% are paid off before term. Because the APR calculation spreads upfront fees over the life of the loan, the longer the assumed life, the lower the APR. The point is illustrated in the chart on the next page, which shows what the APR would be if the loan was terminated in any month over a 30-year period. It applies to a 7% loan with fees equal to 5% of the loan amount.

Suppose a borrower was deciding between this 7% loan with 5% fees and a 7.75% loan and zero fees. The APR on the 7% loan is 7.52%, whereas the 7.75% loan has an APR of 7.75%. But if the borrower expects to be out of his house in 10 years, the 7% loan would have a 10-year APR of 7.76%, and over five years it would be 8.26%. Mortgage shoppers with short time horizons should not use the APR to compare loans. They should use **Interest Cost** calculated over their own time horizon, which they can do using calculators 9a, b, and c on my Web site.

**Ignoring the Paid-Off Loan on a Cash-out Refinance:** The APR is also deceptive for borrowers raising cash who are choosing between a cash-out refinance and a second mortgage. The APR on a cash-out refi ignores the interest rate on the existing mortgage that is being paid off.

For example, you have a $200,000 first mortgage at 7% and you need to raise $20,000 in cash. Assume a second mortgage for $20,000 has an APR of 8.5%, while a cash-out refi for $220,000 has an APR of 7.5%. The APR comparisons make it appear as if the cash-out refi is less costly, but that is not the case. The APR on the cash-out refi ignores the loss to the borrower from increasing the APR on the $200,000 from 7% to 7.5%. An APR that took account of this loss would be well above the 8.5% on the second mortgage.

Borrowers and loan consultants comparing the cost of a second mortgage with that of a cash-out refi should ignore the APRs. They can use calculator 3d on my Web site, "Refinance to Raise Cash or Take Out a Second Mortgage."

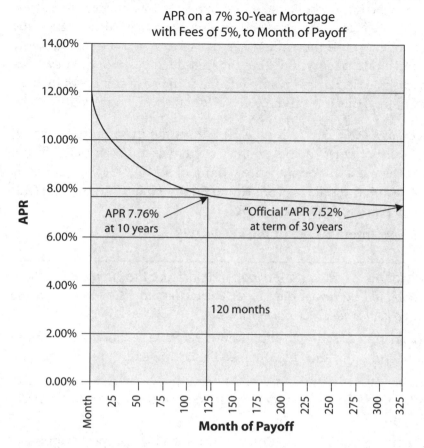

APR on a 7% 30-Year Mortgage
with Fees of 5%, to Month of Payoff

*APR on an ARM:* On an ARM, the quoted interest rate holds only for a specified period. In calculating an APR, therefore, some assumption must be made about what happens to the rate at the end of the initial rate period.

The rule is that the initial rate is used for as long as it lasts, and the new rate or rates are those that would occur if the interest rate index used by the ARM stays the same for the life of the loan. This is a "no-change" or "stable-rate" scenario.

Under a stable-rate scenario, at the end of the initial rate period, the interest rate used in calculating the APR adjusts to equal the "fully indexed rate," or FIR. The FIR is the value of the interest rate index at the time the ARM was written, plus a margin that is specified in the note.

21

When the FIR is above the initial rate, as it was during most of the 90s, the rate increases on a no-change scenario. The APR is above the initial rate, even if there are no lender fees. When the FIR is below the initial rate, as it was during the first three years of the new century, the rate decreases on a no-change scenario. If not offset by high upfront fees, this can produce an APR below the initial rate.

*APR on a HELOC:* The APR on a HELOC is the initial interest rate. It thus does not reflect points or other upfront costs, or expected future rates. The most important price feature of a HELOC, the margin, is not a required disclosure. *See* **Home Equity Line of Credit (HELOC)/ Truth in Lending (TIL) on a HELOC**.

*Also see:* **Interest Cost (IC)/IC Versus APR.**

---

**Application**   *A request for a loan that includes the information about the potential borrower, the property and the requested loan that the solicited lender needs to make a decision.*

In a narrower sense, the application refers to a standardized application form called the "1003" which the borrower is obliged to fill out.

---

**Application Fee**   *A fee that some lenders charge to accept an application.*

It may or may not cover other costs such as a property appraisal or credit report, and it may or may not be refundable if the lender declines the loan.

---

**Appraisal**   *A written estimate of a property's current market value prepared by an appraiser.*

---

**Appraisal Fee**   *A fee charged by an appraiser for the appraisal of a particular property.*

---

**Appraiser**   *A professional with knowledge of real estate markets and skilled in the practice of appraisal.*

When a property is appraised in connection with a loan, the

appraiser is selected by the lender, but the appraisal fee is usually paid by the borrower.

**Approval** *Acceptance of the borrower's loan application.*

Approval means that the borrower meets the lender's **Qualification Requirements** and also its **Underwriting Requirements**. In some cases, especially where approval is provided quickly as with **Automated Underwriting** systems, the approval may be conditional on further verification of information provided by the borrower.

**APR**

*See* **Annual Percentage Rate**.

**ARM**

*See* **Adjustable Rate Mortgage**.

**Assignment** *The transfer of ownership, rights, or interests in property by one person, the assignor, to another, the assignee.*

**Assumable Mortgage** *A mortgage contract that allows, or does not prohibit, a buyer from assuming the mortgage contract of the seller.*

When a home buyer assumes responsibility for a home seller's existing mortgage, the buyer assumes all the obligations under the mortgage, just as if the loan had been made to her.

***Value of Assumptions to Buyers and Sellers:*** The major driving force behind assumptions is the lower interest rate on the assumed mortgage relative to current market rates. If the home seller has a 5.5% mortgage, for example, and the best the buyer can get in the current market is 7%, both parties can be better off if the buyer assumes the 5.5% loan. An assumption also avoids the settlement costs on a new mortgage.

During periods when market rates are low, there is little interest in assumptions. But when rates increase after a long period of low rates, so does the interest in assumptions.

The value of an assumption depends on the difference in rate between the old assumed mortgage and a new one; the balance and period remaining on the old loan; the term of the new loan; on how long the buyer expects to have the mortgage; and the "investment rate"—the rate the buyer could earn on the savings from the lower rate. Assuming that the 5.5% loan has a $100,000 balance with 200 months remaining while the 7% loan would be for 30 years, that the buyer expects to be in the house for five years and can earn 4% on investments, the value is about $7,000. A spreadsheet that makes this calculation is available on my Web site.

The $7,000 of savings does not include the settlement costs on a new loan. On the other hand, the savings would be reduced if the buyer has to supplement the existing loan balance with a new second mortgage at a higher rate. This could well be the case if the existing loan balance has been paid down appreciably, and/or the house has appreciated since that mortgage was taken out. The buyers who do best on assumptions are those who have the cash to pay the difference between the sale price and the balance of the old loan.

However, buyers should not expect to receive the full value of an assumption. The seller must benefit as well; typically, the parties share the savings. The seller's share will be in the form of a higher price for the house. Indeed, some economists believe that the full value of the assumption should be reflected in the price of the house, but this is as implausible as the opposite view, that only the buyer benefits.

*Assumptions a Cost to Lenders:* The benefit to buyer and seller from assuming an old loan comes at the expense of the lender. Instead of having the 5.5% loan repaid, which would allow the lender to convert it into a new 7% loan, the 5.5% loan stays on the books. Back in the '70s and '80s, lenders couldn't do anything about this. Mortgage notes at that time did not prohibit assumptions, and the courts ruled that lenders could not prevent them.

Following that experience, however, lenders began to insert **Due-on-Sale Clauses** in their notes. (An exception is FHA and VA mortgages; see below.) These stipulate that if the property is sold, the loan must be repaid. Even with a due-on-sale clause, the lender may allow an assumption—keeping the loan on the books avoids the cost of making a new loan—but the interest rate will be raised to the current market rate.

***Illegal Assumptions—Wrap-Arounds:*** Raising the interest rate to the current market rate removes most of the benefit of the assumption to the buyer and seller. In some cases, they attempt to retain the benefit by agreeing to a sale using a wrap-around mortgage, without the knowledge of the lender. The seller takes a mortgage from the buyer, which may be for a larger amount than the balance of the old loan and continues to pay the old mortgage out of the proceeds of the new one. The new mortgage "wraps" the old one.

This is a dangerous business, particularly to the seller, who has given up ownership of the house but retained liability for the mortgage. The seller is in deep trouble if the buyer fails to pay, or if the lender discovers the sale and demands immediate repayment of the original loan. I wouldn't do it, even if I were selling the house to my mother.

***Offering Assumability, at a Price, as an Option:*** When borrowers are concerned that interest rates could go much higher, they may be willing to pay for an assumable mortgage. For example, a borrower taking a 6.5% 30-year FRM might be willing to pay 6.875% for the right to allow a home buyer to take it over when he sells his house. The higher rate is akin to an insurance premium. If market rates are above 16% when he sells, as they were in 1981, he will save a bundle.

An assumable mortgage has some similarities to, and some differences from, a **Portable Mortgage**. You sell your home. If your mortgage is assumable, it can be transferred to the buyer; if it is portable, it can be transferred to a new property that you buy. Portability is of no value if you decide to rent, go to a nursing home, or die, whereas an assumable mortgage retains its value in these situations. On the other hand, some portion of the value of an assumable mortgage must be shared with the purchaser. A mortgage that is both assumable and portable would have enhanced value.

Lenders who offer assumable mortgages will require that any new borrower meet the lender's qualification requirements. Borrowers purchasing the option will need to be confident that the lender won't tighten its requirements when market rates increase. The best assurance would be a commitment to accept approval under one of the automated underwriting systems developed by Fannie Mae or Freddie Mac.

**FHA and VA Loans Are Assumable:** Loans insured by FHA or guaranteed by VA have always been assumable. During periods when borrowers are concerned about future rate increases, this gives them an edge.

**Old Loans:** FHA loans closed before December 14, 1989 and VA loans closed before March 1, 1988 are assumable by anyone. Buyers who assume these mortgages don't have to meet any requirements at all, but the seller remains responsible for the mortgage if the buyer doesn't pay.

Any seller who allows assumption by a buyer without a release of liability is looking for trouble. Even if the buyer pays, and that is a crapshoot, the seller's ability to obtain another mortgage will be prejudiced by his continued liability on the old one.

If an old FHA or VA is attractive to a buyer, the seller can request that the agency underwrite the buyer. If the buyer is approved, the seller will be released from liability. At this point, there can't be many of these loans left with balances large enough to be attractive to buyers.

**New Loans:** Assumption of FHA and VA loans closed after the dates shown above requires approval of the buyer by the agencies. The process is much the same as it would be for a new borrower. Upon approval of the buyer and sale of the property, the seller is relieved of liability. FHA allows lenders to charge a $500 assumption fee and a fee for the credit report. VA allows a $255 processing fee and a $45 closing fee, and the VA itself receives a funding fee of ½ of 1% of the loan balance.

FHA and VA loans that were closed during the low-rate years 1996-2003 will become attractive targets for assumption if interest rates rise in future years. Potential sellers who have one of these loans can use the spreadsheet on my Web site to estimate how much the assumption would be worth to a potential buyer.

**Assumption** *A method of selling real estate where the buyer of the property agrees to become responsible for the repayment of an existing loan on the property.*

Unless the lender also agrees, however, the seller remains liable for the mortgage.

---

**Auction Sites**

*See* **Lead-Generation Sites**.

---

**Authorized User** *Someone authorized by the original credit card holder to use the holder's card.*

While authorized users are not responsible for paying any charges, including their own, they are sometimes dunned for the unpaid bills of the card holder. *See* **Credit Score/*Some Misperceptions About Credit*/Authorized Credit Card Users Are Safe**.

---

**Automated Underwriting** *A computer-driven process for informing the loan applicant very quickly, sometimes within a few minutes, whether the application will be approved, denied, or forwarded to an underwriter.*

The quick decision is based on information provided by the applicant that is subject to later verification and other information obtained electronically, including information about the borrower's credit history and the subject property.

---

**Automated Underwriting System** *A particular computerized system for doing automated underwriting.*

Mortgage insurers and some large lenders have developed such systems, but the most widely used are Fannie Mae's "Desktop Underwriter" and Freddie Mac's "Loan Prospector."

---

**Balance** *The amount of the original loan remaining to be paid.*

It is equal to the loan amount less the sum of all prior payments of principal.

**Balloon** *The loan balance remaining at the time the loan contract calls for full repayment.*

---

**Balloon Mortgage** *A mortgage that is payable in full after a period that is shorter than the term.*

In the 1920s most balloon loans were interest-only—the borrower paid interest but no principal. At maturity, usually five or 10 years, the balloon that had to be repaid was equal to the original loan amount. The balloon loans offered today, in contrast, calculate payments on a 30-year amortization schedule, so there is some principal reduction. Assuming a rate of 6.5%, for example, a $100,000 loan would have a balance remaining at the end of the fifth year of $93,611.

***Comparing a Balloon Mortgage to an ARM:*** It is useful to compare five and seven-year balloons with ARMs that have the same initial rate periods. Both offer a rate in the early years below that available on a fixed-rate mortgage, and both carry a risk of higher rates later on. But there are some important differences.

**Favoring the Balloon:**

- Balloon loans are much simpler to understand and therefore easier to shop for.
- The interest rate on a five-year or seven-year balloon is typically lower than that on a 5/1 or 7/1 ARM.

**Favoring the ARM:**

- The risk of a substantial rate increase after five or seven years is greater on the balloon. The balloon must be refinanced at the prevailing market rate, whereas a rate increase on most five- and seven-year ARMs is limited by rate caps.
- Borrowers with five- or seven-year balloons incur refinancing costs at term, whereas borrowers with 5/1 or 7/1 ARMs don't unless they elect to refinance.
- Borrowers who are having payment problems may find it difficult to refinance balloons. The balloon contract allows lenders to decline to refinance if the borrower has missed a single payment in the prior year. This is not a problem with ARMs, which need not be refinanced.

- Borrowers may find it difficult to refinance balloons if interest rates have spiked. The balloon contract allows lenders to decline to refinance if current market rates are more than 5% higher than the rate on the balloon.

**Bimonthly Mortgage** *A mortgage on which half the monthly payment is paid twice a month.*

It should be called a "semi-monthly mortgage" but market practice often trumps logic. In contrast to a biweekly, a bimonthly mortgage involves no extra payments. The 24 half payments a year add to the same total as 12 full payments. Advancing the payment by half a month saves a little interest, but the effect is negligible. A 7% 30-year loan pays off in 29 years, 11 months. Check it out with the bimonthly spreadsheet on my Web site.

**Biweekly Mortgage** *A mortgage on which half the monthly payment is paid every two weeks.*

This results in 26 payments per year, which is the equivalent of 13 monthly payments rather than 12. Because of the extra payment, the biweekly mortgage amortizes before term. For example, a 7% 30-year loan that is converted into a biweekly pays off in 286 months (23 years, 11 months).

***Benefit of a Biweekly:*** Borrowers do not need a biweekly to make extra payments. They can do it themselves in a variety of ways described below, but all require self-discipline. Having a third party set up the procedure and legally obligating borrowers to make the additional payments forces the discipline on them.

***New Biweeklies:*** Borrowers taking out a new loan who need the discipline provided by a biweekly can usually do better with a straight monthly payment loan carrying a shorter term. A 30-year loan converted into a biweekly carries the 30-year rate, whereas 15 and 20-year loans often carry lower rates. 15-year loans in particular generally carry rates 3/8% to 1/2% below those on 30s.

***Rolling Your Own Biweekly:*** Borrowers who already have a 30-year mortgage and are attracted by the prospect of paying it off early, have a number of options. One is to open a new account with a bank that has an automatic payment privilege and arrange for it to make their monthly mortgage payment every month. If they pay half the monthly payment into this account every two weeks, after a year the account will have enough money for a double payment.

This procedure exactly mimics that of a third-party biweekly provider. The only difference is that the borrower rather than the third party earns interest on the account.

*Making a Double Payment Once a Year:* A borrower who makes a double payment once a year will pay off on the same schedule as one using a biweekly. This can be a convenient method for borrowers who regularly receive bonuses or similar compensation at the end of the year.

*Increasing the Monthly Payment by 1/12:* Another simple method is to divide the monthly payment by 12 and add that amount to the payment every month. Paying an extra 1/12 of the payment every month for 12 months is the equivalent of one full extra payment. This method pays off a loan a little sooner than a biweekly or a double payment at year-end because balance reductions begin with the first extra payment rather than after a year. A 30-year 7% loan will pay off in 285 months rather than 286.

*Simple Interest Biweeklies:* On a simple interest biweekly, the biweekly payment is applied to principal every two weeks, which results in a faster payoff. Again, however, the difference is small. The simple interest version pays off the 7% 30-year loan in 284 months.

Readers can check the numbers cited here and test other possibilities with the biweekly spreadsheet on my Web site.

*Also see:* **Paying Off Early/*Monitoring Your Account*.**

---

**Bridge Loan** *A short-term loan, usually from a bank, that "bridges" the period between the closing of a home purchase and the closing of a home sale.*

To qualify for a bridge loan, the borrower must have a contract to sell the existing house. This is the same as a "swing loan." *See*

**Housing Investment/***Buying the Next Home Before the Existing One Is Sold.*

---

**Builder-Financed Construction** *Having the builder borrow the money needed for construction.*

*See* **Construction Financing/***Should the Builder Finance Construction?*

---

**Cap**

*Same as* **Float-Down**.

---

**Cash-Out Refi** *Refinancing for an amount in excess of the balance on the old loan plus settlement costs.*

When the main objective of a refinancing is to raise cash, the relevant question is whether the cost of raising cash in this way is higher or lower than raising the same amount of cash with a second mortgage.

A cash-out refi with an interest rate below the existing rate is likely to be less costly than a second mortgage. If the cash-out refi rate is higher than the existing rate, the second mortgage is likely to be cheaper, even though the second mortgage rate may be well above the cash-out refi rate. The reason is that the second mortgage allows the borrower to retain the lower rate on the existing mortgage.

For example, assume the existing loan has a balance of $200,000 at 7%, the borrower needs $40,000 in cash, the rate on a $240,000 refi is 7.5%, and the rate on a $40,000 second mortgage is 8.5%. The second mortgage is the better deal. While the borrower is paying 1% more on $40,000, he avoids paying .5% more on $200,000.

Other factors are involved, however, including mortgage insurance, settlement costs, and taxes. Calculator 3d on my Web site pulls all of them together to determine the less costly option. If you want to use the cash to consolidate existing debt, use calculators 1b or 1c.

**Warning:** Because the APR on a cash-out refi ignores the loss of the existing first mortgage, comparing it with the APR on a second mortgage is meaningless.

**Closing** *On a home purchase, the process of transferring ownership from the seller to the buyer, the disbursement of funds from the buyer and the lender to the seller, and the execution of all the documents associated with the sale and the loan.*

On a refinance, there is no transfer of ownership, but the closing includes repayment of the old lender.

---

**Closing Costs** *Costs that the borrower must pay at the time of closing, in addition to the down payment.*

*See* **Settlement Costs**.

---

**Closing Date** *The date on which the closing occurs.*

On a purchase transaction, there is no financial advantage to the buyer/borrower in closing on any day of the month, as compared to any other day. Buyers should select the closing date as close as possible to the moving date, regardless of the day of the month that is.

The interest clock on the loan starts ticking on the closing date, because the lender expects to be paid beginning the day the funds are disbursed. There is no point in paying interest before you are prepared to move.

While borrowers pay interest beginning the closing date, they may pay it in different ways, depending on when during the month they close. The first payment on a home loan is due on the first day of a month and includes interest for a full month. Since loans may close anytime within the month, there is always an interest adjustment at closing based on the exact closing date. This is **Per Diem Interest** or "prepaid interest."

If you close on July 29, for example, you pay three days of interest at closing, covering July 30, 31, and August 1. Your first monthly payment is due September 1. So at closing you pay interest for the last three days of July and the first monthly payment on September 1 pays the interest for the full month of August.

Closing on different days during the month will shift the amount of interest you pay at closing, but will not affect the total interest you pay beginning at closing.

In principle, refinancing should work in the same way as a purchase. If you close a refinance on July 29, you should pay the new lender per diem interest for three days and the old lender for 29 days. Unfortunately, because of glitches in the system, it doesn't work out that way. Borrowers often are charged interest by both lenders for one day and sometimes two or three or more.

The major reason is that the funds don't move directly from the new lender to the old lender. The funds are held by an intermediary until the new documents have been recorded, and that process takes time. Because recording offices are usually closed on the weekend, borrowers who close on a Friday are especially likely to pay double interest for several days. So don't close a refinance on a Friday if you can avoid it.

Furthermore, FHA requires that interest be paid for a full month, regardless of when a loan is closed during the month. Those refinancing out of FHA, therefore, should try to close as near to the end of the month as possible.

---

**Co-Borrowers** *One or more persons who have signed the note and are equally responsible for repaying the loan.*

***When One Co-Borrower Has Much Better Credit than the Other:*** A problem that arises frequently with co-borrowers is that one has much better credit than the other. If they buy the house together as co-owners and co-borrowers, the deadbeat's bad credit will result in a bad credit rating for the transaction and a corresponding high interest rate.

One option is for "good-credit" to buy the house alone, leaving "bad-credit" out of the deal. But then the mortgage would be limited to the amount that the income of "good-credit" can support. Whether this option works depends on whether the mortgage that "good-credit" can carry, plus the down payment the partners can make, permit them to purchase the house that they want. *See* **Affordability/*Calculating the Maximum Affordable Sale Price*.**

If the first option doesn't work, the partners can have "good credit" buy the house using a program that does not require verification of income. A number of such programs are available with different twists. (*See* **Documentation Requirements**.) Then the mortgage amount would not be limited by the income of "good-credit." However, programs involving less than full documentation require a higher interest rate, down payment, or both.

Still another possibility is to have a third party with good credit and income replace "bad-credit" as the co-borrower. Usually only a parent would be willing to play this role.

**When Co-Borrowers Split:** Problems can arise when co-borrowers split, whether they are married or not. However, difficulties seem to arise more frequently with unmarried couples, perhaps because unmarried couples purchasing a house together more often do it blindly. When they split, issues that should have been foreseen, but weren't, may prevent a clean and amicable separation.

Here are the major issues to resolve with your partner *before* you buy.

**Split with Sale:** There is much to be said for an agreement that the house must be sold if either partner aborts the relationship. This avoids the thorny issues, discussed below, that can arise when one partner stays with the house.

If a split leads to a sale, the only issue is how the proceeds are to be divided. Equal shares may or may not be equitable. A partner who pays the down payment, or a larger share of current expenses, deserves a larger share of the proceeds.

One approach is to divide the net proceeds by each partner's contribution to the equity in the house when it is sold. Suppose, for example, that the partners pay $100,000 for a house, take a mortgage of $80,000, pay $20,000 down plus $3,000 in settlement costs, and sell it after five years when the loan balance is $74,000. Total contributions of the partners to equity in the house at the time of sale consist of $23,000 in cash at purchase, plus $6,000 in reducing the loan balance. If one partner contributed 60% of the cash and paid 40% of the expenses, that partner's share of net proceeds would be [.6($23,000) + .4($6,000)]/ $29,000, or 56%.

In some cases, this rule would not be fair. For example, one of the partners might unilaterally work on improving the house, which would call for a higher share.

The point is that the partners ought to agree at the outset on the terms of the split. If they can't agree, they should reconsider whether they really want to cohabit.

**Split with One Partner Staying:** The terms of settlement are more complex when one of the partners remains in the house. There is no sale price, so the partners must agree on an appraisal procedure and on who will pay for it. They should also agree on whether a real estate sales commission should be deducted from the valuation used in the settlement. If they wait until the event, this is invariably contentious.

Another problem arises if the partner remaining in the house doesn't have the money to pay off the partner who is leaving. The more equity they have in the house, the more cash the resident partner needs to raise. A home equity loan is not possible unless both partners become responsible, which is the last thing the departing partner wants.

The largest problem, however, is the departing partner's continuing responsibility for the mortgage. Many departing partners believe that they are off the hook because the partner remaining in the house has agreed to assume full responsibility for the mortgage. They (and often their lawyers) overlook the fact that the lender was not a partner to their agreement.

As far as the lender is concerned, the departing partner remains liable. If the departing partner seeks to purchase another house, the old mortgage will show up on his or her credit report, reducing the size of the loan for which he or she can qualify.

Lenders have no incentive to remove one partner from the note. Some can be induced to do it if the partner remaining with the house has a perfect payment record and can document that he or she has been solely responsible for the payments. But in the best situation this takes time, perhaps a year.

If the lender refuses, the only way to get the departing partner off the note is for the remaining partner to refinance in his or her own name. But if this was not part of the original agreement, it is unlikely that the remaining partner will agree later—unless refinancing becomes financially advantageous at the time.

If both the original lender and the remaining partner refuse to help, a new lender may be willing to ignore the old mortgage obligation if presented with evidence that the remaining partner has been meeting the payment obligations. Unlike the old lender, a new lender has something to gain by wiping the departing partner's slate clean.

Of course, if the remaining partner has not been making payments on time, neither lender will be willing to help the departing partner.

If I were drafting an agreement for a loved one, not knowing whether he or she was more likely to be the remaining or the departing partner, it would grant the remaining partner 14 months to make the settlement payment and to remove the departing partner from the note. Otherwise, the house must be sold and the mortgage paid off.

---

**COFI** *Cost-of-Funds Index, one of many interest rate indexes used to determine interest rate adjustments on an adjustable rate mortgage.*

*See* **Adjustable Rate Mortgage (ARM)/ARM Rate Indexes**.

---

**Conforming Mortgage** *A loan eligible for purchase by the two major federal agencies that buy mortgages, Fannie Mae and Freddie Mac.*

Conforming mortgages cannot exceed a legal maximum amount, which was $322,700 in 2003; it is raised every year. They must also meet the agencies' underwriting requirements regarding credit, documentation, property features, and other factors.

A mortgage in excess of the conforming maximum, which is identical in other respects, will have an interest rate about 3/8% higher. Borrowers who need an amount larger than the maximum will often do better taking a conforming loan for the maximum and a second mortgage for the excess.

---

**Construction Financing** *The method of financing used when a borrower contracts to have a house built, as opposed to purchasing a completed house.*

Construction can be financed in two ways. One way is to use two loans, a construction loan for the period of construction, followed by a permanent loan from another lender, which pays off the construction loan. Borrowers who use two loans must decide whether they will take out the construction loan, or have the builder do it. The second approach is to use a single combination loan, where the construction loan becomes permanent at the end of the construction period.

Some lenders (primarily commercial banks) will only make construction loans. Others will only make combination loans. And some will do it either way.

***Two Loans Versus One Loan:*** Two loans mean that you shop twice and incur two sets of closing costs. One loan means that you shop only once and incur only one set of closing costs. But, to do it effectively, you must shop construction loans and permanent loans at the same time.

Construction loans usually run for six months to a year and carry an adjustable interest rate that resets monthly or quarterly. In addition to points and closing costs, lenders charge a construction fee to cover their costs in administering the loan. (Construction lenders pay out the loan in stages and must monitor the progress of construction). In shopping construction loans, one must take account of all of these dimensions of the "price."

Lenders offering combination loans typically will credit some of the fees paid for the construction loan toward the permanent loan. The lender might charge four points for the construction loan, for example, but apply three of the points toward the permanent loan. If the borrower takes the permanent loan from another lender, however, the construction lender retains the three points. This credit plus the one set of closing costs are major talking points of loan officers pushing combination loans.

The rebate offered on combination loans makes it difficult to compare these loans with the two-loan alternative. For example, lender A offers a construction loan at four points with three points applicable to a permanent loan, while B offers an untied construction loan at two points. Going with A means saving one point on the construction loan but this is no bargain if A's terms on permanent loans are not competitive.

Suppose A offers a permanent loan at 6% and three points, while lender C offers the same 6% loan at one point. Then if you selected A, you would pay a total of four points on both loans, but if you had selected B for the construction loan and C for the permanent loan you would have paid only three points in total. A is above the best price available in the permanent loan market by more than it is below the best price available in the construction loan market.

Further, once you accept a combination loan deal that involves a significant rebate from the construction loan, shopping other lenders for a permanent mortgage after construction ends is likely to prove fruitless. So long as the combination lender is not above the market for permanent loans by more than the rebate plus closing costs, you cannot do better by finishing the deal with another lender. You're hooked!

This means that you cannot properly assess a lender's combination loan without comparing that lender's terms on permanent loans with those of other permanent lenders. You should shop construction loans and permanent loans at the same time. If the combination lender is above the market on permanent loans by an amount that is less than the saving on the construction loan plus closing costs, you go with the combination loan. Otherwise, you go with two loans.

If you go the two-loan route, you have the option of having the builder take the construction loan. Then you have only the permanent loan to worry about.

***Should the Builder Finance Construction?*** The advantage of having the builder finance construction is that you need to take out only one mortgage, and you have assurance that the builder has sufficient financial capacity to do the job. Further, a builder paying interest on a construction loan has an incentive to get the job done as quickly as possible.

The downside is that you don't know what you are paying for the financing because it is embedded in the price of the house. Since the builder must include the financing cost in the price before the construction period is known, his inclination may be to assume a longer period (and therefore a higher financing cost) than is actually the case.

In addition, the builder must have title to the land in order to obtain construction financing, and switching title is costly in some states. Finally, a builder who owns the property and is on the hook for the loan may be reluctant to make any modifications in the design that would negatively affect its marketability in the event that the deal falls through.

---

**Contract Chicanery** *Inserting provisions into a loan contract that severely disadvantage the borrower, without the borrower's knowledge, and sometimes despite oral assurances to the contrary.*

Prepayment penalties are perhaps the most frequently cited subject of such abuse. See **Prepayment Penalty/*Surreptitious Penalties*.**

---

**Conversion Option** *The option to convert an ARM to an FRM at some point during its life.*

See **Adjustable Rate Mortgage (ARM)/*Convertible ARMs*.**

---

**Correspondent Lender** *A lender who delivers loans to another (usually larger) lender against prior price commitments the larger lender has made to the correspondent.*

Mortgage brokers sometimes evolve into correspondent lenders when they accumulate enough capital to acquire the credit lines needed to close loans in their own names. But correspondents continue to depend on commitments from other lenders to protect them against the risk that market prices will decline while they are holding loans. *See* **Mortgage Lender/*Retail, Wholesale, and Correspondent Lenders*.**

---

**Co-Signing** *Assuming responsibility for someone else's payment obligation in the event that that party defaults.*

***The Case for Co-Signing:*** When my son graduated from college, he had no credit, but needed a loan to buy a car. I co-signed his car loan. By doing this, I put my credit on the line to help him. It made sense, because I knew my son was a good risk but the lender didn't. My son established his credit-worthiness with this loan, and I never had to co-sign for him again.

***Hazards of Co-Signing:*** The major hazard in co-signing a loan or a lease is that you may be forced to pay. You only do it for someone in whom you have a lot of confidence.

Too often, people co-sign without giving it much thought—until they find themselves being dunned for payment. Then they begin to look for ways to escape.

But there is no escape. Once you co-sign a note, there are only two ways to get off. Either the loan must be repaid in full, by the borrower or you, or the lender must agree to take you off. The lender is not going to let a co-signer off the hook when the borrower stops paying. The risk of non-payment is why the lender required a co-signer in the first place!

A lender might allow a co-signer off a note if the borrower has been making the payments faithfully for some time. But the lender has no financial incentive to do this, and there is no way of knowing in advance how long it will take, or if it will happen at all.

A second possible hazard is that a co-signer may be handicapped in getting a loan of his own because of the contingent obligation represented by the co-signing. This is a loan qualification problem. Lenders impose limits on the amount of existing debt a borrower can carry, and the co-signing obligation is considered debt for qualification purposes.

This problem can usually be remedied if you can document that the borrower for whom you have co-signed has been making the payments on time for a reasonable period. The lender who wants to make a loan will have a reason to remove the debt from your loan application. You remain a co-signer, but the lender is ignoring your obligation to the other lender in assessing your ability to repay a new loan.

---

**Cost-of-Savings Index (COSI)** *One of many interest rate indexes used to determine interest rate adjustments on an adjustable rate mortgage.*

*See* **Adjustable Rate Mortgage (ARM)/***ARM Rate Indexes***.

---

**Credit Report** *A report from a credit bureau containing detailed information bearing on creditworthiness, including the individual's credit history.*

A typical credit report shows some personal information including Social Security number; current and past addresses; employment history; public record information such as liens, foreclosures, bankruptcies, and garnishments; collection accounts; and credit information. The last covers individual credit relationships and shows the creditor, the current status of each account including the amount outstanding and the maximum line if any, prior payment history, and recent activity. A credit report also shows a list of companies that have requested the individual's file and the date the request was made.

There are three major repositories of credit information: Equifax, Experian, and Trans Union. The information provided by the three is not exactly the same because not all credit grantors report information to all three.

At one time, underwriters with responsibility for determining whether or not a mortgage applicant was "creditworthy" spent much of their time studying and interpreting credit reports. Increasingly, however, this judgment is being based on credit scores.

---

**Credit Score** *A single numerical score, based on information in an individual's credit report, that measures that individual's creditworthiness.*

Credit scores are based on statistical studies of the relationship between the different items in a credit report and the likelihood of default. The most widely used credit score is called FICO for Fair Isaac Co., which developed it. FICO scores range from 350 to 850, the higher the better.

### Major Determinants of FICO Scores:

**Payment History:** This is the most important determinant of credit scores. It includes information on the extent to which the subject has made timely payments on mortgage loans, auto loans, credit cards, personal loans, and charge accounts. Delinquencies reduce the score, while timely payments raise it.

Payment history also includes information on bankruptcies, foreclosures, legal judgments, liens, and wage garnishments. These will have a major adverse impact, although the impact declines with the passage of time.

**Amount and Distribution of Current Debts:** This is the next most important determinant of credit scores. Unlike payment history, however, it is not always intuitively obvious whether more or less debt, or whether more or fewer creditors, will improve a score. Past some point, more debt will lower the score by raising questions about the ability of the borrower to pay it all off. But not having debt will not generate a good score because without debt the subject cannot demonstrate a good payment history.

The FICO genie who generates a score does not have information on a subject's income or financial assets. The genie must make judgments about how much debt is too much from information on the debt alone. On debts with debt limits, it focuses on the relationship between the two. It reduces the score when it sees debts that are at or close to the maximum. On installment loans, the genie likes to see the balances going down. A large number of accounts does not disturb the genie, so long as most of them have no balances.

**Age of Accounts:** The FICO genie likes old accounts much better than new ones. Old ones indicate stability in credit relationships, whereas new ones might indicate financial distress—if there are many of them.

The genie understands, however, that shopping multiple credit sources can generate many inquiries without indicating financial distress. All inquiries regarding either mortgage loans or auto loans in any 14-day period are treated as one inquiry, and inquiries within 30 days of a score date are disregarded. The genie also disregards inquiries of your own and inquiries from lenders who are considering you for a loan "pre-approval."

**Mix of Credit:** This is not an important factor in the equation, which is good because Fair Isaac doesn't reveal exactly what it means. Reading between the lines, however, one can surmise that the genie is allergic to finance company loans.

*Reason Codes:* Every FICO score is returned with up to four "score factors," ranked by importance, that indicate why the score was not higher. Examples are "too many delinquencies," "ratio of balances to credit limits is too high," and "too many finance company accounts."

The reason codes mean little to someone with a high score. Those with low scores looking to improve, however, will do well to focus their efforts on the major problem areas indicated by the codes.

*Correcting Errors:* Credit reports often contain mistakes that lower the subject's credit score. Perhaps the most common is the inclusion of someone else's accounts. Borrowers who find mistakes must take the initiative to get them fixed, which means writing to the repository reporting the erroneous information and detailing the particulars of the error.

Under the Fair Credit Reporting Act (FCRA), a repository has five days from receipt of such a letter to contact the credit grantor that reported the erroneous information and another 35 days to complete its investigation and report back to the borrower. The report must indicate that the error was corrected, or there was no error, or the credit grantor did not respond, in which case the disputed item is dropped from the report.

To exercise your rights under FCRA, you must follow the correct procedures. These are spelled out on my Web site (www.mtgprofessor.com/A%20-%20Credit%20Issues/how_do_you_correct_your_credit_file.htm ).

Because fixing errors takes time, it is a good idea for borrowers to check their credit well in advance of entering the market. Your FICO score is available for $14.95 from www.myfico.com.

*Some Misperceptions About Credit:* Many borrowers have misperceptions about how their behavior will affect their FICO score.

**A Skipped Payment Results in One Delinquency:** One misperception is that a skipped payment results in one delinquency record. In fact, however, a skipped payment generates a stream of delinquencies until it is paid.

Under the accounting rules used for amortized mortgages, lenders always credit a payment against the earliest unpaid obligation. If you skip the payment for May, the payment intended for June will be credited to May, leaving the June payment delinquent. Similarly, the payment intended for July will be credited to June, leaving the July payment delinquent.

It would be nice if the mortgage contract allowed a skipped payment now and then. Such contracts exist in the UK and some other countries, but they have appeared in the U.S. only very recently and are not yet widely available. Unless you have one, if you skip a payment but pay regularly thereafter, you remain delinquent (and accumulate late fees) until the skipped payment is made good.

**Paying off Delinquent Loans Improves the Score:** Another misperception is that a credit score will improve if loans that have been delinquent are made current or paid off. This isn't so. Delinquencies lower credit scores because they show a weak commitment toward meeting obligations. This evidence is not wiped away when the loan is repaid. Only the passage of time, along with a better payment record, will wipe it away. The same is true of bankruptcies, tax liens, and judgments. They remain on the record for a period, even after they have been discharged or released.

**Consolidating Balances Improves the Score:** Still another misperception is that the consolidation of credit card balances into a smaller number of cards will increase a credit score. It is true that the FICO genie is much more favorably disposed to four credit cards than to 15. However, the genie is even more concerned with the relationship between the balances on the cards and the maximums. It sees cards that are "maxed out" as an indication of financial distress. So if the consolidation resulted in a smaller number of cards with balances close to their maximums, the score might drop rather than rise.

**Authorized Credit Card Users Are Safe:** Some borrowers have been surprised to find that their credit score has been reduced by delinquencies on credit cards for which they are not responsible. They are authorized users of cards on which the original credit card holder stopped paying. Even though they are not responsible for making the payment, credit grantors sometimes report authorized users to the credit-reporting agencies as delinquent. Unable to collect from the responsible parties, the original card-holders, the credit grantors hope that maybe the authorized users will pay in order to keep their credit records clean.

To fix this, write the credit-reporting agency, as follows:

*I'm an authorized user only and am not financially responsible for this debt. By reporting me delinquent, you are impugning my credit reputation in full violation of the Fair Credit Reporting Act (FCRA). I am aware of my rights under the Act. I intend to enforce them if you don't immediately remove all derogatory information from my credit profile that you placed there as a result of non-payment by the financially responsible party.*

If this doesn't work, go to my Web site for step two. (Look in the table of contents under "Credit Issues"/"Are Authorized Users at Risk?")

**Credit and Income Can Be Separated in a Loan Application:** Some couples want to use the credit score of one spouse (the one with the good score) while qualifying with the income of the other. This doesn't work. Lenders are concerned with the credit score of the borrower whose income they are depending on to service the loan.

***Use of FICO Scores by Lenders:*** Most lenders now incorporate FICO scores in their pricing and qualification requirements, but they do it in all sorts of ways. One lender might have 10 different interest rates corresponding to 10 FICO score categories. Another might only use three categories. Still another might set a single FICO score minimum for all loans, but require higher scores for borrowers who want no-down-payment loans, or less than full documentation. Some lenders use FICO scores but supplement them with other information from the credit report that they believe is not adequately weighted in the score.

Because the different credit repositories may have different information, lenders typically get two FICO scores and use the lower of the two. Sometimes they get three and use the middle score.

Lenders dealing with applicants who have low scores because of a foreclosure or bankruptcy will often request a letter of explanation. The purpose is to determine whether the event was caused by recklessness and, therefore, likely to recur or by unusual and unforeseeable misfortunes that were beyond the applicant's control.

Applicants in this situation should realize that the burden of proof is on them. They must persuade the lender that the misfortune was a one-time event that is very unlikely to recur.

---

**Cumulative Interest**    *The sum of all interest payments to date or over the life of the loan.*

This is not a good measure of the cost of credit to the borrower because it does not include upfront cash payments and it is not adjusted for the time value of money. *See* **Interest Cost**.

**Current Index Value** *The most recently published value of the index used to adjust the interest rate on an indexed ARM.*

*See* **Indexed ARMs**.

---

**Deadbeat** *A borrower who doesn't pay.*

---

**Debt Consolidation** *Rolling short-term debt into a home mortgage loan, either at the time of home purchase or later.*

*The Case for Consolidation:* Borrowers consolidate in order to reduce their finance costs. Usually, the interest rate on the mortgage is below that on short-term debt, and mortgage interest is also tax-deductible. Borrowers also like the convenience of making fewer payments.

*The Case Against Consolidation:* When borrowers consolidate, they convert unsecured debt into secured debt. That is the major reason the mortgage interest rate is usually lower. Borrowers who encounter financial distress and fail to pay their unsecured debts lose their good credit but they don't lose their home. By increasing the size of the claim against their home, they increase the risk of losing it.

If consolidation causes the mortgage amount to exceed the property value, borrowers may also lose their mobility. Sale of the property requires that all mortgages be repaid, which means that the seller must come up with enough cash to cover the deficiency. Borrowers in this situation may also have to pass on opportunities for profitable refinance, since it is very difficult to refinance when debt exceeds value.

Consolidation that reduces the borrowers total monthly payments while eliminating their short-term debt may encourage them to build up that debt all over again. This could result in so much debt they never get out from under.

*Consolidating Intelligently:* To consolidate intelligently, borrowers need to compare their options. Three debt consolidation calculators on my Web site can help you do this. These calculators are designed for three categories of borrowers with non-mortgage debt:

- **Those about to purchase a house.** Their options are to consolidate in the new purchase mortgage, or not.

- **Those with an existing first mortgage.** Their options are to consolidate by refinancing the first mortgage to include the non-mortgage debt, or by taking out a new second, or neither.

- **Those with existing first and second mortgages.** Their options are to a) consolidate existing non-mortgage debt in a new (cash-out refinance) first mortgage, leaving the second mortgage as it is; b) consolidate the existing second mortgage in a new (cash-out refinance) first mortgage, leaving non-mortgage debt as it is; c) consolidate both non-mortgage debt and the second mortgage in a new (cash-out refinance) first mortgage; d) consolidate existing non-mortgage debt in a new (cash-out refinance) second mortgage, leaving the first mortgage as it is; and e) do nothing.

The calculators provide two types of information about each option. One is the total monthly payment, which consists of mortgage payments, mortgage insurance premiums if any, and non-mortgage debt payments if any. Borrowers on tight budgets must be concerned with the monthly payment, but it should not be the major determinant of their choice. It fails to reflect differences in tax savings or debt reduction as between the options.

The second type of information the calculator provides about all the options is their total cost over a period specified by the user. If the user's time horizon is, say, five years, the total cost of each option is the sum of the monthly payments over five years including lost interest, less the tax savings and reduction in total debt over that period.

*Life After Consolidation:* Borrowers who consolidate should use any monthly savings to accelerate the pay down of principal on their mortgage(s). Even better is to shorten the term on the new mortgage(s) so that the new payment is close to the old payment.

Unfortunately, many borrowers interpret a payment-reduction consolidation as a license to take on more non-mortgage debt. A few years later, they look to consolidate again. If their house has appreciated enough, they may be able to, but sooner or later they run out of equity. Then they write me letters like this one.

*We kept adding to our second mortgage to pay off credit card debt ... the rate is now up to 13.75% ... we don't have enough equity to break even if we sell ... we feel trapped.*

They trapped themselves. Don't let it happen to you.

---

**Deed in Lieu of Foreclosure** *Deeding the property over to the lender as an alternative to having the lender foreclose on the property.*

See **Payment Problems/*Position of the Lender*/**Permanent Problem.

---

**Default** *Failure of the borrower to honor the terms of the loan agreement.*

Lenders usually view borrowers delinquent 90 days or more as in default.

See **Payment Problems**.

---

**Deferred Interest**

*Same as* **Negative Amortization**.

---

**Delinquency** *A mortgage payment that is more than 30 days late.*

---

**Demand Clause** *A clause in the note that allows the lender to demand repayment of the balance in full.*

A demand clause is even better (for the lender) than an acceleration clause. An acceleration clause allows the lender to call the loan if the borrower violates some contractual provision, such as a requirement that the loan must be repaid upon sale of the property. A demand clause allows the lender to demand repayment for *any reason*. For example, the lender can force you to accept a higher rate by threatening that if you don't agree, the loan will be called.

The lender asking for a demand clause will no doubt disavow any intention of behaving in such a manner. But you don't put your head on a chopping block just because the executioner promises not to cut it off.

The Truth in Lending Disclosure has a statement that reads "This loan has a demand feature," which is checked "yes" or "no." Some lenders will check "yes," even though the note has an acceleration rather than a demand feature (*see* **Acceleration**). Nonetheless, if it is checked "yes," you want to examine the relevant sections of the note.

**Direct Lender**  *A term that small lenders sometimes use to distinguish themselves from mortgage brokers.*

**Discount Points**

*Same as* **Points**.

**Discretionary ARM**  *An ARM on which the lender has the right to change the interest rate at any time, for any reason, by any amount, subject only to a requirement that the borrower be notified in advance.*

The discretionary ARM is at the opposite pole from **Indexed ARMs** on which rate adjustments are completely rule-based.

Discretionary ARMs were long the standard mortgage in the U.K. and in other English-speaking countries that imported it from the U.K., such as India and South Africa. They never caught on in the U.S., where the indexed ARM prevails.

**Documentation Requirements**  *A lender's requirements regarding how information about income and assets must be provided by the applicant and how it will be used by the lender.*

The following categories have evolved in the market.

*Full Documentation:* Both income and assets are disclosed and verified, and income is used in determining the applicant's ability to repay the mortgage. Formal verification requires the borrower's employer to verify employment and the borrower's bank to verify deposits. In some cases, in order to save time, lenders will accept copies of the borrower's original bank statements, W-2s, and paycheck stubs.

At one time, full documentation was the rule and it remains the standard. In recent years, however, other documentation programs have grown in importance. They make it possible for consumers who are unable to meet standard requirements to qualify for a loan nonetheless.

*Stated Income-Verified Assets:* Income is disclosed and the source of the income is verified, but the amount is not verified. Assets are verified and must meet an adequacy standard such as, for example, six months of stated income and two months of expected monthly housing expense.

*Stated Income-Stated Assets:* Both income and assets are disclosed but not verified. However, the source of the borrower's income is verified.

*No Ratio:* Income is disclosed and verified but not used in qualifying the borrower. The standard rule that the borrower's housing expense cannot exceed some specified percent of income, is ignored. Assets are disclosed and verified.

*No Income:* Income is not disclosed, but assets are disclosed and verified and must meet an adequacy standard.

*Stated Assets or No Asset Verification:* Assets are disclosed but not verified, income is disclosed, verified, and used to qualify the applicant.

*No Asset:* Assets are not disclosed, but income is disclosed, verified, and used to qualify the applicant.

*No Income-No Assets:* Neither income nor assets are disclosed.

While these categories are fairly well established in the market, there are numerous differences between individual lenders in the details. For example, under a stated income program lenders may or may not require that applicants sign a form authorizing the lender to request the applicant's tax returns from the IRS in the event the borrower defaults. Similarly, lenders differ in the amount of assets they require.

The proliferation of different documentation programs reflects a realization by lenders that many consumers with the potential for home ownership were shut out of the market by excessively rigid documentation requirements. It also dawned on lenders that documentation could be viewed as a risk factor that could be priced or offset by other risk factors.

Full documentation is the least risky to the lender, no income/no asset is the most risky, and the others are in between. If the documentation is riskier, lenders will charge more, require risk offsets, or both. The most important risk offsets are large down payments and high credit scores.

The change in attitudes toward both credit rating and documentation requirements has expanded the market. Here are examples of borrowers who would have not qualified under full documentation requirements:

- Jones is a personal trainer with no fixed place of business who makes good money but can't document it. He can document his mutual funds, and his CPA can verify his self-employed status, so Jones qualifies under a stated income/verified assets plan.

- Smith is in the same business and uses the same CPA as Jones but an uncle is gifting him with the cash he needs. Since Smith cannot document assets, he pays a little more under a stated income/stated asset program.

- King can document income and assets but wants to allocate 58% of his income to housing expenses, which far exceeds conventional guidelines. King qualifies under a no-ratio loan.

- Queen is leaving her job to move to a new city where she has no job and will buy a house when she gets there with money from the sale of her existing house. She has no income and cannot document assets because her old house won't be sold until after closing on the new one. Nevertheless, she qualifies under a no income/no asset program. If she has a contract of sale on the old house before closing on the new one, she will be able to document assets and can qualify under a no income program.

---

**Down Payment**  *The difference between the value of the property and the loan amount, expressed in dollars, or as a percentage of value.*

For example, if the house is valued at $100,000 and the loan is for $80,000, the down payment is $20,000 or 20%.

***Down Payment and LTV:*** In percent, the down payment is one minus the LTV—the ratio of loan to value. In the example, the LTV is 80%, and 1 − LTV is 20%. Lender requirements are always expressed in terms of a maximum LTV rather than a minimum down payment because maximum LTV does not generate questions about what a down payment is.

Suppose the house in the example is purchased for $100,000 and the borrower has $20,000 for the down payment, but not the $3,000 needed for settlement costs. The settlement costs are therefore added to the loan amount, raising it to $83,000. The LTV is now 83% and the borrower will be obliged to pay for mortgage insurance.

The borrower may say, "Hold on, I'm putting down the same $20,000 as before." However, the mortgage insurance requirement is set as a maximum LTV of 80% rather than a minimum down payment of 20%, so the argument is over before it begins. In reality, the down payment is $17,000 or 17%.

*Sale Price Versus Appraised Value:* Home purchasers who pay less for a home than its appraised value frequently question whether they can use the difference as their down payment. They cannot. The rule is that the property value used in determining the down payment and the LTV is the sale price or appraised value, *whichever is lower*. The only exception to this is when the seller provides a gift of equity to the buyer, as discussed below.

*Gift of Equity:* Gifts of equity arise when a house is sold for less than its market value, almost always to a family member. In this case, the lender recognizes that the house is being priced below market and will accept the appraisal as the value. Most lenders in such cases require two appraisals, and they take the lower of the two.

Gifts of equity should be structured to avoid gift taxes, which must be paid on gifts from a single donor in excess of $11,000 per recipient per year. The maximum gift equals $11,000 x D x R where D is the number of donors and R the number of recipients. For example, if the donors are a couple gifting a family of four, they can provide a total gift of $88,000 without tax consequences. Donors who want to gift more than the amount calculated from the formula should talk to a tax advisor.

*Cash Gifts:* Lenders will accept cash gifts for some part of the down payment, usually not for all of it. While the rules vary for different programs, it is common to require that the borrower contribute 3% of the down payment.

Lenders require a donor to sign a gift statement affirming that the funds provided are a gift rather than a loan. The lender wants assurance that the transfer of funds imposes no repayment obligation that could put the mortgage loan at risk. Sometimes, however, borrowers induce friends or family members who do not want to make gifts to lend in the guise of a gift.

For example, a house purchaser needs the equity in his current house to make the down payment on a new one, but must close on the new one before the old one is under contract. Because there is ample equity in the old house, the buyer asks a friend or family member to lend the money needed for the down payment, to be repaid when the old house is sold.

This is a bad idea. Not only is it a fraud against the lender, it also involves risk to the donor. Contingencies that could result in not being repaid include a sharp drop in the value of the old house before it is sold, or the sudden death of the home purchaser.

The home buyer in this situation should be advised to take out a home equity loan on the old house, which can be repaid when it is sold. A home equity lender has a lien on the house and has diversified its risk over many loans. The lender pretending to be a donor has neither.

*Land as Down Payment:* Many people acquire land in order to build on it later, and the land serves as part or all of the down payment. If the land has been held for some time, the lender will appraise the completed house with the lot, and the difference between the appraisal and the cost of construction is viewed as the down payment.

For example, if the builder charges $160,000 for the house and the appraisal comes in at $200,000, the land is assumed to be worth $40,000. A loan of $160,000 in this case would have a down payment of 20%, or an LTV of 80%.

If the land was purchased recently, however, the lender will not value it for more than the purchase price. If the price was only

$30,000 in the above example, the lender will value it at $30,000, and the down payment will only be 15.8%, or an LTV of 84.2%.

**Home Seller Contributions:** Home sellers often gift buyers, raising the price by enough to cover the gift. The purpose is to improve the buyer's ability to purchase the house by reducing the required cash. The practice is legitimate, provided it is done openly and conforms to the guidelines of lenders and mortgage insurers. For it to work, the appraiser must say that the house is worth the higher price.

For example, Jones offers his house to Smith for $200,000, which Smith is willing to pay. But under the best financing terms available to Smith, he needs $12,000, which he doesn't have.

So Jones and Smith agree that Jones will raise the price of the house to $206,000 and Jones will gift Smith $6,000. Assuming the appraiser goes along, the amount of cash required of Smith drops from $12,000 to $6,360, making the purchase affordable (see the table below). Jones gets his price and Smith gets his house, so everyone is happy—except, perhaps, the lender.

| How a Seller Contribution Reduces the Buyer's Required Cash | | |
|---|---|---|
| | **Before** | **After** |
| Sale Price | $200,000 | $206,000 |
| Appraised Value | | $206,000 |
| Loan | $194,000 | $199,820 |
| Down Payment (3%) | $6,000 | $6,180 |
| Total Cash Required | $12,000 | $6,360 |
| Down Payment (3%) | $6,000 | $6,180 |
| Settlement Costs (3%) | $6,000 | $6,180 |
| Gift from Seller | 0 | $6,000 |
| Buyer's Stated Equity | $6,000 | $6,180 |
| Buyer's Real Equity | $6-12,000 | $180-6,180 |

Appraisals often ratify sale prices, whether justified or not. If the house is actually only worth the original offer price of $200,000, the buyer has only $180 of real equity—the difference between the original property value and the higher loan amount—rather than $6,180. Less equity means greater loss for the lender if the loan goes into default.

For this reason, lenders and mortgage insurers limit the size of seller contributions. The smaller the down payment requirement, the more critical the issue becomes. On conventional loans (loans not insured by the federal government), it is common to restrict seller contributions to 3% of sale price with 5% down and to 6% with 10% or more down.

*Contributions Under FHA:* On FHA loans, individual sellers can contribute up to 6% of the price to the buyer's settlement costs, but nothing to the down payment. However, FHA allows approved nonprofit corporations to offer down payment assistance using funds provided by sellers. These include www.nehemiah.org, www.partnersincharity.org, and www.ameridream.org. The combination of direct seller contributions to settlement costs on FHAs and indirect contributions through down payment assistance programs, can add up to 9-10% of the sale price.

*Investing in a Larger Down Payment:* A larger down payment is an investment that yields a return that consists in part of the interest rate on the money you aren't borrowing. If you put an additional $10,000 down, for example, you are borrowing $10,000 less and you save the interest that you would have paid on it. But there may be other savings as well that make the return higher than the interest rate on the loan.

First, most borrowers pay points or other loan fees expressed as a percent of the loan amount. If you borrow $10,000 less, you save not only the interest but the upfront fees on the $10,000. Fees of fixed dollar amounts don't affect the return because they aren't reduced when the loan amount is reduced.

A second possibility is that the larger down payment reduces or eliminates mortgage insurance, which must be purchased when the down payment is less than 20% of property value. In such event, the return on the larger down payment includes not only the savings in interest and points but also the mortgage insurance that is eliminated by the larger down payment.

Still a third possibility is that the larger down payment reduces the interest rate by bringing the loan amount below the conforming loan limit, at this writing $322,700. Because the federal secondary market agencies, Fannie Mae and Freddie Mac, cannot purchase mortgages larger than that amount, the market breaks at that point. Interest rates are about 3/8% lower on loans below the maximum.

All these factors are pulled together in calculator 12a on my Web site, "Rate of Return from Investing in a Larger Down Payment." The calculator will show you, for example, that increasing the down payment from 5% to 10% on a 30-year fixed-rate loan at 7% and two points will yield 13.1% before taxes over eight years. If the larger down payment dropped the loan below the conforming loan limit, reducing the rate to 6.625%, the return on the amount invested in the down payment would be 19.37%.

**No-Down-Payment Loans:** The availability of no-down-payment loans (NDPs) is a strength of the U.S. mortgage system and also a weakness. Some families become successful homeowners with the help of NDPs. Others, who shouldn't be homeowners, are enticed to try and fail.

NDPs have high default rates. This has been a finding of every study of mortgage defaults that I have ever seen. One reason is that homeowners who borrow the full value of their property have less to protect should economic adversity strike. If they lose their job, or if property values decline temporarily, they lose less from a default than borrowers with equity.

A second reason is that borrowers unable to accumulate a down payment have not demonstrated budgetary discipline and the ability to plan ahead. People able to save money every month before they buy a home are much more likely to meet their monthly mortgage obligations afterwards.

Why do lenders make NDPs? When property values are rising, as they have most of the time since World War II, the risk of default is reduced. Rising values create equity in houses that were initially mortgaged to the hilt.

In recent years, furthermore, lenders have become more confident in their ability to assess the willingness and capacity of borrowers to repay their mortgages. Using credit scoring and other tools, they judge that it is safe to give less weight to an applicant's ability to accumulate a down payment.

Lenders protect themselves, furthermore, by charging higher rates on NDPs. The rate includes a "risk premium" to cover the losses lenders expect from higher delinquencies and defaults.

Just because a lender is willing to give you a NDP, however, doesn't mean you should take it. The risk premiums protect lenders, not you.

Some people are not cut out to be homeowners. When they default, the costs include not only loss of their house, but also having to find another one with all the disruptions to their lives that that typically involves. Plus their credit rating goes into the tank. If many default-ers live in the same neighborhood, the neighborhood can also tank.

**Securities as Down Payment:** Some investment banks offer home loan plans where they accept the deposit of securities in place of a down payment. If you purchase a house for $200,000, for example, the bank will lend you the entire $200,000, provided you deposit securities worth $40,000 with them. For the bank, the securities provide essen-tially the same protection against default as a down payment, while discouraging the customer from shifting the account to another bank.

These plans delay the accumulation of equity in the house indefi-nitely. The customer begins with no equity, and if the payment only covers the interest for the first 10 years, which is a common feature, the only equity buildup is from appreciation in the value of the prop-erty. The theory behind this is that the consumer's overall wealth will grow more rapidly if the maximum amount is invested in securities.

In the example, the consumer is in effect borrowing an additional $40,000 to invest in securities. Whether this turns out to be a good idea or a bad idea depends on the yield earned on the securities rel-ative to the mortgage rate. It doesn't make sense to borrow $40,000 at 7% to invest in government bonds yielding 5.5%. It may make sense for consumers investing in common stock, which might yield 12% or more over a long period.

**"Dual-Apper"** *A borrower who submits applications through two loan providers, usually mortgage brokers, without their knowledge.*

Home purchasers sometimes submit more than one loan application as a way of protecting themselves against the hazards inherent in committing to one loan provider before the price is locked. Double-apping strengthens their bargaining position in negotiating the lock price. I don't recommend it, however.

Mortgage brokers despise dual-appers because they force the broker to do a lot of work and then bid for the loan or lose it. Being midway through the process with a resentful broker is not a happy prospect. If you run into a major roadblock, a resentful broker may not be willing to go the extra mile to remove it.

Locking does not provide complete protection against skullduggery, furthermore, because the lock price does not finalize the settlement costs other than points. At that point, the settlement costs are merely "estimates." A resentful but resourceful broker will find ways to augment your fees as you move to closing.

There is an alternative to double-apping that protects you better, is fair to the broker and avoids wasted effort. Demand to know the price before the work begins. While the price of the mortgage cannot be set in advance, the price of the broker's services can.

There is now a group of brokers, called Upfront Mortgage Brokers (UMBs), who quote a fee for their services upfront. Separating the price of the broker's services from the price of the mortgage eliminates gamesmanship by the broker and the need for double-apping. *See* **Upfront Mortgage Brokers.**

---

**Dual Index Mortgage** *A mortgage on which the interest rate is adjustable based on an interest rate index, and the monthly payment adjusts based on a wage and salary index.*

Dual index mortgages are not written in the U.S., but they are common in Mexico.

---

**Due-on-Sale Clause** *A provision of a loan contract stipulating that if the property is sold the loan balance must be repaid.*

A mortgage containing a due-on-sale clause is not assumable. This prevents a home seller from transferring responsibility for an existing loan to the buyer when the interest rate on the old loan is below the current market.

**Effective Rate** *The interest rate adjusted for intra-year compounding.*

Because interest on a mortgage is calculated monthly, a 6% mortgage actually has a rate of .5% per month. If there were no principal repayments the first year, $100 invested in a 6% mortgage would actually earn $6.17 of interest during the year because of reinvestment of monthly interest. The "effective rate" is thus 6.17%, while 6% is termed the "nominal" rate. Similarly, a 6% bond on which interest is paid quarterly has an effective rate of 6.14%.

**80/10/10 and 80/15/5 Loan Plans** *Combination first mortgages for 80% of the sale price or value and second mortgages for 10% or 15%.*

*See* **Second Mortgage/*Using a Second to Avoid Mortgage Insurance***.

**Equity** *In connection with a home, the value of the home less the balance of outstanding mortgage loans on the home.*

**Escrow Account** *In a home mortgage transaction, a deposit account maintained by the lender and funded by the borrower, from which the lender makes tax and insurance payments for the borrower as they come due.*

Lenders generally require escrow accounts. The rationale is that it prevents a weakening in the protection provided to the lender by the property. If the taxes are not paid, the tax authority could place a lien on the property that would have a higher priority than the lender's lien. Similarly, if the house burns down or is flooded, the lender's protection goes with it if the insurance premiums had not been paid.

*Size of the Account:* To assure themselves that there will always be enough money in the account, lenders ask for more than they actually need as a "cushion." In years past, many of them maintained unreasonably large cushions. To deal with that, the Department of

Housing and Urban Development (HUD) issued a ruling that placed a ceiling on the size of escrow accounts, which in turn limited the amount the lender could ask the borrower to deposit at closing.

The rule is that the deposit cannot exceed the amount needed to prevent the balance from falling below an amount equal to two-months worth of tax and insurance payments at its lowest point during the year. While HUD does not do a lot of enforcing, my impression is that all but a handful of lenders follow the HUD rules. If you want to check the calculation, I explain how to do it on my Web site, see "How Do I Figure Escrows?"

***Reasons for Avoiding Escrows:*** The least important reason borrowers may want to avoid escrow is to capture the interest earnings on the account for themselves. The amounts involved are small. I explain how to measure the interest earnings on my Web site in "Should I Escrow?"

The more important reason is to establish control over the payments. Lenders require escrow to assure that the payments will be made, and borrowers may want to avoid escrow for the same reason. Lenders occasionally screw up, and when this happens it can be a nightmare for the borrower. *See* **Servicing/Recourse Against Bad Servicing**.

***Ways to Avoid Escrow:*** Most lenders will waive escrow requirements if the borrower makes a down payment of 20% or more. The logic of this waiver is that if the borrower has that much equity in the house, it is safe for the lender to rely upon the borrower's self-interest to pay the taxes and insurance premiums.

So, if you intend to put down 20% or more, let the loan officer know up front that you will not be escrowing.

If you intend to put down less than 20%, it becomes more complicated. In most states, lenders are willing to waive escrows for a fee—usually 1/4 to 3/8 of a point. However, in Washington, D.C., Illinois, New York, and Oregon lenders are barred from charging a waiver fee, which means that they may be less willing to waive escrows in those states.

If you are already escrowing, getting rid of it is not easy. You must convince the lender that it is in his interest to eliminate the requirement in your case.

If the lender is a depository institution servicing its own mortgages, your best shot is to appeal as a customer of the firm. If it isn't too costly, depositories usually want to satisfy their customers or potential customers. Increasingly, however, loans are being serviced not by lenders but by servicing agents working for lenders.

Servicing agents make most of their money from servicing fees paid by lenders and from the interest earnings on escrow accounts. When a loan they are servicing is refinanced, however, the income on this loan ceases unless the agent is the one making the new loan. If the servicing agent understands that if you cannot terminate your escrow account, you intend to refinance your mortgage with another lender (not with him or her), you will get his or her attention. After all, it is better to lose only the escrow interest than to lose both the escrow interest and the servicing fee.

---

**Fallout**  *Loan applications that are withdrawn by borrowers, because they have found a better deal or for other reasons.*

---

**Fannie Mae**  *One of two federal agencies that purchase home loans from lenders. The other is Freddie Mac.*

*See* **Secondary Mortgage Markets** / *Fannie Mae and Freddie Mac.*

---

**FHA Mortgage**  *A mortgage on which the lender is insured against loss by the Federal Housing Administration, with the borrower paying the mortgage insurance premium.*

***What FHA Does:*** By insuring lenders against loss in the event that borrowers default on their loans, FHA encourages lenders to make loans that they might otherwise view as too risky.

FHA began operations in the depths of the depression of the 1930s when lenders had stopped making new loans altogether because a sizeable proportion of existing loans were in default. As the country worked its way out of the depression, the FHA settled into the principal role it has today: helping a segment of the low-and-moderate-income population become homeowners who otherwise might not make it because they have shaky credit, or can't come up with the cash needed for the down payment.

Some FHA programs are subsidized. For example, a special program of mortgage insurance for members of the armed forces is subsidized by the armed forces, while special programs for older declining urban areas and for displaced households are partially subsidized by FHA through insurance premiums that don't cover losses. Its standard (Section 203b) program, however, was designed from the beginning to be self-supporting out of the insurance premiums paid by borrowers. When during the late 80s rising defaults eroded the reserves that FHA maintains to pay losses under this program, the insurance premiums were raised substantially to restore the reserves to an adequate level.

FHA loans are subject to size limits, which vary from state to state and county to county. In 2003, the basic limit was $154,896 but it ranged up to $280,749 in high-cost areas. The limits by state and county are raised every year and can be found at https://entp.hud.gov/idapp/html/hicostlook.cfm.

**Who Should Take an FHA?** FHA loans are for borrowers who can't meet a 5% down payment requirement and have poor credit. Borrowers who can put 10% or more down and have good credit will do better with a conventional loan. The best loan type for borrowers who fall in the middle depends on the specifics of the case.

The great appeal of the FHA program is that it allows 1% down. Private mortgage insurers, in contrast, require 5% down on most loans and only allow 3% down on special programs. FHA is also liberal in allowing gifts to be used for paying settlement costs. *See* **Down Payment/*Home Seller Contributions*.**

FHA borrowers may also have weaker credit than private insurers accept. FHA allows higher ratios of expense to income, is more tolerant of existing debt and will allow the income of co-borrowers who don't live in the house to count fully in measuring income adequacy. It is also quite forgiving about bad credit. For example, a borrower need be out of a Chapter 7 bankruptcy for only two years and out of a Chapter 13 bankruptcy for only one year.

FHA loans are generally available in the market at about the same interest rate and points as conventional loans with the same term. There may be a difference in mortgage insurance premiums, however.

On an FHA 30-year fixed-rate mortgage (FRM), the mortgage insurance premium in 2003 was 1.5% of the loan amount paid up front plus .5% of the loan balance paid monthly. The premium is the same regardless of the down payment.

On conventional loans, the insurance premium depends on the down payment. With 5% down, the premium on a 30-year FRM is about the same as on an FHA. With 10% or more down, the premium on conventional loans is lower.

Borrowers who are unable to make a down payment but have strong credit have another option. Conventional loans are available with no down payment and no mortgage insurance, but borrowers pay a higher interest rate. Cash-poor borrowers with good credit should explore this alternative to an FHA. Veterans also have the option of a VA-guaranteed loan. *See* **VA Loans**.

Some loan officers steer borrowers into FHA loans who would do better with conventional loans. Either they specialize in FHAs and don't want to lose a sale, or they can earn a higher fee on an FHA, or both. If you can put 5% down, or you have good credit (a FICO score of, say, 700 or higher), don't let anyone steer you to an FHA without considering alternatives.

*FHA Loans Are Assumable:* Both FHA and VA loans have the advantage that they can be assumed by a qualified buyer. If a house is to be sold with an FHA or VA mortgage carrying a rate well below the current market, the seller can enhance its marketability by allowing the buyer to assume the old mortgage. Conventional loans carry due-on-sale clauses that require the loan to be repaid when the house is sold. *See* **Assumable Mortgage**.

*FHA and House Quality:* Homebuyers often assume that FHA's involvement as the mortgage insurer protects them against defects in the house. It doesn't. FHA has been bedeviled by this problem since it began operations in 1934.

The assumption that FHA protects the homebuyer is reasonable. FHA requires a property appraisal and that homes meet certain "minimum property requirements." In 1999, furthermore, FHA adopted a new set of rules regarding appraisals that it trumpeted in PR releases as a Homebuyer Protection Plan. The fact is, however, that FHA does not guarantee the value or condition of a home. FHA appraisals are to protect FHA, and homebuyers should protect themselves by ordering a home inspection.

In 2000, FHA developed a form that all purchasers of existing houses taking an FHA mortgage must sign before the date of the sales contract. The form is entitled: "For Your Protection: Get a Home Inspection." Immediately above the signature, it reads:

*I understand the importance of getting an independent home inspection. I have thought about this before I signed a contract with the seller for a home.*

---

### FICO Score
*See* **Credit Score**.

---

**Financing Points**  *Including points in the loan amount.*

*See* **Points/*Financing Points***.

---

**First Mortgage**  *A mortgage that has a first-priority claim against the property in the event the borrower defaults on the loan.*

For example, a borrower defaults on a loan secured by a property worth $100,000 net of sale costs. The property has a first mortgage with a balance of $90,000 and a second mortgage with a balance of $15,000. The first mortgage lender can collect $90,000 plus any unpaid interest and foreclosure costs. The second mortgage lender can collect only what is left of the $100,000.

---

**Fixed-Rate Mortgage (FRM)**  *A mortgage on which the interest rate and the monthly mortgage payment remain unchanged throughout the life of the mortgage.*

**Float** *Allowing the interest rate and points to vary with changes in market conditions, as opposed to "locking" them.*

Floating may be mandatory until the lender's lock requirements have been met. After that, the borrower may elect to lock the rate and points at any time but must do so a few days before the closing.

Allowing the rate to float exposes the borrower to market risk and also to the risk of being taken advantage of by the loan provider. *See* **Locking the Loan/*Choosing When to Lock*.**

---

**Float-Down** *A rate lock, plus an option to reduce the rate if market interest rates decline during the lock period.*

*See* **Locking the Loan/*Lock Versus Float-Down*.**

---

**Forbearance Agreement** *An agreement by the lender not to exercise the legal right to foreclose in exchange for an agreement by the borrower to a payment plan that will cure the borrower's delinquency.*

*See* **Payment Problems/*Position of the Lender*/**Temporary Problem.

---

**Foreclosure** *The legal process by which a lender acquires possession of the property securing a mortgage loan when the borrower defaults.*

*See* **Payment Problems/*Position of the Lender*/**Permanent Problem.

---

**Freddie Mac** *One of two federal agencies that purchase home loans from lenders. The other is Fannie Mae.*

*See* **Secondary Mortgage Markets/*Fannie Mae and Freddie Mac*.**

---

**Fully Amortizing Payment** *The monthly mortgage payment which, if maintained unchanged through the remaining life of the loan at the then-existing interest rate, will pay off the loan at term.*

*See* **Amortization/*Fully Amortizing Payment*.**

---

**Fully Indexed Rate** *On an ARM, the current value of the interest rate index, plus the margin.*

*See* **Adjustable Rate Mortgage (ARM)/*The Fully Indexed Rate*.**

**Generic Prices**  *Prices that assume a more or less standardized set of transaction characteristics that generally command the lowest prices.*

Generic prices are distinguished from transaction specific prices, which pertain to the characteristics of a specific transaction. *See* **Nichification/***Generic Price Quotes*.

**Gift of Equity**  *A sale price below market value, where the difference is a gift from the sellers to the buyers.*

Such gifts are usually between family members. Lenders will usually allow the gift to count as a down payment. *See* **Down Payment/***Gift of Equity*.

**Good Faith Estimate (GFE)**  *The form that lists the settlement charges the borrower must pay at closing, which the lender is obliged to provide the borrower within three business days of receiving the loan application.*

*See* **Settlement Costs** and **Mortgage Scams and Tricks/***Strictly Lender Scams/*Pad the GFE.

**Government National Mortgage Association (GNMA)**  *A federal agency that guarantees mortgage securities that are issued against pools of FHA and VA mortgages.*

*See* **Secondary Markets/***Ginny Mae*.

**Grace Period**  *A number of days, usually 10 to 15, that a borrower is allowed to be late in making the mortgage payment without suffering any penalty.*

**Graduated Payment Mortgage (GPM)**  *A mortgage on which the payment rises by a constant percent for a specified number of periods, after which it becomes fully-amortizing.*

As an example, the payment might increase by 7.5% every 12 months for 60 months, after which it is constant for the remaining term. GPMs had a brief flurry in the 1980s but then largely disappeared.

**Hazard Insurance**  *Insurance purchased by the borrower and required by the lender, to protect the property against loss from fire and other hazards.*

Hazard insurance is also known as "homeowner insurance," and is the second "I" in **PITI**.

**Historical Scenario**  *The assumption that the index value to which the interest rate on an ARM is tied follows the same pattern as in some prior historical period.*

In meeting their disclosure obligations in connection with ARMs, some lenders show how the mortgage payment would have changed on a mortgage originated some time in the past. That is not very useful. Showing how a mortgage originated *now* would change if the index followed a historical pattern would be useful, but nobody does it.

**Homebuyer Protection Plan**  *A plan purporting to protect FHA homebuyers against property defects.*

But it doesn't. *See* **FHA/FHA and House Quality**.

**Home Equity Conversion Mortgage (HECM)**  *A reverse mortgage program administered by FHA.*

*See* **Reverse Mortgage/FHA's Home Equity Conversion Mortgage (HECM)**.

**Home Equity Line**

*Same as* **HELOC**.

**Home Equity Line of Credit (HELOC)**  *A mortgage set up as a line of credit against which a borrower can draw up to a maximum amount, as opposed to a loan for a fixed dollar amount.*

For example, using a standard mortgage you might borrow $150,000, which would be paid out in its entirety at closing. Using a HELOC instead, you receive the lender's promise to advance you *up to* $150,000, in an amount and at a time of your choosing. You can draw on the line by writing a check, using a special credit card, or in other ways.

Most HELOCs are second mortgages and are used to fund intermittent needs, such as paying off credit cards, making home improvements, or paying college tuition. However, an increasing number of HELOCs are first mortgages used to refinance an existing first mortgage.

**Interest Calculated Daily:** Because the balance of a HELOC may change from day to day, depending on draws and repayments, interest on a HELOC is calculated daily rather than monthly. For example, on a standard 6% mortgage, interest for the month is .06 divided by 12 or .5, multiplied by the loan balance at the end of the preceding month. If the balance is $100,000, the interest payment is $500.

On a 6% HELOC, interest for a day is .06 divided by 365 or .000164, which is multiplied by the average daily balance during the month. If this is $100,000, the daily interest is $16.44, and over a 30-day month, interest amounts to $493.15; over a 31-day month, it is $509.59.

**Draw Period and Repayment Period:** HELOCs have a draw period, during which the borrower can use the line and a repayment period during which it must be repaid. Draw periods are usually five to 10 years, during which the borrower is only required to pay interest. Repayment periods are usually 10 to 20 years, during which the borrower must make payments on the principal equal to the balance at the end of the draw period divided by the number of months in the repayment period. Some HELOCs, however, require that the entire balance be repaid at the end of the draw period, so the borrower must refinance at that point.

**Low Up-Front Cost:** A major advantage of a HELOC over a standard mortgage in a refinancing is a lower upfront cost. On a $150,000 standard loan, settlement costs may range from $2,000 to $5,000, unless the borrower pays an interest rate high enough for the lender to pay some or all of it. On a $150,000 credit line, costs seldom exceed $1,000 and in many cases are paid by the lender without a rate adjustment.

*High Exposure to Interest Rate Risk:* The major disadvantage of the HELOC is its exposure to interest rate risk. All HELOCs are adjustable rate mortgages (ARMs), but they are much riskier than standard ARMs. Changes in the market impact a HELOC very quickly. If the prime rate changes on April 30, the HELOC rate will change effective May 1. An exception is HELOCs that have a guaranteed introductory rate, but these hold for only a few months. Standard ARMs, in contrast, are available with initial fixed-rate periods as long as 10 years.

HELOC rates are tied to the prime rate, which some argue is more stable than the indexes used by standard ARMs. In 2003, this certainly seemed to be the case, since the prime rate changed only once, to 4% on June 27. However, in 2001, the prime rate changed 11 times and ranged between 4.75% and 9%. In 1980, it changed 38 times and ranged between 11.25% and 20%.

In addition, most standard ARMs have rate adjustment caps, which limit the size of any rate change. And they have maximum rates 5%-6% above the initial rates, which in 2003 put them roughly at 8% to 11%. HELOCs have no adjustment caps, and the maximum rate is 18% except in North Carolina, where it is 16%.

*Shopping for a HELOC:* Shopping for a HELOC is simpler than shopping for a standard mortgage, if you know what you are doing. The major reason is that important features are the same from one lender to another.

- The interest rate on all the HELOCs is tied to the prime rate, as reported in the Wall Street Journal. In contrast, standard ARMs use a number of different indexes (Libor, COFI, CODI, and so on) which careful shoppers have to evaluate.
- The interest rate on the HELOCs adjust the first day of the month following a change in the prime rate, which could be just a few days. (Exceptions are those HELOCs with an introductory guaranteed rate, but these hold only for one to six months.) Standard ARMs, in contrast, fix the rate at the beginning for periods ranging from a month to 10 years.
- The HELOCs have no limit on the size of a rate adjustment, and most of them have a maximum rate of 18% except in

North Carolina, where it is 16%. Standard ARMs may have different rate adjustment caps and different maximum rates.

**The Margin:** The critical feature of a HELOC that is *not* the same from one lender to another, and which should be the major focus of smart shoppers, is the *margin*. This is the amount that is added to the prime rate to determine the HELOC rate. *Many if not most lenders do not volunteer the margin unless they are asked.*

Here is what can happen when you don't ask. Borrower X, who provided me with his history, was offered an introductory rate of 4.5% for three months. He was told that after the three months the rate "would be based on the prime rate." At the time the loan closed, the prime rate was 4%. Three months later, the prime rate was still 4%, but the rate on his loan was raised to 9.5%. It turned out that the margin, which the borrower never asked about, was 5.5%!

**Warning:** Do not assume that the difference between your HELOC start rate and the prime rate is the margin. It may or may not be. Ask. Bear in mind, as well, that the margin varies with credit score, ratio of total mortgage debt to property value, documentation, and other factors. You need the margin on *your deal*, not the margin they are advertising which is their *best deal*.

**Other HELOC Features:** If the HELOC will be used to meet future contingencies rather than to refinance an existing mortgage, the shopper needs to know whether there is a minimum draw at closing, or a minimum average loan balance. Lenders don't make any money unless the HELOC is used, but they are not always forthcoming about this. Borrowers who are uncertain about future usage don't want to be forced to borrow money they won't need.

Last and least important are the fees. Up-front fees are the same types as on standard mortgages, except that HELOC lenders seldom charge points, and third-party fees tend to be small and are often paid by the lender. In addition, there are some uniquely HELOC charges that you should factor in. These include an annual fee, usually $25-$75 and often waived the first year; and a cancellation fee, perhaps $350-$500, which is usually waived if the account stays open for three years.

**Truth in Lending (TIL) on a HELOC:** The required TIL disclosure on

HELOCs is a travesty. Borrowers must be given an APR, but it is the same as the interest rate. Among other things, it does not reflect points or other upfront costs, as the APR on standard loans does. The borrower described above was given an APR of 4.5% early on, and when his rate jumped to 9.5% he was told that his new APR was 9.5%. TIL does not require disclosure of the margin.

*Shopping Checklist:* Make sure the figures you get apply to *your deal.*

1. Introductory rate and period
2. Margin
3. Minimum draw
4. Required average balance
5. Up-front lender fees
6. Up-front third party fees
7. Annual fee
8. Cancellation fee

## Home Equity Loan

*Same as* **Second Mortgage.**

## Home Keeper *A revers mortgage program administered by Fannie Mae.*

*See* **Reverse Mortgage/*FannieMae's* Home Kepper Mortgage.**

## Homeowner's Equity

*See* **Equity.**

## Housing Bank *A government-owned or -affiliated lender that makes home loans directly to consumers.*

With minor exceptions, government in the U.S. has never loaned directly to consumers, but housing banks have been widespread in many developing countries. In the first two decades after World War II, about 50 housing banks were formed in the same number of countries. At various times over the years I have had occasion to visit and consult with institutions of this type in Iran, Ethiopia, Indonesia, Pakistan, Portugal, Thailand, Brazil, and Fiji.

With one exception, these housing banks have been a disaster. Some have been terminated while others are looking to privatize.

One of the major problems of the housing banks has been high default rates. In some cases, half or more of the borrowers don't repay their loans. Instead of administering "revolving" loan funds, where loan repayments plus interest provide the funds for new loans, the housing banks have needed continuing cash infusions by the government. This is a major reason why governments have become disillusioned.

Chronically high default rates reflect poor loan selection practices and poor collection practices after the loans are made. With private lenders, the dominant criteria used to determine whether or not to make a loan is the likelihood of repayment. With government lenders, politics and favoritism are often involved in a major way. This is especially likely when loan rates are below the market and therefore a bargain, which is often the case.

When housing banks operate side by side with private banks, the housing banks are subject to "adverse selection." The private banks who turn down loan applicants because of bad credit histories refer the applicants to the housing bank.

Housing banks also do very poorly at loan collections. In many cases, their loan collections systems are so poor that borrowers who stop paying do not receive a delinquent notice for six months or longer, by which time it may be too late to remedy the situation.

In dealing with delinquent borrowers, furthermore, housing bank officials usually shrink from exercising the ultimate sanction, which is to take away their house. It isn't their money, so why should they take the political heat? As a consequence, borrowers learn that they can get away with not paying and word gets around. In many cases, the distinction between a loan and a government grant becomes blurred.

The Housing Bank of Thailand is the exception to these comments because it has been well managed, its loan default rates have been comparable to those of private banks, and it has grown without need for continuing investment by the government. The secret of its success is that the government granted it virtually complete autonomy to operate in essentially the same manner as a private bank. The only major difference has been that dividends have been paid to the government rather than to private shareholders.

**Housing Expense**  *The sum of the monthly mortgage payment, hazard insurance, property taxes, and homeowner association fees.*

Housing expense is sometimes referred to as PITI, standing for principal, interest, taxes, and insurance.

**Housing Expense Ratio**  *The ratio of housing expense to borrower income.*

This ratio is one factor used in qualifying borrowers. *See* **Qualification/*Meeting Income Requirements*.**

**Housing Investment**  *The amount invested in a house, equal to the sale price less the loan amount.*

***The House Investment Decision:*** Lenders impose the upper limit on how much a household can spend for a house. When borrowers push the limit, it becomes costly because such borrowers are viewed as more risky to the lender. Small down payments require a higher interest rate or mortgage insurance.

Does a household accumulate more wealth over time by pushing its buying power to the limit? While such an aggressive policy involves taking on more debt at a higher cost, it also generates larger capital gains—3% appreciation on a $200,000 house is twice as much as 3% on a $100,000 house.

Consider two buyers who both have $20,000 in cash, enough income to meet all lender requirements, are in the same tax bracket, and can borrow at 7% for 30 years and zero points. However, one is "aggressive," purchasing a $150,000 house, borrowing $130,000 and paying a mortgage insurance premium of .53% for 10 years. The other buyer is "cautious," purchasing a $100,000 house and borrowing $80,000, thus avoiding mortgage insurance. Which buyer accumulates more wealth over time?

The major component of wealth is the value of the house. This is affected by the assumed rate of price appreciation. Higher price appreciation benefits the aggressive buyer more than the cautious one.

From this must be deducted the balance of the mortgage. Both the rapidity with which the loan balance is reduced and the size of the monthly mortgage payment are affected by the mortgage interest rate. Since the aggressive buyer borrows more than the cautious buyer, higher mortgage rates hurt the aggressive buyer more than the cautious buyer.

We must also deduct the amount paid each month for interest, principal reduction, mortgage insurance, and the lost interest on this amount. This is affected by the assumed "investment rate," which is the rate the buyers could have earned if they invested this money elsewhere. Since the monthly payments are larger for the aggressive buyer, higher investment rates hurt the aggressive buyer more than the cautious buyer. On the other hand, interest is tax deductible so that higher tax rates work in the opposite direction.

The tables below show how long it takes, if ever, for the greater price appreciation enjoyed by the aggressive buyer to offset the effects of the higher costs. For example, if the investment rate is 5% and the buyers are in the 15% tax bracket, the aggressive buyer never catches up if the appreciation rate is 5% or less. At a 6% rate of appreciation, the aggressive buyer catches up in 25 years. Shifting to a tax rate of 35%, the aggressive buyer would catch up in three years.

These numbers suggest that in a "normal" environment, an aggressive purchase policy is difficult to rationalize from a wealth perspective. No buyer should expect 6% appreciation in an environment in which the mortgage rate is 7%, yet 6% appreciation is needed to justify an aggressive policy. On the other hand, no account is taken of the benefits to the aggressive buyer from living in a more expensive house.

Readers can assess their own unique situation using the spreadsheet used to compile these tables. It is on my Web site.

**How Long It Takes an "Aggressive" Buyer to Accumulate More Wealth than a "Cautious" Buyer Using a 7% 30-Year Mortgage**

| Income Tax Rate of Buyer 15% | | | | | |
|---|---|---|---|---|---|
| | **Investment Rate** | | | | |
| **Property Appreciation Rate** | **0%** | **2.5%** | **5%** | **7.5%** | **10%** |
| 3% or Lower | Never | Never | Never | Never | Never |
| 4% | 20 Years | Never | Never | Never | Never |
| 5% | 12 years | 20 Years | Never | Never | Never |
| 6% | 7 Years | 11 Years | 25 Years | Never | Never |
| 7% | 2 Years | 3 Years | 7 Years | Never | Never |
| 8% | 1 Month | 1 Month | 1 Month | 1 Month | 26 Years |
| 9% | 1 Month | 1 Month | 1 Month | 1 Month | 7 Years |

| Income Tax Rate of Buyer 35% | | | | | |
|---|---|---|---|---|---|
| | **Investment Rate** | | | | |
| **Property Appreciation Rate** | **0%** | **2.5%** | **5%** | **7.5%** | **10%** |
| 2% or Lower | Never | Never | Never | Never | Never |
| 3% | 25 Years | Never | Never | Never | Never |
| 4% | 14 years | 28 Years | Never | Never | Never |
| 5% | 7 Years | 12 Years | Never | Never | Never |
| 6% | 1 Year | 1 Year | 3 Years | Never | Never |
| 7% | 1 Month | 1 Month | 1 Month | 1 Month | 23 Years |
| 8% | 1 Month | 1 Month | 1 Month | 1 Month | 11 Years |
| 9% | 1 Month | 1 Month | 1 Month | 1 Month | 1 Month |

**Note:** The aggressive buyer pays a mortgage insurance premium of .53% for 10 years.

*Buying the Next Home Before the Existing One Is Sold:* Many home-buyers are dependent on the equity in their existing house to finance the new one, but the closing date on the new one comes first. The cash needed to close before the sale can be obtained through a swing loan from a bank, or a home equity loan on your current house.

If you have a contract of sale on your current house, many banks will make a "swing" or "bridge" loan for the period between the closing on your new house and the closing on your old house. I used a swing loan on my last purchase, and it was relatively simple and hassle free. While the rate may be high, the interest payment won't amount to much if the period is short.

Banks aren't crazy about swing loans because they realize they are one-shot affairs and they are unlikely to see the borrower again. Go to the institution where you currently hold your deposit, whether it is a commercial bank, savings and loan association, or credit union. Let them know that as a customer, you expect this service.

A home equity loan is likely to be more costly than a swing loan, although the cost will be influenced greatly by the amount of equity in the current property and on how astutely the borrower shops. Pay a higher interest rate if necessary to avoid points (an upfront charge expressed as a percent of the loan amount), other upfront fees, and prepayment penalties. On a three-month loan, a borrower can afford to pay an interest rate up to four percentage points higher to avoid paying a fee equal to 1% of the loan.

---

**Indexed ARMs** *Adjustable rate mortgages on which the interest rate is mechanically determined based on the value of an interest rate index.*

Indexed ARMs are distinguished from **Discretionary ARMs**, in that the first provides the lender with *zero* discretion in setting future interest rates, while the latter provides the lender with *complete* discretion. All ARMs discussed in **Adjustable Rate Mortgage (ARM)** are indexed ARMs, which is the only kind used in the U.S.

---

**Initial Interest Rate** *The interest rate that is fixed for some specified number of months or years at the beginning of the life of an ARM.*

*See* **Adjustable Rate Mortgage (ARM)/***How the Interest Rate on an ARM Is Determined*.

---

**Initial Rate Period**  *The number of months for which the initial interest rate holds on an ARM.*

*See* **Adjustable Rate Mortgage (ARM)/***How the Interest Rate on an ARM Is Determined*.

---

**Interest Accrual Period**  *The period over which the interest due the lender is calculated.*

Assume a 6% mortgage with a $100,000 balance. If the interest accrual period is a year, as it is on some loans in the UK and India, the interest for the year is .06($100,000) = $6,000. If interest accrues monthly, as it does on most mortgages in the U.S., the monthly interest is .06/12($100,000) = $500. If interest accrues biweekly, as on a few programs in the U.S., the biweekly interest is .06/26($100,000) = $230.77. And if interest accrues daily, as it does on HELOCs and some other mortgages in the U.S., the daily interest is .06/365($100,000) = $16.44.

The interest accrual period may or may not correspond to the payment period. On the annual accrual mortgages in the UK, payments are made monthly. On most monthly accrual mortgages in the U.S., payments are also made monthly, but in some cases payments are made biweekly. On biweekly accrual mortgages, payments are made biweekly. On daily accrual mortgages, payments are made monthly or biweekly.

Given the same stated annual interest rate, as 6% in the example, shorter accrual periods result in higher interest earnings over a year because of reinvestment of prior interest. *See* **Effective Rate**.

---

**Interest Cost (IC)**  *A comprehensive and time-adjusted measure of loan cost to the borrower.*

*IC on a Mortgage:* IC is what economists call an "internal rate or return." It takes account of all payments made by the borrower over the life of the loan relative to the cash received up front. On a mortgage, the cash received up front is the loan amount less all upfront fees paid by the borrower. On an ARM, IC captures the effect of interest rate changes on the monthly payment and the balance, but future rate changes must be assumed.

*Formula:* IC is (i) in the formula below:

$$L - F = P_1 + P_2/(1 + i)^2 + \ldots (P_n + B_n)/(1 + i)^n$$

Where:

L = Loan amount

F = Points and all other upfront fees paid by the borrower

P = Monthly payment

n = Month when the balance is prepaid in full

$B_n$ = Balance in month n

*IC Versus APR:* IC differs from APR in the following ways: IC is measured over any time horizon, whereas APR assumes that all loans run to term. IC may be measured after taxes whereas APR is always measured before taxes. On an ARM, IC can be calculated on any interest rate scenario whereas APR always uses a no-change scenario.

---

**Interest Due** *The amount of interest, expressed in dollars, computed by multiplying the loan balance at the end of the preceding period times the annual interest rate divided by the interest accrual period.*

On a monthly accrual mortgage, interest due is computed by multiplying the loan balance at the end of the preceding month times the annual interest rate divided by 12. Interest due is the same as the interest payment except when the scheduled mortgage payment is less than the interest due, in which case the difference is added to the balance and constitutes negative amortization.

---

**Interest-Only Mortgage (Option)** *An option attached to a mortgage, which allows the borrower to pay only the interest for some period.*

A mortgage is "interest only" if the monthly mortgage payment does not include any repayment of principal. So long as the payment remains interest only, the loan balance remains unchanged.

For example, if a 30-year fixed-rate loan of $100,000 has an interest rate of 6.25%, the standard payment is $615.72. This payment is "fully amortizing," meaning that, if it is continued and the rate does not change, the loan will pay off at maturity. The interest-only payment, however, is only $520.84. The $94.88 difference is principal repayment.

***Interest-Only in the '20s and Now:*** If a loan is interest-only until maturity, the loan balance will be the same at maturity as it was at the outset. Back in the 1920s, loans of this type were the norm. Borrowers typically refinanced at term, which worked fine so long as the house didn't lose value and the borrower didn't lose his job.

But the depression of the '30s caused a large proportion of these loans to go into foreclosure. Lenders stopped writing them and switched to fully amortizing loans.

When interest-only loans were revived in this century, most were interest-only for a specified period, usually five to 10 years. At the end of that period, the payment was raised to the fully amortizing level.

***Purpose of Interest-Only (1):*** One purpose is to increase affordability by reducing mortgage payments in the early years. In the example of a 30-year fixed-rate loan of $100,000 at 6.25%, referred to above, the interest-only payment is $94.88 less than the fully amortizing payment of $615.72.

The price of the lower payment during the interest-only period, however, is a higher payment later. If the interest only period on the loan described above is five years, then the fully amortizing payment starting in month 61 would be $659.67. In order to reduce the payment by $94.88 for the first five years, the borrower would pay an additional $43.95 for the next 25.

The longer the interest-only period, the larger the new payment will be when the interest-only period ends. If the same loan is interest-only for 10 years, the fully amortizing payment beginning in month 121 is $730.93. In order to reduce the payment by $94.88 for 10 years, the borrower must pay an additional $115.21 for the next 20.

***Purpose of Interest-Only (2):*** Another purpose of interest-only is to maximize investment leverage. A borrower earning 12% on investments wants to borrow as much at 6.25% as possible. Why pay down the mortgage to earn 6.25% when you can invest it to earn 12%?

That seemed like a plausible policy during the late '90s when stock market returns were extremely high. In the more sober environment of 2002-2003, it didn't make sense for most borrowers. With the stock market in the tank and interest rates very low, mortgage loan repayment was the best investment available to most homeowners.

*Purpose of Interest-Only (3):* Borrowers who have other debt at high interest rates might rationally select an interest-only option on their first mortgage so they can accelerate repayment of the more costly debt. If the rate is 5% on the first mortgage and 8% on the second, it makes sense to allocate as much as possible to repayment of the second.

*Interest-Only ARMs:* The interest-only option on ARMs presents special problems. If the interest rate on an ARM increases, the payment increase is substantially larger if the payment is interest-only than if it is fully amortizing.

Consider, for example, an ARM with an interest-only payment option for 10 years and an initial rate of 4%, which resets every six months. If the rate ratchets up to a maximum of 10% in month 19, the interest-only payment would increase by 150%. A fully amortizing payment, in contrast, would increase by only 82%.

*Misperceptions:* I have been dumbfounded by the claims about interest-only loans reported to me by mortgage shoppers. Whether the claims originate with loan officers or, as one defensive loan officer suggested to me, they arise in the overactive imagination of shoppers who still believe in the tooth fairy, I can't say for sure. Probably it is some combination of the two. All I know for sure is that misperceptions abound. Here are three common ones.

*It is less costly to amortize an interest-only loan.* This is patently ridiculous, but some variant of it keeps popping up in my mail.

Suppose a borrower takes a mortgage with an interest-only option, but decides to make the fully amortizing payment instead. Then the loan will amortize just as it would have if the interest-only option had not been attached. Whether the mortgage did nor did not have the option will affect the way it amortizes not a whit.

*An interest-only loan carries a lower interest rate.* Lenders might charge a higher rate for a loan with an interest-only option, because the risk of default is a little higher on loans that amortize more slowly. But a lower rate would be irrational.

The notion that interest-only loans have lower rates arises from comparisons of apples versus oranges. Adjustable rate mortgages (ARMs) with an interest-only option have lower rates than fixed-rate mortgages (FRMs) without an option. But an ARM with the option does not have a lower rate than the identical ARM without it.

Since the interest-only option is available on both FRMs and ARMs, it is pointless to be sucked into an ARM because of that feature.

*On an ARM with an interest-only option, the quoted interest rate is fixed for the interest-only period.* It is not. This is the most dangerous misperception of all because it can induce borrowers to take ARMs that don't meet their needs.

The interest-only period is the period during which you are allowed to pay interest only. The period for which the initial rate holds is a different matter altogether. On an ARM with a very low rate, the interest-only period is always longer than the initial rate period.

A common ARM in 2003 had an interest-only option for 10 years, but the very low initial rate held only for six months. Numerous borrowers who thought the rate was safe for 10 years face a rude awakening. My impression is that loan officers didn't misinform them, but they didn't bother to correct them either.

---

**Interest Payment** *The dollar amount of interest paid each month.*

The interest payment is the same as interest due so long as the scheduled mortgage payment is equal to or greater than the interest due. Otherwise, the interest payment is equal to the scheduled payment.

**Interest Rate** *The rate charged the borrower each period for the loan of money, by custom quoted on an annual basis.*

A mortgage interest rate is a rate on a loan secured by a specific property.

*Calculating the Interest Due from the Interest Rate:* The interest rate is used to calculate the interest payment the borrower owes the lender. Since the interest payment is calculated monthly, the rate must be divided by 12 before it is used to calculate the payment.

Assume a 6% $100,000 loan. In decimals, 6% is .06 and when divided by 12 it is .005. Multiply .005 times $100,000 and you get $500 as the monthly interest due.

*Interest Rate Versus Total Interest Payments as Cost Measures:* Some loan officers encourage borrowers to view total interest payments, rather than the interest rate, as the measure of cost they seek to minimize. This is a mistake. The lower the interest rate a borrower pays, the better off they are. Interest payments, in contrast, depend not only on the rate but also on the loan amount and the maturity.

Some borrowers bamboozled by this argument pay a higher interest rate or fees for a biweekly mortgage that cuts their interest payments. But the lower interest payments on a biweekly are due to a shortening of the term, which results from making an extra monthly payment every year. *See* **Biweekly Mortgage**.

*Quoted Rates Versus Actual Rates:* Not everybody can borrow at the rates quoted in the media, which are based on numerous favorable assumptions: that the applicant's credit is good, they have enough income to qualify, they can fully document their income and assets, they will occupy the house as their primary residence, and on and on. If a particular applicant doesn't meet all the assumptions, his or her rate will be higher. *See* **Nichification**.

*Determinants of Mortgage Rates:* A major determinant of all interest rates is inflation. Rates paid by prime borrowers on 30-year FRMs reached 15% in 1981 when the inflation rate was unusually high (for the U.S.). In 2003, the rate was generally below 6% because the inflation rate was very low.

A second factor that affects mortgage rates is the efficiency of the housing finance system. In most respects, the U.S. system is more efficient than those in most other countries. As a result, mortgage rates to prime borrowers in the U.S. are only 1%-1.5% above long-term government bond yields. In many other countries, the spread is twice as large or more.

*Predicting Mortgage Rates:* The general level of interest rates is not predictable, but specific interest rates that lag the general market may be. Before the development of secondary mortgage markets, mortgage rates had some degree of predictability because they lagged bond yields by anywhere from two to eight months.

Today, however, the mortgage market is thoroughly integrated into the broader capital market. A large proportion of all mortgages are placed in pools against which mortgage-backed securities (MBSs) are issued. MBSs trade actively in the market and are considered close substitutes for bonds. This means that MBS yields and bond yields change together. Since lenders base their rates to borrowers on MBS yields, there is no longer a leading indicator of mortgage rates.

---

**Interest Rate Adjustment Period** *The frequency of rate adjustments on an ARM after the initial rate period is over.*

The rate adjustment period is sometimes but not always the same as the initial rate period. As an example, using common terminology, a 3/3 ARM is one in which both periods are three years while a 3/1 ARM has an initial rate period of three years after which the rate adjusts every year. *See* **Adjustable Rate Mortgage (ARM)/***How the Interest Rate on an ARM Is Determined*.

---

**Interest Rate Ceiling** *The highest rate possible under an ARM contract; same as "lifetime cap."*

It is often expressed as a specified number of percentage points above the initial interest rate. *See* **Adjustable Rate Mortgage (ARM)/** *How the Interest Rate on an ARM Is Determined*.

---

**Interest Rate Decrease Cap** *The maximum allowable decrease in the interest rate on an ARM each time the rate is adjusted.*

It is usually one or two percentage points. *See* **Adjustable Rate Mortgage (ARM)/*How the Interest Rate on an ARM Is Determined***.

---

**Interest Rate Floor** *The lowest interest rate possible under an ARM contract.*

Floors are less common than ceilings. *See* **Adjustable Rate Mortgage (ARM)/*How the Interest Rate on an ARM Is Determined***.

---

**Interest Rate Increase Cap** *The maximum allowable increase in the interest rate on an ARM each time the rate is adjusted.*

It is usually one or two percentage points. *See* **Adjustable Rate Mortgage (ARM)/*How the Interest Rate on an ARM Is Determined***.

---

**Interest Rate Index** *The specific interest rate series to which the interest rate on an ARM is tied, such as "Treasury Constant Maturities, One-Year," or "Eleventh District Cost of Funds."*

*See* **Adjustable Rate Mortgage (ARM)/*ARM Rate Indexes***.

---

**Internet Mortgages** *Mortgages delivered using the Internet as a major part of the communication process between the borrower and the lender.*

Three types of mortgage Web sites are discussed in this book. *See* **Lead-Generation Sites**, **Referral Sites**, and **Single-Lender Web Sites**.

---

**Jumbo Mortgage** *A mortgage larger than the maximum eligible for purchase by the two federal agencies, Fannie Mae and Freddie Mac.*

The maximum was $322,700 in 2003. However, some lenders use the term to refer to programs for even larger loans, such as greater than $500,000.

---

**Junk Fees** *A derogatory term for lender fees that are expressed in dollars rather than as a percent of the loan amount.*

*See* **Settlement Costs/*Fees Paid to Lender*/Lender Fees Expressed in Dollars**.

**Late Fees** *Fees assessed by lenders when payments are late.*

Late fees are usually 4% or 5% of the payment. A borrower with a 6% mortgage for 30 years who pays a 5% late charge every month raises his or her interest cost over the life of the loan to 6.46%.

**Late Payment** *A payment made after the grace period stipulated in the note, usually 10-15 days.*

**Lead-Generation Sites** *A mortgage Web site designed to provide leads to lenders.*

A "lead" is a packet of information about a consumer in the market for a loan. Lenders pay for leads, and these sites are an important source of them.

Prospective borrowers fill out a questionnaire covering the loan request, property, personal finances, and contact information. The sites use this information to select the lenders to whom the information is sent. Lenders then prepare offers to the borrower based on the same information.

*Lender Screening:* Lender selection by lead generation sites should be valuable to borrowers with one or more challenging features, such as poor credit, incomplete documentation, or little cash. Such borrowers can avoid wasting time soliciting lenders who won't deal with them.

Lender screening also provides some protection against falling into the hands of rogues—lenders or mortgage brokers out to extract as much revenue as possible from every customer. The sites have every reason to bounce a lender who attracts multiple complaints from borrowers.

*Promoting Lender Competition:* Lead-generation sites are sometimes called "auction sites" because they purport to provide a group of lenders, usually up to four, who will bid for the borrower's business. Selecting from among lenders provided by an auction site, however, is as difficult for most borrowers as selecting among any other group of lenders.

The sites don't require that the initial price quotes provided by their lenders be sufficiently complete to allow borrowers to make intelligent choices. It is no easier to get settlement cost data, or the complete specs on an ARM, from these lenders as from any others. Neither can the sites protect borrowers against "sharp practices" by lenders during the period between initial price quotes and the time when the price is "locked."

### Guidelines for the Most Effective Use of Lead-Generation Sites:

- Decide beforehand whether you want a fixed or adjustable rate mortgage, as well as your preferred loan term, down payment, and points. If you are uncertain about any of these, do some homework.

- Fill out the questionnaire as accurately and completely as you can. That information is used to match you with the lenders most likely to be interested in your loan.

- Mortgage price information comes from the lenders who contact you, not from the site. The amount of price information they give you may depend on what you ask for. Remember that on fixed-rate mortgages you need the interest rate, points, and dollar fees. While some lenders are not in the habit of providing their dollar fees in initial price quotes, you can insist upon it.

- If you are interested in an ARM, you need to know more than the rate, points, and loan fees. *See* **Adjustable Rate Mortgage (ARM)/ Gambling on Future Interest Rates/**Required ARM Information.

- Receiving price quotes over the telephone is looking for trouble. Ask lenders to e-mail or fax their prices to you.

- The interest rate and points quoted by a lender apply only to the day you receive them. The prices that really matter are those quoted to you on the day you "lock" the loan with the lender. The lock means that the lender is committed to the prices. Lender locking requirements vary widely, ranging from very little, to a signed application, to a signed application plus a non-refundable payment. You are entitled to know at the outset exactly what each lender's requirements are, and how long it should take if you do everything expected of you. Ask!

- Since you selected the lender based on the initial price quote but it is the locked price that you are going to pay, you have a right to know how the lender will set the price on the day you lock. The lock price should be the same as the price the lender is quoting to new customers on the identical loan on the same day. Ask if the lender has a Web site that contains up-to-date prices that you can use to monitor your price day by day. If it does not, ask the loan officer how he intends to demonstrate that you have received the correct price.

- Unlike rates and points, loan fees are not market driven. Unless you change one or more of the loan characteristics, there is seldom a good reason for these fees to change between the time you receive the initial price quote and the time you close. Some lenders will guarantee their fees in writing if you ask. Lenders can't guarantee the fees of third parties, but they may be willing to include appraisal fees and credit charges in a guarantee because they order them and know how much they cost.

For a list of lead-generation sites in 2003, *see* **Mortgage Shopping/ *Solicit Price Quotes*/Sources**.

---

## Lender

*See* **Mortgage Lender**.

---

**Loan Amount** *The amount the borrower promises to repay, as set forth in the loan contract.*

The loan amount may exceed the original amount requested by the borrower if he or she elects to include points and other upfront costs in the loan.

---

**Loan "Flipping"** *The process of raising cash periodically through successive cash-out refinancings.*

This is a scam initiated by mortgage brokers that victimizes wholesale lenders, with the connivance of borrowers. *See* **Mortgage Scams/*Strictly Broker Scams*/Successive Refinancings Using Rebate Loans**.

**Loan Officer** *Employees of lenders or mortgage brokers who find borrowers, sell and counsel them, and take applications.*

Loan officers employed by mortgage brokers may also be involved in loan processing. In the case of a one-person mortgage broker firm, that person is both the broker and the loan officer.

While loan officers are employees, they act more like independent contractors. They are compensated largely, if not entirely, on a commission basis. The typical commission rate is 1/2 of 1% of the loan amount, and successful loan officers earn six figure incomes.

Both lenders and mortgage brokers post prices with loan officers to be offered to consumers. The loan officers usually have limited discretion to reduce the price if necessary to meet competition, and full discretion to raise the price if they can. The difference between the posted price and the price charged the consumer is called an **Overage**, and the loan officer usually gets a share of it.

**Loan Provider** *A mortgage lender or mortgage broker.*

**Loan-to-Value Ratio (LTV)** *The loan amount divided by the lesser of the selling price or the appraised value.*

The LTV and down payment are different ways of expressing the same facts. *See* **Down Payment/*Down Payment and LTV*.**

**Lock Commitment Letter** *A letter from a lender verifying that the price and other terms of a loan have been locked.*

Borrowers who lock through a mortgage broker should always demand to see the lock commitment letter.

**Locking the Loan** *An option exercised by the borrower, at the time of the loan application or later, to "lock in" the rates and points prevailing in the market at that time.*

When lenders "lock," they commit to lend at a specified interest rate and points, provided the loan is closed within a specified "lock period." For example, a lender agrees to lock a 30-year fixed-rate mortgage of $200,000 at 7.5% and one point, good for 30 days.

*The Need for Locking:* The need for locking arises out of two special features of the home loan market: volatility and process delays. Volatility means that rates and points are reset each day, and sometimes within the day. Process delays refer to the lag between the time when the terms of the loan are negotiated, and the time when the loan is closed and funds disbursed.

If prices are stable, locking isn't needed even if there are process delays. If there are no process delays, locking isn't needed even if prices are volatile. It is the combination of volatility and process delays that creates the need for locking.

For example, Smith is shopping for a loan on June 5 for a house purchase scheduled to close July 15. Smith is comfortable with the rates and points quoted on June 5, but a rate increase of 1/2% within the following 40 days could make the house unaffordable, and Smith doesn't want to take that risk. Smith wants a lock, and lenders competing for Smith's loan will offer it.

*Cost of Locking to Lenders:* If locks were equally binding on lender and borrower, locks would not cost the borrower anything. While lenders would lose when interest rates rose during the lock period, they would profit when interest rates fell. Over a large number of customers they would break even.

In reality, however, borrowers are not as committed as lenders. The number of deals that don't close, known as "fallout," increases during periods of falling rates, when borrowers find they can do better by starting the process anew with another lender. Fallout declines during periods of rising rates.

This means that locking imposes a net cost on lenders, which they in turn pass on to borrowers. The cost is included in the points quoted to borrowers, which are higher for longer lock periods. The lender who quoted 7.5% and one point for a 30-day lock, for example, might charge 1.125-1.25 points for a 60-day lock.

*Controlling Lock Costs:* Years ago, lenders controlled lock costs by requiring borrowers to pay a commitment fee in cash. The fee was returned to them at closing but forfeited if they walked from the deal. But today, commitment fees have mostly died out. Borrowers don't like them, and lenders and mortgage brokers don't want to place themselves at a competitive disadvantage by requiring them.

To control lock costs today, many lenders refuse to lock until borrowers demonstrate commitment to the deal by completing one or more critical steps in the lending process. This may include submission of a completed application along with an appraisal and credit report. But some lenders will lock based on submission of only an abbreviated lock request form.

Lenders who make it difficult to lock will have lower fallout and may therefore offer better prices, but the locking delays that arise from their requirements impede effective shopping. Lenders who make it easy to lock have large fallout costs but they allow borrowers to shop and lock in a short period.

A mortgage shopper needs to know what each lender requires to lock, and how quickly the process can be completed if the shopper does his or her part. A good mortgage broker can help enormously. Brokers know lender lock requirements, can help expedite the process, and will keep the lender honest if the market changes during the lock process.

**Choosing When to Lock:** Borrowers developing a lock strategy should forget about trying to guess the direction of interest rates. Interest rates are not predictable.

The first thing borrowers should consider is their capacity to take the risk of a rise in market rates. If they barely qualify at today's rates and an increase would knock them out of the market, or force them to accept other unfavorable terms, they should lock ASAP.

If they can withstand a rise in rates, and are confident that the loan provider will offer the true market price when they finally lock, there is a benefit in delaying it. As noted above, the price is lower for shorter lock periods because the lender takes less risk with a shorter lock. This means that if market interest rates don't change, the lock price will fall as the lock period shortens.

Borrowers can only capture this benefit, however, if the market price quoted to them when they finally do lock, is accurate. Borrowers will know that the price is accurate if they can access the price on the lender's Web site, or are dealing with an "Upfront Mortgage Broker." (They give you the best price quoted by their wholesale lenders and will show you the price sheets.) They won't know, and should expect the worst, if the market price on the lock day is what the loan provider says it is over the telephone. In that event, "lock ASAP" remains the best advice.

This is particularly the case with home purchasers, who lose the ability to walk away from their loan provider as the closing date approaches. Borrowers who are refinancing can always change loan providers if they get a fast shuffle on the lock day.

***Paying for Insurance You Don't Get:*** Borrowers who lock through mortgage brokers are exposed to a special hazard: the broker may inform the borrower he is locked but actually allows the rate to float. If the market is stable, the broker can pocket the difference between the lock price quoted to the borrower and the price at which the loan is finally locked. This scam, and how to avoid it, is discussed in **Mortgage Scams and Tricks/*Strictly Broker Scams*/Charging for a Lock Without Locking with the Lender**.

***Is the Borrower Committed Under a Lock?*** I have changed my position on this question. Originally my view was that borrowers were committed. Now my view is that borrowers can't be held to a commitment they don't make. If lenders lock at their own risk to get the borrower's business, lock-jumping is just another cost of business.

The prevailing practice of brokers and lenders is to leave the borrower's commitment under a rate lock unstated. They want borrowers to consider themselves committed by rate locks. However, they fear that if they ask the borrower for a written acknowledgement of commitment, the borrower might be frightened into the arms of another loan provider who didn't require it. This is the same reason that loan providers don't require a commitment fee that borrowers would lose if they jump the lock.

If the borrower's commitment under a rate lock is left ambiguous, then the borrower is entitled to interpret that ambiguity as he or she pleases. Lock-jumping is OK, in other words, unless the borrower acknowledges in writing that it is not OK.

**Lock Versus Float-Down:** Where a lock freezes the rate and points, a float-down freezes them only in the event that market rates increase. If they decrease, the rate under a float-down will decline correspondingly.

Since a float-down carries more value to the borrower than a lock, and is more costly to the lender to provide, it carries a higher price. For example, a lender who charges one point to lock the interest rate for 60 days might charge 1.5 points for a 60-day float-down.

The exact terms of float-downs vary from lender to lender. Questions to ask include: when can I exercise, how often can I exercise, is there any minimum price reduction for exercise, and how is the current market price communicated to me? If the market price is what the loan provider says it is over the telephone, the borrower is vulnerable to being scammed.

To avoid being scammed, borrowers should ask the loan provider to agree to show the price sheet with the relevant price circled, at the borrower's request, anytime within the exercise period. A Web site that clearly identifies the price niche into which the deal falls is even better.

**Locking the Rate but Not the Points:** Since the interest rate and points are two dimensions of the price, locking only one makes no sense. It is the equivalent of locking the price of a box of doughnuts but not the number of doughnuts in the box.

**Lock Expirations:** Sometimes locks expire before the loan can be closed. There are many possible reasons why the work does not get done on time. When this happens, lenders typically will extend the lock period only if interest rates have not increased. If rates are higher, they will relock at the higher rate.

The only situation where a lender will extend a lock when interest rates have risen would be where the lender acknowledges that he or she is solely to blame for the delays that caused the lock expiration. This does not happen very often. Typically, there are too many people involved in the process for the lender to assume full responsibility. These include the borrower, mortgage broker, appraisers, escrow agents, and others.

Deals that don't get done on time are more likely to be refinances than home purchases. Lenders generally give purchasers a priority. Delayed refinancings can be rescheduled, but not completing purchase mortgages on time can jeopardize the deals, at high cost to buyers. It could also jeopardize lenders' relationships with real estate brokers, upon whom many depend for borrower referrals.

Here are some tips for minimizing the chances of a lock expiration:

- When you select the lock period at the beginning, ask how long the lender's current turn-around time is. Lenders usually report this to mortgage brokers every day on their price sheets. During a refinance boom, it makes sense to add 15 days more than you think you need.

- Be sure you know all the documents needed by the broker or lender, and assemble them so they can be produced when needed.

- Be available to answer questions or provide additional documents during the entire period the loan is in process, and respond to questions in a timely manner.

- Stay on top of the mortgage broker, who should be the key coordinator of all players. In interviewing the broker at the outset, seek assurance that he has the time to handle your deal effectively. Deals from harassed brokers who take on more than they can handle effectively, are most likely to languish in the lender's pile of incomplete applications.

**Recourse When Locks Expire That Shouldn't:** When interest rates spiked in July-August 2003, my mailbox was suddenly flooded with messages from frustrated borrowers whose locks had expired. In some cases borrowers held the broker responsible, in other cases the lender, but they all ended with the same question to me: "What is my recourse?"

In cases where the broker informed the borrower in writing that the loan was locked but did not lock with the lender, it would be relatively easy to prove the broker's culpability. (If the broker told the borrower the loan was locked but did not commit it to writing, it would be one recollection against another.)

Obtaining a court judgment and then collecting from a broker, however, is another matter. It might work against some substantial broker firms, but many brokers are individual operators who may be here today and gone tomorrow.

Lenders who allowed locks to expire by deliberately slowing down the process are more attractive targets for a lawsuit, but proving their culpability in any individual case is difficult. Lenders can claim that the borrower should have selected a longer lock period, or that the borrower was slow in meeting the lender's reasonable requests for information. They can also claim that unforeseen circumstances for which they are not responsible slowed down the process. Hence, filing an individual suit against a lender is not likely to provide redress.

Borrowers can and should make their case to the lender's regulatory authority. If the authority receives a large number of such complaints, they might audit the lender's operations to see if there was an actual policy in place to accelerate the number of lock expirations. Class action lawyers might also get wind of the complaints, and initiate an action that will force the lender to provide information that would not be obtainable in any individual action. Even if this provides little redress to the borrowers who were hurt, it can send a useful message that may help the next cohort of borrowers.

---

**Lock-Jumper** *A borrower, usually refinancing rather than purchasing a home, who allows a lock to expire when interest rates go down in order to lock again at the lower rate.*

*See* **Mortgage Scams and Tricks/***Scams by Borrowers***/**Lock Jumping.

---

**Lock Period** *The number of days for which any lock or float-down holds.*

The longer the period, the higher the price to the borrower.

---

**Mandatory Disclosure** *The array of laws and regulations dictating the information that must be disclosed to mortgage borrowers, and the method and timing of disclosure.*

*See* **Annual Percentage Rate (APR)** and **Good Faith Estimate (GFE)**.

**Manufactured Home**  *A home built entirely in a factory, transported to a site, and installed there.*

Manufactured homes are distinguished from "modular," "panelized," and "pre-cut" homes. Manufactured houses usually are built without knowing where they will be sited, and are subject to a federal building code administered by HUD. The other types of factory-built housing are not assembled until the site is identified, and they must comply with the local, state, or regional building codes that apply to that site.

Because of efficiencies in factory production, manufactured houses cost significantly less per square foot than housing constructed on-site. Manufactured housing is an important source of affordable housing, especially in the South and in rural areas.

There are major differences within the manufactured housing market, so much so that it makes sense to think of two different markets. A major difference is that one segment is shut out of the mainstream mortgage market and the other segment isn't.

**The Deprived Market:** Many purchasers of manufactured housing must find loans in a parallel market, which is much like the unsecured personal loan market. Lenders in this parallel market assume that loss rates on manufactured house loans will be high, as they are on personal loans, and they price them accordingly. They view manufactured houses as poor collateral that provides them with little protection.

One reason for this view is that manufactured houses can be moved. Before the HUD building code went into effect in 1976, manufactured houses were called "mobile homes," and this term is still widely used. Even though few ever leave their first site, they remain tarnished by the image of mobility.

Lender concern that the collateral can disappear is well grounded when the house sits on rented land, which is the case for about half of all manufactured houses. Most leases are short, and if the landowner decides that it is more profitable to use the land in some other way, the manufactured house owner must move it or leave it. Since the cost of moving is very high, and in many cases the property is worth little more than the debt, owners sometimes just walk away. The lender's collateral ends up in the trash heap.

In the deprived market, few owners of manufactured houses have built equity the way owners of site-built houses do. A major part of the appreciation in the value of site-built houses is due to rising land values. If you don't own the land, you don't realize this benefit. Furthermore, many purchasers of manufactured houses began with no or negative equity, putting nothing down, and including settlement costs (and sometimes furniture and insurance) in the loan.

Manufactured houses in the deprived sector also seem to have more defects than site-built homes. Because they are geared to low-income purchasers, the materials used have often been inferior. Sometimes mishaps occur in moving houses from factory to site, and sometimes the installation is defective.

Getting defects in a manufactured house fixed can be a hassle because responsibility is divided and finger pointing is common. The factory owner says the mover did it, the mover says the installer did it, and the installer says it happened at the factory.

**The Healthy Market:** In this part of the market, buyers of manufactured houses have them installed permanently on their own land, and qualify for mainstream mortgage financing. It is even possible to qualify under a lease, provided the lease is long enough and provides adequate legal protections to the house owner and lender.

The quality of houses in this segment is good. Quality has been improving generally since Congress passed the Manufactured Housing Improvement Act (MHIA) in 2000. The Act provided an improved system for keeping the HUD building code up to date, and required states to improve the quality of installation and to set up dispute resolution programs.

In California, some developers have used manufactured housing in lieu of on-site construction, marketing and financing them in the same way. This avoids many of the problems referred to above that have tarnished the industry.

**Guidelines:** Here are some guidelines for avoiding the deprived market.

**Do Not Buy a Home from a Dealer in a Package That Includes Installation, Site, and Financing:** Tempting as it may be, one-stop shopping in this market is a sure fire recipe for overpaying and not getting what you want. Take it one step at a time. It is easiest to compare the houses offered by different dealers if the price applies only to the house. Bundling muddies the waters.

**Find the Site First:** Before I did anything else, I would decide where I want my house, and whether on rented or owned land. If your credit is good and you have enough cash to buy your own plot, you will be eligible for mainstream mortgage financing. The savings in financing costs and in rent, if converted into a "present value," will probably be well in excess of the cost of the land.

If you rent because you can't find a plot or don't have the cash to buy one, but your credit is good, you may still be eligible for mainstream financing. This requires that you obtain a proper lease, which is one that has a term of at least five years, and provides the other legal protections required by lenders.

Freddie Mac will buy mortgages on manufactured houses secured by leaseholds in some but not all states. Freddie's requirements are complicated and you may need a lawyer to determine whether any particular lease is in compliance.

If you can't purchase a plot or obtain an eligible lease, you will be obliged to settle for personal loan-type financing, paying 2%-3% more. Even so, you will want to pay careful attention to the lease terms, which can vary widely. If you accept a monthly term, or the landlord's right to approve a purchaser, you will be at the landlord's mercy. Before you sign, talk to residents of the park about their experience.

**Get a Warranty on Installation:** Installation of manufactured houses remains trouble-prone. The dealer may want to include installation in the price. That is one type of bundling that makes sense, provided the dealer assumes responsibility with a strong warranty. If the dealer includes installation in the price but will not provide an adequate warranty, either ask for a price without installation, or walk.

If you buy the house without installation, you have to hire an installer yourself. This is no small matter, which is why so few buyers do it. The MHIA requires states to develop installation programs that include installation standards, training and licensing of installers, and inspections, but compliance has been spotty. Ask local owners for recommendations, ask installers for references, and make sure they are insured.

**Arrange Your Own Financing:** The dealer will try to package financing into the deal. He can get you approved fast and easily, which is an attractive lure. If you can qualify for mainstream financing, however, you will do better to find your own loan. If you don't qualify, it might not matter.

---

**Margin** *On an ARM, an amount (usually two to three percentage points) that is added to the interest rate index to obtain the interest rate charged the borrower after the initial rate period ends.*

*See* **Adjustable Rate Mortgage (ARM)** / *How the Interest Rate on an ARM Is Determined.*

---

**Market Niche** *A particular combination of loan, borrower, property, and transaction characteristics that lenders use in setting prices and underwriting requirements.*

*See* **Nichification**.

---

**Maturity** *The period until the last payment is due.*

The maturity is usually but not always the same as the period used to calculate the mortgage payment. *See* **Term**.

---

**Maximum Loan Amount** *The largest loan size permitted on a particular loan program.*

For programs where the loan is targeted for sale to Fannie Mae or Freddie Mac, the maximum will be the largest loan eligible for purchase by these agencies. On FHA loans, the maximums are set by the Federal Housing Administration, and vary somewhat by state and county. On other loans, maximums are set by lenders.

---

**Maximum Loan-to-Value Ratio** *The maximum allowable ratio of loan-to-value (LTV) on any loan program.*

Generally, these are set by mortgage insurers or by lenders and can range up to 100%, although some programs will go above 100%.

**Maximum Lock** *The longest period for which the lender will lock the rate and points on any program.*

On most programs, the longest lock period is 90 days; some go to 120 days and a few to 180 days.

It is extremely important that the lock period selected be long enough to cover your home purchase closing. On a refinance, the period must be long enough for the loan to be processed. This can vary widely, depending on the lender's workload. Discuss the time required with the broker or lender.

**Minimum Down Payment** *The minimum allowable ratio of down payment to sale price on any loan program.*

If the minimum is 10%, for example, it means that you must make a down payment of at least $10,000 on a $100,000 house or $20,000 on a $200,000 house.

The minimum down payment ratio is equal to one minus the maximum LTV. If the maximum LTV is 95%, for example, the minimum down payment is $1 - .95 = .05$, or 5%.

**Monthly Debt Service** *Monthly payments required on credit cards, installment loans, home equity loans, and other debts but not including payments on the loan applied for.*

**Monthly Housing Expense**

*Same as* **Housing Expense**.

**Monthly Total Expense**

*Same as* **Total Expense**.

**Mortgage** *A written document evidencing the lien on a property taken by a lender as security for the repayment of a loan.*

The term "mortgage" or "mortgage loan" is used loosely to refer both to the lien and to the loan. In most cases, they are defined in two separate documents: a mortgage and a note.

## Mortgage Auction Site

*Same as* **Lead Generation Site**.

## Mortgage Bank

*Same as* **Mortgage Company**.

*See* **Mortgage Lender/*Mortgage Banks Versus Portfolio Lenders***.

**Mortgage Broker** *An independent contractor who offers the loan products of multiple lenders, called wholesalers.*

Mortgage brokers do not lend. They counsel borrowers on any problems involved in qualifying for a loan, including credit problems. Brokers also help borrowers select the loan that best meets their needs and shop for the best deal among the lenders offering that type of loan. Brokers take applications from borrowers and lock the rate and other terms with lenders. They also provide borrowers with the many disclosures required by the federal and state governments.

In addition, brokers compile all the documents required for transactions, including the credit report, property appraisal, verification of employment and assets, and so on. Not until a file is complete is it handed off to the lender, who approves and funds the loan.

*How Brokers Make Money:* The lenders that mortgage brokers deal with quote a "wholesale" price to the broker, leaving it to the broker to add a markup in order to derive the "retail" price offered the consumer. For example, the wholesale price on a particular program might be 7% and zero points, to which the broker adds a markup of one point, resulting in an offer to the customer of 7% and one point. But if the broker adds a two-point markup, the customer would pay 7% and two points.

What determines the markup? Most have a target, sometimes in points (say 1.5 to 2), sometimes in dollars (say $3,000), which they try to adjust to the anticipated workload. Some brokers set the markup in each case as high as they can get away with. An unsophisticated customer who shows no inclination to shop the competition will be charged more than a sophisticated customer who makes clear an intention to shop.

Indeed, mortgage brokers often rationalize the high markups they charge some customers on the grounds that these are needed to off-set the excessively small markups they are forced to accept on other deals. Some borrowers do turn the tables on mortgage brokers by threatening to bail out of a deal after most of the work has been completed unless the mortgage broker agrees to cut the price.

*How Much Brokers Make:* A survey taken in 1998 of about 1,000 broker firms found that the average income per loan was $2,443, which was 2.02% of the average loan amount of $120,744. This is gross income—none of the brokers' expenses are deducted.

A study I did covering 774 loans brokered in December 2000 and January 2001 provides more detailed information on factors affecting mortgage broker income. The brokers covered are larger firms employing multiple loan officers, and they operate in relatively upscale markets. Their average income per loan was $3,191, which was 2.10% of the average loan of $152,031.

Brokers make more money on large loans than on small ones. For loans of $80,000 and less, the brokers averaged $1,600 per loan. For loans greater than $225,000, they averaged $5,453 per loan. Income per loan was higher on FHA loans than on conventional loans. For example, on loans between $80,000 and $110,000, brokers averaged $3,234 on FHAs and $2,093 on conventionals.

*Advantages of Dealing with Brokers:* Borrowers with special needs do better dealing with a broker. No one lender offers loans in every market niche. For example, many lenders won't offer loans to borrowers with poor credit, borrowers who can't document their income, borrowers who can't make any down payment, borrowers who want to purchase a condominium as an investment, borrowers with very high existing debts, borrowers who need to close within 72 hours, or borrowers who reside abroad. The list goes on and on. But there are lenders in every one of these niches, and brokers, who deal with multiple lenders, can find them when needed.

In addition, brokers are experts at shopping the market. Brokers are far better positioned than consumers to select the best deal available from competing lenders on the day the terms of the loan are "locked." In addition, brokers keep lenders honest on lender fees specified in dollars, sometimes called "junk fees." Some retail lenders view these fees as an added source of revenue because borrowers often don't know what they are at the time they select the lender. But wholesale lenders don't play this game.

Lenders quote wholesale prices to brokers because of the work that brokers do for them that lenders would otherwise have to do themselves. While there are no published statistics on the wholesale/retail price difference, informed observers say that it averages about 1.5 points.

The price savings to the borrower thus consist of the wholesale-retail price spread plus the savings from better shopping. On the other side of the ledger is the broker's fee. If the price savings exceed the fee, the borrower pays less dealing with a broker.

**Disadvantages of Dealing with Brokers:** A lender will honor a mistake in the customer's favor made by one of its employees, but it won't honor a mistake made by a mortgage broker. In addition, some borrowers find comfort in dealing with a large lender with a recognizable name. Brokers are not known nationally, although they may be well known locally, especially by the real estate agents from whom they receive referrals.

It is not at all clear that an unsophisticated borrower is more likely to be taken advantage of by a broker than by a lender. Predators come from both groups. Lender predators may actually be more difficult to spot because they are subject to less rigorous disclosure rules than brokers. Nonetheless, there are some unscrupulous brokers, and it is very difficult for borrowers to distinguish them from the scrupulous ones.

**The Broker as the Borrower's Agent:** One strategy I recommend is to find a mortgage broker who is willing to work as your agent. The prevailing practice is for brokers to operate as independent contractors.

A broker operating as an independent contractor adds a markup to the wholesale prices received from lenders, quoting a retail price to the borrower. The borrower doesn't know what the markup is. But if you retain a broker as your agent, you pay the broker a fee agreed upon in advance, which includes your payment and any compensation the broker receives from the lender. The broker passes through the whole-sale prices, which are disclosed to you, without any markup.

Implementing this strategy requires finding a broker prepared to work as your agent for an agreed-upon fee. Upfront Mortgage Brokers, listed on my Web site, prefer to work in this way. But many other brokers would be willing to if customers requested it.

Successful implementation requires that the broker's compensation from your transaction be stipulated at the outset, in writing, signed by the broker and by you. This avoids misunderstandings or surprises. The document should state:

*The total compensation to [name of broker], including any rebates from the lender, will be _____. A separate processing fee will be _____.*

See **Upfront Mortgage Broker**.

---

**Mortgage Company** *A mortgage lender that sells all the loans it origi-nates in the secondary market.*

See **Mortgage Lender/*Mortgage Banks Versus Portfolio Lenders***.

---

**Mortgage Equations** *Equations used to derive common measures used in the mortgage market, such as monthly payment, balance, and APR.*

*Fully Amortizing Payment:* The following formula is used to calcu-late the fixed monthly payment (P) required to fully amortize a loan of L dollars over a term of n months at a monthly interest rate of c. [If the quoted rate is 6%, for example, c is .06/12 or .005.]

$$P = L[c(1 + c)^n] / [(1 + c)^n - 1]$$

*Balance After a Specified Period:* The next formula is used to calcu-late the remaining loan balance (B) of a fixed payment loan after p months.

$$B = L[(1 + c)^n - (1 + c)^p] / [(1 + c)^n - 1]$$

*Annual Percentage Rate (APR):* The APR is what economists call an "internal rate of return" (IRR), or the discount rate that equates a future stream of dollars with the present value of that stream. In the case of a home mortgage, the formula is

$$L - F = P_1 + P_2 / (1 + i)^2 + \ldots (P_n + B_n) / (1 + i)^n$$

where:

$i$ = IRR

$L$ = Loan amount

$F$ = Points and all other lender fees

$P$ = Monthly payment

$n$ = Month when the balance is paid in full

$B_n$ = Balance in month n

This equation can be solved for i only through a series of successive approximations, which must be done by computer. Many calculators will also do it provided that all the values of P are the same.

The APR is a special case of the IRR, because it assumes that the loan runs to term. In the equation, this means that n is equal to the term and $B_n$ is zero.

Note that on ARMs, the payments used to calculate the APR are those that would occur under the assumption that the index rate does not change over the life of the loan.

*Future Values:* Many of my calculators measure financial results in terms of "future values"—the borrower's net wealth at the end of a specified period.

The future value of a single sum today is:

$$FV_n = S(1 + c)^n$$

where:

$FV_n$ is the value of the single sum after n periods

$S$ is the amount of the single sum now

$c$ is the applicable interest rate

$n$ is the length of the period

The future value of a series of payments of equal size, beginning after one period, is:

$$FV_n = P[(1+c)^n - 1]/c$$

where $P$ is the periodic payment and the other terms are as defined above.

**Mortgage Insurance** *Insurance provided the lender against loss on a mortgage in the event of borrower default.*

In the U.S., all FHA and VA mortgages are insured by the federal government. On other mortgages, the general practice is to require mortgage insurance from a private mortgage insurer when the loan amount exceeds 80% of property value. Borrowers pay the insurance premium in all cases. *See* **Private Mortgage Insurance**.

**Mortgage Insurance Premium** *The upfront and/or periodic charges that the borrower pays for mortgage insurance.*

There are different mortgage insurance plans with differing combinations of monthly, annual, and upfront premiums.

**Mortgage Lender** *The party advancing money to a borrower at the closing table in exchange for a note evidencing the borrower's debt and obligation to repay.*

*Retail, Wholesale, and Correspondent Lenders:* Lenders who perform all the loan origination functions themselves are called "retail lenders." Lenders who have certain functions performed for them by mortgage brokers or correspondents are called "wholesale lenders." Many large lenders have both retail and wholesale divisions. Wholesale lenders will have different departments to deal with correspondent lenders and mortgage brokers. The division of functions is shown in the table on the next page.

Correspondent lenders are typically small and depend on wholesale lenders to protect them against pipeline risk. A correspondent lender locks a price for a borrower at the same time as the correspondent locks with a wholesale lender.

*Mortgage Banks Versus Portfolio Lenders:* Mortgage banks sell all the loans they make in the secondary market because they don't have the long-term funding sources necessary to hold mortgages

| Function | Retail Lender | Wholesale Lender | Correspondent Lender | Mortgage Broker |
|---|---|---|---|---|
| Find and counsel customers | ✔ |  | ✔ | ✔ |
| Take application | ✔ |  | ✔ | ✔ |
| Process loan | ✔ |  | ✔ | ✔ |
| Lock loan terms | ✔ | ✔ | ✔ |  |
| Assume price risk | ✔ | ✔ |  |  |
| Underwrite loan | ✔ | ✔ | ✔ |  |
| Close and fund loan | ✔ | ✔ | ✔ |  |

permanently. They fund loans by borrowing from banks or by selling short-term notes, repaying when the loans are sold.

Mortgage banks now dominate the U.S. market. Of the 10 largest lenders in 2002, nine were mortgage banks and only one was a portfolio lender. However, most of the large mortgage banks are affiliated with large commercial banks.

Portfolio lenders include commercial banks, savings banks, savings and loan associations, and credit unions. They are sometimes referred to as "depository institutions" because they offer deposit accounts to the public. Deposits provide a relatively stable funding source that allows these institutions to hold loans permanently in their portfolios.

Mortgage banks often offer better terms on fixed-rate mortgages than portfolio lenders, while the reverse is more likely for adjustable rate mortgages. It would be a mistake to place too much reliance on this rule, however, because the variability within each group is very wide.

---

**Mortgage Payment** *The payment of principal and interest made by the borrower.*

---

**Mortgage Price** *The interest rate or rates and upfront fees paid to the lender and mortgage broker.*

Some upfront charges are expressed as a percent of the loan, and some are expressed in dollars. The price includes the total of each type.

On a fixed-rate mortgage (FRM), one interest rate is preset for the life of the loan. On an adjustable rate mortgage (ARM), the rate is preset for an initial period, ranging from one month to 10 years, and then can change. For ARM shoppers who are uncertain about how long they will be in their house, the price includes ARM features that affect the ARM rate after the initial rate period ends. These include the *margin, maximum rate, rate adjustment period*, and *rate adjustment caps.*

The *margin* is the amount that is added to the index used by the ARM in determining the rate after the initial rate period ends. In a stable interest rate environment, the ARM rate will become the index plus margin, called the "fully indexed rate." Both the index and the margin are specified in the ARM contract.

The *maximum rate* is the highest rate permitted by the ARM contract. It tells shoppers how high the ARM rate can go in a rising rate environment.

The *rate adjustment period* and *rate adjustment caps* indicate how often the rate is changed and the maximum amount of any change. Hence, they indicate whether any rate increases at the end of the initial rate period will be abrupt or gradual.

---

**Mortgage Price Quotes** *Rates and points quoted by loan providers.*

You cannot safely assume that mortgage price quotes are always timely, niche-adjusted, complete, or reliable.

**Timeliness:** Most mortgage lenders change their prices daily, generally in the morning after secondary markets open, and sometimes they will change them during the day as well. This is a major problem for shoppers using traditional distribution channels, since prices collected from lender 1 on Monday and from lender 2 on Tuesday will not be comparable if the market has changed in the meantime.

Prices advertised in newspapers are out of date when they are read. A newspaper that publishes price information in its Monday edition, for example, is reporting Friday's prices. On Monday when the paper hits the street, lenders have already posted new prices.

The Internet can ease the pain of shoppers trying to stay abreast of the market. On Monday morning when the newspapers are reporting Friday's prices, some Web sites are reporting Monday's prices. In addition, it is easy to compare prices of different lenders on the Internet, so having to repeat the process on successive days is not a burden.

Not all mortgage Web sites provide current data, however. Some of the prices posted on the Internet are even more out of date than those in the newspapers. Almost always, however, the date of the quote is given, so you can ignore those that are not current. If the date is not given, you can assume the quote is not current.

**Niche-Adjusted:** Most mortgage price quotes are based on the most favorable assumptions possible about your niche. For a list of such assumptions, *see* **Nichification/*Generic Price Quotes.*** If your deal does not correspond to these assumptions, the price you ultimately receive will be higher.

Niche-adjusted prices are available from a loan officer by volunteering the information needed to determine the correct price. Usually, the loan officer will ask you to fill out an application in the process, which makes it difficult to shop. The easier way to shop niche-adjusted prices is at Web sites that offer a "customized" price. To receive it, you must first fill out a form that provides the required information about your deal, but you don't have to apply. Multiple Web sites can be shopped in one sitting.

**Completeness:** Most price quotes consist of rate and points only. They omit fixed-dollar fees, and on ARMs they also omit features that affect the ARM rate after the initial rate period ends. *See* **Mortgage Price**.

Complete price quotes are available on some Web sites. *See* **Single-Lender Web Site**.

**Reliability:** A reliable price quote is one that, assuming the market does not change, the loan provider intends to honor when you lock.

Some loan providers offer low-ball quotes they have no intention of honoring. The objective is to rope you in. They figure that once you are in the application process, they have a good chance of landing you as a borrower.

If you are purchasing a house, the cost of terminating the process with one loan provider and starting again with another becomes increasingly high as you move toward the home closing date. Your bargaining power recedes with the passage of time.

I know a mortgage broker who aims to make at least a 1.5-point markup on all loans but includes only a 0.5 point markup on prices he quotes over the telephone. When he lands a customer, he finds a way to recover the point (or more) before the loan terms are locked.

For example, suppose market interest rates rise after the initial quote, with the original wholesale quote of 8.25% and one point now 8.25% and 1.5 points. The broker tells you "Sorry, the market has gone against us. The loan you want is now at 8.25% and three points." The broker makes an extra point by pretending that the increase in market rates was larger than it was.

Conversely, if the wholesale quote falls to 8.25% and zero points, the broker can make his 1.5-point markup by providing you with the terms originally quoted. The broker merely ignores the decline in market rates.

How do they get away with it? Loan providers legally can't be held to a price quote. Since the market is volatile, yesterday's price may not apply today. All loan providers warn borrowers that price quotes aren't firm until they are locked.

You can attempt to forestall this trickery by monitoring changes in the market after you get a price quote, but probably you won't get far.

The broker will point out that your market information is general and does not accurately describe the specific segment of the market relevant to your loan. Only the broker has that information. You will probably lose this argument because you're fighting on the broker's turf, and you have a closing date on the near horizon.

It would be a different story if the broker agreed initially to share his or her market information with you. If the broker in my example revealed the wholesale lenders' price quotes, you would know exactly how the market relevant to you had changed. But then the broker would not be able to modify his or her low-ball markup, which is why most brokers keep wholesale prices to themselves.

On the Internet, you are less vulnerable to low-ball offers that disappear under the cloud of "market change adjustments." Loan providers who quote prices on the Internet can't tell you market rates rose by ½% between the day you applied and the day you locked unless they did, because their rates are posted for you to see on both days. (*See* **Single-Lender Web Site**.) An attractive alternative is to hire an Upfront Mortgage Broker to shop prices for you. (*See* **Upfront Mortgage Brokers**.)

---

**Mortgage Program** *A bundle of mortgage characteristics that lenders view as comprising a distinct category.*

The characteristics used include whether it is an FRM, ARM, or Balloon, the term, the initial rate period or the index on an ARM, whether it is FHA-insured or VA-guaranteed, and if it is not FHA or VA whether it is "conforming" (eligible for purchase by Fannie Mae or Freddie Mac) or "non-conforming."

---

**Mortgage Referrals** *Advice on where to go to get a mortgage.*

A borrower can always select a loan provider by throwing a dart at the Yellow Pages. A referral is of value if it raises the probability of a good outcome above that from throwing the dart. The four major sources of referrals are real estate sales agents, other borrowers, Internet referral sites, and builders.

*Real Estate Sales Agents:* Home purchasers accept more referrals from real estate sales agents than from all other sources combined. Sales agent referrals generally are to individual loan officers or brokers, as opposed to firms. An agent with great confidence in a loan officer will continue to refer clients even when the loan officer switches firms.

Sales agents have the same interest as buyers in completing transactions. Hence, they refer clients to loan providers who can generally be depended upon to close on time. This is the agent's major concern, and it is a concern of borrowers as well.

Sales agents have no comparable interest in the mortgage price or whether the borrower is placed in the right kind of mortgage.

However, the agent doesn't want the price to be so far out of line or the service provided so abysmal that the borrower throws a fit and blames the agent. Hence, referrals from sales agents are significantly better than throwing a dart at the Yellow Pages.

***Other Borrowers:*** Referrals from other borrowers are usually based on a single transaction. They are better than the Yellow Pages, but not much better. I have seen borrowers who were very pleased with their experience because they were not aware that they had seriously overpaid. I have also seen the reverse—borrowers who bad-mouthed their loan provider, who had done the best possible job under adverse circumstances, and had earned very little on the deal. Before acting on a borrower referral, grill the borrower about the basis for his or her opinion.

***Internet Referral Sites:*** These Web sites provide price information for a large number of lenders and mortgage brokers, usually listed by state. They also provide quick entree to the Web sites of each loan provider listed. In theory, a borrower can sort through the list of loan providers, identify those with the lowest prices, and visit the individual Web sites to make a final selection. In practice, I found that referral sites were no better than the Yellow Pages. *See* **Referral Site**.

***Builder Referrals:*** Builder referrals are usually to a lender with whom the builder has a financial arrangement. Hence, they are suspect. In some cases, preferred lenders price loans above the market and kick back some of the excess to the builder. This makes builder referrals inferior to the Yellow Pages.

But builders can trap you into using their preferred lender. They do this by offering a price concession conditional on your using the preferred lender. The builder pads the house price, then offers back part of what has been taken from you. If you don't accept it, you lose even more. *See* **Mortgage Scams and Tricks/*Scams by Home Sellers*/ Builder Concessions**.

***Self-Referrals:*** Responding to self-referrals (solicitations) usually is a bad idea. Not all lenders who solicit are predators, but all predators solicit. Your chances of avoiding one are better if you throw a dart at the Yellow Pages.

**Mortgage Scams and Tricks**  *Deceptive practices used by mortgage loan providers and other participants in the mortgage process.*

*Scams by Loan Providers:* Lenders and mortgage brokers may employ a number of tricks to increase their income from originating a loan, at the borrower's expense.

**Make Low-Ball Offers:** To draw customers, some loan providers will advertise low-ball prices that they have no intention of honoring. Once they get you in the door, they will play *bait and switch*, or *let 'em dangle.*

"Bait and switch" is the game played by some appliance merchants and others who advertise a low-ball price but when you arrive at the store they happen to be out of the advertised special and try to interest you in something else. "Let 'em dangle" means keeping you on the hook in the hope that market rates might drop enough to make the advertised special profitable.

Mortgage shoppers should place little credence in media or oral price quotes, especially when the price is below that of all other loan providers.

**Overstate the Market Price:** The loan provider making a low-ball offer can attempt to validate it in another way. He can overstate the market price when it comes time to lock the terms. This practice, however, can be deployed regardless of whether the original price was understated. I sometimes refer to it as "float abuse."

Assume that after shopping prices at several lenders, Jane Doe selects lender X and submits an application. The prices quoted by X, upon which Jane based her decision, "float" with the market until they are locked by the lender.

Floating is mandatory between the initial price quote, which may be the basis for selection of the loan provider, and the time when the lender is willing to lock. This period can range from a day to several weeks or longer, depending on the lender's requirements to lock and on how long it takes the applicant to comply. Some applicants extend the float period in the hope that interest rates will decline.

At the end of the float period, the lender should lock at the price that he would quote to the applicant's identical twin if the twin walked through the door on the lock date as a new customer shopping the exact same deal. In practice, the quote may be higher because the applicant is at least partially committed while the twin is only shopping. This is probably the most pervasive scam in the market.

One way to avoid it is to deal with a lender whose locking requirements can be met within the day, or overnight at worst. A second way is to deal with a lender whose Internet site posts the applicant's price every day. Less effective but better than nothing is to ask the loan provider to acknowledge the twin-sibling principle in writing, and monitor general movements in the market using the rates posted on www.hsh.com.

**Pocket the Borrower's Rebate:** Some unwary borrowers are steered into high-rate loans on which they should receive a rebate from the lender but don't. For example, the loan officer's price sheet shows 6% at zero points, 5.75% at two points, and 6.25% at a two-point rebate. If the borrower is willing to pay 6.25% without argument, the rebate is retained by the loan provider. *See* **Overages**.

This abuse can be avoided by asking first about "the lowest rate possible" and how many points it would require. If you want a rebate deal, you can work yourself down to high rate/rebate combinations. Ask to see the schedule of rates and points from which the quote given to you has been extracted. Press to see them on the fax price sheet or computer screen. If the loan officer insists on transcribing them to a separate piece of paper, ask point-blank if she is adding an overage.

**Exploit Shifts in Borrower Niche Preferences:** Borrowers sometimes change their minds about some feature of the transaction that has pricing implications. If the borrower is in too deep to back out, the loan provider may pad the new price.

For example, the borrower decides to shift from a 30-year to a 15-year FRM. On a day when a shopper soliciting rates quotes would find the quote on a 15-year to be 3/8% below that on a 30, a committed applicant might receive only a 1/4% reduction. Other preference shifts where the same thing can happen include changing the combination of interest rate and points, changing between FRM and ARM, and electing to escrow or not escrow.

**Offer No-Cost Loans That Aren't:** Some loan providers tout deals as "no-cost" when the settlement costs are added to the loan balance. These deals should be referred to as "no-cash." This is a scam if the borrower doesn't understand that he or she is borrowing more to pay the settlement costs. *See* **No-Cost Mortgage**.

**Surreptitiously Change the Contract:** Borrowers who accept whatever they are told may find that the note includes a provision favorable to the lender, about which the borrower has no knowledge. A favorite is a prepayment penalty, which increases the value of a loan by 1% or more. A loan provider who includes it in the contract without your knowledge can put the point in his pocket—rather than in yours, where it belongs. *See* **Prepayment Penalty/*Surreptitious Penalties***.

### Strictly Lender Scams:

**Sell Biweeklies Under False Pretenses:** The biweekly mortgage meets the needs of some borrowers, either to help them budget or as a forced-saving device to pay off the loan early. (*See* **Biweekly Mortgage**.) Some lenders, however, promote the simple-interest biweekly as a way of substantially accelerating the rate of payoff, compared with a standard biweekly. They offer to refinance borrowers into their simple-interest biweekly at rates 2% to 3% above those the borrower is paying.

On a standard biweekly, an extra monthly payment is credited to the borrower's account after 12 months. On a simple-interest biweekly, a half-payment is credited to the borrower's account every two weeks. This does result in an earlier payoff and reduced total interest outlays. The advantage over a standard biweekly, however, is very small.

For example, on a 6% 30-year loan with biweekly payments, a borrower would be justified in paying only 6.063% for the simple interest equivalent. This is the rate that would equalize the payoff date and total interest outlays. It is a far cry from the 8% or 9% that would be charged. Readers can make the same comparisons using the biweekly spreadsheets on my Web site. *See* **Biweekly Mortgage/*Simple Interest Biweeklies***.

**Deliberately Allow Locks to Expire in a Rising Market:** When interest rates spiked in July-August 2003, my mailbox was flooded with complaints from borrowers who lost their locks. Their lenders could not get the loans processed in time. In as many as half of these cases, the borrower was at least partially at fault for not selecting a long enough lock period or for not providing needed documents on a timely basis. But in many other cases, it seems clear that the lender deliberately slowed the process so the lock would expire. I draw this inference from the flimsy excuses they provided the borrowers, who relayed them to me.

**Deceive Borrowers Regarding ARMs:** Because ARMs are complicated, the loan officers selling them tend to focus on one or two major features. In doing this, they sometimes cross the line between acceptable "puffery" and unacceptable deception. Expecting lenders to police the sales practices of loan officers is probably unrealistic. Some lenders, however, provide their loan officers with tools that aid and abet deceptive practices.

For example, mortgage applicants have sent me exhibits prepared for them showing schedules of interest rates, monthly payments, and balances on obviously favorable assumptions regarding future interest rates. But the assumptions are not indicated. In one case, the footnote to the table says, "Actual results may vary.... Consult your regulation Z."

At a minimum, ARM borrowers should have amortization schedules based on the assumption that a) the index rate does not change and b) the ARM rate increases by the maximum amount permitted by the note. These are "no-change" and "worst-case" scenarios. Borrowers can develop these schedules (and many others) themselves using calculator 7b or 7c on my Web site.

**Pad the GFE:** The Good Faith Estimate of settlement or GFE shows the borrower all the settlement costs connected to the loan. Unfortunately, lenders are not bound to the numbers shown there, and there are no penalties for discovering new charges or increasing existing ones at the 11th hour—which is exactly what some lenders do. At the time of writing, HUD was developing regulations that would eliminate this scam.

**Servicing Scams:** My mailbox is stuffed with letters from borrowers complaining about their servicing. It is difficult, however, to distinguish poor service from scams. The basic problem is that servicing provides lenders with many opportunities to profit from their own mistakes.

For example, sometimes lenders don't pay taxes on time, but is it deliberate? Some lenders purchase hazard insurance on the borrower's house and add the premium to the loan balance, even though the borrower already has insurance. Were they really unaware that the borrower was already insured? Occasionally a lender won't credit borrowers for extra payments, for one reason or another.

If you believe you have been mistreated, you can't fire your servicer, but you can file a written complaint with the lender, addressed to Customer Service. Do not include it with your mortgage payment, which you should continue to make separately. State the following:

*Your loan number.*

*Names on loan documents.*

*Property and/or mailing address.*

*This is a "qualified written request" under Section 6 of the Real Estate Settlement Procedures Act (RESPA).*

*I am writing because:*

*[Describe the problem and the action you believe the lender should take.]*

*[Describe any previous attempts to resolve the issue, including conversations with customer service.]*

*[If it is relevant to the dispute, request a copy of your payment history.]*

*[List a daytime telephone number.]*

*I understand that under Section 6 of RESPA you are required to acknowledge my request within 20 business days and must try to resolve the issue within 60 business days.*

If this doesn't do the trick, you can file a complaint with HUD. You can also sue. According to HUD, "A borrower may bring a private lawsuit, or a group of borrowers may bring a class action suit, within three years, against a servicer who fails to comply with Section 6's provisions."

You can also file a complaint with the government agency that regulates the servicing agent. Here are Web sites you can use to contact these agencies:

- For national banks, www.occ.treas.gov/customer.htm.

- For federally chartered savings and loan associations, www.ots.treas.gov/contact.html.
- For state-chartered banks and savings and loans, www.lend-ingprofessional.com/licensing.html.
- For mortgage banking firms, www.aarmr.org/lists/members-IE.html.

If you don't know the proper agency, you can send the complaint to the Consumer Protection Division of the state attorney general. It will forward it to the relevant state or federal agency.

All borrowers should periodically check their transaction history to make certain that a) payments are always applied to the balance at the end of the preceding month, b) tax and insurance payments from escrow are correct and there have been no double payments, c) rate adjustments on ARMs are in accordance with the method stipulated in the note, and d) there isn't anything in the history that looks "funny."

Any borrower who does not receive a complete transaction statement at least annually should periodically submit a "qualified written request" for one, using the form described above.

**Strictly Broker Scams:** Some scams are initiated only by mortgage brokers. The first one described below is directed against the borrower, the second against the lender.

**Charging for a Lock Without Locking with the Lender:** Locking the mortgage rate assures borrowers that the interest rate and points they have agreed to pay will be honored at closing, even if market rates rise in the meantime. Some mortgage brokers tell their clients that the interest rate has been locked with the lender when that is not the case. They substitute their lock for the lenders without informing the borrower.

Brokers do this to increase their markup. For example, a lender might quote 6% plus 0.5 points for a 10-day lock, and 6% plus one point for the 60-day lock an applicant requires. The lying broker tells the applicant she is locked for 60 days at 6% plus one point. If the market doesn't change, the broker locks 10 days from closing at .5 point, and pockets the other .5%.

Brokers rationalize this lie by saying that they are assuming the lock risk themselves and will deliver the "locked" rate and points to the borrower even if they have to take a loss. In a stable or declining rate market, they can get away with this, perhaps for years at a time.

But sooner or later interest rates will suddenly spike and brokers locking at their own risk will not be able to deliver. For example, in the two-month period January-March 1980, mortgage rates jumped from 12.88% to 15.28%. A broker who locked for 60 days at 12.88% would have to pay a lender about 15 points to accept a loan with that rate in a 15.28% market. The broker would either go out of business or deny that a lock was given. (Broker locks are oral commitments.) The borrower would be left high and dry in either case.

Indeed, many non-locking brokers deserted their customers following the much smaller rate increase that occurred in July-August 2003. Unlike lenders who can always come up with an excuse, a non-locking broker who is challenged by a borrower cannot produce a lock commitment from a lender. About all the broker can do is apologize or run.

Broker locks are a deceitful practice because the borrower is led to believe that the lender is providing the lock. To protect themselves, borrowers locking through a broker should insist on receiving the rate lock commitment letter from the lender identifying them as the applicant. They must demand this at the time of the lock, not after the lock fails.

**Successive Refinancings Using Rebate Loans:** This scam is directed toward wholesale lenders and requires the cooperation of venal borrowers who participate in it. The larger the loan, the more profitable the scam.

Lenders pay rebates on high-rate loans. For example, a lender who offers a 30-year FRM at 7.875% and zero points might pay a rebate of four points for a 9.5% loan. Lenders know that 9.5% loans have relatively short lives because borrowers refinance them as soon as they can. Nonetheless, the lender will recover the four points through the above-market rate in 30 months, and most such loans last longer than that. Or rather, they last longer unless there is a scam to pay off in three months.

On a loan of $350,000, the lender pays a rebate of 4% of $350,000, or $14,000. Over three months, the lender collects only about $1,400 in excess interest. The broker pays the borrower's closing costs of about $4,000 and $1,400 to cover the higher interest payment on the 9.5% loan for three months. The balance of $8,600 is split between them, with the broker keeping most of it. After three months, they do it again, but with a different lender in order to avoid disclosure.

I classify this as a broker scam because the broker initiates and executes it, but the broker requires a corrupt borrower as an accomplice.

**Scams by Borrowers:** Borrower scams are directed mainly against mortgage brokers. Because borrowers are in the market only intermittently, however, they have less incentive and fewer opportunities than loan providers to develop and refine scams. Not surprisingly, those they come up with often don't work, or even backfire on them.

**"End-Run" Around the Broker:** Some borrowers believe they can beat the system by using a broker to find the right lender, then going directly to that lender. They think they can cut out the markup in this way. This is a sleazy practice because the broker won't be compensated for his or her time and for the use of his or her knowledge and expertise on the borrower's behalf. It is why even the most scrupulous brokers keep the identity of the lender concealed until an application has been submitted.

Nor does it work the way the borrower expects it to. Lenders who lend both directly to borrowers and indirectly through brokers have separate retail and wholesale departments. The borrower who dumps the broker to go directly to the lender will be directed to the retail department and be offered retail prices, which are higher. They could be higher than the price the borrower would have paid going through the broker.

**Net-Jumping:** Net-jumping involves using a broker's time and expertise to become informed and creditworthy, then jumping to the Internet to get the loan. Here's a broker's story.

When Jones came to me six months ago, his credit score wouldn't have qualified him to purchase a doghouse. But I worked with him while he disputed his credit report with the bureaus, and negotiated with collection agencies. His credit score went from "D" to "A." While he was working with me, he learned his responsibilities as a future homeowner.... Then he informed me that he was going to shop for a loan on the Internet.

Brokers could protect themselves against Net-jumping by charging a non-refundable fee. Few do this, however, for fear it would place them at a competitive disadvantage.

**Multiple-Apping:** Another borrower trick is to submit multiple applications through different brokers—two, three, or even more. All the brokers check credit, shop loan programs, and fill out the application, but only the one offering the best deal on the lock date will be compensated. The others waste their time.

Borrowers who submit multiple applications also waste their own time, but the practice is evidence of how difficult it is to shop traditional mortgage channels. Borrowers typically can't obtain a complete listing of loan fees and charges until they submit an application, which encourages "shopping by application."

But multiple-apping can boomerang. If the application runs into a major roadblock, a resentful broker may have little motivation to go the extra mile that may be needed to remove it.

**Lock-Jumping:** Under a loan lock agreement, the lender and the borrower are committed to the interest rate and other specified terms. Some borrowers, however, act as though the agreement only binds the lender. If interest rates rise prior to closing, the lender is committed to the rate specified in the agreement. But if rates decline, the borrower feels free to go to another broker and relock at a lower rate.

Borrowers who want both the benefit of a rate decline and protection against a rate increase should purchase a "float-down." It allows the rate to remain locked if market rates rise, but if market rates decline the borrower can relock at a lower rate. A float-down costs a little more than a straight lock.

Unfortunately, in many cases borrowers are never put on notice that the lock commits them as well as the lender. Many brokers fear that if they mention the "C" word, they will lose the client. This makes lock-jumping morally ambiguous.

Lock-jumping is much more common among refinancers, who are more flexible on when they close than purchasers who must close on a specified date. This means that lenders could largely eliminate lock-jumping if they offered only float-downs to refinancers.

**The Double House Purchase:** A buyer who wants to buy two houses but can qualify for a mortgage on only one, arranges to have them close on the same day. That way, the debt from one is not counted in the expense-to-income ratio of the other.

However, the application for whichever loan closed second would contain false information because it would not reveal the loan that closed first. This could be caught in a post-closing audit of either loan. It would also be caught if both loans ended up being serviced by the same entity. Since servicing is becoming increasingly concentrated in the hands of a few large players, the chances of that happening are not insignificant.

*Scams by Home Sellers:* Scams by home sellers are directed against lenders or borrowers.

**Fictitious Down Payments:** Down payment assistance programs are widespread and often involve gifts by home sellers offset by a price increase equal to the gift. The practice is legitimate, provided it is done openly and conforms to the guidelines of lenders and mortgage insurers. *See* **Down Payment/*Home Seller Contributions*.**

Down payment assistance becomes a scam when it is done without the knowledge or permission of the lender. For example, buyer and seller agree on a price of $289,000 but the buyer cannot meet the down payment requirement of $15,000. So they agree to raise the price to $304,000 and for the seller to lend the borrower the $15,000 needed for the down payment. After the closing, the loan is forgiven. This is a scam because the lender is tricked into believing that the borrower has made a down payment when that is not the case.

For this scam to work, the appraisal of the property must come in at $304,000. The appraiser either is hoodwinked by the fictitious sale price or is a party to the scam.

The buyer is a party to the scam as well. For the loan to close, the buyer is obliged to lie about the source of the funds used for the down payment.

Assuming the deception is not caught and the loan goes through, it might be caught in a post-closing audit, in which event the lender could elect to call the loan. All mortgage loans contain an "acceleration clause," which allows the lender to demand immediate repayment if any information provided by the borrower turns out to be false.

Borrowers with good credit don't need to cheat in order to get 100% financing. It is available in the form of combination loans—80% first mortgage and 20% second mortgage. 100% first mortgages are also available. Find a mortgage broker familiar with these options.

**Builder Concessions:** Many builders have a financial interest in a lender to which they want to refer business. While the law prohibits builders from requiring buyers to use their preferred lenders, they can offer financial concessions contingent on using those lenders.

Since the builder will include the concession in the price of the house, buyers who agree to the price are going to find it difficult not to deal with the preferred lender. The lender can charge an above-market rate or points, but with the concession buyers are still better off than if they financed elsewhere.

Suppose, for example, the builder pads the sale price by $5,000, but offers a concession of $5,000 for using the preferred lender. If the lender prices the loan $3,000 above the market, the buyer using that lender is still ahead by $2,000.

The only way a buyer can avoid this trap is to refuse deals that tie concessions to use of a preferred lender. Offer the builder the asking price less the concession.

**"Wrapping" a Mortgage:** Home sellers sometimes have compelling reasons to avoid repaying their mortgage when they sell their house. The interest rate might be well below the current market rate. Or they might have a willing buyer who is unable to qualify for a new mortgage.

To keep the old mortgage going, the seller may lend to the buyer him or herself while continuing to make the payments on the old loan. For example, S, who has a $70,000 mortgage on his home, sells his home to B for $100,000. B pays $5,000 down and borrows $95,000 from S on a new mortgage. This mortgage "wraps around" the existing $70,000 mortgage because the lender-seller will make the payments on the old mortgage.

Wrap-arounds, like down payment gifts, are OK if the lender

knows about them and agrees. They are a scam when used to circumvent restrictions on assuming old loans. The home seller who does this violates his or her contract with the lender and may or may not get away with it. In some states, escrow companies are required by law to inform a lender whose loan is being wrapped. If a wraparound deal on a non-assumable loan does close and the lender discovers it afterwards, watch out! The lender will either call the loan or demand an immediate increase in interest rate and probably a healthy assumption fee.

---

**Mortgage Shopping** *Trying to find the best deal on a mortgage.*

It isn't easy to do it right, as a summary of the major steps involved will demonstrate. This guide is based on the regulatory structure in September 2003. Reforms proposed by HUD, which were pending at the time this was written, should make shopping for a mortgage much easier. *See* **RESPA/*Proposals for RESPA Reform***.

**Step 1: Decide if You Are a Potential Shopper:** Not everyone is a potential shopper. Some will do a lot better entrusting that responsibility to someone else. Read the following statements, giving yourself one point if a statement marked "1" best describes you, two points if a statement marked "2" describes you best, and 1.5 points if you are in between.

*A1. I like to bargain and have no hesitancy in speaking up if I think someone is trying to take advantage of me.*

*A2. I avoid confrontation at all costs.*

*B1. I feel that I either know or have the capacity to learn as much about mortgages as I will need to know to take care of myself in the marketplace.*

*B2. I feel overwhelmed by the complexity of mortgages, and I don't have the time, energy, or desire to educate myself about them.*

*C1. When significant money is at stake, I like to control things myself.*

*C2. When significant money is at stake, I like to find someone I can trust to make critical decisions for me.*

*D1. I feel very comfortable using a computer.*

*D2. I am computer-phobic.*

If your total score is above six, find a mortgage broker to be your agent in shopping for a mortgage. I recommend Upfront Mortgage Brokers (UMBs) because they are prepared to provide this service at a set fee, negotiated in advance. Once the fee is established, your interest and that of the broker are closely aligned. *See* **Upfront Mortgage Broker**.

Potential shoppers score six or lower. What follows is directed primarily at them.

***Step 2: Decide Which Mortgage Features You Want:*** Before entering the market, shoppers should decide on the type of mortgage, term, points, down payment, and lock period.

You can't compare prices of different loan providers accurately unless you can specify exactly what you are shopping for. When you shop for an automobile, you decide beforehand that you want, e.g., a four-door Toyota Corolla with accessory package 101. You must do the same when you shop for a mortgage.

It is especially important to know exactly what you want before you lock the price. If you change your mind after you lock and market prices have risen in the meantime, many lenders will allow a change only at the higher price.

***Step 3: Determine Your Market Niche:*** The interest rate and/or points on a mortgage vary with a number of borrower, property, and transaction features. Loan officers quoting prices will assume the features commanding the lowest price. *See* **Nichification/*Generic Price Quotes***.

For example, if you don't say anything about the property, the loan officer will assume it is a single-family detached house constructed on the site. If in fact it is in a low-rise condominium, a four-family structure, or a manufactured house, the price will probably be higher. To obtain valid price quotes, shoppers must indicate all such deviations between their deal and the generic deal.

Make a list of your "Niche Adjustments"—all the deviations between your deal and the generic assumptions. Whenever you are soliciting price quotes, you offer the list.

***Step 4: Formulate Your Price Selection Strategy:*** Selecting the best price on a mortgage is not like selecting the best price on a toaster. Mortgages have three (or more) price components, toasters only one.

**Pricing Strategy on Fixed-Rate Mortgages (FRMs):** Once you know your loan amount, convert all upfront charges into a single total dollar figure. Multiply all upfront fees expressed as a percent of the loan times the loan amount. (This includes points, origination fee if there is one, and broker fee if it is defined as a percent.) Add fixed-dollar fees charged by the lender and broker. For example, if the loan is for $150,000 at one point ($1,500), with lender fees of $800 and broker fees of $3,000, total dollars amount to $5300.

Ignore the cost of title-related services and settlement services. If you are in an area in which it can pay to shop for them, you can do it after selecting the loan and lender. Also ignore any government charges, escrows, and per diem interest. You can't shop these. Hazard insurance you buy on your own.

When you have two price components—the interest rate and total dollars upfront—there are two ways to make a selection decision. One way is to fix the interest rate (call it your "shopping rate") and ask for quotes on total dollars at that rate. It is convenient that interest rates are generally quoted in 1/8% increments.

You thus ask the loan provider "If these are my mortgage features and niche adjustments, what are your points and total fees at (say) 5.875%?" You must be clear that "total fees" refers to payments to the lender and the broker, excluding payments to third parties, per diem interest, and escrows.

The best shopping rate for your purpose can only be found through trial and error. If you begin with a shopping rate that elicits larger total dollar quotes than you want to pay, for example, raise it. As your shopping rate goes up, the total dollar quotes will go down.

An alternative to soliciting total dollar quotes for a given shopping rate is to combine different rate and total dollars into a single measure of **Interest Cost (IC)**. Economists call this measure an "internal rate of return," or IRR. The annual percentage rate (APR), which is a mandatory disclosure, is an IRR. The problem with the APR is that it is calculated over the entire term of the loan, which makes it a biased measure for borrowers with short horizons.

If you know you will be in your house for 10 years or longer, you can use the APR because the error is small. Otherwise, you should compare interest costs over your own shorter time horizon. You can do that using calculator 9c on my Web site.

There is one way to shop a single price that has become popular in recent years. This is to shop for the lowest interest rate with zero settlement costs. The lender pays all costs, including third-party charges. This approach makes it almost as easy to compare mortgage prices as toaster prices. Just make sure all costs are covered except per diem interest and escrows, and nothing is added to the balance. *See* **No-Cost Mortgage**.

This is a great strategy if your time horizon is less than five years. The lender pays your settlement costs in exchange for higher interest payments, but these payments don't go on long enough to wipe out the benefit. After about five years, however, the higher interest payments convert the strategy into a loser.

**Pricing Strategy on ARMs and Balloon Loans:** Both ARMs and balloons have fixed rates for some initial period. For balloons, that period is almost always either five or seven years. For ARMs, it can range from a month to 10 years.

If you know that you will be out of the house before the initial rate period ends, you can use the same price selection strategy as on an FRM. As far as you are concerned, it is an FRM. In using calculator 9c to measure interest cost, enter the initial rate period as the period you expect to stay in your house. The calculator will ignore what happens after that period.

The problem is that virtually no one can be certain that they will be gone by the end of any initial rate period. Life has a bad habit of changing our minds. You should be aware of what can happen at the end of that period and factor that into your decision process.

In the case of balloon loans, that is not difficult. At the end of the initial rate period, you must refinance at the market rate prevailing at that time. Since all balloons are equally bad in that regard, select the one that is the best deal over the initial rate period. The pricing strategy for a balloon thus turns out to be the same as that for an FRM.

ARMs, however, have built-in protections against rate increases after the initial rate period, and these may differ from one ARM to another. If two five-year ARMs have the same interest cost over the five years, you want the one that exposes you to less risk of a rate increase at the end of five years.

Unfortunately, this is not easy to determine because it is affected by a number of ARM features that won't be provided to you in a comprehensible form unless you ask. Print out Information Needed to Evaluate an ARM from my Web site and have the lender fill it in for any ARM you are considering. You then have what you need to use calculators 7b or 7c and 9a or 9b. These calculators will tell you what will happen to your interest rate and monthly payment at the end of the initial rate period if 1) the interest rate index doesn't change, 2) the index goes through the roof (a "worse case"), or 3) the index follows any other future scenario you choose to examine.

### Step 5: Solicit Price Quotes:

**Validity:** To be valid, mortgage price quotes must be:

- Complete, which means inclusive of lender and broker fees expressed in dollars, as well as those expressed as a percent of the loan. On adjustable rate mortgages (ARMs), it also means inclusive of information on features affecting the interest rate and payment when the initial rate period ends.

- Timely, which means that the prices are live at the time they are conveyed to the shopper.

- Niche-adjusted, which means that the prices are adjusted for all the ways in which the shopper's transaction differs from the generic assumptions used by lenders in developing their best prices.

- Honest, which means that the loan provider would be willing to lock the rate and points quoted, rather than low-balling to get the business, and is willing to guarantee fixed-dollar fees.

**Sources:** One source of price quotes is individual loan officers recommended by your sales agent if it is a purchase transaction, or by other borrowers. Provide them with your mortgage features and niche adjustments. If you are shopping an ARM, include the blank table on Information Needed to Evaluate an ARM from my Web site.

Request that quotes include fixed-dollar fees and that they be e-mailed or faxed.

A second source of price quotes is Internet mortgage auction sites. These sites ask you to fill out a questionnaire covering the loan request, property, personal finances, and contact information. (It is their version of your mortgage features and niche adjustments.) The sites use this information to select the lenders, usually up to four, to whom the information is sent. The selected lenders then send price quotes to you based on the same information, hopefully on the same day.

This is a quick and easy way to obtain up to four price quotes. However, the niche adjustments may or may not be complete, they may not ask you about your mortgage preferences, and they may not include information on fixed-dollar fees or on important ARM features. Hence, you probably will need to request a second round. The integrity of the quotes is no more verifiable than those you get by directly soliciting loan officers yourself.

Auction sites include:

- CityLoans.com
- GetSmart.com
- LendingTree.com
- InterestRatesOnline.com
- LoanApp.com
- LoanAtlas.com
- LoanHounds.com
- LoanWeb.com
- LowestMortgage.com
- MortgageExpo.com
- MortgageTrader.com

A third source of price quotes is single-lender Internet sites. They are less convenient than auction sites, since you can only get one quote per site. However, you choose your mortgage features, and the price quotes are more likely to be complete. Furthermore, if your loan is priced on-line it is an honest price. They can't give you a low-ball quote to snare your business, then raise the price when you lock, because you can monitor the price when you lock.

Single-lender sites vary greatly in the extent of their niche adjustments. The more questions they ask the user, the more complete the niche adjustment can be. However, many lenders are afraid to ask too many questions on their Web sites for fear the user will become discouraged and leave. The trick, therefore, is to determine whether the questions posed by a site have captured your particular niche adjustments. If you are buying a two-family house, for example, and you are asked about "Type of Property" with "Two-Family House" as one possible answer, then you know that they adjust for that.

The following are some Internet sites that provide fairly complete niche adjustments, though no two are exactly the same:

- Citimortgage.com
- ELOAN.com
- HomeLoanCenter.com
- IndyMac.com
- Infoloan.com
- Mortgage.com
- Mortgagebot.com
- Mortgage.ETrade.com
- WaMuHomeLoans.com.

To make it easier to shop single-lender sites, I developed the "Upfront Mortgage Lender" certification. The requirements include filling out a niche table, which allows a shopper to tell at a glance whether the niche into which the shopper falls is priced on-line by the lender. Complete pricing is also a requirement. At this writing, only ELOAN.com complies fully.

***Step 6: Select the Loan Provider:*** Lenders who price high often argue that service quality is equally important. "You wouldn't hire a lawyer or an architect based strictly on price, would you?" The problem with this argument is that there is very little reliable information available to borrowers on the service quality of loan providers. Furthermore, there is no reason whatever to believe that lenders who price high provide better service.

There is one particular service, however, that shoppers may want to consider in making their final selection. This is the lender's requirements for locking the price.

Some lenders refuse to lock until a borrower demonstrates commitment to the deal by completing one or more critical steps in the lending process, including an application. Other lenders will lock based on very little. We would expect that lenders who make it easy to lock would quote higher prices because they have higher lock costs. Some shoppers will lock with them as protection against a rate increase while they continue to shop for a better deal elsewhere. However, it doesn't always work out that way.

If two lenders have the same price, but one will lock you today while the other won't lock you for three days, you should go with the first. This is especially the case if you have no way to verify the validity of the changes in the market that occur over the three days.

**Step 7: Lock the Price:** Most borrowers lock as soon as possible, and you can't get into trouble doing that. Allowing the price to "float" until shortly before closing can be either a good gamble, meaning that the odds are in your favor, or a bad gamble. It is has nothing to do with whether market interest rates go up or down over the period, because that is not predictable.

Allowing the price to float is a good gamble only if all the following conditions are met:

- You can afford the hit if market rates go up. If your income is only marginally adequate to qualify, it would be foolish to risk being disqualified by a rate increase.

- You can monitor your price day by day. In general, this is possible only if your specific deal is priced on the lender's Web site.

- The lender charges lower prices for shorter lock periods. This means that if the market is stable, your price will drop as the lock period shortens.

For example, you have 60 days to closing and the quote is 5% and one point for a 60-day lock, .875 points for a 45-day lock, .75 points for a 30-day lock, and .625 points for a 15-day lock. If you float until five days before closing and the market does not change, you save .375 points, the difference between the 60-day and the 15-day lock prices. Some mortgage brokers do this as a matter of course, i.e., they "lock" the borrower at their own risk at the 60-day price but don't lock with the lender until they can get the 15-day price.

This is a good gamble because you win if interest rates neither rise nor fall, but it remains a gamble because you lose if interest rates rise. If the lender charges the same price for a 15-day as for a 60-day lock, it is no longer a good gamble, since you don't profit in a stable market. If you can't monitor your price, it is a bad gamble because you are then at the mercy of the lender to tell you what the market price is.

Locking the price should end the shopping process, but unfortunately it doesn't. When it comes to mortgages, "it isn't over till it's over." If you don't watch yourself, you can be victimized by "lender fee inflation" and/or by "contract chicanery."

### Step 8: Cover Your Rear:

**Lender Fee Inflation:** When you lock the price of the loan, you are not locking the whole price. You are locking the market-sensitive part, consisting of interest rate and points. Lender fees specified in dollars are not market-sensitive and are not locked. Further, such fees do not usually appear in media ads that show mortgage price and are seldom volunteered to shoppers. They are shown on the Good Faith Estimate of settlement (GFE), along with all other settlement costs. However, the GFE need not be provided to borrowers until three business days after receipt of an application. This is too late to help shoppers.

But it gets worse. Lenders are not bound by the numbers on the GFE, which are "good faith estimates." The GFE concept made some sense with regard to third-party services, such as title insurance. It never made any sense with regard to lender charges, however, because lenders know their own charges with certainty. The GFE has thus provided a cloak behind which some rogue lenders extract additional fees from unsuspecting borrowers. *See* **Mortgage Scams and Tricks/*Strictly Lender Scams*/P**ad the GFE.

This is not a problem if you are dealing with a mortgage broker. Brokers know the fees of each lender they deal with and will not tolerate lenders taking advantage of their clients. Fee inflation puts no money in brokers' pockets. The problem arises in dealing with lenders.

Some Internet lenders include their fixed-dollar fees in their price quotes and guarantee that these will be the fees charged at closing. These lenders include ELOAN.com, HomeLoanCenter.com, IndyMac.com, Mortgage.com, and Mortgage.ETrade.com.

In soliciting price quotes from other lenders, ask them to guarantee their fixed-dollar fees. If they agree and you want to push your luck, ask if they will include credit check and property appraisal charges, which they order but you pay for. They may be reluctant because these charges can vary from case to case. Your fallback is to ask them to guarantee not to mark them up. To make sure you have no surprises at closing, get it in writing. Fixed-dollar fees should be on the lock confirmation statement.

**Contract Chicanery:** The mortgage note is a contract between the lender and the borrower, but ordinarily the borrower does not see the contract until the closing, and few read it even then. Generally this is not problematic, but it can be if the lender slips something in that disadvantages the borrower, without the knowledge of the borrower. This is contract chicanery.

When this happens, the offensive provision is likely to be in a rider to the contract. Judging from my mailbox, the most common such rider is a prepayment penalty. The inducement is a significant enhancement in the value of the note, part of which will probably go into the pocket of the loan officer.

It is remarkably easy to prevent this from happening. There is a line on the Truth in Lending (TIL) form you are given after you submit your application that says, *"If you pay off your loan early, you [ ] may [ ] will not have to pay a penalty."* If there is a check in front of "may," it means that your loan does have a prepayment penalty, no maybes about it. If you have not agreed to a prepayment penalty, then is when you should catch it.

I also see contract chicanery in connection with adjustable rate mortgages (ARMs). In the typical case, the borrower is sold an ARM based on one or two features, and never confronts the remaining features that are included in the note. Unlike a prepayment penalty, which must come to light if the borrower tries to refinance, disadvantageous ARM features can remain undetected indefinitely. To prevent this, collect all the relevant information about the ARMs for which you shop.

**Negative Amortization** *A rise in the loan balance when the mortgage payment is less than the interest due. Sometimes called "deferred interest."*

See **Adjustable Rate Mortgage/*How the Monthly Payment on an ARM Is Determined*/**Negative Amortization ARMs.

**Negative Amortization Cap** *The maximum amount of negative amortization permitted on an ARM, usually expressed as a percentage of the original loan amount (e.g., 110%).*

See **Adjustable Rate Mortgage/*How the Monthly Payment on an ARM Is Determined*/**Negative Amortization ARMs.

**Negative Points** *Points paid by a lender for a loan with a rate above the rate on a zero point loan.*

For example, a lender might quote the following prices: 8%/0 points, 7.5%/3 points, 8.75%/-2.5 points. Negative points, often referred to as "rebates," are used to reduce a borrower's settlement costs. When negative points are retained by a mortgage broker, they are called a "yield spread premium." See **Points/*Points and Rebates as Borrower Options***.

**Net Branch** *A facility offered by some lenders to mortgage brokers where de jure the brokers become employees of the lender but de facto they retain their independence as brokers. One of the advantages of this arrangement to brokers is that they need not disclose yield spread premiums received from lenders.*

**Net Jumping** *Using a broker's time and expertise to become informed and creditworthy, then jumping to the Internet to get the loan.*

See **Mortgage Scams and Tricks/*Scams by Borrowers*/**Net-Jumping.

**Nichification** *Proliferation in the number of loan, borrower, property, and transaction characteristics used by lenders to set mortgage prices and underwriting requirements.*

Nichification is unique to the U.S. and reflects the importance of secondary markets there. Any characteristic identified by investors in the secondary market as affecting risk or cost is priced in the secondary market, and then in the primary market. The following is a partial list of factors used in pricing or in setting qualification requirements.

### Transaction Characteristics:

*Loan Amount*

*Desired Lock Period* (in days)

*Down Payment* (as percent of property value)

*Term*

*Prepayment Penalty* (if any)

### Borrower Characteristics:

*Credit Score*

*Ratio of Borrower Income to Monthly Housing Expense*

*Ratio of Borrower Income to Total Housing Expense*

### Property if Not Single-Family Detached:

*Two-Family*

*Three-Family*

*Four-Family*

*Co-op* (building is owned by a cooperative association in which members own shares)

*Condominium* (borrower owns unit in a project in which some facilities are owned in common)

*Condominium More than Four Stories High*

*Manufactured* (house was not built on site)

*Attached* ("Twin," "Triplex," "Row")

*Planned Unit Development* (house is located in a PUD with a homeowners association that charges dues)

### Loan Purpose if Not Purchase for Permanent Occupancy:

*Purchase Second Home* (Vacation Home)

*Refinance*

*Cash-Out Refinance* (loan is larger than old loan balance by an amount larger than the settlement costs)

*Investment* (home is being purchased to rent out)

### Documentation if Not Standard:

*Alternative Documentation* (borrower wants to provide payroll and bank statements rather than wait for verification of information from employer and bank)

*Documentation for Self-Employed* (borrower wants to use special documentation requirements available for the self-employed)

*No Income Verification* (borrower doesn't want reported income to be verified by the lender)

*No Asset Verification* (borrower doesn't want reported assets to be verified by the lender)

*"No Docs"* (borrower doesn't want reported income or assets to be verified by the lender)

*No Income Ratios* (borrower doesn't want income to be used in determining qualification)

*Streamlined Refinance* (borrower wants the reduced documentation requirements available on refinances only)

### Special Borrower Features:

*Non-Occupant Co-Borrower* (one of the borrowers won't be living in the house)

*Subordinate Financing* (there will be a second mortgage on the property when the new loan is made)

*Non-Permanent Resident Alien* (borrower is employed in U.S. but is not a U.S. citizen or permanent resident)

*Non-Permanent Non-Resident Alien* (borrower is not a U.S. citizen and is not employed in the U.S.)

*Waiver of Escrows* (borrower wants to be responsible for payment of taxes and insurance)

**Numbers of Niches:** The number of potential niches is enormous because of all the different combinations of niche characteristics. Software developed by GHR Systems, Inc., which many major lenders use to make pricing adjustments, allows lenders to enter up to *40 million prices for each loan program*. A second loan program could have a different 40 million. While no one lender uses any significant part of this capacity, in combination the lenders using the system price for several million niches at least.

***Implications for Mortgage Shopping:*** First, shoppers need to understand that no lender operates in every niche, and the narrower the niche, the fewer the lenders. In a survey of 15 national lenders that I once did, I found that all 15 made investor loans on 30-year fixed-rate mortgages. However, only nine of them made investor loans to borrowers who were doing a cash-out refinance, and only four were also willing to waive standard loan documentation requirements. On adjustable rate mortgages, furthermore, the number fell to two.

Second, the lender offering the best deal in one niche is very unlikely to be the one offering the best deal in another niche. In a study of 13 lenders operating in 19 niches that I did some time ago, I found that 12 of them offered the best deal in at least one niche. Further, no one of the lenders offered the best deal in more than three of the 19 niches.

Third, nichification is a major reason why mortgage brokers have become such a major part of the market in recent years. Since mortgage brokers deal with multiple lenders, usually 30 or more, they are well positioned (as consumers are not) to identify the lenders who operate in a particular niche, and select the best of the available deals.

Finally, in collecting price data from loan providers, shoppers must be sure that they have provided each loan provider with the information required to place them in the correct market niche. Otherwise, the shopper does not know whether the prices apply or not.

***Generic Price Quotes:*** Casual mortgage shoppers who ask loan providers for "their rate and points" will receive a generic price quote: one based on a series of favorable assumptions. Here are typical assumptions underlying generic price quotes:

- The transaction is a home purchase or no-cash refinance.
- The loan amount is below the conforming loan limit ($322,700 in 2003) and larger than some minimum, such as $50,000, which can vary.

- There will not be a second mortgage on the property when the loan closes.
- The property is single-family, detached, and constructed on the site.
- All co-borrowers will occupy the house as their permanent residence.
- The FICO score of all co-borrowers is above some level, often 720-740.
- The borrowers can document that they have enough cash for the down payment and closing costs.
- The borrowers can document that they have sufficient income to meet the maximum income/expense ratios on the program selected.
- The borrowers are U.S. citizens or permanent resident aliens.

Any deviations from these assumptions will call for a higher price.

---

**No-Asset Loan**  *A documentation requirement where the applicant's assets are not disclosed.*

*See* **Documentation Requirements**.

---

**No-Change Scenario** *On an ARM, the assumption that the value of the index to which the interest rate is tied does not change from its initial level.*

---

**No-Cost Mortgage** *A mortgage on which all settlement costs except per diem interest and escrows are paid by the lender and/or the home seller.*

A no-cost mortgage should be distinguished from a "no-points mortgage," which will have other settlement costs, and a "no-cash-outlays mortgage," on which settlement costs are added to the loan balance. Calling the latter "no-cost" is extremely deceptive.

A true no-cost mortgage is one where the interest rate is high enough to command a rebate from the lender that covers the closing costs (except for per diem interest and escrows, which borrowers always pay). In general, they make sense only for borrowers who expect to hold their mortgages for no more than five years. A borrower with a longer time horizon and who has the cash to pay settlement costs ought to avoid the no-cost option.

Lenders demand a high interest rate for rebates because they assume they won't enjoy it very long. The average life of high-interest-rate loans is short. A borrower who pays the high rate for a long time gets a bad deal. It is akin to a healthy person buying life insurance from a company that mainly insures diabetics and smokers and prices its insurance accordingly.

The critical number for potential borrowers is the "break-even period" (BEP) for a no-cost loan, relative to the same loan with a lower rate on which the borrower pays the costs. Over periods shorter than the BEP, the no-cost loan has lower costs. Beyond the BEP, the no-cost loan has higher costs. The BEP can be calculated in any real situation using calculators 11a and 11b on my Web site.

One important side benefit of no-cost mortgages is that shopping for them is relatively easy. The shopper needs quotes on only one price dimension—the interest rate. *See* **Mortgage Shopping/*Step 4: Formulate Your Price Selection Strategy*/Pricing Strategy on Fixed-Rate Mortgages (FRMs)**.

---

**No-Income Loan** *A documentation requirement where the applicant's income is not disclosed.*

*See* **Documentation Requirements**.

---

**Non-Conforming Mortgage** *A mortgage that does not meet the purchase requirements of the two federal agencies, Fannie Mae and Freddie Mac, because it is too large or for other reasons, such as poor credit or inadequate documentation.*

---

**Non-Permanent Resident Alien** *A non-citizen with a green card employed in the U.S.*

Non-permanent resident aliens are subject to somewhat more restrictive qualification requirements than U.S. citizens. Permanent resident aliens are not.

**No-Ratio Loan** *A documentation option where the applicant's income is disclosed and verified but not used in qualifying the borrower.*

The conventional maximum ratios of expense to income are not applied. *See* **Documentation Requirements**.

---

**Note** *A document that evidences a debt and a promise to repay.*

A mortgage loan transaction always includes a note evidencing the debt, and a mortgage evidencing the lien on the property.

---

**100% Loan** *A loan with no down payment.*

*See* **Down Payment/*No-Down-Payment Loans***.

---

**125% Loan** *A mortgage loan for 125% of property value.*

Since such loans are only partly secured, they have many of the characteristics of unsecured loans, including relatively high interest rates. Rates are largely determined by the borrower's credit score, however, and can be quite reasonable when the score is high. A drawback is that borrowers have difficulty refinancing 125% loans and can't sell their house without defaulting unless they can come up with the additional cash required to pay off the 125% loan.

---

**Origination Fee** *An upfront fee charged by some lenders, expressed as a percent of the loan amount.*

It is the same as points except that points vary with the interest rate and the origination fee does not.

---

**Overage** *The difference between the price posted to its loan officers by a lender or mortgage broker and the price charged the borrower.*

Loan officers who work for lenders or mortgage brokers receive updated prices from their head office every morning. These consist of rates and points for different loan programs. They are the "posted prices."

The loan officer who executes a deal at the posted price gets paid a commission that may be .5%-.7% of the loan amount. On a $100,000 loan, the commission might be $500-$700. But if the loan officer can induce the borrower to pay more than the posted price, the commission rises. It now includes an overage.

For example, the posted price on a particular loan is 5% and zero points but the loan officer induces the borrower to pay 5% and one point. That point is the overage. It is worth $1,000 on a $100,000 loan, and typically the loan officer gets half. An overage can thus double the loan officer's commission.

Overages are heavily concentrated on high-rate loans with negative points, or "rebates." For example, the lender posting a price of 5% and zero points might also quote 5.25% and -2 points. Loan officers push higher-rate plus rebate combinations because they can collect an overage without taking any cash out of borrowers' pockets. If the loan officer in the example above quotes 5.25% and -1 point to the borrower, the other point of rebate becomes the overage. The borrower pays for the overage in the interest rate for the next five or 10 years, but that's down the road.

Overages associated primarily with rebate loans are an equal opportunity abuse, practiced by lenders and mortgage brokers alike. The only difference is that mortgage brokers who retain rebates from lenders leave a trail in the Good Faith Estimate of disclosure, where it can be discovered by the borrower, although usually too late to do anything about it. Rebates retained as overages by loan officer employees of lenders disappear without a trace.

Defenders of overages argue that they merely reflect the wheeling and dealing characteristic of many markets. They point out that sometimes borrowers turn the tables, forcing loan officers to cut the price below the posted price, which results in an "underage." The automobile market works essentially the same way.

The weakness of this argument is that almost everyone who buys an automobile understands that wheeling and dealing is part of the game, but many mortgage borrowers don't. They are innocents. That's why the number of underages is miniscule compared with the number of overages.

To avoid overages, borrowers must either confront the loan officer or switch to a distribution channel where there are no overages. Confrontation means letting the loan officer know that you know that mortgage prices are not engraved in cement and that you have or will explore other options. If you find this disagreeable, either retain an Upfront Mortgage Broker (UMB) to act as your agent in shopping for a loan or deal with an online lender, such as ELOAN.com or Mortgage.ETrade.com, which do not allow employees to deviate from posted prices.

*Also see* **Loan Officer** and **Mortgage Scams and Tricks/***Scams by Loan Providers/***Pocket the Borrower's Rebate.**

---

**Partial Prepayments (or Paying Off Early)** *Making a payment larger than the fully amortizing payment as a way of retiring the loan before term.*

*Making Extra Payments as an Investment:* Suppose you add $100 to the scheduled mortgage payment. This makes the loan balance at the end of the month $100 less than it would have been without the extra payment. In the months that follow, you save the interest on that $100. Since the interest payment that you would have made is determined by the interest rate on your mortgage, the yield on your $100 investment is equal to that rate.

Absent any prepayment penalty, principal repayment yields a return equal to the interest rate on the loan. A prepayment penalty would reduce that yield.

*Factoring Taxes into the Equation:* Many borrowers want to reduce the yield on mortgage repayment by the amount of the lost tax saving. If the borrower is in the 36% tax bracket, for example, his or her after-tax yield on an 8% mortgage is $(1 - .36) \times 8$, or 5.12%.

If the yield on mortgage repayment is being compared with the yield on other taxable investments, however, it doesn't matter whether yield is measured before tax or after tax. If mortgage repayment is compared with a 6% taxable bond, for example, the before-tax comparison is 8% versus 6%, while the after-tax comparison is 5.12% versus 3.84%. The conclusion, that mortgage repayment earns the higher return, remains the same.

On the other hand, if the alternative investment is tax-exempt, you should compare only after-tax yields.

**Partial Prepayments Versus Other Investments:** To determine whether paying more principal is a good investment, the yield should be compared with the yield on alternative investments, with allowance for differences in risk. An investment in mortgage repayment carries zero risk.

Mortgage repayment will always carry a higher return than other riskless investments—insured certificates of deposit and U.S. government securities. However, investments that shelter income, such as contributions to a 401(k) plan, will usually generate a higher after-tax return than mortgage repayment. In addition, a diversified portfolio of common stock may yield 12-15% over a long time horizon, provided the borrower is prepared for the risk of short-term fluctuations in portfolio value.

**Seniors Versus Juniors:** Investing in mortgage repayment is generally smarter for a senior than for anyone else. Many seniors no longer have income to shelter; even those that do have a lower after-tax return because the tax deferment period is short. Furthermore, where a diversified portfolio of common stock is a prudent risk for people in their 30s or 40s, it is less prudent for those in their 70s or older. A single stock market tumble could crack their nest egg. For this reason, mortgage repayment is a preferred investment for many older investors.

This does not necessarily mean, however, that they should repay the entire mortgage balance at one fell swoop, as explained below. The partial prepayment decision and the repayment in full decision are very different.

**Partial Prepayment Versus Repayment in Full:** Whether to allocate excess cash flow to mortgage repayment is a relatively easy decision because borrowers get to change it every month if they want. They prepay if the mortgage rate is higher than the rate that can be earned *this month* on newly acquired financial assets. Next month, the investment rate could be higher and the decision different.

Whether to repay the entire mortgage balance by liquidating financial assets, in contrast, is a single, irrevocable decision. Either the assets are liquidated to pay off the mortgage or they aren't.

While the principle, that the decision should be based on comparison of the mortgage rate and the investment rate, is the same, borrowers can't adjust to future changes in the investment rate. They have to look ahead and anticipate what these changes might be as well as how long they will be around.

To help deal with this problem, I developed a spreadsheet that allows borrowers to enter any scenario for future interest rates and compare their wealth in every future month in the two cases: where they liquidate their assets to repay the mortgage at the outset and where they retain both the mortgage and the assets. The spreadsheet is available on my Web site.

For example, assume the mortgage rate is 6% while the current investment rate is 2%, but the borrower assumes that in two years it will jump from 2% to 7%, and stay there. The spreadsheet shows that for the first 67 months, the borrower's wealth would be greater in the case where he or she repaid the mortgage. After 67 months, this person's wealth is greater in the case where he or she didn't. The borrower then must decide whether he or she is likely to be around for more than 67 months.

In general, the sooner interest rates increase, the larger the increase when it happens, and the longer the borrower expects to live, the weaker the case for liquidating assets to pay off the mortgage. Seniors having to make this decision may find it instructive to play with the spreadsheet.

***Mechanics of Paying Early:*** To repay early, just increase the amount of your monthly check. With the exception noted below, you don't have to tell the lender to apply the extra payment to principal. There isn't anything else the lender can do with it except steal it, and if he wants to steal it, nothing you write on the check will stop him.

For example, if the regular monthly payment is $600 of which $500 is interest, the other $100 is used to reduce the loan balance. If you make a payment of $650, the loan balance will decline by $150. Since the interest has already been paid, the additional $50 is used to reduce the balance by the same amount.

999 times out of 1,000 the lender's computerized servicing system does this automatically. Of course, if your lender's account records

are maintained by a guy with a quill pen and a green eye shade sitting on a stool, you may have to watch what he does.

But don't make an extra payment equal to the exact amount of your regular payment without telling the lender what you want done with it. If your monthly payment for April is $600, for example, and you send in a check for $1,200, the lender does not know, unless you tell him, whether you wish to reduce the principal by another $600 or to make your May payment early. If you intend it as a reduction of principal but don't inform the lender, the lender may interpret it as the May payment sent early, in which case the lender gets the interest on the $600 during April instead of you.

Excepting simple interest mortgages, the benefit of early prepayment is *not* affected by when it is received within the month. Thus, $100 received by the lender on May 1 or on May 20 both reduce the loan balance on May 31, on which the interest payment due June 1 is calculated, by $100. On simple interest mortgages, however, extra payments reduce the balance on the day they are received and posted.

***Effect of Early Payment on Monthly Payments:*** Extra payments to principal affect different types of mortgage differently.

**FRMs:** On an FRM, extra payments shorten the period to final payoff but do not affect the monthly installment payment. This is sometimes a source of frustration to borrowers who come into a sizeable amount of money that they would like to use to reduce their installment payment burden. They can't do it except by refinancing the reduced loan balance.

On balloon mortgages, the monthly installment payment is not affected either. However, the balance that must be rolled over at the end of the five- or seven-year rollover period is lower than it would be otherwise. And this means that the new installment payment is lower than it would be otherwise.

**ARMs:** Where it is difficult to reduce the monthly installment payment on an FRM, it is difficult to shorten the payoff period of an ARM. The reason is that every time the mortgage payment is recalculated to reflect changes that have occurred in the interest rate, the calculation assumes that the loan will pay off in the period remaining of the original term.

For example, if the interest rate on a 30-year ARM is adjusted after five years, the payment for year six would be calculated over 25 years. Hence, any additional principal payments made during the first five years would result in a lower monthly payment, but no change in the payoff period.

It is possible to shorten the payoff period of an ARM by making extra payments, but you must increase the extra payment at every payment adjustment date so as to offset the decline in the scheduled payment resulting from prior prepayments. This is a pain, but spreadsheets on my Web site can ease the pain substantially. Each time the rate changes, the borrower can find the extra payment required for a target payoff date at the new rate. The spreadsheets can also be used to monitor the lender's calculations.

***Figuring the Payoff Month:*** Calculators 2a, 2b, and 2c on my Web site will help borrowers who want to pay off early. 2a is for those who want to know when their loan will pay off and how much interest they will save if they allocate a certain amount to extra payments. 2b is for borrowers who want to know how much extra they must pay to pay off their loan within a specified period. 2c is for borrowers who want to know when their loan will pay off and how much interest they will save if they shift to a biweekly payment schedule.

***Monitoring the Lender:*** Many borrowers worry about whether or not lenders have properly credited them for partial prepayments. While I don't think that any lenders misappropriate payments, mistakes happen and it is a good idea to keep an eye out for them. A few lenders have begun to provide borrowers with access to their payment history on the Internet, but it will be a while before this becomes standard practice.

Meanwhile, you can use two Excel spreadsheets I developed for just this purpose that are accessible on my Web site. The spreadsheets can be saved to your computer so you can maintain a permanent record of your mortgage.

The spreadsheets show an entire amortization schedule for an FRM or an ARM, with an empty column for prepayments. The ARM version also has a column for the interest rate. When you enter an extra payment, the entire schedule is recalculated. The resulting balance can then be compared with the balance shown in the lender's statement.

*Closure at Payoff:* After the mortgage is fully paid, you should receive a "satisfaction of mortgage" from the lender, along with your note. This is the evidence you need that your loan has been paid off.

If you don't receive these documents, contact the lender, but give him a few weeks at least. You must also make sure that the lender has filed the satisfaction of mortgage with the county where your mortgage was registered so that it no longer appears on your property record. Check with the county, but give the lender at least six weeks.

If your taxes are escrowed, you must also notify the tax office or offices that henceforth tax notices should be sent directly to you. Also see **Biweekly Mortgages**.

---

**Pay-Down Magic** *Belief that there is a special way to pay down the balance of a home mortgage faster, if you know the secret.*

Since many if not most borrowers don't fully understand how mortgage amortization works, they are susceptible to wishful thinking-type myths. As a mortgage counselor, I hear these myths frequently. Most make no sense at all, such as those that advocate early payment of specific future principal payments. A few, however, have some foundation in fact.

*Making a Large Extra Payment as Soon as the Loan Closes:* According to my respondents, two books promote this as a way to pay off a loan early and save lots of interest. Instead of borrowing $190,000, they suggest you borrow $200,000 and immediately repay $10,000. If the loan is for 30 years at 6%, doing it their way will result in a payoff in 316 months instead of 360 and a saving of $32,042 in interest. These numbers are correct.

The reason for the early payoff and interest savings is that, if you borrow $200,000 and repay $10,000, your monthly mortgage payment is calculated on $200,000 rather than $190,000, making it $60 higher. This additional $60 a month is the entire secret. You will get exactly the same result by borrowing $190,000 and making the payment for $200,000.

This does not mean that the two alternatives are equivalent. If you borrow $200,000 and immediately repay $10,000, you have a required payment of $1,199. If you borrow $190,000, your required payment is $1,139, and the extra $60 is optional. Which is better depends on whether you prefer the discipline of having to make the higher payment or the flexibility of having it optional.

Borrowing the larger amount also increases all the settlement costs that depend on the loan amount, including points and origination fees, title insurance and per diem interest. These will be calculated on $200,000 rather than $190,000. In addition, you will pay another full month's interest on $200,000 if the lender's accounting system does not recognize an extra payment before the first installment payment is due.

The upshot is that, in an apples-to-apples comparison where the monthly payment is the same, borrowing $200,000 and repaying $10,000 immediately will cost more than the alternative of borrowing $190,000.

**Refinancing into a Simple Interest Biweekly:** While the "magical" device described above costs little to those who act on it, the same cannot be said for this one. I have found borrowers who were bankrupted by it. It is a biweekly mortgage with daily interest accrual, as described in **Mortgage Scams and Tricks/***Strictly Lender Scams***/Sell Biweeklies Under False Pretenses**.

In the merchandising of this scam, loan officers paint a magical aura around the way their mortgages pay down. They use words like "reamortize" to connote a unique process that saves borrowers money despite the higher interest rate. In fact, every borrower I have encountered who has taken one of these mortgages has been duped.

---

**Payment Adjustment Cap** *Limit on the size of payment change on an adjustable rate mortgage.*

*See* **Adjustable Rate Mortgage/***How the Monthly Payment on an ARM Is Determined***/Negative Amortization ARMs**.

---

**Payment Adjustment Interval** *The period between payment changes on an ARM, which may or may not be the same as the interest rate adjustment period.*

**Payment Period** *The period over which the borrower is obliged to make payments.*

On most mortgages, the payment period is a month but on some it is biweekly. It is not necessarily the same as the **Interest Accrual Period**.

---

**Payment Problems** *When a borrower has difficulty making the scheduled payment.*

Many homeowners faced with payment problems do nothing, allowing the problem to overwhelm them when it hits. That is not smart. When you know a tidal wave is coming, you should minimize the damage by preparing for it the best way you can.

*Position of the Lender:* A good place to start is by understanding the position of the lender. A game plan for survival should be based on a realistic view of what the lender is likely to be willing to do.

**Temporary Problem:** When a borrower is unable to pay but the problem is temporary, the lender has an interest in finding a way to help the borrower ride it out. A tool for this purpose is a forbearance agreement combined with a special repayment plan.

A forbearance agreement means that the lender suspends and/or reduces payments for a period, usually less than six months, although it can go longer. At the end of the period, the repayment plan kicks in. The borrower agrees to make the regular payment plus an additional agreed-upon amount that will cover all the payments that were not made during the forbearance period. The repayment period is usually no longer than a year.

When successful, the borrower is brought current after a lapse and the lender suffers no loss. However, a lender will consider this approach only if convinced that the borrower's problem is temporary. The burden of proof is on the borrower.

**Permanent Problem:** If the borrower's problem is permanent, the lender's objective is to minimize loss. The ultimate remedy is foreclosure, where the lender goes through a lengthy legal process to acquire possession of the house. The lender then sells the house to recover the loan balance, unpaid interest, and expenses—provided there is sufficient equity in the property to cover it all.

Lenders often do not come out whole on a foreclosure, and they do not like forcing people out of their homes. They look for alternatives to foreclosure that will cost them less, but they don't want to be scammed by borrowers in the process.

If a borrower's income has been reduced to the point where he or she can't pay the current mortgage but could pay a smaller amount, the lender might consider a loan modification. This could be a lower interest rate, a longer term, a different loan type, or any combination of these. It could also include adding past unpaid interest to the loan balance.

A lender is likely to be most receptive to a loan modification where the borrower has little equity in the house, but wants to keep living there. With no equity, foreclosure would be costly. But the lender must be convinced that the borrower's inability to pay is completely involuntary.

If the borrower's inability to pay is long-term and the borrower is resigned to giving up the house, the lender will consider several alternatives to foreclosure. If the borrower has a qualified purchaser who will take title in exchange for assuming the mortgage, the lender may allow it. This is called a **Workout Assumption**.

Alternatively, the lender might allow the borrower to put the house on the market and accept the sale proceeds as full repayment, even though it is less than the loan balance. This is called a **Short Sale**.

If the borrower is unable to sell the house, the lender might accept title to the house in exchange for discharge of the debt. This is called a **Deed in Lieu of Foreclosure**.

Knowing what a lender *can* do is useful, but it does not tell you what a particular lender *will* do in any specific situation. Lenders differ in how they respond to payment problems. It may depend on whether they own the loan or merely service it. It may depend on who answers the phone. It will certainly depend on the borrower's behavior.

**The Borrower's Game Plan:** Borrowers having payment problems should develop a game plan before they become delinquent, based on a realistic understanding of the position of the lender. While some actions you can take on your own, such as selling your house, other actions have to be negotiated with the lender.

**Document Your Loss of Income.** This will position you to demonstrate to the lender that your inability to pay is involuntary, should this be necessary later on.

**Estimate Your Equity in the House.** Your equity is what you could sell it for net of sales commissions, less the balance of your mortgage. This will help you develop a strategy for dealing with the lender.

**Determine Whether Your Financial Reversal Is Temporary or Permanent.** A temporary reversal is one where, if you are provided payment relief for up to six months, you will be able to resume regular payments at the end of the period and repay all the payments you missed within the following 12 months. You must document the case for the reversal being temporary. If you cannot make a persuasive case that the change in your financial condition is temporary, the lender will assume it is permanent.

Your game plan should take account of whether or not you have substantial equity in the house, and on whether the change in your financial status is temporary or permanent.

*Best Strategy When You Have Substantial Equity:* If you have substantial equity in your house, the least costly action to the lender may be foreclosure. While foreclosure is costly, the lender is entitled to be reimbursed from the sales proceeds for all foreclosure costs plus all unpaid interest and principal.

While foreclosure makes the lender whole, it is a disaster for you. Your equity is depleted, you incur the costs of moving, and your credit is ruined. Hence, you must avoid foreclosure, if necessary by selling your house.

*If your financial reversal is temporary* and you can persuade the lender of this, the lender may be willing to suspend payments for a period, followed by a repayment plan. The lender will probably prefer to keep your loan, rather than foreclose on it, but only if convinced it is a good loan. The burden of proof is on you in this situation to demonstrate that temporary payment relief will really work.

*If your financial reversal is permanent,* sell the house before you begin accumulating delinquencies. This way, you at least retain your equity and your credit rating.

Obtaining full value for your home may take some time—you don't want to be forced into a fire sale. If delinquency is looming, take out a home equity line of credit to keep your payments current.

**Best Strategy When You Have Little or No Equity:** If you have little or no equity, your bargaining position is actually stronger because foreclosure is a sure loser for the lender.

*If your financial reversal is temporary* and you want to remain in your house, it will be easier to persuade the lender to offer payment relief.

*If your financial reversal is permanent, but not major,* the lender may be favorably disposed to a contract modification that will permanently reduce the payments.

*If your financial reversal is permanent and major,* the lender probably will be willing to accept either a short sale or a deed in lieu of foreclosure. In both cases your debt obligation usually is fully discharged. They do appear on your credit report, but are not as bad a mark as a foreclosure.

The lender will turn a wary eye on borrowers with negative equity who have the means to continue making payments but would like to rid themselves of their negative equity through short sale or deed in lieu. While these options are less costly to the lender than foreclosure, lenders view borrowers as responsible for their debts, regardless of the depletion of their equity. How they respond depends on how convinced they are that the borrower's problems are truly involuntary and on the likelihood of success in collecting more if they go after the borrower for the deficiency.

---

**Payment Rate**   *The interest rate used to calculate the mortgage payment.*

The interest rate and the payment rate are often the same, but they need not be. They must be the same if the payment is fully amortizing (*see* **Fully Amortizing Payment**). If the payment rate is higher than the interest rate, the payment will be more than fully amortizing and, if continued, the loan will pay off before term. If the payment rate is below the interest rate, the payment will be less than fully amortizing and, if continued, the loan will not be fully paid off at term.

**Payment Shock**  *A very large increase in the payment on an ARM that may surprise the borrower.*

*See* **Adjustable Rate Mortgage/***How the Monthly Payment on an ARM Is Determined***/Negative Amortization ARMs.**

The term is also used to refer to a large difference between the rent being paid by a first-time home buyer and the monthly housing expense on the purchased home.

---

**Payoff Month**  *The month in which a zero loan balance is reached.*

The payoff month may or may not be the loan term.

---

**Per Diem Interest**  *Interest from the day of closing to the first day of the following month.*

To simplify the task of loan administration, the accounting for all home loans begins as if the loan was closed on the first day of the month following the day the loan is closed. For example, if the loan is closed and the money disbursed on May 15, the clock begins ticking on that loan as if it were closed on June 1, with the first payment due July 1. But since the lender actually gave you the money on May 15, the lender expects to be paid interest for the period between May 15 and June 1. That payment is the "per diem interest," which is due at closing.

If the loan in the example above was $100,000 and the interest rate 6%, the per diem interest would be $100,000 x .06/365 x 17, or $279.

In some cases, especially when a loan is closed early in the month, the lender is willing to rebate interest to the borrower for those few days and collect the first payment a month earlier. If the loan above was closed May 3, for example, the lender would pay three days of interest at closing and collect the first monthly payment on June 1.

---

**Permanent Buydown**

*Same as* **Points**. *Also see* **Temporary Buydown/***Temporary Versus Permanent Buydowns***.**

---

**Pipeline Risk**  *The lender's risk that, between the time a lock commit-*

ment is given to the borrower and the time the loan is closed, interest rates will rise and the lender will take a loss on selling the loan.

See **Locking the Loan/*Cost of Locking to Lenders***.

**PITI** *Principal, interest, taxes, and insurance.*

These are the components of the monthly housing expense. *See* **Qualification/*Meeting Income Requirements*/Expense Ratios**.

**PMI**

See **Private Mortgage Insurance**.

**Points** *An upfront cash payment required by the lender as part of the charge for the loan, expressed as a percent of the loan amount; e.g., "3 points" means a charge equal to 3% of the loan amount.*

When points are negative, the lender credits the borrower or the mortgage broker. Negative points are termed "rebates." When retained by a mortgage broker, they are termed "yield spread premiums."

***Points and Rebates as Borrower Options:*** The points/rebate system is unique to the U.S. It offers borrowers more options at the cost of greater complexity. The following is a typical schedule for a 30-year fixed rate mortgage.

5.375% and 2.75 points
5.50% and 2.0 points
5.625% and 1.375 points
5.750% and 0.75 points
5.875% and 0.125 points
6% and 0.5 rebate
6.125% and 1.0 rebate
6.25% and 1.5 rebate
6.375% and 2.0 rebate
6.5% and 2.3755 rebate

For borrowers who have the cash and expect to remain in their house for a long time, paying points to reduce the rate makes economic sense. The benefit from the lower rate extends over a long period. In addition, borrowers who have difficulty qualifying because their income is low relative to their monthly housing expense may pay points to reduce their monthly payment.

In contrast, borrowers with a short time horizon do better with high-rate/rebate combinations because they don't pay the high rate very long. In addition, borrowers who are cash-short prefer to pay interest rates high enough to command rebates, which can be used to cover their settlement costs.

***Sharpening the Rate/Point Decision:*** Borrowers who are neither cash-short nor income-short can sharpen the decision process using one of the calculators on my Web site. Calculators 11a and 11b, covering FRMs and ARMs, respectively, compare the future costs of a low-rate/high-points combination with those of a high-rate/low-points combination over any period specified by you. These calculators also show the "break-even period," which is the minimum period you must hold the mortgage to come out ahead with the low-rate/high-points combination.

A different approach to the decision is to look at the payment of points as an investment that yields a return that increases the longer you stay in your house. This return can be compared to the return on other investments available to you. This approach is used in calculators 11c and 11d.

***Paying Points Versus Making a Larger Down Payment:*** An advantage of viewing the payment of points as an investment decision is that it allows you to compare the return from paying points with the return from increasing the down payment. (You can find the latter using calculator 12a.)

In both cases, the borrower makes an upfront cash outlay and receives a stream of income in the future. With a larger down payment, the income is the reduction in monthly payment that results from the smaller loan and mortgage insurance premium. With points, the income is the reduction in monthly payment that results from the lower interest rate. The better investment is the one that yields the higher return over the period you retain the mortgage.

The return on investment in points is extremely sensitive to how long you stay in the home. For example, if you are in the 25.5% tax bracket, pay four points to reduce the rate on a 30-year fixed-rate mortgage from 6% to 5%, and stay in your house for three years, your after-tax return is a negative 12.6%. But if you stay for 15 years your return is a positive 16.4%.

In contrast, the return on an investment in a larger down payment declines over time, though not very much. If you increase your down payment from 5% of the property value to 10%, for example, which reduces the mortgage insurance premium on a 6% 30-year FRM from .78% to .52% of the loan amount, the after-tax return over three years is 10.0%; over 15 years it is 8.8%.

Hence, if your time horizon is short, you should invest in a larger down payment, and if it is long, you should invest in higher points. But how long is "long"?

In most cases the crossover point where the returns are the same occurs in eight years or less. However, the crossover point is affected by a number of factors, including your tax bracket, PMI premiums, the rate reduction you receive for a given increase in points, and appreciation of your house, which affects how long you'll carry PMI. The beauty of calculators 11c, 11d, and 12a is that you can take account of all the specifics of your own particular situation.

*Financing Points:* Points can be included in the loan amount, but usually it isn't a good idea if you can avoid it. The break-even periods are usually longer, as illustrated in the table below. The first number in each cell assumes the borrower pays the points in cash while the number in parentheses assumes the points are financed.

| Break-Even Periods in Months on a 30-Year Mortgage Used for Purchase: 6% at 0 Points Versus 5% at 4 Points | | | |
|---|---|---|---|
| Savings Rate | Tax Rate 0% | Tax Rate 28% | Tax Rate 40% |
| 0% | 49 (63) | 49 (85) | 49 (103) |
| 5% | 56 (59) | 55 (80) | 54 (99) |
| 10% | 68 (55) | 63 (75) | 61 (94) |

Financing points lengthens the break-even period if the savings rate—the rate the borrower could earn on cash not used to pay points—is below the rate on the high-rate/low-points mortgage. This usually is the case. On purchase transactions, furthermore, financing points spreads the tax deduction over time, whereas points paid in cash are deductible in the year paid. Financing points is worthwhile only where the savings rate is above the mortgage rate and the tax rate is low.

The break-even periods shown in the table on the previous page assume that financing the points does not raise any other costs to the borrower. Borrowers should be wary of the following exceptions.

First, the increase in the loan amount might bring it from an amount below to an amount above the maximum size loan eligible for purchase by the two government-sponsored entities, Fannie Mae and Freddie Mac. In 2003, the maximum was $322,700. Rates are higher on loans exceeding the maximum.

Second, the increase in the loan amount might bring it into a higher mortgage insurance premium category. Mortgage insurance premiums are based on the ratio of loan amount to property value, with three premium categories: 80-85% (the lowest), 85-90%, and 90-95%.

If the larger loan that results from financing the points triggers an increase in the interest rate or the mortgage insurance premium, there will be no break-even.

---

**Portable Mortgage** *A mortgage that can be moved from one property to another.*

Ordinarily, you repay your mortgage when you sell your house and take out a new mortgage on the new home you purchase. With a portable mortgage, you transfer the old mortgage to the new property.

*An Innovation in 2003:* Portable mortgages were talked about for a long time, but did not appear until 2003, when they were introduced by E*TRADE Mortgage. E*TRADE offers the portability option on 30-year fixed-rate mortgages only, at an interest rate 3/8% higher than the rate on the identical mortgage without the option. Borrowers must be purchasing single-family homes as their permanent residence (refinancing doesn't qualify), they must have squeaky-clean credit, and they must provide full documentation.

*Benefits to the borrower:* There are two. One is that it avoids the costs of taking out a new mortgage. This cost must be set against the cost of paying 3/8% more in rate, which rises the longer the period between the first purchase and the second. The break-even period comes out to roughly four years on a $150,000 loan. If you expect that you won't be buying your next house within four years, the cost saving on the future mortgage won't cover the cost penalty imposed by the 3/8% rate premium. The period is a little shorter on a larger loan, longer on a smaller loan.

The second benefit is that it allows you to avoid any rise in market interest rates that occurs between the time you purchase one house and the time you purchase the next one. Since World War II, mortgage rates have been as low as 4% and as high as 18%. When rates are about 6%, there is clearly much greater potential for rise than for decline. If rates increase, the portable mortgage protects you, and if they decrease, you can get the benefit by refinancing. There is no prepayment penalty.

Borrowers who confidently expect to move within five or six years and fear that a major spike in rates could seriously crimp their plans may find the 3/8% rate increment a reasonable insurance premium. It is less valuable for borrowers who expect to move every three years, since the transfer option can only be used once.

Portability is also less valuable for borrowers who expect to trade down when they move. Since they will need a smaller mortgage at that point, the rate protection is not worth as much. However, E*TRADE will recalculate their payment if the new mortgage is more than $10,000 smaller than the old one.

Borrowers who trade up cannot increase the original loan. E*TRADE will give them a second mortgage at the market rate on first mortgages at that time, but the sum of first and second mortgages cannot exceed 80% of property value. The borrower will have to pay settlement costs on the second—the same costs that a new borrower would have to pay at that time. Borrowers trading up could well find that they would do better getting a second mortgage from another lender.

Borrowers with the excellent credit needed to qualify for a portable mortgage should be confident that they can maintain that record. Borrowers in bankruptcy or behind in their payments cannot exercise the transfer option. In such a situation, they would have paid the 3/8% rate increment for nothing.

**Portfolio Lender** *A lender that holds the loans it originates in its portfolio rather than selling them.*

See **Mortgage Lender/*Mortgage Banks Versus Portfolio Lenders***.

---

**Pre-Approval** *A lender commitment to make a mortgage loan to a specified borrower, prior to the identification of the property that will be mortgaged.*

On a pre-approval, unlike a pre-qualification, the lender verifies the financial information provided and checks the credit of the potential borrower.

Prospective homebuyers seek pre-approvals because they believe it helps them in shopping for a house. Lenders offer pre-approvals in the hope that the homebuyers receiving them will come back to them for a loan after they contract to purchase.

The lender's commitment under a pre-approval is usually expressed in terms of the monthly mortgage payment that the prospective buyer has the income to meet. Converting the mortgage payment into a loan amount requires an assumption regarding the interest rate, which is not known at the time of the pre-approval. Since the lender is not committed to an interest rate, an increase in rates could reduce the approved loan amount.

---

**Predatory Lending** *A variety of unsavory lender practices designed to take advantage of unwary borrowers.*

Predatory lending covers much the same ground as **Mortgage Scams and Tricks/*Scams by Loan Providers***. The difference is that the term "predatory lending" has been associated with practices in the sub-prime market that specifically target unsophisticated and vulnerable borrowers. Scams operate across a wider spectrum and usually don't leave quite as much human wreckage in their wake.

*Predatory Practices:* The two most important types of predatory lending are "equity grabbing" and "price gouging."

**Equity Grabbing:** This is lending that is intended by the lender to lead to default by the borrower so the lender can grab the borrower's equity.

Equity grabbing may be associated with cash-out refinancing to cash-dazzled customers. In one case, a borrower with significant equity in his home refinanced a low interest-rate loan into one carrying a high interest rate plus heavy fees, with the fees included in the new loan. The inducement was the cash, more than the borrower had ever seen at one time. But the borrower was saddled with a larger repayment obligation that he couldn't meet, resulting in default and loss of the home.

Home improvement scams work in a similar manner. Gullible homeowners are sweet-talked into contracting for repairs for which they are overcharged, and then the cost of the repairs plus high loan fees are rolled into a mortgage that they cannot afford. Default follows and the borrower loses the home.

Equity grabs are extremely difficult to regulate away because they represent an abusive application of legitimate activities. Most borrowers who do a cash-out refinance retain their equity, and this is true as well for most of those who take out home improvement loans. There are no remedies that won't curb legitimate transactions, except perhaps for counseling directed at potential victims. But people can't be compelled to seek counsel or to listen when they receive it.

**Price Gouging:** This involves charging interest rates and/or fees that are excessive relative to what the same borrower would have paid had they shopped the market. It also includes packaging of related services such as credit life insurance, which are over-priced and made to appear as if they are required.

A large number of the newspaper columns I write are designed to help potential borrowers avoid price gouging. Informed borrowers who shop, even if it is only to check prices on the Internet, are very unlikely to be gouged.

Still, there are many uninformed borrowers who don't shop, and government ought to protect them if there were ways to do it that didn't seriously harm other borrowers. Unfortunately, the regulatory reaction to price gouging is to set maximum prices, which prevents borrowers from being gouged only by depriving other borrowers of access to credit altogether. The tradeoff between protection and harm becomes increasingly unfavorable as the market widens to provide market access to more and more consumers. As offensive as price gouging is, price controls are not a good remedy.

*Targets of Predators:* To educate myself on what makes a victim, I studied 51 case histories of households victimized by mortgage lenders. The histories were provided by ACORN, which has been in the forefront of the struggle against predators. While every case is different, victims share certain features that make them vulnerable to predators.

**Passive:** Perhaps the most pervasive characteristic of victims by far is that they are passive. They don't select a loan provider; the loan provider selects them. In more than half the cases compiled by ACORN, the victims were solicited by the lenders. In most of the remaining cases, the victims approached a lender they knew from prior experience, either their own or someone they knew.

Borrowers who passively go with a loan provider who solicits them run a high risk of getting a predator. While not all lenders who solicit are predators, all predators solicit. This means that a borrower would do better by throwing a dart at the loan providers listed in the Yellow Pages than by responding to a solicitation.

Borrowers who allow themselves to be selected by loan providers stay selected. Passive borrowers don't shop alternatives. They also don't ask as many questions as they should, which is one of the reasons they usually end up confused about the transaction.

**Confused:** Almost all of the case histories provided by ACORN involved confusion by the borrower about one or another feature of the transaction. In some cases, borrowers were under the impression that they were getting unsecured loans rather than mortgages. In many cases, they purchased credit life insurance under the impression that it was required. Often, they thought that they were paying a lower interest rate than was in fact the case. The total amount of fees packed into the loan balance usually surprised them. A large number did not know that their contract included a prepayment penalty until years later when they went to prepay.

Why so much confusion? Victims often don't read documents or, if they do read, they are afraid to ask questions about what they don't understand. The "Plain English" movement has not impacted mortgage documents, although there isn't a segment of the economy that needs it more.

Predators thrive on confusion, which provides a smoke screen for their shenanigans. To a predator, a reading-challenged borrower is an invitation to take advantage in every possible way. And mortgages provide lots of ways.

Confusion and passivity go hand in hand, and must be overcome together. It is the loan provider's responsibility to eliminate confusion. If he doesn't do it, walk out the door.

**Indebted:** Victims are often heavily in debt, and therefore vulnerable to the siren call of debt consolidation. Debt consolidation was the primary motivation in about 2/3 of the ACORN cases.

The argument is compelling: make one lower payment and enjoy tax benefits besides. While these advantages can be real, they tend to disappear in dealing with a predator. Sometimes the payment is higher rather than lower, because of the stiff interest rate. Even if the payment is lower, the borrower's equity is depleted by the inclusion of large upfront fees in the loan. Consolidate debts with a predator and you end up worse off than you were before.

Consumers who have accumulated too much short-term debt have an option other than debt consolidation. They can instead work out a debt management plan with a credit counselor. In exchange for agreeing to take on no new debt and to pay off the old debt within a prescribed period, the counselor can get the creditors to agree to a reduction in interest rates. The consumer makes one payment to the agency, which in turn pays the creditors.

A debt management plan is protection against falling into the hands of a predator. It also avoids one of the perils of a successful debt consolidation, which is that it paves the way for a new credit binge.

**Cash-Dazzled:** Many victims are cash-dazzled—the prospect of pocketing a significant sum of money causes a complete lapse of judgment. They ignore where the money is coming from and what it is costing them.

Cash-dazzled victims are prime candidates for cash-out refinancing—refinancing into loans that are larger than the outstanding balance of the old loans. Frequently, the new loan has a higher interest rate than the old one and the refinancing fees are added to the loan balance. Some borrowers will refinance again and again, a practice known as "flipping," until they have used up all their equity.

There are many legitimate cash-out refinance transactions. They become predatory when the cash-dazzled victim agrees to terms that are far more costly than the borrower could have obtained by shopping alternative sources.

The worst rip-off is cash-out refinancing of zero-interest loans, a problem that has plagued the Habitat for Humanity program. The Coalition for Responsible Lending estimates that 10% of all Habitat borrowers between 1987 and 1993 subsequently refinanced their zero-interest loans into loans carrying rates of 10-16%. Borrowers who did this were paying interest costs of 60% and up for the cash in their pockets. Cash-dazzled victims don't see it.

**Payment-Myopic:** Victims often base decisions solely on the affordability of monthly payments; they are payment-myopic. They don't consider interest costs or how the decisions will affect the equity in their homes.

Here is the kind of deal that payment-myopic/cash dazzled borrowers find irresistible. The borrower has paid down his 8% loan to $100,000 and has only 12 years to go. He is offered a 30-year loan for $110,000 at 9%. The monthly payment would fall from $1,082 to $885, and he puts $10,000 in his pocket tax-free. What a deal!

Of course, five years down the road, he would have owed only $69,449 had he stayed with his original mortgage. With the new mortgage he will owe $105,468—even more if there are upfront fees included in the new loan, which is almost always the case. Payment-myopic borrowers don't look down the road.

---

**Prepayment**  *A payment made by the borrower over and above the scheduled mortgage payment.*

If the additional payment pays off the entire balance it is a "prepayment in full"; otherwise, it is a "partial prepayment." *See* **Partial Prepayments**.

**Prepayment Penalty**  *A charge imposed by the lender if the borrower pays off the loan early.*

The charge is usually expressed as a percent of the loan balance at the time of prepayment or a specified number of months' interest. Some part of the balance, usually 20%, can be prepaid without penalty. Usually, the penalty declines or disappears as the mortgage ages. For example, the penalty might be 3% of the balance net of the exclusion within the first year, 2% in the second year, and 1% in the third year.

A penalty may or may not apply to prepayment resulting from a home sale. A penalty that applies whether the loan is prepaid because of a sale or because of a refinancing is referred to as a "hard" penalty. A penalty that applies only to a refinancing is a "soft" penalty.

***Advantage of a Prepayment Penalty for Prime Borrowers:*** Prime borrowers can usually negotiate a lower interest rate in exchange for accepting a prepayment penalty. Investors who buy loans from lenders in the secondary market are willing to accept a lower rate in exchange for a prepayment penalty. The benefit of the penalty to them is that it discourages refinancing if interest rates decline in the future. Lenders will then pass the benefit on to knowledgeable borrowers who ask for it.

Whether it is a good deal depends on the rate reduction, and the size and scope of the penalty. I would consider a 1/4% reduction in rate in exchange for a 2-3% penalty during the first three to five years, payable only on a refinancing, as a good deal. It would be an exceptionally good deal for someone who expects to be in the house a long time.

***Penalties on Loans to Sub-Prime Borrowers:*** In contrast to prime loans, where penalties are an option, penalties are required on most sub-prime loans. Lenders demand them because the risk of refinancing is higher on sub-prime loans than on prime loans. Sub-prime borrowers profit from refinancing if their credit rating improves, even when the general level of mortgage rates does not change. Because of high origination costs and high default costs, sub-prime lending is not profitable if the good loans walk out the door after only two years.

But that doesn't mean sub-prime borrowers have no negotiating power. While they may not be able to negotiate away the penalty entirely, they may well be able to negotiate the specifics. Tell the loan officer, "No longer than five years, no higher than 3%, partial pre-payments up to 20% of the balance allowed in any year without penalty, no penalty on sale of the property."

***Surreptitious Penalties:*** During the heavy refinance periods after 1998, I received hundreds of letters from borrowers who claimed that they were unaware that their loan carried a prepayment penal-ty until they went to refinance it. In many cases, they alleged that the loan officer had explicitly told them that there was no penalty.

Considering that the penalty must be in the note, and also in the Truth in Lending Disclosure Statement (TIL), both of which are signed by the borrower, how could they not have known?

My best guess, and it is just a guess, is that about half of them did know, but preferred to forget. But that leaves half who were hood-winked.

It is all too easy, because so many borrowers are so overwhelmed with documents that they sign without reading. Or they read, but what is important in the document doesn't register. It is extremely easy to overlook a prepayment penalty on the TIL.

"Prepayment" lies at the bottom of the TIL, the last piece of infor-mation on a long form. It reads as follows:

*PREPAYMENT: If you pay off your loan early, you*

[ ] *may* [ ] *will not have to pay a penalty*

[ ] *may* [ ] *will not be entitled to a refund of part of the finance charge*

This is a strange set of choices. The negative is definite—"you ... will not have to pay a penalty"—but the affirmative is qualified. The dictionary says that "may" refers to "a possibility"; "may" and "may not" thus mean exactly the same thing. Use of the word "may" sug-gests falsely that there may not be a penalty. It would not be surpris-ing if this misleading phraseology put borrowers off their guard.

Since a mortgage loan either has a prepayment penalty clause or it doesn't, the disclosure should be rephrased as follows:

*PREPAYMENT: Your loan*

[ ] *does* [ ] *does not have a prepayment penalty clause*

The second line under "Prepayment" on the existing TIL form indicates whether or not, in the event of early payment, the lender will refund "part of the finance charge." There is no good reason for this being here. Lenders *never* refund fees to borrowers, and even if they did, borrowers need not be warned about the possibility of lender generosity.

What this item does is cause confusion. Because this confusing and wholly unnecessary statement is placed immediately below the already weak notice of a prepayment penalty, it weakens the penalty notice further by diluting the borrower's attention. The effectiveness of disclosure declines as the amount of other information with which it is packaged rises. The borrower trying to figure out what the refund option means is not concentrating on the penalty option.

It is thus readily understandable why many borrowers signed a TIL but were later surprised to find that they were subject to a prepayment penalty. Don't expect improvements in the TIL anytime soon. Meanwhile, borrowers receiving a TIL for the first time should understand that a check mark against "may" on the first line under "Prepayment" means they have a penalty clause without any doubt whatever and they should just ignore the second line.

## Pre-Qualification

*Same as* **Qualification**.

**Price Gouging** *Charging unwary borrowers interest rates and/or fees that are excessive relative to what the same borrowers could have found had they shopped the market.*

*See* **Predatory Lending/*Predatory Practices***.

**Primary Residence** *The house in which the borrower will live most of the time, as distinct from a second home or an investor property that will be rented.*

**Principal** *The portion of the monthly payment that is used to reduce the loan balance.*

*See* **Amortization**.

**Principal Limit** *The present value of a house, given the elderly owner's right to live there until she dies or voluntarily moves out, under FHA's reverse mortgage program.*

*See* **Reverse Mortgage/FHA's Home Equity Conversion Mortgage (HECM)/Principal Limit**.

---

**Private Mortgage Insurance (PMI)** *Mortgage insurance provided by private mortgage insurance companies (PMIs).*

As distinguished from mortgage insurance provided by the government under FHA and VA.

*Insurance Premiums:* Premiums are most often quoted as annual rates that are paid monthly. Some typical premium rates are shown below. They vary by type of mortgage, down payment, and term. In the future, it is likely that insurance premiums will be tied to other transaction features that affect risk.

To obtain the monthly premium in dollars, the figures shown in the table on the next page are multiplied by the loan balance and divided by 1,200. If the premium rate is .92 and the loan is for $100,000, for example, the monthly premium is $92,000 divided by 1,200, or $76.67.

The premiums charged by different companies are either identical or so close that the difference isn't worth bothering with.

*Alternative Premium Plans:* There are a number of ways of paying for PMI but several of them are historical relics and rarely used. Today, about 90% of the policies carry the monthly premiums shown in the table on the next page.

An attractive alternative to the monthly premium plan is the financed upfront premium, where a one-time premium is included in the loan amount. On a $100,000 loan with a monthly premium of $32.50, the upfront premium is 2.35%, which increases the loan amount to $102,350. Assuming an interest rate of 8%, the mortgage payment would increase by $17.25. Further, $15.66 of the additional payment is additional interest that is tax-deductible. For a borrower in the 28% tax bracket, the increase in mortgage payment net of tax savings is only $12.87. This is less than half of the premium under the monthly plan, which is not deductible.

| Typical Monthly Private Mortgage Insurance Premiums | | | |
|---|---|---|---|
| Loan Amount as Percent of the Lower of Sale Price or Appraised Value | | | |
| | 95.1 to 97% | 90.1 to 95% | 85.1 to 90% | 80.1 to 85% |
| **FRMs** | | | | |
| 30 Years | .90 | .78 | .52 | .32 |
| 25 Years | .81 | .56 | .28 | .21 |
| 20 Years | .81 | .56 | .23 | .19 |
| 15 Years | .79 | .56 | .23 | .19 |
| **ARMs 1** | | | | |
| 30 Years | NA | .88 | .61 | .33 |
| 25 Years | NA | .82 | .55 | .27 |
| 20 Years | NA | .82 | .55 | .27 |
| 15 Years | NA | .77 | .50 | .22 |
| **ARMs 2** | | | | |
| 30 Years | NA | .92 | .65 | .37 |
| 25 Years | NA | .86 | .54 | .26 |
| 20 Years | NA | .86 | .54 | .26 |
| 15 Years | NA | .81 | .54 | .26 |

**Notes:** ARMs that have five years or more of level payments are considered FRMs. ARMs 1 are those with rate adjustment caps of 1% or less. All other ARMs are ARMs 2. "NA" indicates that insurance is not available.

The downside of the financed upfront premium plan is that the borrower will have a higher loan balance when the loan is repaid. However, loan repayment in the early years results in a partial refund of the premium. In the example above, refunds are 92% after one year, declining to 50% after six years and zero after 12 years.

Unfortunately, few borrowers are aware of this attractive alternative because most lenders don't offer it. Fannie Mae and Freddie Mac require lenders to obtain special authorization to use this program on loans that are sold to them. Most lenders prefer to avoid this inconvenience and they aren't pressed because few customers are aware of the option.

***The Cost of PMI:*** PMI is useful to borrowers because it allows loans that exceed 80% of value. So does a second mortgage. If you wanted to compare the two, the cost of PMI should be measured on the portion of the loan that exceeds 80% of value.

For example, assume you can obtain a 15-year fixed rate mortgage at 7.5% and zero points to purchase a $100,000 house. Without mortgage insurance, you could borrow up to $80,000, whereas with mortgage insurance you could borrow up to $95,000 (95% of property value). The insurance premium on the $95,000 loan is .79% of the balance per year for the first 10 years, after which it drops to .20%.

The loan of $95,000 consists of two loans: one for $80,000 which has an interest cost of 7.5% consisting solely of the interest rate, and one for $15,000, the cost of which includes both the interest rate and the insurance premium. The interest cost on the $15,000 loan turns out to be 12.7% if you stay in your house for up to 10 years, declining slowly after that to 12% if you stay a full 15 years.

Since the insurance premium is only .79%, how can the cost of the $15,000 loan be 5.2% higher than the cost of the $80,000 loan? The reason is that while you are borrowing an additional $15,000, you pay the premium on the entire $95,000.

The cost calculation above assumes that you take a fixed-rate mortgage with a loan-to-value ratio of 95% and pay mortgage insurance for 10 years. Change the assumptions and you change the cost. For example:

- On 85% and 90% loans, the cost is 13.4% and 12.5%, respectively. While the insurance premiums are smaller, the incremental loans are also smaller.
- On smaller loans within the same mortgage insurance premium bracket, the cost is higher. For example, the cost of insurance on a 91% fixed-rate loan, which has the same premium as a 95% loan, is 14.3%.
- Adjustable rate mortgages have higher insurance premiums, and therefore higher costs, than fixed-rate mortgages.

Here is a handy rule of thumb for estimating the interest cost on the incremental loan made possible by mortgage insurance, assuming the loan runs 10 years. Divide the total loan by the incremental loan and multiply the result by the annual insurance premium, e.g., $95,000 divided by $15,000 equals 6.33, which multiplied by .79% equals 5%. Adding that to the interest rate gives an estimated cost of 12.5% on the incremental $15,000 loan.

Shoppers who want to do a more careful analysis of the cost of a mortgage with PMI relative to an 80% mortgage plus a second should use calculator 13a on my Web site. The calculator takes account of several cost factors that are not included in the interest cost figures given above, including taxes.

**Why Aren't PMI Premiums Deductible?** The IRS says that mortgage insurance premiums are not deductible. In this, they are inconsistent.

Interest payments on home mortgages are deductible, and no distinction is made by the IRS between the portion of the interest payment that represents compensation for the time value of money and the portion that represents compensation for risk. If a low-risk borrower pays 7%, for example, while a high-risk borrower pays 9%, the entire interest payment of the high-risk borrower is deductible. However, if the lender charges both borrowers 7% but requires that the high-risk borrower purchase mortgage insurance, with the mortgage insurer now collecting the 2% or its equivalent, the IRS will not allow the 2% to be deducted. That is inconsistent.

The IRS classifies mortgage insurance premiums as payments by borrowers for services provided by the lender, similar to an appraisal fee, and as a general matter such payments are not deductible. The problem with this position is that the lender is not in fact providing any service in connection with mortgage insurance. The mortgage insurance premium is a payment for risk, in exactly the same way that the 2% rate increment charged the high-risk borrower is a payment for risk. Apart from possible differences in price, the borrower doesn't care whether the lender receives the payment and takes the risk or the mortgage insurance company receives the payment and takes the risk.

**Why Do Borrowers Pay the Premiums?** It is more historical accident than anything else. When the modern PMI industry began in the late 1950s, many states had legal ceilings on interest rates. If lenders paid for mortgage insurance and passed on the cost to borrowers as a higher interest rate, they might have bumped up against those ceilings. If the borrower paid the premium, this potential roadblock was avoided.

Unfortunately, a borrower-pay system is much less effective than a lender-pay system. Borrowers do not shop for mortgage insurance but are locked into arrangements established by lenders, who decide the insurance carrier with which *they* want to do business.

When the borrower pays, lenders have little interest in minimizing insurance costs to the borrower because these costs do not influence a consumer's decision regarding the selection of a lender. Insurers do not compete for the patronage of consumers, but for the patronage of the lenders who select them. Such competition is directed not at premiums but at the services provided by the insurers to the lenders. Its effect is to raise the costs to insurers and ultimately the cost borne by borrowers.

Under a lender-pay system, lenders would shop for the lowest premiums. Because lenders buy in bulk, they would have the market clout to push premiums down. As a result, the higher interest rates under a lender-pay system would be lower than the combined cost of interest plus insurance premiums under the current borrower-pay system. Furthermore, the rate increase that the lender tacks on to cover the cost of insurance is deductible to the borrower, where a mortgage insurance premium paid by the borrower is not. A lender-pay system also would eliminate confusion over when insurance can be terminated, as noted below.

***Mortgage Insurance Versus Higher Rate:*** Some lenders offer a higher interest rate in lieu of PMI. The sales pitch is that interest is tax-deductible whereas PMI premiums are not. The other side of the coin, however, is that the borrower must pay the higher interest rate for the life of the mortgage, while mortgage insurance is terminated at some point.

Calculator 14a on my Web site provides a cost comparison of the options. It takes account of the borrower's tax bracket, the period the borrower expects to be in the house, the PMI premium, the rate increment to avoid the premium, and the number of years until PMI terminates.

*Terminating PMI:* Until 1999, borrowers could terminate PMI only with the permission of the lender. Because borrowers paid the premiums, however, lenders had no financial incentive to agree. Some lenders allowed PMI termination under certain specified conditions. Others had more stringent conditions. Still others did not allow it at all. Many borrowers, furthermore, were unaware of the possibility of terminating insurance and paid premiums for years longer than necessary.

What Congress should have done to deal with this problem was mandate that lenders pay PMI premiums. If lenders paid for mortgage insurance and passed on the cost in the interest rate, lenders would decide when to terminate based on whether or not they felt the insurance was still needed. This would also have reduced the cost of PMI, for reasons indicated above. Instead, Congress in 1999 elected to do it the hard way, by enacting mandatory termination rules. Unfortunately, the rules are unavoidably complicated.

Under federal law, lenders are required to cancel PMI on loans made after July 29, 1999, when amortization has reduced the loan balance to 78% of the value of the property at the time the loan was made. Cancellation is automatic. Loans made before July 29, 1999, are not covered by the law.

In addition, under the 1999 law, lenders must terminate insurance *at the borrower's request* when the loan balance hits 80% of the original value. Borrowers who take the initiative can thus terminate earlier than those who wait. However, the lender need not comply if the property has a second mortgage or has declined in value. Furthermore, the borrower cannot have had a payment late by 30 days or more within the year preceding the cancellation date, or late by 60 days or more in the year before that.

Loans sold to Fannie Mae or Freddie Mac, however, are subject to the termination rules of the agencies regardless of when the loan was made. And these rules are more favorable to homeowners because they are based on the current appraised value of the property rather than the value at the time the loan was made.

Under the rules of the agencies:

- Borrowers can terminate after two years if the loan balance is no more than 75% of current appraised value, and after five years if it is no more than 80%.

- Borrowers must request cancellation and obtain an appraisal acceptable to the agencies and to the lender.
- The ratios required for termination are lower if there is a second mortgage, if the property is held for investment rather than occupancy, or if the property is other than single-family.
- The agencies will not accept termination if a payment has been 30 days late within the prior year or 60 days late in the year before that.

Loans made before July 29, 1999, and not sold to Fannie or Freddie remain subject to the termination rules of the lender. However, California, Connecticut, Maryland, Minnesota, Missouri, New York, North Carolina, Oregon, Texas, and Virginia also have termination rules.

The best strategy for borrowers is to assume that they are subject to the liberal Fannie/Freddie rules. After two years, they should begin periodically to estimate the current value of their house. Web sites offering tools that can help include HomeGain.com, DataQuick.com, and Domania.com.

When it appears that the agencies' requirements have been met, contact the lender and ask whether the mortgage is held by one of the agencies. If it is, confirm the ratio of balance to current value that permits termination in your case and ask about acceptable appraisers.

If the loan isn't held by one of the agencies, ask the lender for a written statement of its own termination policy. If the loan was made after July 29, 1999, follow the most liberal of the lender's rules, the federal law, or state law if the property is in one of the states listed above. If the loan was made before July 29, 1999, you are stuck with the lender's rules or possibly state law.

---

**Processing** *Compiling and maintaining the file of information about the transaction, including the credit report, appraisal, verification of employment and assets, and so on.*

Mortgage brokers usually process the loans they handle. The processing file is handed off to underwriting for the loan decision.

**Qualification** *The process of determining whether a prospective borrower has the ability to repay a loan.*

*Qualification Versus Approval:* To be approved for a loan, a prospective borrower must demonstrate both the ability to repay and the willingness to repay. The borrower's willingness to repay is assessed largely by the applicant's past credit history. Qualified borrowers may ultimately be turned down because, while they have demonstrated the capacity to repay, a poor credit history suggests that they may be unwilling to pay.

*Meeting Income Requirements:* Lenders ask two basic questions about the borrower's ability to pay. First, is the borrower's income large enough to service the new expenses associated with the loan, plus any existing debt obligations that will continue in the future? Second, does the borrower have enough cash to meet the upfront cash requirements of the transaction? The lender must be satisfied on both counts.

**Expense Ratios:** Lenders assess the adequacy of the borrower's income in terms of two ratios that have become standard in the trade. The "housing expense ratio" is the sum of the monthly mortgage payment including mortgage insurance, property taxes, and hazard insurance, divided by the borrower's monthly income. The "total expense ratio" is the same except that the numerator includes the borrower's existing debt service obligations. For each of their loan programs, lenders set maximums for these ratios, such as, e.g., 28% and 36%, which the actual ratios must not exceed.

**Debt Service:** The debt service portion of total expenses includes alimony but not income taxes, which doesn't make a lot of sense. It also does not include student loans if repayment is deferred for a year or longer, although the underwriter can elect to include it if the amount involved is very large or the borrower's credit is weak. If there are co-borrowers, the debts of both must be included.

**Variations in the Ratios Among Loan Programs:** Maximum expense ratios may vary from one loan program to another. Hence, an applicant only marginally over the limit may need to do nothing more than find another program with higher maximum ratios.

**Variations in Ratios with Other Transaction Characteristics:** Within any program, maximum expense ratios may vary with other characteristics of the transaction. For example, the maximum ratios are often lower (more restrictive) if the property is two- to four-family, co-op, condominium, second home, manufactured, or acquired for investment rather than occupancy. On the other hand, if the applicant makes a down payment larger than the minimum, the maximum expense ratios may be higher.

**Applicant's Ability to Get the Maximum Ratios Raised:** The maximum ratios are not carved in stone. The following are illustrative of circumstances where the limits may be waived:

- The borrower is just marginally over the housing expense ratio but well below the total expense ratio—29% and 30%, for example, when the maximums are 28% and 36%.
- The borrower has an impeccable credit record.
- The borrower is a first-time homebuyer who has been paying rent equal to 40% of income for three years and has an unblemished payment record.

**Reducing Expense Ratios by Reducing the Term:** If expense ratios exceed the maximums, one possible option is to reduce the mortgage payment by extending the term. If the term is already 30 years, however, there is very little that can be done. Few lenders offer 40-year loans, and extending the loan to 40 years doesn't reduce the mortgage payment much anyway.

**Using Excess Cash to Reduce Expense Ratios:** Borrowers paying more than the minimum down can shift the excess over the minimum to reduce expense ratios. They can pay points to reduce the interest rate, pay off other debt, or fund a temporary buydown. Except for the last, however, the impacts are quite small. They won't work at all, furthermore, if the reduced down payment increases the mortgage insurance premium.

The mortgage insurance premium categories, defined in terms of the ratio of down payment to property value, are 5 to 9.99%, 10 to 14.99%, and 15 to 19.99%. An applicant putting down 10%, 15%, or 20% cannot reduce the down payment without moving into a higher mortgage insurance premium category. But an applicant putting down 7.5 %, 12.5%, 17.5%, or 22.5% can.

The most effective way to reduce expense ratios is to use a temporary buydown, which some lenders allow on some programs. With a temporary buydown, cash is placed in an escrow account and used to supplement the borrower's payments in the early years of the loan. *See* **Temporary Buydown**.

**Income Used to Qualify:** Lenders disregard income that is viewed as temporary, such as overtime or bonuses. But sometimes income from such sources can be expected to continue. The burden of proof is on the applicant to demonstrate this. The best way to do this is to show that they have in fact persisted over a considerable period in the past.

Borrowers who intend to share their house with another party can also consider making that party a co-borrower. In such case, the income used in the qualification process would include that of the co-borrower. Of course, the co-borrower would be equally responsible for repaying the loan. This works best when the relationship between the borrower and the co-borrower is permanent.

Lenders will not take account of anticipated growth in income, even if it is highly probable, such as in the case of a physician just out of medical school. They are not going to base a loan on anticipated income that may or may not materialize. And they will not include income from a job the borrower is confident of getting but doesn't have.

Lenders include investment income, if it can be documented as relatively stable. This includes income from property, as when a homebuyer elects to rent rather than sell an existing home. The lender in this situation will assume that some part of rental income (usually 75%) will remain after paying for utilities, maintenance, etc. From this, they subtract the mortgage payment, taxes, and insurance. If the difference is positive, they add it to income, but if it is negative, they add it to debt service payments.

**Getting Fired Before the Loan Closes:** If this happens, the applicant should tell the lender immediately because the lender will get the bad news anyway when they send out an employment verification request. If they hadn't been told, they will be annoyed at having their time wasted and probably won't be as helpful as they might have been otherwise.

Being helpful means exploring the possibility of recasting the loan so that the borrower's income can be disregarded. However, this could require a substantial increase in down payment or interest rate, which could make the loan unworkable.

**Is an ARM Needed to Qualify?** Because the interest rate used to qualify applicants is generally lower on an ARM than on a FRM, some borrowers need an ARM to qualify. Yet some borrowers who appear to require an ARM in fact could qualify with an FRM using one or more of the approaches discussed above. It just takes a little more work by the loan officer. If the loan officer is lazy or is primarily interested in selling ARMs, the effort may not be made.

*Meeting Cash Requirements:* More borrowers are limited in the amount they can spend on a house by the cash requirements than by the income requirements. Cash is needed for the down payment, and also for points and other fees charged by the lender, title insurance, escrows, and a variety of other charges. Settlement costs vary from one part of the country to another and, to some degree, from deal to deal. *See* **Settlement Costs**.

**Down Payment Requirements:** Down payment requirements range from 30% to zero and below—in some cases, lenders will lend more than the value of the property. The requirements depend on the type of program, loan amount, property characteristics, and the borrower's credit rating.

VA-guaranteed loans (available only to veterans) require no down payment on loans up to $203,000. FHA-insured loans require only 1% down. Loan limits in 2003 ranged from $154,896 to $280,749.

On conventional (non-VA, non-FHA) prime loans, the lowest down payment requirement is generally 5% on loans up to $400,000. It notches up quickly after that and is generally 40% on a $1,000,000 loan. Some special affordability programs are available from Fannie Mae and Freddie Mac with 3% down. The loan limit on these in 2003 was $322,700.

On sub-prime loans, which carry higher interest rates, some lenders will advance up to 125% of property value to borrowers with good credit ratings.

Down payment requirements will be higher whenever a transaction has characteristics that lenders view as risky. The million-dollar loan has a high requirement, for example, because it is secured by an expensive house that may have unique features that appeal to a limited number of potential buyers and is therefore subject to much greater price variability than a less expensive house. For similar reasons, lenders will usually require a larger down payment if the borrower has a poor credit record, is purchasing a house as an investment rather than for occupancy, wants to refinance for an amount significantly larger than the existing balance, and so on.

**Sources of Funds for Down Payment:** In general, lenders prefer that borrowers meet the down payment requirement with funds they have saved. This indicates that the borrower has the discipline to save, which bodes well for the repayment of the loan. Other sources of funds may be problematic.

Gifts and secured loans are acceptable but only within limits. On conventional loans having down payments of less than 20% of property value, at least 5% of the down payment must come from the applicant's own funds. (There are some special programs for which the own-funds requirement is only 3%.) The balance can come from a gift or a secured loan. With a 20% down payment, the entire amount can come from gifts or secured loans.

Secured loans must be reported as existing debt and the payments on them are included in total housing expenses. If this total as a percent of income exceeds the lender's guidelines, a secured loan may not work where a gift would work.

Lenders want to be sure that an alleged gift is really a gift. If it comes from a family member, they may ask that member to sign a gift affidavit. The concern is that the "gift" is really an unsecured loan and that if the borrower gets into financial difficulty, he or she will give first priority to paying off the family member.

If the "gift" is from the home seller, the concern is that the sale price has been correspondingly inflated. This would mean that the equity in the property is less than it appears. For this reason, lenders tend to set a limit on "gifts" by sellers, which are typically referred to (more accurately) as "seller contributions." *See* **Down Payment/ Home Seller Contributions**.

***Qualifying Self-Employed Borrowers:*** The system is somewhat more complicated and onerous for self-employed borrowers, but it does work. I have been in countries where it is impossible for a self-employed person to obtain a mortgage loan from an institutional lender. The only sources of funding, other than family members, are money-lenders, who charge extortionate rates and break the borrowers' legs if they don't pay.

The major problem with lending to the self-employed is documenting an applicant's income to the lender's satisfaction. Applicants with jobs can provide lenders with pay stubs, and lenders can verify the information by contacting the employer. With self-employed applicants, there are no third parties to verify such information.

Consequently, lenders fall back on income tax returns, which they typically require for two years. They feel safe in relying on income tax data because any errors will be in the direction of understating rather than overstating income. Of course, they don't necessarily feel safe that the W-2s given them are authentic rather than concocted for the purpose of defrauding them. For this reason, they will require that the applicant authorize them to obtain copies directly from the IRS.

The support it provides to self-employed loan applicants is an unappreciated benefit of our income tax system. It may not be fully appreciated, of course, by applicants who have understated their income. In countries where virtually no one pays income taxes because cheating is endemic, tax returns are useless for qualifying borrowers.

The second problem with lending to the self-employed is determining the stability of reported income. For this purpose, the lender wants to see an income statement for the period since the last tax return and in some cases a current balance sheet for the business.

The two government-sponsored enterprises, Fannie Mae and Freddie Mac, have developed detailed guidelines for qualifying self-employed borrowers. Lenders looking to sell such loans to the agencies must follow the guidelines. The problem is that implementation can be complicated and time-consuming, especially when the declared income comes from a corporation or a partnership. If you own 25% or more, you are considered as "self-employed."

Most lenders offer reduced documentation loans to self-employed applicants who cannot demonstrate two years of sufficient income from their tax returns. (*See* **Documentation Requirements**.) These programs vary from lender to lender, but they all provide less favorable pricing and/or tougher underwriting requirements of other types. Lenders invariably require larger down payments and may also require a better credit score or higher cash reserves. In addition, they may limit the types of properties or types of loans that are eligible.

**Qualification Rate** *The interest rate used in calculating the initial mortgage payment in qualifying a borrower.*

The rate used in qualifying borrowers may or may not be the initial rate on the mortgage. On FRMs with **Temporary Buydowns**, the qualifying rate is the "bought down" rate. On ARMs, the borrower may be qualified at the **Fully Indexed Rate** rather than the initial rate.

**Qualification Ratios** *Requirements stipulated by the lender that the ratio of housing expense to borrower income and the ratio of housing expense plus other debt service to borrower income cannot exceed specified maximums, e.g., 28% and 35%.*

These may reflect the maximums specified by Fannie Mae and Freddie Mac; they may also vary with the loan-value ratio and other factors. *See* **Qualification**.

**Qualification Requirements** *Standards imposed by lenders as conditions for granting loans, including maximum ratios of housing expense and total expense to income, maximum loan amounts, maximum loan-to-value ratios, and so on.*

Qualification requirements are less comprehensive than underwriting requirements, which take account of the borrower's credit record.

**Rate**

*See* **Interest Rate**.

**Rate/Point Break-Even** *The period you must retain a mortgage in order for it to be profitable to pay points to reduce the rate.*

*See* **Points/*Sharpening the Rate/Point Decision***.

**Rate/Point Options** *All the combinations of interest rate and points that are offered on a particular loan program.*

On an ARM, rates and points may also vary with the margin and interest rate maximum.

**Rate Protection** *Protection for a borrower against the danger that rates will rise between the time the borrower applies for a loan and the time the loan closes.*

Rate protection can take the form of a lock, where the rate and points are frozen at their initial levels until the loan closes, or a float-down, where the rates and points cannot rise from their initial levels but they can decline if market rates decline. In either case, the protection only runs for a specified period. If the loan is not closed within that period, the protection expires and the borrower will have to either accept the terms quoted by the lender on new loans at that time or start the shopping process anew. *See* **Locking the Loan**.

**Rebate**

*Same as* **Negative Points.**

**Recast Clause** *A contract provision that adjusts the payment on an ARM periodically to make it fully amortizing.*

*See* **Adjustable Rate Mortgage (ARM)/***How the Monthly Payment on an ARM Is Determined/*Negative Amortization ARMs.

**Referral Site** *A mortgage Web site that shows mortgage prices posted by participating lenders, in some cases hundreds of them.*

Referral sites are similar to newspapers in that lenders and brokers pay for the privilege of posting their mortgage prices on the site. However, they provide more information than newspapers. At least some of the price information on referral sites, furthermore, is posted on the day the user looks at the screen, whereas all price information in newspapers is obsolete when it is published. Some referral sites are Bankrate.com, BestRate.com, CompareInterestRates.com, Domania.com, Interest.com, and LoanPage.com.

For referral sites to be useful, shoppers must be able to select the lenders quoting the best prices, then visit the Web sites of each of them to make a final selection. This won't work for ARMs because the referral sites don't provide complete information about ARMs. While they do provide complete price information about fixed-rate mortgages, the process breaks down when the lender's own Web site is poor. I found that some of the lenders quoting the best prices on the referral sites were either quoting higher prices on their own sites or not providing complete information.

---

**Refinance** *Paying off an old loan while simultaneously taking a new one.*

Borrowers may refinance to reduce **Interest Cost** or to raise cash. These are very different decisions based on different considerations.

*Refinancing to Lower Interest Cost:* To lower interest cost by refinancing, the new interest rate must be lower than the old one.

It is possible to reduce interest payments (as distinct from interest cost) by refinancing into a new loan with a higher interest rate combined with higher payments. The higher payments shorten the payoff period and reduce total interest payments. You don't need to pay a higher rate, however, to shorten the payoff period. *See* **Mortgage Scams and Tricks/ *Strictly Lender Scams*/Sell Biweeklies Under False Pretenses**.

**Measuring the Costs and Gains:** The best way to measure the costs and gains from refinancing is to compare all costs of the existing mortgage and a new mortgage over a future period. The period should be your best guess as to how long you will have the new mortgage. If the total costs are lower with the new mortgage, you should refinance.

Calculator 3a on my Web site shows all the costs over a specified period of an existing and a new mortgage side by side. It also shows the break-even period, which is the *minimum* length of time the borrower must hold the new mortgage to make the refinancing pay. So if you are confident that you will have the mortgage longer than the break-even period, you know the refinance pays. If you hate calculators, use the break-even tables below.

A side benefit from using a calculator is that it forces you to collect all the information that affects the profitability of a refinance. Once all the relevant information is at hand, it is clear that no two cases are exactly alike. But the calculator will handle them all.

**Avoid This Common Rule of Thumb:** Loan officers often calculate a break-even period by dividing the cost of the loan by the reduction in the monthly mortgage payment. For example, if it costs $4,000 to refinance and the monthly payment falls by $200, the break-even would be 20 months.

This rule of thumb does not take account of differences in how rapidly you pay down the balance of the new loan as opposed to the old one, it does not allow for differences in tax savings (which depend on the borrower's tax bracket), and it ignores differences in lost interest on upfront and monthly payments. All these factors are taken into account by calculator 3a.

**Financing Upfront Costs:** Lenders ordinarily allow refinancers to fold the settlement costs into the loan amount without classifying it as a "cash-out." For example, if the balance on the old loan is $100,000 and settlement costs including the lender's fees are $3,750, the new loan could be for $103,750.

Financing the settlement costs, however, reduces the gains from refinancing because the borrower must pay interest on the costs at the mortgage rate. Financing the costs, furthermore, can flip the loan amount above 80% of property value, which triggers mortgage insurance. If the borrower is already paying mortgage insurance, it can raise the premium. Calculator 3a includes a financing option and automatically factors mortgage insurance into the cost calculation, if it arises.

**No-Cost Refinance:** A no-closing-cost loan is one where the interest rate is high enough to command a rebate from the lender that covers the closing costs. This is very different from a no-cash outlay loan, where closing costs are added to the loan balance. Note that even with a legitimate no-cost loan, borrowers should always expect to pay per diem interest and escrows at closing.

The no-cost option is for borrowers who are sure to have the mortgage for no more than five years. Either they plan to sell the house within that period or they are convinced that interest rates will fall further and they will refinance again. For further discussion, *see* **No-Cost Mortgage**.

**Refinancing Versus Contract Modification:** Many borrowers wonder why they can't induce their lender to agree to a modification of the rate on the existing loan. If the old loan stays on the books, the settlement costs required by a new loan are avoided and both the borrower and the lender can be better off.

Contract modifications do occur, but not very often. In most cases, the lenders to whom borrowers send their payments don't own the loans. They are the servicing agents of the owners. Ordinarily, owners will not grant servicing agents the right to modify the interest rate. Owners fear that agents would agree to rate reductions too readily in order to retain their servicing income, which is not affected by a reduction in the interest rate.

Even when the servicing agent owns the loan, it will not volunteer a rate reduction. The lender's objective is to drop the rate only if necessary to prevent the borrower from refinancing with another lender. Borrowers who understand this will take the initiative to let the lender know their intentions. The best way to do this is to request a payoff statement. This tells the lender that you have begun a refinance process with another lender.

**Don't Confuse "Better Off" with "Best":** The fact that a refinancing lowers your cost doesn't mean you should do it. Another mortgage may be available that would save you even more. If you are happy with your savings at a rate above the market, the loan officer will be happy too.

**Refinance Versus Extra Payments:** Many borrowers get confused over how the decision to make extra payments bears on their decision to refinance. It is complicated, but here are some guidelines:

- Ignore extra payments made in the past: that's water over the dam.

- Looking ahead, consider first whether you want to repay your loan in full. Repayment is an investment on which the yield is the rate at which you could refinance with no upfront costs. (If you can refinance your current loan at 6%, for example, you earn 6% by paying it off.) Compare this with the returns on your investment alternatives. If you repay in full, the process ends.

- If you elect not to repay in full, consider whether refinancing pays if you make the extra monthly payments that you can afford. Extra payments reduce the benefit from refinancing. You factor them into your analysis, using my refinance calculators, by shortening the term of your new mortgage. If you plan to refinance into a 15-year loan, for example, but extra payments would result in payoff in 10 years, you use 10 years as the term. You can determine the payoff period from any extra payments using my calculator 2a. If refinancing is beneficial assuming extra payments, you refinance—end of process.

- If refinancing is not profitable with the extra payments, do the analysis again without the extra payments. If refinancing remains unprofitable, you don't refinance. But if refinancing is profitable without the extra payments, you flip a coin: heads you refinance without extra payments, tails you make extra payments without refinancing.

**Refinancing When You Have Two Mortgages:** Two mortgages complicate the refinance decision. You can refinance the first alone (provided the second mortgage lender allows it, *see* **Subordination Policy**), you can refinance the second alone, you can refinance both into two new mortgages, and you can refinance both into one new mortgage.

You can analyze the first three possibilities using my calculator 3a and the 4th using 3b. You must obtain price quotes on a new first for the amount of the balance on the existing first, on a new second for the amount of the balance on the existing second, and a new first for the amount of the balance on both existing loans.

**Effect of Prior Refinances on the Current One:** When interest rates drop, some homeowners who had refinanced earlier are discouraged from refinancing again, for reasons that make no sense.

Some homeowners assume that there must be a waiting period before they are allowed to refinance again. This is not the case.

Of course, lenders hate serial refinancing with a passion, but it is a cost of doing business. While loan contracts may discourage refinancing with a prepayment penalty, in jurisdictions where such penalties are allowed, that is a different issue.

Some homeowners are reluctant to refinance the second time because it means they "have to start all over again." One borrower commented that "I have already paid five months of the term and am reluctant to give that up."

But she gives up nothing. In the five months she had the loan, she reduced the balance by an amount equal to the five principal payments she made. If she refinances, it will be on this lower balance, so her savings remain intact.

It is true that if she refinances into another 30-year loan, she will be staring at 360 new payments. Lenders won't write a loan with a term of 355 months. That is easily remedied, however, by making a small increase in the monthly payment, sufficient to pay off in 355 months.

Some borrowers are reluctant to refinance a second time because they haven't yet recovered the costs of the previous refinance. For example, one borrower told me that he had paid $4,500 to refinance eight months ago and he wanted to wait 17 months to refinance again because it would take that long for his savings to cover the $4,500.

But the $4,500 is gone and should not affect his current decision. My calculator 3a, which can be used to determine whether or not it pays to refinance now, must be given information about a number of things, including the interest rates on the current and new loans and the points and other costs of the new loan. But the costs incurred on the previous refinance are not there, because they are irrelevant to whether another refinance pays.

**Refinancing May Cost More than a Purchase Loan:** One would think that if the borrower, property, and loan are the same, a loan used to purchase a home would be priced the same as a refinance. Historically, this was in fact the case. During the prolonged refinance boom in 2000-2003, however, refinancing loans began to be priced higher than purchase loans.

The boom stretched to the limit the capacity of lenders to process loans. Reluctant to add more employees when the boom could fizzle out at any time, lenders preferred to lengthen the processing period and let borrowers queue up for longer periods. But purchasers often have closing dates they must meet and lenders strive to give them priority over refinancers. Pricing refinance a little higher is one way to do this because it cuts the number of refinancers in the queue.

Another factor was at work as well. It costs lenders more to lock the interest rate on refinance loans than on purchase loans. In the past, this was never important enough to cause a difference in pricing, but that also changed during the refinance boom.

If loan applicants who lock always went to closing, over time, lenders would gain as much from rate declines as they lost from rate increases. But in practice borrowers do not always close and the fallout, as it is called, is larger when rates are falling. Some applicants are "lock-jumpers." They lock and, if rates subsequently decline, they find another loan provider and lock again at a lower rate. Locking thus imposes a net cost on lenders.

This cost is larger on refinancings than on purchases because lock-jumping is more common among refinancers. Borrowers who are refinancing usually are flexible on when they close. Most purchasers, in contrast, must close on a specific date and don't have time to restart the process with another lender.

The prolonged refinance boom increased the number of refinancing lock-jumpers. An unusually large number of borrowers refinanced multiple times within just a few years, learning the ropes in the process. One thing they learned is how to lock-jump. This widened the difference in lock cost to lenders between refinancings and purchase loans.

***Refinancing to Raise Cash:*** While not all lenders define "cash-out refinance" in the same way, the most widely used definition is that of the two federal secondary market purchasers, Fannie Mae and Freddie Mac. Their rules define a cash-out refinance by exclusion, i.e., they define an ordinary or no-cash-out refinance, and any refinance that does not meet that definition is considered a cash-out.

A non-cash-out refinance is one that a) is used to pay off a first mortgage and/or junior mortgages that were used in their entirety to buy the subject property, and b) is for an amount not in excess of the loan balance, plus settlement costs, plus 2% of the new loan amount or $2,000, whichever is less. If the borrower has a mortgage balance of $150,000 and settlement costs are $5,000, for example, the loan can be no larger than $157,000.

Any refinance that does not meet these specs is a cash-out refinance and will carry a higher interest rate.

**Why Cash-Out Refinancing Carries a Higher Rate:** The major reason for the higher rate is that studies of delinquency and default indicate that borrowers who do a cash-out subsequently have poorer payment records than borrowers who don't. The presumed reason for this is that borrowers who need cash are financially weaker than borrowers who don't, and in some cases they may be in financial distress.

**Refinancing a Second Is Cash-Out:** The agencies assume that refinancing borrowers who want to repay second mortgages that they acquired after they purchased their house are cut from the same cloth as refinancing borrowers who want a large amount of cash. While those refinancing a second don't need cash now, they did need cash when they took a second mortgage. If they were in financial distress then, perhaps they still are. The presumption of distress does not apply, however, if the second mortgage was taken out when the house was purchased.

**Loan on a Property with No Mortgage Is Cash-Out:** If a homeowner who paid all cash for a property or who has paid off all mortgages elects to take a new mortgage, the agencies consider it cash-out. This is also based on the presumption that the need for cash may signal financial distress.

**Portfolio Lenders May Be More Flexible:** Lenders who originate loans to hold rather than to sell in the secondary market may be more flexible in their definitions of what constitutes a cash-out. They may not view a loan for the purpose of repaying a second mortgage as cash-out if the borrower has had the loan for some time or if the loan had been used to improve the property. Property improvement might also exempt a loan on a property with no mortgage. Borrowers should be prepared to document the improvements, however.

**Cash-Out Versus Second Mortgage:** Borrowers who want to raise cash should compare the cost of a cash-out refinance against the cost of a home equity loan. This will depend on the interest rates, points and terms of both loans, the amount of cash required relative to the loan balance, the borrower's tax rate, and other factors.

Calculator 3d on my Web site computes all costs of both options over a future time period specified by the user. It also shows a break-even interest rate on the second mortgage—the highest rate you can pay on the second and come out ahead of the refinance option.

**Cash-Out Refinance by Predators:** Cash-out refinance is a tool used by some predators to exploit unwary borrowers who are dazzled by the prospect of putting a sizeable amount of money in their pocket. This applies to many of those who have become homeowners with assistance from Habitat for Humanity, who have refinanced the zero interest rate loans provided them by the program into high-rate loans—in order to get cash. *See* **Predatory Lending/ *Targets of Predators*/**Cash-Dazzled.

*Refinancing with the Current Lender:* Borrowers interested in refinancing face the problem of whether they approach their current lender, go to another loan provider, or both. Here are the pros and cons.

**The Pros:** Perhaps the major reason people approach their current lender is that it is convenient. They are spared having to decide who and where to shop. If their payment record has been good, furthermore, their existing lender has immediate access to their record, where other lenders would have to investigate. There is comfort in "being known" and a belief that this should earn them special treatment.

There is some validity to this belief. The current lender—defined as the firm to which you now remit your payments—may be in a position to offer lower settlement costs than a new lender. How much lower, however, can vary from case to case.

The greatest potential for lower settlement costs arises where the current lender was the originating lender and still owns the loan, a common situation with loans made by banks and savings and loan associations. If the payment record has been good, the current lender may forgo a credit report, property appraisal, title search, and other risk control procedures that are otherwise mandatory on new loans. This is strictly up to the lender.

If the current lender was the original lender but later sold the loan and is now servicing it for the owner, the potential for lower settlement costs is less. A lender servicing for others must follow the guidelines set down by the owner. If the owner is one of the federal secondary market agencies, Fannie Mae or Freddie Mac, the guidelines are theirs. While both agencies have provisions for "streamlined refinancing documentation," the discretion granted the lender, and therefore the potential cost savings, is quite limited.

The potential for lower settlement costs is least when the current lender is neither the originating lender nor the current owner. This is a fairly common situation that arises when the contract to service the loan is sold. In this case, the lender may not be in a position to use all of the streamlined refinancing procedures because its files do not contain some of the information those procedures require, such as the original appraisal report.

**The Cons:** The major argument against refinancing with your current lender is that that lender may not give you the market price. It will try to minimize its loss by taking advantage of your preference for staying put and your reluctance to shop the market. Any settlement cost benefits your current lender can offer that other lenders cannot may serve to draw attention away from the fact that the rate and points offered are not competitive.

Above-market offers are especially likely if the lender takes the initiative in soliciting its own customers. Lenders who do that are likely to base their offer on the borrower's existing rate. For example, in a 5% market, the borrower with a 7% mortgage might be offered 6% while a borrower with a 6% mortgage (but who is otherwise identical) might be offered 5.5%. The objective is to provide a saving over the existing loan that is attractive enough to discourage the borrower from looking elsewhere. This way, the lender gives up as little as possible.

An even greater hazard is that the borrower dealing with the existing lender will get the run around because that lender has no interest in completing the deal. Why rush to convert a 7% loan into a 5.5% loan? I saw one situation where the lender charged an unsuspecting borrower a lock fee and then let him dangle indefinitely.

**The Preferred Strategy:** In general, the best strategy is to first inquire about the settlement cost savings the existing lender can offer, then find the market price by shopping elsewhere, and then return to the existing lender.

*Title Insurance on a Refinance:* Borrowers who refinance do not need a new owner's title policy. They must purchase a new policy for the lender, however, because the lender's policy terminates with the repayment of the old mortgage. Such policies are customarily available at a discount, which is usually larger the shorter the period from the previous policy.

---

**Required Cash** *The total cash required of the home buyer/borrower to close the purchase plus loan transaction or the loan transaction on a refinance.*

Required cash includes the down payment, points and fixed dollar charges paid to the lender, any portion of the mortgage insurance premium that is paid upfront, and other settlement charges associated with the transaction such as title insurance and per diem interest. It is shown on the Good Faith Estimate that every borrower receives. *See* **Good Faith Estimate**.

---

**RESPA** *The Real Estate Settlement Procedures Act, a federal consumer protection statute first enacted in 1974.*

RESPA was designed to protect home purchasers and owners shopping for settlement services by mandating certain disclosures and prohibiting referral fees and kickbacks.

*Current Disclosure Requirements:* Different disclosure rules kick in at different stages of the home-buying or borrowing process.

**At Time of Loan Application:** Within three business days of receipt of a loan application, the lender must provide the applicant with a Special Information Booklet which describes the various real estate settlement services; a Good Faith Estimate (GFE) of settlement costs, which lists the estimated charges the borrower may have to pay at closing (*see* **Settlement Costs**); and a Mortgage Servicing Disclosure Statement, which discloses whether the lender intends to service the loan or transfer it elsewhere.

**Before Closing:** Before settlement service provider A refers an applicant to service provider B, A must provide the applicant with an Affiliated Business Arrangement (AfBA) Disclosure if A has an ownership or other beneficial interest in B. An applicant may request the HUD-1 Settlement Statement, which shows all charges imposed on buyer/borrowers and sellers, one day before settlement.

**At Settlement:** The borrower receives the final HUD-1 Settlement Statement at settlement and an Initial Escrow Statement that itemizes the estimated taxes and insurance premiums to be paid from the escrow account and the amounts to be paid into the account.

**After Settlement:** Borrowers must be provided with an Annual Escrow Statement which shows all inflows and outflows to and from the escrow account, and the balances, during the year. If the firm servicing the loan transfers the servicing to another firm, the borrower must be notified at least 15 days before the effective date of the transfer.

### Practices Currently Prohibited:

**Kickbacks, Referrals, and Unearned Markups:** RESPA prohibits any settlement service provider from giving or receiving anything of value for the referral of business in connection with a mortgage or charging fees or markups when no additional service has been provided.

**Seller Required Title Insurance:** A home seller is prohibited from requiring a borrower to use a particular title insurance company.

**Escrow Accounts Larger than Necessary:** A lender may not require a borrower to pay into an escrow account more than 1/12 of the total payments out of the account during the year, plus any shortages. The cushion a lender holds for unexpected disbursements cannot exceed 1/6 of the disbursements for the year.

**Loan Servicing Complaints:** RESPA provides a complaint procedure for borrowers who are being taken advantage of by the firm servicing their loan. *See* **Servicing/Predatory Servicing**.

**Proposals for RESPA Reform:** The existing HUD rules have not prevented a number of market abuses and have not been effective in driving down settlement costs. In response, in July 2002, HUD announced a wide-ranging set of proposals "to simplify and improve the process of obtaining home mortgages and reduce settlement costs for consumers." Because these proposals threatened the interests of several powerful groups, they were still being debated in September 2003, when this was written.

**Disclosing Mortgage Broker Compensation:** One proposal would change the way in which the compensation of mortgage brokers is reported, so that a broker's total compensation is transparent to borrowers. It is designed to deal with the practice of steering unwary borrowers into high-rate loans that command rebates from lenders, which the broker pockets. *See* **Mortgage Scams and Tricks/***Scams by Loan Providers*/**Pocket the Borrower's Rebate**.

Under the proposed new rules, rebates would be reported on the Good Faith Estimate as a payment by the lender to the borrower. The borrower would have to authorize the rebate to be paid to the broker—as if it were coming directly out of the borrower's pocket, which for all practical purposes it is. Most brokers are against this rule, but their only serious argument is that lenders are not being held to the same standard.

**Revising the Good Faith Estimate (GFE):** The second of HUD's proposals would change the format of the GFE, on which lenders and mortgage brokers disclose settlement costs, to make it more useful to borrowers as a shopping tool. The existing GFE lists each individual settlement charge, which encourages borrowers to focus on individual charges. This distracts them from what should be their major focus, which is the total of settlement charges. *See* **Settlement Costs/***Fees Paid to Lender*.

The existing GFE is also open-ended, inviting lenders to add new charges, which some do. In addition, the existing GFE makes no distinction between charges that lenders can control, and those they cannot. All are "estimates" subject to change. And they often are changed, after borrowers pass the point of no return, and always to the borrower's disadvantage. *See* **Mortgage Scams and Tricks/***Strictly Lender Scams*/**Pad the GFE**.

The proposed GFE is not simple, because the content is not simple, but it is light-years ahead of the existing GFE. The major difference is that settlement costs are consolidated into a number of major groups and only the total is reported for each group. A second major difference is that the new GFE limits the extent to which the costs may change. These limits are different for services controlled by the lender and services for which the borrower may shop independently.

**Guaranteed Mortgage Package (GMP):** The most far-reaching and controversial of HUD's proposals is to authorize lenders and others to offer borrowers complete (or almost complete) packages of loans and settlement services at a single price. This is permissive rather than obligatory. Lenders who package would use a Guaranteed Mortgage Price Agreement (GMPA) in lieu of the proposed new obligatory GFE.

GMPs could be offered by lenders or other entities such as real estate companies or title insurers. A package must include a loan at a guaranteed interest rate plus a guaranteed dollar price for all settlement services excepting per diem interest, hazard insurance, and escrows. Packagers can deal freely with their own affiliates and are exempt from kickback prohibition rules.

The major purpose of the GMP is to drive down settlement costs. Under existing arrangements, competition in the markets for settlement services is "perverse"—it tends to drive up prices or to prevent them from falling in response to deployment of more efficient technology. Perverse competition arises whenever one party selects the seller of the service and another party pays for it.

For example, lenders select the mortgage insurer but borrowers pay the premiums. Instead of competing for customers by lowering prices and improving service, service providers compete for the favor of the lenders.

While kickbacks for the referral of business are illegal, mortgage insurers and others have found legal ways to accomplish the same thing. The only difference is that the legal ways are more costly.

Under the GMP proposal, it is expected that competition will force down the prices that packagers pay for settlement services. Because the price of a package will consist solely of the interest rate plus a single dollar price for all settlement services, it will be relatively easy for borrowers to shop and compare. The major concern is whether there will be enough packagers to ensure that they will compete.

Because I share this concern, I support an alternative two-package proposal advanced by title insurers. One package, offered only by lenders, would consist of lender-related services. These are services provided directly by the lender or by third parties, such as independent appraisers, at prices known by the lender. This package would have the same rate guarantee as the GMP, but the price guarantee would cover only lender-related services.

The second package, offered by title insurance, real estate, or other non-lender firms, would consist of all real-estate-related services. These are all the services needed in the settlement of the real estate transaction. The price of real-estate-related services would also be guaranteed. Both groups of packagers would have the same type of exemptions (from restrictions on referral fees, for example) as GMP packagers.

The two-package approach would materially increase the number of competitive options available to borrowers. Many lenders reluctant to offer GMPs will be willing to offer lender packages because, except for the guarantee, it is what they do now. A few forward-looking lenders already guarantee their settlement service package. Real estate firms that are disinclined to become subcontractors to lenders offering GMPs will take advantage of the opportunity to develop their own distribution networks.

Under the two-package approach, borrowers could buy a complete GMP or they could buy separate lender and real estate packages. It would be a simple matter to compare the price of a GMP package with the sum of the prices on a lender package and a real estate package.

At the time this was written, HUD was wrestling with the issue of one package versus two.

---

**Retail Lender** *A lender who offers mortgage loans directly to the public. See* **Mortgage Lender/Retail, Wholesale, and Correspondent Lenders**.

---

**Reverse Mortgage** *A mortgage loan to an elderly homeowner on which the borrower's debt rises over time, but that need not be repaid until the borrower dies, sells the house, or moves out permanently.*

The "forward" mortgages that are used to purchase homes *build equity*—the value of the home less the mortgage balance. Borrowers pay down the balance over time, and by age 62, when they become eligible for a reverse mortgage, loan balances are either paid off or much reduced.

Reverse mortgages, in contrast, *consume equity* because loan balances rise over time. If there is a balance remaining on a forward mortgage at the time a reverse mortgage is taken out, it is paid off with an advance under the reverse mortgage.

***Need:*** Most of the elderly are homeowners. For many, especially those with low incomes, homeowner equity constitutes a major part of their net worth. Most of them built that equity during their working lives, in part by paying down their mortgages.

As their incomes decline in their later years, many would like to consume their equity rather than leave it to heirs who don't need it. Without reverse mortgages, however, the only way to do that is to sell the house and live elsewhere. Reverse mortgages allow elderly homeowners to consume some or all of the equity in their homes without having to move—ever.

***Suspicion:*** In the 1970s and early '80s, when I was actively involved in trying to develop reverse mortgage programs and bring them to the market, the need was as great as it is today. However, they were a very tough sell. I was involved in two projects that offered excellent products, but neither project survived.

The major problem was that elderly homeowners were extremely cautious and suspicious. Even when they seemed convinced, they often backed out at the last moment. Unfortunately, some programs being offered around that time did not guarantee lifetime occupancy—borrowers could be forced out of their homes if they lived too long. The complexity of reverse mortgage programs was also a deterrent.

This situation began to change in 1988 with the development of a federal program under the FHA. The borrower protections built into this program, along with the imprimatur of the federal government, paved the way toward increasing acceptance by elderly homeowners. The AARP also entered the picture as a major information source (*see* www.aarp.org/revmort). Complexity continues to be a problem, however, which is why the FHA requires that applicants be counseled before entering the program.

In 1999, a sample of homeowners who had taken FHA reverse mortgages was surveyed regarding their experience under the program. The survey found that about 80% were either "very satisfied" or "satisfied," and only about 15% were "very dissatisfied" or "dissatisfied."

In early 2003, reverse mortgages were being written at a rate of about 1,500 a month, which was an all-time high. Yet the volume remained small relative to the size of the potential market. About 95% of the new loans were FHA-insured. Other reverse mortgage programs were available from Fannie Mae and from Financial Freedom Senior Funding Corporation, a subsidiary of Lehman Brothers Bank, FSB. In addition, some limited special purpose programs were available from some states and cities.

**Safeguards:** Under all the programs cited in the paragraph above, borrowers have the right to live in their house until they sell it, die, or move out permanently, regardless of how much their mortgage debt grows. If the debt comes to exceed the value of the property, the lender takes the loss, except that on the FHA program, FHA reimburses the lender for any loss out of insurance premiums paid by borrowers.

In addition, loans under these programs are without recourse. This means that lenders cannot attach other assets of borrowers or their heirs in the event that the reverse mortgage debt comes to exceed the property value.

Borrowers do have obligations under these programs, but they are no more than one would expect. Under the three major programs, the lender can demand repayment of the loan if the borrower fails to pay property taxes or insurance, doesn't maintain the home, changes the names on the title, takes out a second mortgage, takes in boarders, or uses the home as a business.

**Eligibility:** To be eligible for the major programs, all owners must be 62 or older and must occupy the home as their permanent residence. There are no income or credit requirements, since borrowers don't assume any payment obligation, but all the reverse mortgage programs require counseling.

Eligible properties generally include one-family units, condominiums, manufactured housing, and houses in planned unit developments. Two- to four-family units may or may not qualify. Mobile homes and co-ops are not eligible, although co-ops may soon become eligible under the FHA program.

The house may have an existing mortgage, but it will have to be repaid out of the reverse mortgage proceeds. An exception would be where the existing lender is willing to subordinate his claim to that of the reverse mortgage, meaning he wouldn't get paid until the reverse mortgage is repaid. No institutional lender would be willing to do that, but some special purpose reverse mortgage programs may allow it.

***Debt-Based Versus Equity-Based Products:*** While the term "reverse mortgage" implies a debt secured by property, it is possible to fashion instruments for the same purpose that are equity-based—meaning that the investor acquires an ownership interest in the property. Investors are willing to pay more to acquire a house outright than they will on a reverse mortgage, where they only earn interest on the amounts they advance the owner.

Indeed, the oldest known instrument for "home equity conversion" was of this type. At least as far back as the 19th century, notaries in France arranged deals between homeowners and individual investors where the investor paid the owner an annuity for life. Such deals were very simple. The annuity was determined by dividing the current value of the property by the owner's life expectancy. The investor took possession of the house upon the owner's death, whether that happened after a month or after 40 years.

However, these deals were extremely risky to both parties. Occasionally the owner would outlive the investor. And occasionally the owner would die before the ink was dry on the contract. While investors can diversify their risk by writing many contracts, owners cannot because each owner has only one house with which to transact.

Combined debt/equity arrangements are also possible, and several of these have appeared in the U.S. In these deals, the investor makes a loan and also receives either a share of the appreciation in the home's value or a share of the value at termination. The equity participation feature permits the investor to pay the owner more than in a straight debt transaction.

None of the programs of this type have been successful, however. The American Homestead program during the 1980s failed because the expected rate of appreciation did not materialize and investors did not earn an adequate return. In 2000, Fannie Mae terminated an equity option in connection with its Home Keeper reverse mortgage for essentially the opposite reason.

In exchange for paying up to 10% of the value of their home at the termination of the contract, owners received larger payments under Home Keeper than if they took a straight loan. With this equity option, owners who terminate early pay a lot more than those who terminate late. When a syndicated columnist wrote up the news that early terminators were paying a high cost, as if it were a scandal, Fannie Mae was embarrassed, and in 2000 it terminated the equity option.

***Available Payment Amounts:*** The amounts available on a reverse mortgage depend on the value of the house, age of the youngest co-borrower, interest rate, upfront costs, servicing fee, method of payment, and whether there is an equity option. The tables on the next page apply to the FHA's Home Equity Conversion Mortgage program, which provides the largest payments for the property values of $100,000 and $200,000 assumed in the table, but not necessarily for larger values that exceed FHA loan limits. Upfront costs are assumed to be $2,000 plus 2% of the house value, while the servicing fee is $30 a month. There is no equity option.

The first table shows the maximum credit line, which is the amount the borrower can withdraw immediately as a lump sum. For example, at 6%, a 75-year-old with a $100,000 house could withdraw $58,433. Note that because some costs are a fixed amount, the credit lines on a $200,000 house are more than twice as large as those on a $100,000 house.

The second table shows different combinations of credit line plus monthly payments for a 75-year-old with a $100,000 house at 6%. The largest credit line of $58,433 allows no monthly payments. If the bor-

| Credit Line or Maximum Immediate Lump Sum Withdrawal | | | | | | |
|---|---|---|---|---|---|---|
| **Interest Rate** | **Age of Youngest Co-Borrower** | | | | | |
| | **65** | **70** | **75** | **80** | **85** | **90** |
| | Property Value = $100,000 | | | | | |
| 5% | $59,488 | $62,992 | $66,692 | $70,819 | $75,012 | $79,233 |
| 6% | $48,107 | $53,128 | $58,433 | $64,054 | $69,737 | $75,244 |
| 7% | $38,423 | $44,383 | $50,815 | $57,653 | $65,544 | $71,257 |
| 8% | $30,455 | $36,771 | $43,948 | $51,619 | $59,532 | $67,263 |
| | Property Value = $200,000 | | | | | |
| 5% | $128,588 | $135,292 | $140,292 | $150,019 | $157,712 | $165,223 |
| 6% | $105,207 | $115,028 | $123,333 | $136,154 | $146,937 | $157,144 |
| 7% | $83,323 | $95,083 | $107,715 | $121,053 | $134,344 | $147,057 |
| 8% | $66,955 | $79,471 | $93,648 | $108,719 | $124,132 | $138,963 |

| Credit Line Plus Monthly Payment Combinations for a 75-Year-Old with a $100,000 Property at 6% | | | | |
|---|---|---|---|---|
| **Credit Line** | **Monthly Payments** | | | |
| | **Tenure** | **15 Years** | **10 Years** | **5 Years** |
| 0 | $475 | $555 | $723 | $1,247 |
| $10,000 | $401 | $468 | $610 | $1,052 |
| $20,000 | $327 | $382 | $498 | $857 |
| $30,000 | $253 | $295 | $385 | $663 |
| $40,000 | $178 | $208 | $272 | $468 |
| $50,000 | $104 | $122 | $159 | $274 |
| $58,433 (Max) | 0 | 0 | 0 | 0 |

rower only takes a $30,000 line, however, she can also receive $253 a month for life, $295 for 15 years, $385 for 10 years, or $663 for five years.

**Available Calculators:** Jerry Wagner, an expert's expert on reverse mortgages, has developed calculators used in determining the amounts a homeowner can receive under the FHA and Fannie Mae programs. Different versions of these calculators are available at Jerry's own Web site (www.revmort.com), at the AARP's site (www.rmaarp.com), and at the site of the National Reverse Mortgage Lenders Association (www.nrmla.org), where you will also find a list of reverse mortgage lenders. Financial Freedom has its own calculator, available at www.ffsenior.com, that covers all three programs.

None of these calculators show changes in the borrower's mortgage debt and homeowner equity in the future. Lenders and loan counselors have calculators that do this, however, and they can meet borrowers' requests for such information.

**Total Annual Loan Costs (TALC):** Federal law requires lenders to report a single interest cost figure for all reverse mortgages. The TALC is designed to allow borrowers to compare one lender's offerings (or one type of reverse mortgage) with another, and also to illustrate how the cost of a reverse mortgage declines as the transaction ages.

The TALC is somewhat analogous to the APR required on forward mortgages, except that the TALC covers all costs and the APR does not. In addition, the TALC is calculated over two years, half of life expectancy, life expectancy, and 1.4 times life expectancy, whereas APR is calculated over the term of the loan.

Under the market conditions of early 2003, the TALC was pretty much a fifth wheel for comparison shopping, especially on the FHA program. Interest rates did not vary from one lender to another, and FHA capped the origination fee and servicing fee. Third-party settlement costs varied with the area of the country, but were not likely to vary between lenders in the same area.

Because origination and closing costs are incurred upfront, the TALC always declines over time. A typical pattern in early 2003 for a 79-year-old taking a tenure (lifetime) payment on a HECM would be a TALC of 30% if the borrower terminated after two years, 10% over five years, 6.5% over nine years, and 5.5% over 13 years. Reverse mortgages are not a good deal for borrowers who expect to be out of their homes within a few years.

**Single-Purpose Programs:** Much the simplest type of reverse mortgages are those offered by some states and cities, which are either for property improvement or for the payment of property taxes. These loans require no repayment so long as the borrower lives in the house. Loans for property improvement are one-time advances, while those for payment of property taxes are annual advances.

Single-purpose programs are invariably good deals, but they usually have eligibility criteria that limit their availability. The criteria may apply to income, house value, age, area, or borrower health. There is no one comprehensive source of information on these programs, but a good place to start looking is the directory of "homes and communities organized by state" on www.hud.gov.

***FHA's Home Equity Conversion Mortgage (HECM):*** The largest program by far is FHA's HECM program. In 2003, it accounted for about 95% of all reverse mortgages. The great strengths of this program are the security provided by the federal guarantee and the payment options available to the borrower. These options are available at the outset and also throughout the life of a transaction in that borrowers can shift from one to another.

The weakness of HECM is that it is complicated, which is why Congress made it mandatory that borrowers undergo a counseling session before they sign on. But as I write this, no one involved with HECM has much of an idea of how good or bad the counseling is. Wise borrowers will do the homework they need to counsel themselves.

**Options:** Borrowers can choose from five payment plans. All of them require that the borrower maintain the property as his or her principal residence.

- **Tenure:** The borrower receives a fixed monthly payment for as long as he or she remains in the house.
- **Term:** The borrower receives a fixed monthly payment for a period specified by him or her.
- **Line of Credit:** The borrower may make withdrawals at times and in amounts selected by him or her, within a specified maximum draw. This includes drawing the maximum amount as a lump sum at the outset.
- **Modified Tenure:** A combination of tenure and line of credit.
- **Modified Term:** A combination of term and line of credit.

These options are designed to meet diverse needs. A borrower who wants to repay what is left on his or her existing mortgage can do it with a line of credit. A borrower who plans to sell in five years but needs more income in the meantime can elect a term loan for five years. And so on.

**Principal Limit:** A critical number in each HECM is called the "principal limit." It is the present value of the house, given the owner's right to live there until he or she dies or voluntarily moves out.

If the house is worth $100,000, for example, the principal limit might be only $64,000. $100,000 is what the owner can get if he or she gives up the house immediately. $64,000 is what he or she can get if he or she retains the right to live there for an indefinite period.

The principal limit is determined by three factors: the borrower's age, which determines how long the investor is likely to have to wait to be repaid; the expected interest rate, which measures the cost of having to wait; and the property value, which affects the risk that the debt won't be fully paid when it comes due because it will exceed the property value.

There is an important proviso attached to the last factor, however. If the property value exceeds the FHA loan limit in the county in which the property is located, the loan limit is used in calculating the principal limit. This limit makes other reverse mortgages more attractive to seniors with higher-valued homes.

The owner cannot withdraw cash equal to the full principal limit. She can withdraw the *net* principal limit, which is the principal limit less the HECM settlement costs, including any required repairs and repayment of existing debt, and less a servicing fee hold-back or "set-aside" (see *Costs* below). The net principal limit is the maximum line of credit you can get at the outset if you exercise the credit line option; it is also used to determine tenure or term payments. For example, if the net principal limit is $60,000, you could take a credit line for that amount or you could take a credit line for $30,000 and use the remaining $30,000 to purchase tenure or term payments.

**Property Value Versus FHA Loan Limits:** The greater the value of the borrower's property, the larger should be the credit advances and/or monthly payments available under the program. But this is true only so long as the property value does not exceed the FHA loan limit in the county where the property is located. Borrowers receive no credit for value in excess of the loan limit, which in 2003 ranged from $154,896 to $280,749. For a borrower living in a county where the FHA limit is $190,000, the credit line and tenure or term payments are the same for a house worth $190,000 and a house worth $500,000.

This is not a major problem for borrowers who view a HECM as a stop gap measure and want to retain as much equity as possible. A borrower who takes a term payment for five years, for example, intending to sell at the end of that period, will retain the equity that FHA did not use in calculating his payment.

But borrowers who want to live in their house until they die, who are usually viewed as the major intended beneficiaries of reverse mortgage programs, are disadvantaged. The borrower with a $585,000 house must pay the same insurance premium as the borrower with the $185,000 house, but there is a substantial difference in risk of loss to FHA. A borrower in this situation might consider a reverse mortgage from Fannie Mae, which has a higher loan maximum, or from Financial Freedom, which has no maximum.

**Note:** FHA loan limits are raised at the beginning of every year. You can find them at https://entp.hud.gov/idapp/html/hicost-look.cfm.

**Tenure Payments:** Tenure payments in the HECM program are priced on the assumption that the borrower, whether age 62 or 92, male or female, will live to be 100! Borrowers who want payments for life and are not concerned with leaving equity to their heirs do better taking a lump sum under a credit line and using it to purchase an immediate annuity from a life insurance company. Just make sure the company is highly rated, because you are leaving the realm of federal insurance when you do this. I found immediate annuity quotes on www.immediateannuity.com, which also shows the quality ratings of each company.

You want a fixed annuity, one that pays the same guaranteed amount every month, beginning immediately. If you don't yet need the payments, you can take the credit line and sit on it—it will grow over time. Alternatively, you can wait until you need the income before taking out the credit line (see **Credit Lines** below).

**Warning:** Do not use a lump sum drawn under a reverse mortgage credit line, whether a HECM line or any other, to invest. There are no safe investments available that pay a return higher than the cost of the reverse mortgage to you. Borrowing at 6% to invest at 3% is dumb.

**Interest Rates:** Among the complexities of the HECM program is that it uses two interest rates. The rate the borrower pays is the one-year Treasury rate plus a margin. This rate determines how fast the borrower's debt rises over time. But borrowers have a choice between two variants of it. They can select between a) monthly rate adjustments, a margin over the Treasury rate of 1.5%, and a limit on rate change over the life of the loan of 10% and b) annual adjustments, a margin of 2.1%, and a limit on rate change of 5% over the life of the loan and 2% in any one year. Most borrowers select a), which is what I would select.

The second rate, called the "expected rate," is used in calculating the credit line/payments borrowers can receive. It is the 10-year Treasury rate, plus the margin used in the rate selected by the borrower. In contrast to the first rate, which adjusts regularly, the expected rate is fixed for each borrower. If a borrower changes the payment plan, the expected rate used in calculating the new payment is the one set at the outset of the transaction.

**Credit Lines:** Most borrowers who take reverse mortgages under HECM elect credit lines rather than term or tenure payments. In calculating credit lines, FHA assumes that properties will appreciate 4% a year between the time the reverse mortgage is taken out and the time the investor acquires the property. On the other hand, the calculation of term and tenure payments is very stingy. The calculation for term payments assumes that no one dies during the term and the calculation for tenure payments assumes the borrower will live to be 100.

In addition, a credit line has more flexibility than tenure or term payments. A borrower could draw the same amounts under a credit line as under tenure or term payments, while retaining the flexibility to stop it or expand it at any time. Further, the unused portion of the HECM credit line increases every year at the same rate as the borrower pays on accumulated debt.

A question faced by many seniors with no immediate need for

funds is whether their HECM credit lines will be larger in, say, five years if they take it immediately or if they wait for five years. Waiting increases the credit line, both because the borrower will be five years older and because the house value used in calculating the line is likely to be higher.

For example, using the interest rates that prevailed in early 2003, a borrower 75 years old with a $100,000 house would have a credit line of $63,100, which if unused would grow to $74,500 after five years. If the borrower waited five years but the house did not appreciate, the credit line in five years would be $68,000, with the increase due entirely to the borrower being five years older. If the borrower waited five years and the house appreciated by 3% a year, so that in five years it was worth $115,900, the credit line in five years would be $79,600.

In general, therefore, if you don't need the money now, it is better to wait until you do. Even if the house does not appreciate, if it is currently valued well above the FHA loan limit, the annual increase in the limit will increase the line. The only situation where it is not better to wait is when the house is currently valued at less than the FHA loan limit and has no prospect of appreciation.

Note that under Fannie Mae's Home Keeper Plan, discussed below, the credit line does not increase over time at all. Hence, the only way you can get a larger line is to delay doing the deal. In contrast, credit lines increase under the Financial Freedom plan even faster than they do under HECM, so sitting on a credit line may be a more viable strategy.

**Refinancing:** In many cases, borrowers who have taken out reverse mortgages under HECM in the past and still live in their house could increase the amount they draw by refinancing. Because they are older and their house is likely to have appreciated, a recalculation of the net principal limit will provide an increased line. Even if the house has not appreciated, if its value exceeded the FHA loan limit at the outset, increases in the limit have the same effect as appreciation. In addition, interest rates may be lower than when they took out their loan.

Refinancing does require a new set of settlement costs, including a new insurance premium. At this writing, the market was waiting for HUD to issue new regulations implementing legislation passed by Congress whereby mortgage insurance would be charged only on the increment to property value above that on the first loan. Implementation of that rule should encourage more borrowers to refinance.

**Costs:** HECMs and other reverse mortgage programs involve upfront costs, which can generally be financed. FHA allows lenders to charge an origination fee of $2,000 or 2% of the house value, whichever is less. FHA charges an insurance premium of 2% of value at closing, while a monthly premium of ½% per year is included in the interest rate you pay on your loan balance. Other closing costs vary by area but run about $3,000. The calculator at www.nrmla.org shows all these costs, which are deducted from the credit line.

A servicing fee is also added to the loan balance each month. It is $30 if rate adjustments are annual and $35 if they are monthly. In addition, to ensure that there is enough money available to pay for servicing over the life of the loan, the present value of these payments is deducted from the credit line as a servicing fee "set-aside." It is not debt, but it is deducted from the principal limit in calculating the net principal limit.

***Fannie Mae's Home Keeper Mortgage:*** Fannie Mae is the major investor in FHA HECMs and also has its own reverse mortgage product, called Home Keeper. It carries a higher interest rate than the HECM, but it does not have an insurance premium. Home Keeper offers a line of credit, tenure payments, and combinations of the two, but no term payments. Credit lines are fixed, rather than increasing over time as they do with the HECM.

On homes with values that do not exceed the FHA loan limit, owners do better with an HECM than with a Home Keeper. But because Fannie Mae's loan limit is higher than the highest FHA limit, an owner whose house value exceeds the FHA limit may get a larger credit line under Home Keeper. This doesn't necessarily mean that Home Keeper is preferable in such a case, but it might be, depending on the preferences of the owner.

Here is an example as of early 2003. An owner age 79 has a $300,000 house in a county where the FHA loan limit is $184,666. Fannie Mae's limit is $322,700. Both mortgages are adjustable monthly.

|  | FHA HECM | Home Keeper |
|---|---|---|
| **Initial Interest Rate** | 3.41% | 4.77% |
| **Maximum Credit Line** | $120,252 | $132,753 |
| **Credit Line in 5 Years** (assuming no draws on line) | $146,869 | $132,753 |
| **Tenure Payment** | $883.16 | $1,162.06 |
| **Mortgage Balance at Age 95** (assuming tenure payments) | $252,868 | $363,860 |

If this owner had no heirs and wanted the largest possible monthly payment for life starting immediately, Home Keeper would be the right choice. She probably would do better taking the full credit line and purchasing an annuity from a life insurance company, rather than taking tenure payments. However, the purchased annuity would be larger under Home Keeper because the credit line is larger.

On the other hand, if the owner wanted to leave an estate and could afford to take the lower HECM payment, she might elect the HECM because of the smaller buildup of debt. She also might go that route if her immediate need for cash was small, because the unused portion of the line grows under the HECM program.

If the owner has no immediate need for funds, she should select neither program. The best option in such case is to wait because the passage of time increases the potential draw.

***Financial Freedom's Cash Account:*** This is a private program that offers only a line of credit and has no limit on property value. Costs are higher than on HECM or Home Keeper, but the draws will be higher on high-value properties.

The break point in property value depends on the age of the borrower. An owner aged 79 will receive a larger draw on the Cash Account than on HECM or Home Keeper if her house is worth $400,000. But an owner aged 62 has to have a house worth $700,000 before she can draw more under a Cash Account.

Financial Freedom also offers an equity participation feature on Cash Account that will increase the draw but use more equity. The interest rate used to calculate the credit line is reduced by 1% in exchange for the payment of 5% of property value at termination. The return on the transaction to Financial Freedom is capped at 8% above the initial interest rate.

*Lenders:* Elderly homeowners interested in a reverse mortgage should select a lender who belongs to the National Reverse Mortgage Lenders Association (NRMLA). The 120 or so members subscribe to a code of conduct that appears on www.reversemortgage.org. That site also contains a list of lenders by state and shows the reverse mortgage programs that each lender offers.

---

**Scheduled Mortgage Payment** *The amount the borrower is obliged to pay each period, including interest, principal, and mortgage insurance, under the terms of the mortgage contract.*

Paying less than the scheduled amount results in delinquency; paying more results in a partial prepayment.

On FRMs and ARMs that do not allow negative amortization, the scheduled payment is the fully amortizing payment, unless the loan has an interest-only option for some period at the beginning, such as five or 10 years. In that case, the scheduled payment is the interest-only payment until the end of the interest-only period, when it becomes the fully amortizing payment.

On ARMs that allow negative amortization, the scheduled payment may be determined by the lender in a number of ways, which can change over the life of the instrument. Some of these ARMs also allow the borrower to elect from alternative payment plans during the early years of the loan. Whatever form the scheduled payment takes in the early years, however, at some point it becomes the fully amortizing payment.

---

**Second Mortgage** *A loan with a second-priority claim against a property in the event that the borrower defaults.*

*Second Mortgages Versus Home Equity Lines:* A second mortgage is any loan that involves a second lien on the property. Some second mortgages are for a fixed dollar amount paid out at one time, in the same way as a first mortgage. As with firsts, such seconds may be fixed rate or adjustable rate.

A home equity line of credit (HELOC) is usually a second mortgage also, but instead of being paid out at one time, it is structured as a line of credit. (They are frequently referred to as "home equity lines.") A HELOC allows the borrower to draw an amount at any time up to some maximum. They are always adjustable rate. *See* **HELOC**.

A line of credit is most convenient when cash needs are stretched out over time. A common example is a series of home improvements, one followed by another. Fixed-dollar seconds are best when all the money is needed at one time. Many home purchasers take out such seconds to avoid mortgage insurance on the first mortgage or the higher interest rate on a jumbo loan.

When taking a fixed-dollar second, borrowers can select between fixed and adjustable rates, as they prefer. When taking a HELOC, they take an adjustable, and if they want a fixed they can refinance into a fixed-dollar second after they have drawn as much as they intend to borrow on the line.

**Seconds Priced Higher than Firsts:** Second mortgages are riskier to lenders than first mortgages. In the event of default, the second mortgage lender gets repaid only if there is something left after the first lender is fully repaid. Hence, the rate will be higher on the second, provided everything else (mortgage and property type, borrower credit, etc.) is the same. Of course, if the second mortgage is a line of credit with an adjustable rate, it may well be priced below the rate on a first mortgage with a fixed rate.

**Refinancing a First with a Second:** As a general rule, it is not a good idea to take out a second to pay off a first, because seconds are priced higher. If you take out a second mortgage to repay the first, the second becomes the first, which is a gift to the lender: you are paying a second mortgage price on a first mortgage.

But there is at least one exception to this rule. Borrowers with a high-rate first mortgage with a small balance may find it more advantageous to pay off the first with a second rather than refinance the first. This reflects the higher settlement costs on the first.

Some borrowers lower their rate by refinancing a first with a

HELOC. In the process, however, they are exposing themselves to the risk of future rate increases. HELOCs are much more exposed than standard ARMs.

***Using a Second to Avoid Mortgage Insurance:*** Borrowers who put down less than 20% on a first mortgage usually must purchase mortgage insurance. However, a borrower can take an 80% first mortgage combined with a 5%, 10%, or 15% second mortgage, and avoid mortgage insurance. Such combination loans are referred to as 80/5/15s, 80/10/10s, and 80/15/5s. An 80/15/5 is an 80% first, 15% second, and 5% down.

Whether a combination loan saves the borrower money depends on a variety of factors. For example, a combination loan is more advantageous than a single loan with mortgage insurance the smaller the difference in interest rate between the two mortgages, the shorter the term on the second mortgage relative to the term on the first, and the higher your income tax bracket.

These and other factors affecting the costs of both options are pulled together in calculator 13a on my Web site. The calculator shows all the costs of both options over any future period, and the "break-even rate" on the second mortgage, which is the highest rate it makes sense to pay. The combination loan will save you money if the market rate on the second is below the break-even rate.

***Using a Second to Avoid Jumbos:*** Jumbo loans are larger than the maximum size loan that Fannie Mae and Freddie Mac can purchase. In 2003, the maximum was $322,700. Jumbos carry interest rates from 1/4% to 1/2% higher than the "conforming" loans purchased by the agencies.

Borrowers who need a loan above the conforming loan maximum, but not too much above it, may save money by taking a first mortgage for the maximum and a second for the amount required above the maximum. Calculator 13a can be used to determine whether a conforming loan plus a second will be less costly than a jumbo.

### Second Mortgage Versus Cash-Out Refinance:

*See* **Refinance/*Refinancing to Raise Cash*/Cash-Out Versus Second Mortgage**.

*Second Mortgage Versus 401(k) Loan:* Many borrowers have the choice of borrowing on a second mortgage or borrowing against their 401(k) plan. Several factors bear on this decision.

**Relative Interest Cost:** The general rule is that you select the one offering the lowest after-tax cost. On a second mortgage, the after-tax cost is the interest rate less the tax savings. You can calculate this by multiplying the interest rate by one minus your tax rate. For example, if the rate on a home equity loan is 8.5% and you are in the 28% tax bracket, the after-tax cost is $8.5 \times (1 - .28)$ or 6.12%.

The cost of borrowing from your 401(k) is not the rate you charge yourself because that goes from one pocket to another. The cost is what your loan would have earned had you kept the money in the 401(k). This is sometimes called an "opportunity cost." Since your 401(k) accumulates tax free, the total return on the fund is a close approximation of the after-tax cost.

Of course, taxes must eventually be paid on the earnings on your 401(k). But this doesn't happen until you retire, and even then the tax payments will be stretched out over time unless you elect to withdraw a lump sum.

**Consequences of Unemployment:** The two fund sources have different consequences should you be laid off. Unless the 401K loan is repaid within a month or two of losing your job, it is considered by the IRS as a taxable distribution on which income taxes, and perhaps a 10% early withdrawal penalty, are due. A second mortgage loan need not be repaid if you are laid off. On the other hand, you must continue making the payments on the second mortgage or risk losing your home.

Some other possible negative consequences of second mortgages that borrowers should factor into their decision are discussed immediately below.

*Loss of Flexibility from Negative Equity:* A second mortgage reduces the equity in your house, in some cases converting positive equity to negative equity. Borrowers with negative equity lose flexibility. It becomes difficult or impossible to refinance should a favorable opportunity to do so arise, and it may also be impossible to sell. Second mortgages cannot be transferred to a new house. The sale requires that all liens be paid off, so if the liens add up to more than the house is worth, the seller must come up with the needed cash.

*Subordination by Second Mortgage Lender:* A borrower with a second mortgage can't refinance the first mortgage unless either the second is refinanced as well or the second mortgage lender agrees to allow it by signing a subordination agreement. Without such an agreement, paying off the first mortgage automatically converts the second mortgage into a first mortgage and any new mortgage would become a second.

The problem is that second mortgage lenders have varying policies toward subordination. Some will do it for a modest fee. Some will do it subject to conditions, such as that any new first mortgage not be cash-out, which would weaken the second mortgage. And some won't do it at all! Lenders' policies toward subordination are not a required disclosure, and very few borrowers find out what their lender's policy is until they try to refinance their first mortgage.

If you do take a second mortgage, ask the lender about its subordination policy immediately after asking about the interest rate. *If the lender doesn't allow subordination, march out the door.* There's another second mortgage lender down the street. If they say they do allow it, ask about any conditions, if there is a fee, and how long it will take. If the answers are satisfactory, get it in writing and make sure it is incorporated in the loan documents so that if the loan is sold the new lender will be bound by it.

*Negative Amortization ARM May Prevent a Second Mortgage:* Mortgage lenders may be unwilling to make a second mortgage loan if the first mortgage is an ARM that allows negative amortization.

Second mortgage lenders assess the risk on a second by the amount of equity available to pay them. The equity equals the property value less the balance on the first mortgage. Since the loan balance on the great majority of first mortgages goes down every month, the equity available for the second rises every month.

But a negative amortization ARM is a different story. On these loans, the balance can *rise* over time, which reduces the equity protecting the second mortgage. Some lenders will reject second mortgage applications out of hand when the first is a negative amortization ARM, without considering whether or not the equity protecting them might be adequate.

For example, I ran into a case where the balance on the negative amortization ARM was only 60% of the current property value and could not rise by more than 25% in a worst case. This would bring it to 75% of current value in a worst case. The application was rejected, although the same lender would make seconds in cases where the balance on a FRM was 80% or even higher. The lender heard the dreaded words "negative amortization" and shut its ears.

---

**Secondary Mortgage Markets** *Markets in which mortgages or mortgage-backed securities are bought and sold.*

**"Whole Loan" Markets Versus Securities Markets:** Secondary mortgage markets are of two general types. "Whole loan" markets involve the sale of mortgages themselves, sometimes on a loan-by-loan basis but more often in blocks. Such markets, which arose in the U.S. soon after World War II, primarily involve the one-time sale of newly originated mortgages to traditional mortgage lenders.

In the 1970s, markets also developed in mortgage-backed securities issued against pools of mortgages. Instead of selling, e.g., $50 million of whole loans, the loans are segregated in a pool and $50 million of securities are issued against the pool. These securities are actively traded after the initial issuance, and they are attractive to investors that would not ordinarily hold mortgages, such as pension funds or mutual funds.

Mortgage-backed securities always have some kind of "credit enhancement," or guarantees of payment beyond the promises of the individual mortgage borrowers. The most important of the guarantors are Ginny Mae, Fanny Mae, and Freddie Mac (see below).

**Impact on Interest Rates:** Secondary markets reduce mortgage interest rates in several ways. First, they increase competition by encouraging the development of a new industry of loan originators. Called different names in different countries (in the U.S. they are called "mortgage companies" or "mortgage banks"), they all have in common that they require little capital and tend to be aggressive competitors.

Absent secondary markets, the only institutions originating mortgage loans are those with the capacity to hold them permanently, termed "portfolio lenders." In small communities especially, borrowers may be at the mercy of one or a few local banks or savings and loan associations. The entry of mortgage companies that can sell into the secondary market breaks up these local fiefdoms, much to the benefit of borrowers. The development of whole loan markets in the U.S. is largely responsible for the growth of this industry.

Secondary markets also increase efficiency by encouraging a specialization of lending functions that reduces costs. Portfolio lenders typically do everything connected to originating and servicing loans, even though they may do some things quite inefficiently. Secondary markets, in contrast, create pressures to break functions apart and price them separately, and this imposes a discipline on mortgage companies to concentrate on what they do best. Many mortgage companies have ceased servicing loans, for example, because they can do better selling the servicing to companies that specialize in that function.

In addition, conversion of mortgages into mortgage-backed securities permits a better distribution of the risk of holding fixed-rate mortgages (FRMs). As one example, depository institutions don't want to take the risk of funding long-term assets with short-term liabilities. But they can originate FRMs, convert them to securities, and sell the securities to pension funds, which have long-term liabilities.

Mortgage-backed securities also are "liquid" while mortgages themselves are not. This means that in most cases mortgage-backed securities can be sold for full value within the day whereas selling the same amount of mortgages could take weeks. Because most investors value liquidity and are willing to accept a lower yield to get it, converting illiquid mortgages to liquid securities puts downward pressure on the rates charged to borrowers.

***Widening the Market:*** Secondary markets have also vastly expanded the size of the borrower pool. Portfolio lenders generally restrict their loans to "A-quality" borrowers, in large part because of regulatory concerns about their safety and soundness. Secondary markets, in contrast, can access investors who are prepared to hold risky loans if the price is right. The result has been the emergence of the so-called "sub-prime market" and a new category of borrowers—borrowers who previously had recourse only to family, friends, home sellers, and loan sharks.

**Shopping Complexities:** The downside of secondary markets from a borrower's perspective is that shopping for a mortgage becomes more complex. The secondary market is largely responsible for market nichification, which makes it difficult for a borrower to determine whether a price quote applies to his or her particular deal, and price volatility, which makes it risky to compare a price quote on Monday with one from another loan provider on Tuesday. Nichification and volatility underlie several common scams perpetrated on borrowers by loan providers. *See* **Mortgage Scams and Tricks/ Scams by Loan Providers**.

**Ginny Mae:** The mortgage-backed security market was begun in 1970 by Ginny Mae, a wholly-owned agency of the federal government. The agency guaranteed the payments on securities issued by lenders against pools of FHA and VA mortgages. This program makes money for the Treasury and has been relatively free of controversy.

**Fannie Mae and Freddie Mac:** These firms are "government-sponsored enterprises" (GSEs), which means that they are privately owned, but receive support from the federal government and assume some public responsibilities. The two GSEs today are among the largest corporations in the world and are highly controversial.

**Operations:** The GSEs purchase "conforming" mortgages from the lenders that originate them. They hold some, which are funded by issuance of debt. The remainder are "securitized"—sold in the form of securities that the GSEs guarantee.

Conforming mortgages are those that meet the underwriting requirements of the agencies and are no larger than the largest loan the GSEs are allowed by law to purchase. In 2003 the maximum was $322,700. It is raised every year in line with increases in home prices. Conforming mortgages account for roughly 80% of the conventional (non-FHA/VA) home loan market.

**Government Support:** The major support the GSEs receive from the Federal Government is a special claim for government assistance in the event they ever get into financial trouble. This claim is grounded on their right to borrow from the U.S. Treasury, and on their history—both were public institutions before they became privately owned. As a result, investors consider the notes they issue and the mortgage securities they guarantee almost as good as securities issued by the federal government itself.

**Absence of Competitors:** The GSEs have no competitors in the conforming loan market. Because of their government backing, the GSEs can sell notes and securities at a lower yield than any strictly private secondary market firm. This gives them a monopoly—or rather a duopoly, since there are two of them—in the market in which they operate.

The GSEs do have emulators, however, in the non-conforming market. While the cast of players changes, at any one time there are usually 15 or more strictly private firms that purchase non-conforming loans and securitize them in much the same way as the GSEs.

**Why the Special Treatment?** The government did not select the two firms for special treatment. Both the GSEs began as government entities and the major objective in privatizing them (while retaining government support) was to encourage development of a private secondary market. The other firms arose later, based on the GSE model, so that objective was achieved.

While logic might dictate that the special treatment is no longer required, it has continued. The GSEs are unwilling to give it up and they have become so powerful politically that they have managed to thwart the several attempts that have been made to take it away.

**The Public Stakes:** If you are a potential borrower eligible for a conforming loan, your interest rate will probably be about 3/8% lower than it would be absent the GSEs. This reflects their relatively low funding costs, part of which is passed through to borrowers.

In addition, if you are a low or low-to-moderate-income borrower and/or reside in an underserved area, you might find a loan through a GSE. As part of their public responsibility, the GSEs commit to purchase specified numbers of such loans. How many would not be made without the GSEs, however, is not clear.

As a taxpayer, on the other hand, you have a cause for concern. The low borrowing costs of the GSEs are based on implicit government backing for their $3 trillion-plus of debt and guarantees. If the GSEs ever have a financial disaster, the government will have to bail them out and tax payers will be on the hook for the cost.

A few years ago Congress gave responsibility for monitoring the safety and soundness of GSEs to the Department of Housing and Urban Development (HUD). However, very few informed observers believe that HUD is up to the task.

**A Way Out:** It is possible to gradually reduce the risk of a financial disaster by removing government support without hurting investors who have relied on that support. This could be done by revoking the credit lines the GSEs now have with the Treasury and providing an explicit federal guarantee of all debt and GSE guarantees outstanding on the date the credit line is revoked. An explicit guarantee on the old claims would prevent any repercussions in the financial markets, yet put the markets on notice that new ones are not guaranteed. Over time, the volume of guaranteed claims would gradually decline.

---

**Self-Employed Borrower** *A borrower who must use tax returns to document income rather than information provided by an employer.*

This complicates the process somewhat. *See* **Qualification/*Qualifying Self-Employed Borrowers*.**

---

**Seller Contribution** *A contribution to a borrower's down payment or settlement costs made by a home seller, as an alternative to a price reduction.*

*See* **Down Payment/*Home Seller Contributions*.**

---

**Servicing** *Administering loans between the time of disbursement and the time the loan is fully paid off.*

Servicing includes collecting payments from the borrower, maintaining payment records, providing borrowers and investors with account statements, imposing late charges when the payment is late, and pursuing delinquent borrowers. In many cases, servicing agents also pay property taxes and insurance with money placed in escrow by the borrower.

***The Poor Quality of Servicing Overall:*** From a borrower perspective, the quality of servicing is generally low. The Department of Housing and Urban Development (HUD) reports that two of every five complaints they receive from borrowers involve servicing issues. J.D. Powers and Associates, which measures consumer satisfaction with business services of many kinds, reports that only 10% of borrowers are happy with their servicing agent.

The financial incentives to provide good service, which work in other sectors of our economy, don't work for loan servicing. The borrower selects a lender or mortgage broker, not a servicing agent. The major focus is the price of the loan. Rarely if ever does the expected quality of servicing come into the picture.

Information on the quality of servicing is not generally available, and even if it was, the borrower has no way to know that the lender making the loan will also be servicing it. Most loans are sold shortly after origination, and while servicing sometimes is retained by the seller, often it isn't. In addition, servicing contracts are bought and sold in an active market, much like bonds. This means that any borrower at any time can find his loan suddenly being serviced by a different firm.

The fact that borrowers have little say in who services their loan would not be so bad if they could fire their servicing agent for poor performance, but they can't. The only way to rid yourself of a servicing agent is to refinance, but then you are gambling that the new one will be better, which is a bad bet.

Since borrowers can neither choose nor fire their servicing agents, quality of service has no impact on an agent's bottom line. For most, there is no business reason to provide quality service to borrowers.

***Quality Servicing by a Few:*** A few enlightened firms have adopted the view that the borrowers they are servicing are potential customers for new services. A business strategy of "targeted cross-selling" requires attention to service quality. A borrower who is miffed because his taxes weren't paid on time is a poor candidate for cross-selling. Unfortunately, this approach has not made major inroads in the industry.

**Predatory Servicing:** At the opposite pole are the servicing predators, whose business strategy is to extract as much additional revenue from the borrowers they service as the law allows. Here is an outrageous example:

A borrower made his monthly payment on the 16th of the month—one day after the grace period. Without notice, the lender imposed a late charge on that payment, and then proceeded to collect that charge by deducting it from the following month's payment. That payment was made on time but recorded as late because of the deduction of the late charge from the previous month, which generated still another late charge. Seven consecutive payments were made on time but recorded as late because of the deduction of late charges on the prior payments.

Predatory servicing agents who purchase servicing will examine each note to determine whether they are entitled to shorten the grace period or raise the late fee. If there is some excuse for considering the property to be underinsured, the agent will purchase over-priced insurance and add the cost to the loan balance. Extra payments to principal will not be credited in a timely fashion and the borrower will not know because monthly statements are incomplete.

**Recourse:** Since borrowers can't fire their servicing agents, what can they do to protect themselves? If you have been mistreated, you should file a written complaint with the lender addressed to customer service. Do not include it with your mortgage payment, which you should continue to make separately. State:

*Your loan number.*

*Names on loan documents.*

*Property and/or mailing address.*

*This is a "qualified written request" under Section 6 of the Real Estate Settlement Procedures Act (RESPA).*

*I am writing because:*

*[Describe the problem and the action you believe the lender should take.]*

*[Describe any previous attempts to resolve the issue, including conversations with customer service.]*

*[If it is relevant to the dispute, request a copy of your payment history.]*
*[List a daytime telephone number.]*

*I understand that under Section 6 of RESPA you are required to acknowledge my request within 20 business days and must try to resolve the issue within 60 business days.*

If this doesn't do the trick, you can file a complaint with HUD. You can also sue. According to HUD, "A borrower may bring a private law suit, or a group of borrowers may bring a class action suit, within three years, against a servicer who fails to comply with the provisions of Section 6."

You can also file a complaint with the government agency that regulates the servicing agent. Here are Web sites you can use to contact these agencies:

- For national banks, www.occ.treas.gov/customer.htm.
- For federally-chartered savings and loan associations, www.ots.treas.gov/contact.html.
- For state-chartered banks and savings and loans, www.lendingprofessional.com/licensing.html.
- For mortgage banking firms, www.aarmr.org/lists/members-IE.html.

If you don't know the proper agency, you can send the complaint to the Consumer Protection Division of the state attorney general. It will be forwarded to the relevant state or federal agency.

**Preventative Measures:** Borrowers should periodically check their transaction history to make certain that a) payments are always applied to the balance at the end of the preceding month, b) tax and insurance payments from escrow are correct and there have been no double payments, c) rate adjustments on ARMs are in accordance with the method stipulated in the note, and d) there isn't anything in the history that looks "funny."

Any borrower who does not receive a complete transaction statement at least annually should periodically submit a "qualified written request" for one using the form described above.

**Servicing for Borrowers:** Under existing arrangements, servicing systems are designed to meet the needs of lenders and they won't meet the needs of borrowers until they are redesigned for that purpose. This is possible and may be in the cards. Borrowers must be willing to pay for the service.

A servicing system for borrowers (SSB) would not replace existing servicing systems. The firms providing the services described below could be called "second-tier servicers." Borrowers would make their payments to second-tier servicers, which would then make payments to the primary servicers.

With the payments going through its hands, the second-tier servicer has command of information on the borrower's payment history. In contrast to the primary servicer, however, the second-tier servicer will use the information to provide useful services to the borrower. The services, for which the borrower will pay a modest monthly fee, will be provided over the Internet.

**Access to Payment History:** The major purpose is to provide peace of mind that the lender is properly crediting mortgage payments. The SSB would allow borrowers to monitor their accounts continuously and the "what-if" capacity would allow them to experiment with different future payment patterns.

**Access to Details of ARM Rate Adjustments:** The major purpose is to provide peace of mind that the new rate has been properly calculated. The SSB would show the details of the ARM rate adjustment, rather than just the resulting new rate, which is all borrowers get now. Borrowers will also be able to forecast what the new rate will be months in advance so they can prepare for a possible refinancing.

**Cost-Reduction Refinance Opportunities:** The purpose is to flag profitable refinance opportunities. The SSB would continually monitor the relationship between the borrower's interest rate, current market rates, and the borrower's credit as affected by his or her mortgage payment record.

**Cash-Raising Opportunities:** The purpose is to provide borrowers who request it with a tool for assessing alternative ways to raise cash. The system would already know many of the required data inputs, including the borrower's existing mortgage balance and terms, as well as current market terms. Other data inputs, such as the amount of cash needed, would be entered by the borrower.

**PMI Termination:** The purpose is to give the borrower a "heads-up" that it may be possible to terminate mortgage insurance. Automatic termination under the federal legislation passed in 1999 does not take account of extra payments to principal or house price appreciation. Earlier termination that does take account of these factors requires that the borrower take the initiative.

**Alternative Payment Options:** The purpose is to allow borrowers to pay biweekly, bimonthly, or weekly. Borrowers may prefer one of these options because they find the schedule more convenient or because they want to build an early payoff plan around shorter payment periods.

---

**Servicing Agent** *The party who services a loan, who may or may not be the lender who originated it.*

*See* **Servicing**.

---

**Settlement Costs** *Total costs charged to the borrower that must be paid at closing, by the borrower, the home seller, or the lender.*

In dealing directly with a lender, settlement costs can be divided into the following categories:

1. Fees paid to lender.
2. Lender-controlled fees paid to third parties.
3. Other fees paid to third parties.
4. Other settlement costs.

*Fees Paid to Lender:* Lender fees fall into two categories: those expressed as a percent of the loan and those expressed in dollars.

**Fees Expressed as Percent of Loan:** These consist of points and origination fees. Origination fees are points in disguise. Reporting services that publish information on mortgage rates and points do not show origination fees, so lenders that charge an origination fee may appear to have lower fees. This is pure gamesmanship. The borrower's concern is the total of all charges expressed as a percent of the loan amount, whatever they are called.

**Lender Fees Expressed in Dollars:** Some of the common lender fees expressed in dollars cover processing, tax service, flood certification, underwriting, wire transfer, document preparation, courier, and lender inspection. They are almost always itemized, a deplorable practice that goes back to the days when interest rates were regulated and lenders had to justify their fees in terms of reimbursement for costs.

From the borrower's perspective, what these fees are called doesn't matter, and whether they are cost-justified doesn't matter. All that matters is their sum total, which borrowers should use in shopping.

Shoppers take account of points in selecting a lender because lenders always report points alongside the interest rate. Dollar fees and origination fees, however, are not reported in the media and generally are not volunteered by lenders. For this reason, shoppers often fail to consider them in selecting a lender. Trying to negotiate them afterwards is usually fruitless.

Shoppers should ask for dollar fees and should expect the lender to guarantee them through to closing. In contrast to guaranteeing a rate and points, which exposes a lender to market risk, there is virtually no risk in guaranteeing dollar fees. The same is true of an origination fee.

Some retail lenders guarantee their dollar fees now. These include ELOAN.com, IndyMac.com, HomeLoanCenter.com, Mortgage.com, Mortgage.etrade.com, and Countrywide.com. If they can do it, any lender can, and they will if shoppers demand it. Under HUD proposals pending at the time of writing, the guarantee would be mandatory.

***Lender-Controlled Fees to Third Parties:*** These are fees for services ordered by lenders from third parties and include the costs of appraisals, credit reports, and (when needed) pest inspections. Lenders know the prices of these services and can easily guarantee them in addition to their own fees. Countrywide.com, Mortgage.com, and Mortgage.etrade.com include appraisals and credit reports in their guarantees.

***Other Fees Paid to Third Parties:*** These fees are not controlled by and may not be known by the lender. The most important are title-related services and settlement services. If you are in an area in which it can pay to shop for them, you can do it after selecting the lender. Mortgage.com includes third-party fees in its guarantee, except for charges of governments.

***Other Settlement Costs:*** These are a miscellany of charges, which require little vigilance by the borrower.

- Government charges, such as transaction taxes, are what they are.

- Per diem interest is interest for the period between the closing date and the first day of the following month. At worst, the lender might try to tack on an extra day or two.

- Escrow reserve is your money placed on deposit with the lender so the lender can pay your taxes and insurance. The amount is based on a HUD formula.

- Hazard insurance is your homeowner's policy, which you purchase from a carrier of your choice.

***Good Faith Estimate (GFE):*** Under the Real Estate Settlement Procedures Act of 1974 (RESPA), lenders are required to provide borrowers with a Good Faith Estimate of settlement costs. It is a confusing and largely useless document. The GFE encourages itemized pricing by providing space on the form for any expense category a lender wishes to use. Further, the GFE intermixes lender charges with charges of third parties (for insurance, taxes, and the like) and *total lender charges are not shown anywhere.* The GFE thus provides borrowers with all the detail for which they have no use, but no total, which is the only number they really need.

Furthermore, because some third-party charges are not known with certainty until late in the process, all costs are viewed as "estimates," including the lenders' own charges, which obviously are known with certainty. Viewing lender charges as estimates encourages the practice of some less scrupulous loan officers and mortgage brokers of "overlooking" certain charges at the outset, only to discover them later when it is too late for the borrower to back out.

***Strategy in Shopping Lenders:*** In shopping lenders, you want the total of points, including the origination fee if any, dollar fees, and lender-controlled fees paid to third parties. Ask if they will guarantee all these fees except points in writing.

The common mistake that shoppers make is to select a lender without knowing any of the lender charges except points, then try to negotiate other charges afterwards. Typically they do this after they receive a Good Faith Estimate (GFE).

But challenging individual cost items is not an effective way to control lender fees. Typical borrowers have little to no factual basis for challenging a cost item. Even if they have such knowledge, their bargaining power is weak. Having already selected the lender, few are prepared to walk from the deal, and the lender knows this.

Furthermore, even if a determined borrower succeeds in bludgeoning the lender into making a change, the determined lender can get it back somewhere else. The costs shown on the GFE are "estimates" and can be different at closing than they were the day before closing. This is a game the borrower can't win.

***Shopping Total Settlement Costs:*** Some shoppers adopt a different strategy, which seems to make a lot of sense. They reason that what matters is total settlement costs, so they select the lender on that basis. Instead of shopping lender fees, they shop total settlement costs.

Indeed, this approach is the foundation of new rules regarding settlement costs that have been proposed by HUD. Under these rules, borrowers will be able to obtain one binding price covering all settlement costs from lenders electing this option. Until that happens, however, borrowers can't use this strategy effectively because lenders will not commit to any figures on total settlement costs that they might quote to shoppers.

Suppose, for example, you are deciding between 7% 30-year fixed-rate mortgages offered by two lenders. Lender A quotes total settlement costs of $4,000, compared with $4,200 for lender B. Lender A looks like the better deal.

Closer inspection reveals, however, that A's own fees are $2,000 and A has estimated other costs of $2,000. B's own fees, in contrast, are $1,900 and B has estimated other costs at $2,300. The correct choice is B because B has the lower lender fees, which lenders can guarantee. The other costs are estimates. While we don't know which is closer to the mark, we do know that the actual figure will almost certainly not be affected by whether the shopper selects A or B.

Since lenders being shopped for total settlement costs have an incentive to err on the low side, we can guess that B's estimate probably will be closer to the mark. Whether A deliberately low-balled to get the business or made a "good faith" mistake, there is no way to know.

The bottom line is that, until HUD changes the rules, shoppers who want to control their settlement costs should focus on lender fees only. The alternative is to shop for a no-cost loan, on which lenders do accept responsibility for most settlement costs. The price is a higher interest rate, not a good deal for people who expect to be in their homes a long time. *See* **No-Cost Mortgage**.

*Dealing with a Mortgage Broker:* If the shopper is dealing with a mortgage broker rather than a lender, the process is more complicated in the sense that the broker's fee is one more settlement cost to consider. But it is simpler in the sense that the broker keeps the lender honest on fixed-dollar fees.

While some retail lenders view fixed-dollar fees as an easy way to generate additional revenue from unwary borrowers, wholesale lenders don't because it would cause them problems with brokers. For this reason, lender fees differ very little from one wholesale lender to another. Dealing with a mortgage broker pretty much eliminates fixed-dollar lender fees as an issue to the shopper. Mortgage brokers can also help borrowers find third-party services at competitive prices.

The upshot is that shoppers who deal with a mortgage broker can shift their focus from shopping settlement costs to negotiating the broker's fee. Just make sure that the broker fee includes any payment to the broker from the lender. For example, if you agree on a fee of $3,000 and the broker gets $1,500 from the lender, your payment should be the difference of $1,500. Upfront Mortgage Brokers operate this way as a matter of course, but many other brokers are willing to do business this way with educated borrowers who understand the value of broker services.

---

**Shared Appreciation Mortgage (SAM)** *A mortgage on which the borrower gives up a share in future price appreciation in exchange for a lower interest rate and/or interest deferral.*

SAMs in the private market had a brief flurry in the early '80s but died out quickly and an attempt to revive them in 2000 was unsuccessful. Some cities on the West Coast offer second mortgage SAMs to residents with incomes below some maximum. Reverse mortgage SAMs have also appeared in small numbers.

**Shopping Site**   *A multi-lender Web site that offered borrowers the capacity to shop among multiple competing lenders.*

At one point, there were five such sites, including one sponsored by Microsoft and one by Intuit. By 2003, they were all gone.

**Short Sale**   *An agreement between a mortgage borrower in distress and the lender that allows the borrower to sell the house and remit the proceeds to the lender.*

A short sale is an alternative to foreclosure or a deed in lieu of foreclosure. *See* **Payment Problems/*Position of the Lender*/**Permanent Problem**.

**Silent Second**   *A second mortgage offered at preferential (subsidized) terms to those who qualify.*

For example, a labor union may offer members who are first-time home buyers a silent second to finance closing costs or the down payment. The second might bear no interest and might not be repayable until the first mortgage is repaid or the property is sold.

**Simple Interest**   *A transaction in which interest is not paid on interest—there is no compounding.*

For example, if you deposit $1,000 in an account that pays 5% a year simple interest, you would receive $50 interest in year one and another $50 in year two. If interest were compounded annually, you would receive $52.50 in year two.

All deposit accounts compound interest, however, because if they didn't, depositors would shuffle accounts between banks. In my example, you could withdraw the $1050 at the end of year one, put it into another bank, and earn $52.50 in year two.

**Simple Interest Biweekly Mortgage** *A biweekly mortgage on which biweekly payments are applied to the balance every two weeks, rather than monthly, as on a conventional biweekly.*

See **Biweekly Mortgage/*Simple Interest Biweeklies***.

**Simple Interest Mortgage** *A mortgage on which interest is calculated daily based on the balance on the day of payment, rather than monthly, as on the standard mortgage.*

See **Amortization/*Simple Interest Mortgages***.

**Single-Lender Web Site** *A Web site of an individual lender offering loans to consumers.*

They are easy to identify because the name of the lender usually will be prominently displayed on the screen. They are not easy to shop, however, because very few of the thousands of sites provide prices that are customized to the individual transaction. I have tried to help by evaluating a number of the better sites against this and other criteria, publishing the results on my Web site. However, it takes a determined and fairly sophisticated shopper to use this type of information effectively. It is not what most shoppers want.

Most Internet shoppers want a list of lenders in whom they can have confidence, who will provide them with the information they need to make an informed decision *before* applying for a mortgage, and who also guarantee them fair treatment during the period *after* they apply through to closing. To meet this need, I developed the Upfront Mortgage Lender (UML) program. *See* **Upfront Mortgage Lenders**.

**Stated Assets** *A documentation rule where the borrower discloses assets and their source but the lender does not verify the amount.*

See **Documentation Requirements/*Stated Assets or No Asset Verification***.

**Stated Income** *A documentation rule where the borrower discloses income and its source but the lender does not verify the amount.*

See **Documentation Requirements/*Stated Income-Verified Assets***.

**Streamlined Refinancing** *Refinancing that omits some of the standard risk control measures and is therefore quicker and less costly.*

The rationale for streamlined refinancing is that, while it is an entirely new loan, the information from the previous loan available to the lender retains validity. In addition, valuable information may be available on the borrower's payment history.

The extent to which a lender can offer streamlining depends on how much information and how much discretion the lender has. A new lender that was the original lender and still owns the loan has the greatest leeway. A new lender that was the original lender but is now servicing the loan for someone else has the same information but less discretion. A new lender that was not the original lender and is not servicing the old loan doesn't have the information needed to justify streamlined refinancing.

*See* **Refinance/*Refinancing with the Current Lender*.**

---

**Subordinate Financing** *A second mortgage on a property that is not paid off when the first mortgage is refinanced.*

The second mortgage lender must allow subordination of the second to the new first mortgage. *See* **Second Mortgage/*Subordination by Second Mortgage Lender*.**

---

**Subordination Policy** *The policy of a second mortgage lender toward allowing a borrower to refinance the first mortgage while leaving the second in place.*

*See* **Second Mortgage/*Subordination by Second Mortgage Lender*.**

---

**Sub-Prime Borrower** *A borrower who does not meet the underwriting requirements of mainstream lenders.*

Sub-prime borrowers pay more than prime borrowers and are sometimes taken advantage of. *See* **Predatory Lending.**

---

**Sub-Prime Lender** *A lender who specializes in lending to sub-prime borrowers.*

## Swing Loan

*Same as* **Bridge Loan**.

---

**Tax Deductibility (of Interest and Points)** *The provision of the U.S. tax code that allows homeowners to deduct mortgage interest payments from income before computing taxes.*

Points and origination fees are also deductible, but not lender fees expressed in dollars or any other settlement costs. Interest deductibility is politically untouchable in the U.S., although it is often criticized by economists and is found in few other countries.

Interest deductibility enters a number of decisions made by homeowners or purchasers, sometimes when it shouldn't.

***Borrow for the Deduction?*** It never makes sense to borrow for the sole purpose of obtaining a tax deduction, even if you are in the highest tax bracket. If you are in the 40% bracket, for example, and you borrow $100,000 at 5%, you pay $500 of interest in month one and save $200 in taxes. Your net loss is $300.

If you invest the $100,000, the interest earnings reduce the loss. However, borrowing at 5% to invest does not become a profitable strategy unless you can earn *more than* 5% on the investment. Since this is not possible without incurring default risk, the required return on the investment must be above 5% plus an increment sufficient to compensate for this risk.

Assuming that the interest on investment is taxable, comparisons of mortgage rate with investment return can be made either before tax or after tax. For example, if the borrower in the 40% tax bracket would pay 5% on the mortgage and earn 4% on investment, the investment is a loser before tax (5% less 4%), or after tax (3% less 2.4%). If the investment is tax-exempt, however, its return should be compared with the after-tax cost of the mortgage.

Note that the very same principles hold when the issue is whether to invest in mortgage loan repayment, as opposed to acquiring some other type of investment. *See* **Partial Prepayments (or Paying Off Early)/*Making Extra Payments as an Investment***.

***Should Mortgage Insurance Also Be Deductible?*** The IRS is inconsistent in not allowing mortgage insurance premiums to be deducted in the same way as interest. *See* **Private Mortgage Insurance/***Why Aren't PMI Premiums Deductible?*

---

**Teaser Rate** *The initial interest rate on an ARM, when it is below the fully indexed rate.*

   *See* **Adjustable Rate Mortgage (ARM)/***Fully-Indexed Rate*.

---

**Temporary Buydown**  *A reduction in the mortgage payment made by a homebuyer in the early years of the loan in exchange for an upfront cash deposit provided by the buyer, the seller, or both.*

*How Temporary Buydowns Work:* Temporary buydowns are a tool for borrowers purchasing a home who don't have enough income, relative to their monthly mortgage payment and other expenses, to meet lender requirements. To use a temporary buydown, the borrower must have access to extra cash. The cash can be the borrower's or it can be contributed by a home seller anxious to complete a sale. The cash funds an escrow account from which the payments that supplement the borrower's payments are drawn.

While the borrower's payments are reduced in the early years, the payments received by the lender are the same as they would have been without the buydown. The shortfalls from the borrower are offset by withdrawals from the escrow account.

Temporary buydowns are not a type of mortgage. They are an option that can be attached to any type. Most temporary buydowns, however, are attached to fixed-rate mortgages.

*Temporary Versus Permanent Buydowns:* Another way in which borrowers with excess cash can reduce their mortgage payment is by paying additional points in order to reduce the interest rate. This is sometimes called a "permanent buydown" because the reduced payment holds for the life of the loan. For the same number of dollars invested, however, temporary buydowns reduce the monthly payment in the first year, which is the payment used to qualify the borrower, by a larger amount than a permanent buydown. This reflects the concentration of the payment reduction in the early years of the loan.

The table illustrates the three most common temporary buydowns. On a 3-2-1 buydown, the mortgage payment in years one, two, and three is calculated at rates 3%, 2%, and 1%, respectively, below the rate on the loan. On a 2-1 buydown, the payment in years one and two is calculated at rates 2% and 1% below the loan rate. And on a 1-0 buydown, the payment in year one is calculated at 1% below the loan rate.

The 3-2-1 buydown involves the largest reduction in the borrower's payment in the first year, but also requires the largest amount placed in escrow, as shown on the bottom line.

| Payments by Borrowers and Payments from Escrow Accounts on a $100,000 30-Year 7% Fixed-Rate Mortgage with 3-2-1, 2-1, and 1-0 Temporary Buydowns | | | | | | | |
|---|---|---|---|---|---|---|---|
| | | 3-2-1 Buydown | | 2-1 Buydown | | 1-0 Buydown | |
| Year | Payment Received by Lender | Payment by Borrower | Payment from Escrow | Payment by Borrower | Payment from Escrow | Payment by Borrower | Payment from Escrow |
| 1 | $665.31 | $477.42 | $187.89 | $536.83 | $128.48 | $599.56 | $65.75 |
| 2 | $665.31 | $563.83 | $128.48 | $599.56 | $65.75 | $665.31 | 0 |
| 3 | $665.31 | $599.56 | $65.75 | $665.31 | 0 | 0 | 0 |
| 4-30 | $665.31 | $665.31 | 0 | 0 | 0 | 0 | 0 |
| Needed Escrow | | | $4,586 | | $2,331 | | $789 |

The required escrow shown in the table assumes that no interest is paid on the account. If the borrower were credited with 4% interest on the 3-2-1 illustrated above, the required deposit to the buydown account would fall from $4,586 to $4,369. Only a few lenders credit interest, however.

Some lenders not only do not pay interest on the buydown account, but dispense with the account altogether, replacing it with additional points equal to the sum of the buydown digits. That is, they charge an additional 6 points for a 3-2-1, 3 points for a 2-1, and 1 point for a 1-0. This is a ripoff.

Calculator 7d on my Web site will allow you to experiment with a variety of temporary buydown options that are available in the marketplace. In general, you will want the smallest buydown you need to qualify. The calculator will also show you the proper deposit to escrow for any buydown.

**Temporary Lender** *A lender that sells the loans it originates, as opposed to a portfolio lender that holds them.*

*Same as* **Mortgage Company**.

---

**Term** *The period used to calculate the monthly mortgage payment.*

The term is usually but not always the same as the maturity, which is the period over which the loan balance must be paid in full. On a seven-year balloon loan, for example, the maturity is seven years but the term in most cases is 30 years.

### Selecting the Term:

**Impact on Monthly Payment:** The longer the term, the lower the mortgage payment but the slower the growth of equity. Borrowers who want to make their payments as small as possible select the longest term available. The reduction in payment from lengthening the term, however, becomes less and less effective as the term gets longer. This is illustrated in the table at the top of the next page, which shows the mortgage payment on a $100,000 loan at various interest rates and terms.

For example, at 6% extending the term from 10 years to 20 years reduces the payment by $394, but extending it to 30 years and 40 years reduces the payment by only $116 and $50, respectively. The furthest you can possibly go in extending the term is to infinity, which is an interest-only loan—you never repay any part of the loan. On a 6% loan, the monthly interest is $500, only $50 less than the payment at 40 years.

Extending the term to reduce the payment also becomes less effective at higher interest rates. For example, at 6% extending the term from 20 to 30 years reduces the payment by $116, but at 12% the reduction is only $72. (See table at the top of the next page.)

**Impact on Equity Growth:** Borrowers who want to build equity in their home as quickly as possible select the shortest term they can afford. As illustrated in the table in the middle of the next page, the shorter the term, the more rapid the increase in equity. For example, after 10 years the borrower with a 15-year term at 7% has repaid 54.6% of the original balance, whereas the borrower with a 30-year

| Mortgage Payment Per $100,000 of Loan Amount | | | | | | | |
|---|---|---|---|---|---|---|---|
| | 6% | 7% | 8% | 9% | 10% | 11% | 12% |
| 5 Years | $1,933 | $1,980 | $2,028 | $2,076 | $2,125 | $2,174 | $2,224 |
| 10 Years | $1,110 | $1,161 | $1,213 | $1,267 | $1,322 | $1,378 | $1,435 |
| 15 Years | $844 | $899 | $956 | $1,014 | $1,075 | $1,137 | $1,200 |
| 20 Years | $716 | $775 | $836 | $900 | $965 | $1,032 | $1,101 |
| 25 Years | $644 | $707 | $773 | $839 | $909 | $980 | $1,053 |
| 30 Years | $600 | $665 | $734 | $805 | $878 | $952 | $1,029 |
| 40 Years | $550 | $621 | $695 | $771 | $849 | $928 | $1,008 |
| Interest Only | $500 | $583 | $667 | $750 | $833 | $917 | $1,000 |

term at the same rate has repaid only 14.2% of the balance. Since 15-year loans usually carry a lower rate than 30-year loans, this understates the difference in the rate of equity buildup.

| Percent of Loan Balance Repaid After Specified Periods at 7% | | | | | | | |
|---|---|---|---|---|---|---|---|
| Term | After 5 Years | After 10 Years | After 15 Years | After 20 Years | After 25 Years | After 30 Years | After 40 Years |
| 5 Years | 100% | 100% | 100% | 100% | 100% | 100% | 100% |
| 10 Years | 41.4% | 100% | 100% | 100% | 100% | 100% | 100% |
| 15 Years | 22.6% | 54.6% | 100% | 100% | 100% | 100% | 100% |
| 20 Years | 13.7% | 33.2% | 60.8% | 100% | 100% | 100% | 100% |
| 25 Years | 8.8% | 21.4% | 39.1% | 64.3% | 100% | 100% | 100% |
| 30 Years | 5.9% | 14.2% | 26.0% | 42.7% | 66.4% | 100% | 100% |
| 40 Years | 2.7% | 6.6% | 12.1% | 19.8% | 30.9% | 46.5% | 100% |

**Interest Rate Differences:** The two most common terms are 30 years and 15 years. 15-year FRMs typically carry interest rates from .25% to .50% below those on comparable 30-year FRMs. This rate difference strengthens the case for the 15 by reducing the payment advantage of the 30 and increasing the advantage of the 15 in the rate at which equity grows.

But note that 10-year terms may not carry rates below 15s and the rates on 20s and 25s are likely to be closer to those on 30s than to those on 15s.

***Shorter Term Versus Extra Payments:*** A borrower can always shorten the realized term of a mortgage by making extra payments. For example, a borrower who selects a 15-year loan but wants to pay it off in 10 years can make an extra payment every month to bring the payment to what it would be on a 10. Assuming the interest rate is the same, the outcome is the same.

For example, the monthly payment on a $100,000 loan at 6% for 15 years is $843.86. On a 10-year loan at the same rate, it is $1,110.21. If you take the 15-year loan and make an extra payment every month equal to the $266.35 difference, you will pay it off in 10 years.

This is hardly surprising, since the sum of $843.86 and $266.35 is $1,110.21, which is the payment on the 10-year loan. The extra payment in effect converts the 15-year loan into a 10-year loan.

There is one difference, however, between the 10-year loan and the 15-year loan with the extra payment. With the 10-year loan, $1,110.21 is the **Scheduled Payment**, the amount you are obliged to pay every month. With the 15-year loan, the scheduled payment is only $843.86; the extra payment of $266.35 is optional. Which is better for you depends on whether you attach greater value to discipline or to flexibility.

You can't apply this logic to the selection of a 30 versus a 15, however, because the 15 has a lower rate. If you convert a 30 into a 15 by making an extra payment, you will pay more than you would have by selecting a 15 at the outset.

***Investing Excess Cash Flow on the 30:*** Most borrowers electing a 30-year term do it because they can't afford the monthly payment on a shorter term. Some elect the 30-year term, however, because they plan to invest the difference in payment. There is nothing wrong with this, provided they understand how much they must earn on other investments to make it a paying strategy. The yield on other investments must exceed the yield on investment in the shorter term, which is generally high.

An investment in a shorter-term mortgage is a little different than most other investments. Typically, an investment consists of a lump sum paid out at the beginning and the return is a series of payments received over time. This is the way it is, for example, with an investment in a deposit or bond.

By contrast, when you invest in a shorter-term mortgage, your investment is a series of payments equal to the difference between the monthly payment at the shorter term and the payment at a longer term. And the return is a lump sum, equal to the larger proceeds you receive at time of sale because of the smaller loan balance that must be repaid at the end of the period.

Let's say you are borrowing $100,000 and choosing between a 30-year fixed-rate mortgage (FRM) at 7.5% and a 15-year FRM at 7.125%. The .375% difference is typical. Monthly payments of principal and interest are $699.22 for the 30-year loan and $905.84 for the 15-year. The difference is $206.62 each month. That's your investment.

You expect to stay in your home seven years. At that point, the balance of the 30-year loan will be $91,833 and the balance of the 15-year loan will be $66,137, for a difference of $25,696. That's your return. On an annual basis, it amounts to 10.72%. If the difference in interest rate had been greater than .375%, the return on investment would be higher, and vice versa.

The calculation above assumes the interest rate is the only difference between the two loans. But if the down payment you expect to make is less than 20%, you will have to pay for mortgage insurance, and the premiums are higher on the 30-year loan. This increases the return on the 15-year loan considerably. If you anticipate paying 5% down, for example, the higher premium on the 30-year FRM will raise the seven-year return on the 15 from 10.72% to 15.74%.

An important feature of this type of investment is that the return is inversely related to how long you expect to have the mortgage. If you remain three years instead of seven, for example, the return on your investment in the case without mortgage insurance rises from 10.72% to 16.21%. If you remain for 15 years, the return falls to 8.60%. That's because you must wait 15 years to realize the return.

Calculator 15a on my Web site lets you calculate the return on your own deal. You enter two terms, their interest rates, your anticipated down payment and your expected period in the house. The calculator determines your rate of return.

***Staying on Schedule When Refinancing:*** Some borrowers want to refinance while staying on the same amortization schedule. For example, they took out a mortgage seven years ago that has 23 years to run and they want to stay on that schedule, rather than start with a new 30-year schedule.

Lenders won't ordinarily make a 23-year loan. The best option, therefore, is to refinance for 30 years, but increase the payment by the exact amount required to amortize over 23—or any other period you wish. Use calculator 2c on my Web site. You tell the calculator when you want the loan to pay off, and it will tell you the extra payment required to do it.

---

**3/2 Down Payment** *Programs offered by some lenders under which a borrower who is able to secure a grant or gift equal to 2% of the down payment will only have to provide a 3% down payment from their own funds.*

---

**Title Insurance** *Insurance against loss arising from problems connected to the title to property.*

A home may go through several ownership changes and the land on which it stands through many more. There may be a weak link at any point in that chain that could emerge to cause trouble. For example, someone along the way may have forged a signature in transferring title. Or there may be unpaid real estate taxes or other liens. Title insurance covers the insured party for any claims and legal fees that arise out of such problems.

***Lender Versus Owner Policies:*** All mortgage lenders require title insurance to protect their lien against the property. A lender policy is for an amount equal to the loan and lasts until the loan is repaid. As with mortgage insurance, the borrower pays the premium, which is a single payment made upfront.

To protect his or her equity in the property, the owner needs an owner's title policy for the full value of the home. In many areas, sellers pay for owner policies as part of their obligation to deliver good title to the buyer. In other areas, borrowers must buy it as an add-on to the lender policy. It is advisable to do this because the additional cost above the cost of the lender policy is relatively small.

***Coverage Period:*** With the exception noted below, title insurance only protects against losses arising from events that occurred prior to the date of the policy. Coverage ends on the day the policy is issued and extends backward in time for an indefinite period. This is in marked contrast to property or life insurance, which protect against losses resulting from events that occur after the policy is issued, for a specified period into the future.

On a title policy, the owner's protection lasts as long as the owner or any heirs have an interest in or any obligation with regard to the property. When they sell, however, the lender will require the purchaser to obtain a new policy. That protects the lender against any liens or other claims against the property that may have arisen since the date of the previous policy.

***Extended Coverage:*** The standard title insurance policy provides no protection against false claims that arise after the property is purchased. Yet such events occur. Identity theft can result in a new mortgage the owner knows nothing about. Or a neighbor could build on the land without the owner's knowledge and, after a period without challenge, could acquire ownership rights.

A new policy is available in most states that protects against such contingencies. It is usually referred to as the ALTA Homeowner's Policy. It may cost a bit more than the standard policy.

***Title Insurance on a Refinancing:*** A borrower who refinances does not need a new owner's policy, but the lender will require a new lender policy. Even if the borrower refinances with the same lender, the lender's policy terminates when the old mortgage is paid off. Furthermore, the lender is concerned about title issues that may have arisen since the purchase. However, insurers generally offer discounts on policies taken out within short periods after the preceding policy. In some cases, discounts are available as far out as six years from the date of the previous policy.

***Cost Structure of Title Insurance:*** Because title insurance protects against what may have happened in the past, most of the expense incurred by title companies or their agents is in loss reduction. They look to reduce losses by finding and fixing defects before the policy is issued, in much the same way as firms providing elevator or boiler insurance. These types of insurance are very different from life, property, or mortgage insurance, which protect against losses from future events over which the insurers have no control.

***Cross-Subsidization:*** The cost of providing title insurance is not much different for a small policy than for a large one. The reason is that most title insurance costs arise in preventing loss rather than paying claims, and prevention costs are not related to the size of a policy. Despite this, premiums are scaled to the amount of coverage, the amount of the mortgage, or the value of the property, which suggests that smaller policies may be underpriced and larger policies overpriced.

***Geographic Variations in the Cost of Title Insurance:*** The cost of title insurance varies widely from one area to another. One major reason is that the services covered by the title insurance premium vary in different parts of the country. In some areas, the premium covers not only protection against loss but also the costs of search and examination, as well as closing services. In other areas, the premium covers protection only, and borrowers pay for the other related services separately.

To complicate it further, in some states the charges for title-related services are paid to title insurance companies, which perform the functions but charge separately for them. In other states, borrowers may pay attorneys or independent companies called abstractors or escrow companies.

Of course, what matters to the borrower is the sum total of all title-related charges. These also differ from one area to another in response to a variety of factors. The 50 states have 50 different regulatory regimes, which affect charges. So do local costs, competition in local markets, and other factors.

***Shopping for Title Insurance:*** Most borrowers leave it to one of the professionals with whom they deal—real estate agent, lender, or attorney—to select the title insurance carrier. This means that competition among title insurers is largely directed toward these professionals who can direct business rather than toward borrowers.

Borrowers may be able to save money by shopping for title insurance themselves, although it is difficult to generalize because market conditions vary state by state, and sometimes within states. I would certainly shop in states that do not regulate title insurance rates: Alabama, District of Columbia, Georgia, Hawaii, Illinois, Indiana, Massachusetts, Oklahoma, and West Virginia.

There is no point shopping in Texas or New Mexico because these states set the prices for all carriers. Florida also sets title insurance premiums but not other title-related charges, which can vary.

In the remaining states, the situation is murky and it may or may not pay to shop. Insurance premiums are the same for all carriers in "rating bureau states": Pennsylvania, New York, New Jersey, Ohio, and Delaware. These states authorize title insurers to file for approval of a single rate schedule for all carriers through a cooperative entity. Yet in some there may be flexibility in title-related charges. More promising are "file and use" states—all those not mentioned above—which permit premiums to vary among insurers.

It is a good idea to ask an informed but disinterested local whether it pays to shop in the area where the property is located. Just keep in mind that those likely to be the best informed are also likely to have an interest in directing your business in the direction that is most advantageous to them.

---

**Total Annual Loan Costs (TALC)** *A measure of interest cost on a reverse mortgage.*

See **Reverse Mortgage/*TALC***.

---

**Total Expense Ratio** *The ratio of total housing expense to borrower income.*

This ratio is used (along with other factors) in qualifying borrowers. See **Qualification/*Meeting Income Requirements*/Expense Ratios**.

**Total Housing Expense** *Housing expense plus current debt service payments.*

---

**Total Interest Payments** *The sum of all interest payments to date or over the life of the loan.*

This is an incomplete measure of the cost of credit to the borrower because it does not include upfront cash payments, and it is not adjusted for the time value of money. *See* **Interest Cost**.

---

**Truth in Lending (TIL)** *The federal law that specifies the information that must be provided to borrowers on different types of loans. Also, the form used to disclose this information.*

Truth in Lending (TIL) is a great idea, in principle. The idea is to require lenders to provide one uniform set of price disclosures that are consistent from loan to loan and from lender to lender. Then consumers can make apples-to-apples price comparisons across loan types and across lenders.

The idea has worked concerning the methodology used to calculate interest cost. Borrowers no longer have to contend with noncomparable ways to calculate interest: discount rates, add-on rates, and internal rates of return. The last has become the standard; *see* **Mortgage Formulas**.

Unfortunately, in all other respects, TIL as it has been applied to mortgages is a disaster.

*APR:* The internal rate of return used to measure interest cost on a mortgage is called the annual percentage rate, or APR. The APR on a mortgage is misleading because upfront fees are a major cost, yet only some of them are included in the APR. In addition, the APR assumes all loans run to term, when in fact most mortgages are paid in full well before term. *See* **Annual Percentage Rate**.

*Useless Information:* The TIL also includes useless information that distracts borrowers and causes confusion.

**Total payments:** This is the monthly payment multiplied by the term.

**Amount financed:** This is the loan amount less *"prepaid finance charges,"* which are the selected upfront charges that are included in the calculation of the APR. If the loan is $100,000 and fees are $3,000, the amount financed is $97,000.

**Finance charge:** This is the sum of all interest payments over the term of the loan, plus the prepaid finance charges.

All these numbers are totally useless for comparing loans of different type or for shopping different loan providers.

***Notice of Prepayment Penalty:*** This is hopelessly confusing, worse than no disclosure at all. *See* **Prepayment Penalty/*Surreptitious Penalties***.

***What Isn't Disclosed That Should Be:*** In addition to making the prepayment disclosure comprehensible to borrowers, the TIL should replace the useless information listed above with information that is critically important to borrowers.

**Total Lender Fees:** In addition to points, which are an upfront charge expressed as a percent of the loan, lenders also charge a variety of fees that are expressed in dollars that do not change with the size of the loan. These fees are disclosed on the TIL only indirectly. Subtracting the "amount financed" from the loan amount will yield the fees. If one borrower in 100 knows enough to do this, I would be surprised. (**Note: The Good Faith Estimate (GFE)** shows individual lender fees but mixes them with third-party charges, provides no total, and does not commit the lender, since the numbers are "estimates".)

The TIL should also commit the lender to these fees. When borrowers "lock" the price of a loan, the lender is committed to the rate and points but not to fees, paving the way for larceny at the closing table. The Federal Reserve, which administers TIL, could easily prevent this by requiring that all locks apply to the APR, which is calculated from the rate and all lender fees.

**Margin on ARMs:** The margin on an ARM is the lender's markup—the amount the lender adds to the interest rate index on a rate adjustment date to obtain the new interest rate. It can be 1.5%; it can also be 6.5%.

Lenders always quote the initial rate on an ARM but they seldom quote the margin, and it is not a required disclosure. On an increasing number of ARMs, the initial rate holds only for one to three months. (This includes all flexible payment or option ARMs and all home equity lines.) On these loans, the borrower knows the interest rate for the first few months, but often doesn't know the lender's markup over the remaining 29 plus years. It should be a required disclosure.

**Is the Loan Simple Interest?** On simple interest loans, interest accrues daily instead of monthly, imposing a stiff penalty on borrowers who pay past the due date. *See* **Amortlzation/*Amortization on a Simple Interest Mortgage***. Most borrowers who write me about their problems with simple interest loans never knew they had one until the problems emerged. TIL should require lenders to disclose it.

**Subordination Policy on Second Mortgages:** Very few borrowers who take out a second mortgage are aware that the second mortgage lender can prevent them from refinancing their first mortgage. When the existing first mortgage is repaid, the existing second mortgage automatically becomes the first mortgage *unless* the second mortgage lender is willing to subordinate his claim to that of the lender providing the new mortgage into which the borrower is refinancing. *See* **Second Mortgage/*Subordination by Second Mortgage Lender***.

Policies of second mortgage lenders regarding subordination vary all over the lot, from a small fee and no conditions to absolute prohibition. Borrowers taking a second mortgage should see the lender's subordination policy on the TIL.

---

**12 MTA** *An interest rate index that is used on some ARMs.*

*See* **Adjustable Rate Mortgage/*ARM Rate Indexes***.

---

**Underage** *Fees collected by a loan officer from a borrower that are lower than the target fees specified by the lender or mortgage broker who employs the loan officer.*

An underage is the opposite of an **Overage**.

**Underwriting** *The process of making a final determination on approval or rejection of a loan application.*

Underwriting involves verifying the information that has been obtained from the borrower and that served as the basis for qualification, as well as assessing information on the applicant's credit worthiness.

**Underwriting Requirements** *The standards imposed by lenders in determining whether a borrower can be approved for a loan.*

These standards are more comprehensive than qualification requirements in that they include an evaluation of the borrower's creditworthiness.

**Upfront Mortgage Broker (UMB)** *A mortgage broker who sets a fee for services, in writing, at the outset of the transaction and acts as the borrower's agent in shopping for the best deal.*

Customers of UMBs pay the broker's fee plus wholesale loan prices, which are disclosed at the customer's request. In contrast, other mortgage brokers (MBs) add a markup to the wholesale prices and quote only the resulting "retail prices" to customers. Most MBs reveal their markup only in required disclosures after an application has been submitted.

UMBs credit customers with any rebates they receive from lenders or home sellers that would otherwise increase the broker's fee beyond what was agreed upon. Such rebates are often an added source of revenue to MBs.

Once the UMB's fee has been established, the UMB's interests are largely aligned with those of customers. In contrast, MBs are in a conflict situation with customers.

A list of UMBs, showing their Web site addresses and the states in which they operate, is available on my Web site.

Many brokers who are not listed as UMBs are willing to operate in the same manner with borrowers who understand the value of broker services and won't faint when they hear the fee. Here is a form you can use.

*Broker Compensation*

*The total compensation to [Name of broker], including any rebates from the lender, will be: _____*

*A separate processing fee will be: _____*

I developed the UMB program in 2001. At the time of writing, there were 53 UMBs listed on my Web site.

---

**Upfront Mortgage Lender** *A lender offering loans on the Internet who provides mortgage shoppers with the information they need to make an informed decision before applying for a mortgage and guarantees them fair treatment during the period after they apply through to closing.*

The specific requirements, and how they meet the needs of shoppers, are as follows:

**Requirement 1:** *A UML provides quick access to the market niches it prices on-line.* Shoppers need a quick way to determine whether a particular lender prices the niche in which that shopper falls. If not, the shopper can go elsewhere without wasting time.

If the shopper's niche *is* priced on-line:

- The shopper can make valid comparisons of one UML's prices against those of another, prior to paying any fees and prior to filling out an application.

- After selecting the lender and applying for the desired loan, the applicant is not exposed to a future price change based on information that the lender claims not to have had at the time of the original quote.

- The applicant who elects to move to a different niche, say to a 15-year from a 30, or to pay more points to reduce the rate, can check online to ensure that the new niche has been correctly priced.

- The applicant who elects to float rather than lock can monitor the price as it is reset daily with the market, and therefore will not be overcharged on the lock day.

UMLs comply with this requirement by filling out a table on their Web site called Market Niches Priced On-Line. The table format is the same at every UML, making it easy for a shopper to tell at a glance whether the lender is pricing the shopper's niche.

**Requirement 2:** *A UML includes its fixed-dollar fees, including credit and appraisal charges, in its price and guarantees them to closing.* This assures borrowers that new fees won't be added or existing ones increased after they have committed themselves to working with the selected lender.

**Requirement 3:** *A UML provides a clear explanation of its lock requirements:* Mortgage shoppers need to know when they have the discretion to lock. The explanation should include any required payments, processes that must be completed, how expired locks are handled, and whether the borrower is committed as well as the UML.

**Requirement 4:** *A UML discloses all the information about its ARMs needed by shoppers to make intelligent decisions.* It is very difficult today to obtain the information about ARMs that is needed to make an informed decision. Loan officers selling ARMs stress one or another feature, usually the index, and leave the remainder of the ARMs' features in the dark. Shoppers need information on potential ARM performance—what will happen to the interest rate and mortgage payment under assumptions about future interest rates that make sense to the shopper.

UMLs can comply with this rule in two ways. One way is to offer schedules of monthly payment and interest rate under no-change and worst-case scenarios. The first assumes that the most recent value of the index remains unchanged through the life of the loan, while the second assumes that the ARM rate increases by the maximum amount allowed in the contract.

The alternative is to provide the information needed for the shopper to calculate these (and perhaps other) scenarios using calculators on my Web site or other sites. The required information is shown on a form that is identical for all UMLs.

**Requirement 5:** *A UML informs borrowers if its loan officers are compensated in a way that gives them a financial incentive to overcharge the borrower.* Off the Internet, many lenders credit loan officers with overages. An overage is a price higher than the price delivered to the loan officer by the lender's pricing department. For example, if the price shown on the loan officer's price sheet is 6% at zero points and the loan officer sells the deal for 6% and one point (an upfront charge equal to 1% of the loan), there is an overage of one point. If the loan officer gets a piece of it, there is a conflict situation that the customer ought to know about.

At the time of writing in 2003, the Upfront Mortgage Lender (UML) program had just been launched, with one participating lender: Eloan.com.

---

**VA Mortgage** *A mortgage with no down payment requirement, available only to ex-servicemen and women, on which the lender is insured against loss by the Veterans Administration.*

Subject to a proviso, VA loans are advantageous for veterans who need a no-down-payment loan. In most areas, VA loans can be larger than FHA loans. FHA also requires at least 1% down and the insurance premium is higher than on VAs. Conventional loans with no down payment carry interest rates .75% higher and up, depending on the borrower's credit score.

The proviso is that VA borrowers may pay a higher price (rate or points) than is available on either FHAs or conventionals. They shouldn't—in the competitive wholesale market where lenders quote prices to mortgage brokers, the prices are much the same. But the retail market is something else. Some loan providers view veterans who need no-down-payment loans, and who trust the loan provider to give them the market rate, as sheep to be fleeced.

To protect themselves, veterans should consult a Web site that prices all three types of loans. There aren't many sites that price VAs, but one that does it well is www.Countrywide.com. It shows about the same rate and points for VA, FHA, and conventional loans. Use it to shop.

The VA Web site, www.homeloans.va.gov, will tell you who is eligible, how you go about obtaining a Certificate of Eligibility, whether eligibility can be used more than once, the types of properties that can be purchased with a VA loan, the range of insurance premiums for different categories of veterans and different loan purposes, the conditions under which VA loans can be assumed by a buyer, the types of VA home loans, and more.

---

**Waiver of Escrows** *Authorization by the lender for the borrower to pay taxes and insurance directly.*

This is in contrast to the standard procedure, where the lender adds a charge to the monthly mortgage payment that is deposited in an escrow account, from which the lender pays the borrower's taxes and insurance when they come due. On some loans lenders will not waive escrows, and on loans where the waiver is permitted lenders are likely either to charge for it in the form of a small increase in points or to restrict it to borrowers making a large down payment. *See* **Escrow Account**.

---

**Warrantable Condo** *A condominium project with features that lenders view as favorable in terms of their risk exposure on loans secured by individual condo units.*

The requirements of warrantability include such features as the following: the project (including all common areas) is fully completed and the common areas are insured, the Homeowners Association has been controlled by unit owners (as opposed to the developer) for some period, most units are owner-occupied, and no one person owns more than 10% of the units. Loans on units in warrantable condos receive better terms than loans on units in non-warrantable condos.

---

**Wholesale Lender** *A lender that provides loans through mortgage brokers or correspondents.*

*See* **Mortgage Lender/Retail Versus Wholesale Lenders**.

---

**Workout Assumption** *The assumption of a mortgage, with permission of the lender, from a borrower unable to continue making the payments.*

*See* **Payment Problems/Position of the Lender/Permanent Problem**.

---

**Worst-Case Scenario** *On an ARM, the assumption that the interest rate rises to the maximum extent permitted by the loan contract.*

*See* **Adjustable Rate Mortgage/***Scenarios***.

**Wrap-Around Mortgage**  *A mortgage loan transaction in which the lender assumes responsibility for an existing mortgage.*

Usually, but not always, the lender is the home seller. For example, S, who has a $70,000 mortgage on his home, sells his home to B for $100,000. B pays $5,000 down and borrows $95,000 from S on a new mortgage. This mortgage "wraps around" the existing $70,000 mortgage because S will continue to make the payments on the old mortgage.

A wrap-around can be attractive to home sellers because they may be able to sell their home for a higher price. In addition, if the current market interest rate is above the rate on the existing mortgage, the seller can earn an attractive return on the cash foregone from the sale. For instance, if the $70,000 mortgage in the example has a rate of 6% and the new mortgage for $95,000 has a rate of 8%, S earns 8% on his $25,000 investment plus the difference between 8% and 6% on $70,000. The total return is about 13.5%. I have a spreadsheet on my Web site that calculates the yield on a wrap-around.

But the high return carries a high risk. The new mortgage owned by S is a riskier asset than the house he previously owned. The new owner has only $5,000 of equity in the property. If a small decline in market values erases that equity, the owner has no financial incentive to maintain the property. If the buyer defaults on his mortgage, S will be obliged to foreclose and sell the property in order to pay off the old mortgage.

Only assumable loans are legally able to be wrapped. Assumable loans are those on which existing borrowers can transfer their obligations to qualified house purchasers. Today, only FHA and VA loans are assumable without the permission of the lender. Other fixed-rate loans carry "due on sale" clauses, which require that the mortgage be repaid in full if the property is sold.

Sometimes wrap-arounds arise on loans with due-on-sale clauses without the knowledge of the lender. This is looking for big trouble. *See* **Assumptions/***Illegal Assumptions***/Wrap-Arounds.**

**Yield-Spread Premium**  *A payment made by a lender to a mortgage broker for delivering an above-par loan.*

A par loan is one on which the lender charges zero points. Lenders charge points on loans carrying interest rates below that on the par loan and pay points or rebates on loans carrying rates above that on the par loan. *See* **Points/*Points and Rebates as Borrower Options***.

On loans involving mortgage brokers, the rebate on above-par loans is credited to the broker, and is referred to euphemistically as the "yield-spread premium" (YSP). YSPs are a major part of broker income.

Because borrowers pay YSPs indirectly in the interest rate, they resist them less than they would broker fees paid directly out of their pockets. But a comparable form of "rebate abuse" also occurs with lenders. *See* **Mortgage Scams and Tricks/ *Scams by Loan Providers/* Pocket the Borrower's Rebate**.

In its proposals for RESPA reform that were pending in 2003, HUD would require lenders to credit rebates to borrowers rather than brokers. The borrower would have to authorize payment of the rebate to the broker. *See* **RESPA/*Proposals for RESPA Reform/* Disclosing Mortgage Broker Compensation**.

**Zero Balance**  *The amount the borrower owes at maturity.*

## Refinance Break-Even Tables

### *Purpose of the Tables*

These tables are for borrowers who incur costs to refinance to a lower interest rate, whether the costs are paid in cash or added to the balance of the new loan. The savings from the lower rate accumulate over time, and at some point completely offset the upfront refinance costs. This point is called the "break-even period," or BEP.

The BEP is the period you must hold the new loan to break even. If you hold it longer, you profit from the refinance. The shorter the BEP, the more advantageous the refinance.

The table is designed for borrowers who want to refinance into a fixed-rate mortgage (FRM). However, the error in using it for new adjustable rate mortgages (ARMs) is negligible if the initial rate period on the ARM is five years or longer.

You don't need Refinance Break-Even Tables if you can refinance to a lower interest rate without incurring any refinance costs. In that event, you are ahead after one month.

You cannot use these tables if you now have two mortgages or if you want to take cash out of the transaction. Financing the costs is not taking cash out.

### *How to Use the Tables*

1. Find the table that shows the number of points on your loan. (Points are an upfront charge expressed as a percent of the loan balance. One point equals 1% of the loan.) The tables cover zero, 1, 2, and 3 points.

2. Subtract the interest rate on your new loan from the interest rate on your old loan. This is the "Interest Rate Reduction," shown in the leftmost column. Run down the column until you get to the number that is closest to yours. This is your rate reduction row.

3. Add up all closing costs other than points, escrows, and per diem interest. Divide this number by the loan amount. Run across the column headings at the top, showing "Other Closing Costs as a Percent of Loan Amount," until you get to the number that is closest to yours. This is your closing cost column.

4. Your break-even period is shown in the cell where your rate reduction row and your closing cost column intersect.

**An example:** The old loan has an interest rate of 7.5%, 300 months to go, and a balance of $135,000. The new loan will have a rate of 6% for 30 years, with one point, and other closing costs of $2,700. The buyer is in the 40% tax bracket and will pay points and other closing costs in cash.

The relevant page, covering one point, is shown on the next page. The rate reduction row is 1.5% and is in bold. Other closing costs are 2% of the loan. The 2% column is also in bold. The break-even period, where the bold row and the bold column intersect, is 48 months.

## Notes

"Income Tax Bracket" is the tax rate you pay on your last dollar of income, including federal and state and/or local income taxes.

"Term Left on Current Loan" is the number of months until the balance is paid off if borrowers continue to make the mortgage payments they are making now.

"Term on New Loan" is the term being contemplated on the loan used to refinance.

"Points and Costs" are either financed (included in the new loan balance) or paid in cash by the borrower.

The tables assume that no mortgage insurance premiums are paid on either the old or new mortgage and that the user would earn 2% before tax on upfront and monthly payments had they been saved instead of spent.

| Break-Even Periods (in Months) | | | | | | | | | | | |
|---|---|---|---|---|---|---|---|---|---|---|---|

Term Left on Current Loan: 300 months
Term on New Loan: 30 years
Points: 1.00%

Income Tax Bracket: 40.00%
Points and Costs: Financed

| Other Closing Costs as a Percent of Loan Amount | | | | | | | | | | | |
|---|---|---|---|---|---|---|---|---|---|---|---|
| Interest Rate Reduction | .25% | .5% | .75% | 1.00% | 1.25% | 1.50% | 1.75% | 2.00% ** | 2.50% | 3.00% | 3.50% | 4.00% |
|---|---|---|---|---|---|---|---|---|---|---|---|---|
| 0.125% | None | None | None | None | None | None | None | **None** | None | None | None | None |
| 0.25% | None | None | None | None | None | None | None | **None** | None | None | None | None |
| 0.375% | None | None | None | None | None | None | None | **None** | None | None | None | None |
| 0.5% | 74 | 111 | None | None | None | None | None | **None** | None | None | None | None |
| 0.625% | 51 | 65 | 83 | 108 | None | None | None | **None** | None | None | None | None |
| 0.75% | 40 | 50 | 61 | 74 | 88 | 107 | 135 | **None** | None | None | None | None |
| 0.875% | 33 | 41 | 49 | 58 | 68 | 79 | 92 | **106** | 156 | None | None | None |
| 1% | 28 | 35 | 42 | 49 | 56 | 65 | 73 | **83** | 106 | 139 | None | None |
| 1.125% | 25 | 30 | 36 | 42 | 48 | 55 | 62 | **69** | 86 | 106 | 132 | 177 |
| 1.25% | 22 | 27 | 32 | 37 | 42 | 48 | 54 | **60** | 73 | 89 | 106 | 127 |
| 1.375% | 20 | 24 | 29 | 33 | 38 | 43 | 48 | **53** | 64 | 77 | 90 | 106 |
| **1.5% | **18** | **22** | **26** | **30** | **34** | **39** | **43** | **48** | **57** | **68** | **79** | **92** |
| 1.625% | 17 | 20 | 24 | 28 | 31 | 35 | 39 | **43** | 52 | 61 | 71 | 82 |
| 1.75% | 16 | 19 | 22 | 25 | 29 | 32 | 36 | **40** | 47 | 56 | 64 | 74 |
| 1.875% | 14 | 17 | 20 | 24 | 27 | 30 | 33 | **37** | 44 | 51 | 59 | 67 |
| 2% | 14 | 16 | 19 | 22 | 25 | 28 | 31 | **34** | 40 | 47 | 54 | 62 |
| 2.125% | 13 | 15 | 18 | 21 | 23 | 26 | 29 | **32** | 38 | 44 | 50 | 57 |
| 2.25% | 12 | 14 | 17 | 19 | 22 | 25 | 27 | **30** | 35 | 41 | 47 | 53 |
| 2.375% | 11 | 14 | 16 | 18 | 21 | 23 | 26 | **28** | 33 | 39 | 44 | 50 |
| 2.5% | 11 | 13 | 15 | 17 | 20 | 22 | 24 | **27** | 31 | 36 | 42 | 47 |
| 2.625% | 10 | 12 | 14 | 17 | 19 | 21 | 23 | **25** | 30 | 34 | 39 | 44 |
| 2.75% | 10 | 12 | 14 | 16 | 18 | 20 | 22 | **24** | 28 | 33 | 37 | 42 |
| 2.875% | 9 | 11 | 13 | 15 | 17 | 19 | 21 | **23** | 27 | 31 | 35 | 40 |
| 3% | 9 | 11 | 13 | 14 | 16 | 18 | 20 | **22** | 26 | 30 | 34 | 38 |
| 3.125% | 9 | 10 | 12 | 14 | 16 | 17 | 19 | **21** | 25 | 28 | 32 | 36 |
| 3.25% | 8 | 10 | 12 | 13 | 15 | 17 | 18 | **20** | 24 | 27 | 31 | 35 |
| 3.375% | 8 | 10 | 11 | 13 | 14 | 16 | 18 | **19** | 23 | 26 | 30 | 33 |
| 3.5% | 8 | 9 | 11 | 12 | 14 | 15 | 17 | **19** | 22 | 25 | 29 | 32 |
| 3.625% | 8 | 9 | 10 | 12 | 13 | 15 | 16 | **18** | 21 | 24 | 28 | 31 |
| 3.75% | 7 | 9 | 10 | 12 | 13 | 14 | 16 | **17** | 20 | 23 | 27 | 30 |
| 3.875% | 7 | 8 | 10 | 11 | 13 | 14 | 15 | **17** | 20 | 23 | 26 | 29 |
| 4% | 7 | 8 | 9 | 11 | 12 | 14 | 15 | **16** | 19 | 22 | 25 | 28 |

# Refinance Break-Even Tables

| Break-Even Periods (in Months) | | | | | | | | | | | |
|---|---|---|---|---|---|---|---|---|---|---|---|
| Term Left on Current Loan: 120 months<br>Term on New Loan: 15 years<br>Points: 0.00% | | | | | | Income Tax Bracket: Pre-Tax<br>Points and Costs: Financed | | | | | |
| Other Closing Costs as a Percent of Loan Amount | | | | | | | | | | | |
| Interest Rate Reduction | .25% | .5% | .75% | 1.00% | 1.25% | 1.50% | 1.75% | 2.00% | 2.50% | 3.00% | 3.50% | 4.00% |
|---|---|---|---|---|---|---|---|---|---|---|---|---|
| 0.125% | None | None | None | None | None | None | None | None | None | None | None | None |
| 0.25% | None | None | None | None | None | None | None | None | None | None | None | None |
| 0.375% | 11 | None | None | None | None | None | None | None | None | None | None | None |
| 0.5% | 7 | 17 | None | None | None | None | None | None | None | None | None | None |
| 0.625% | 6 | 12 | 21 | None | None | None | None | None | None | None | None | None |
| 0.75% | 5 | 10 | 15 | 23 | 39 | None | None | None | None | None | None | None |
| 0.875% | 4 | 8 | 13 | 18 | 24 | 34 | None | None | None | None | None | None |
| 1% | 4 | 7 | 11 | 15 | 20 | 25 | 33 | 46 | None | None | None | None |
| 1.125% | 3 | 6 | 9 | 13 | 17 | 21 | 26 | 32 | None | None | None | None |
| 1.25% | 3 | 6 | 8 | 11 | 14 | 18 | 22 | 26 | 38 | None | None | None |
| 1.375% | 3 | 5 | 8 | 10 | 13 | 16 | 19 | 23 | 31 | 42 | None | None |
| 1.5% | 3 | 5 | 7 | 9 | 12 | 14 | 17 | 20 | 27 | 35 | 47 | None |
| 1.625% | 2 | 4 | 6 | 8 | 11 | 13 | 15 | 18 | 24 | 30 | 39 | 50 |
| 1.75% | 2 | 4 | 6 | 8 | 10 | 12 | 14 | 16 | 21 | 27 | 34 | 42 |
| 1.875% | 2 | 4 | 6 | 7 | 9 | 11 | 13 | 15 | 20 | 25 | 30 | 37 |
| 2% | 2 | 4 | 5 | 7 | 9 | 10 | 12 | 14 | 18 | 23 | 27 | 33 |
| 2.125% | 2 | 3 | 5 | 6 | 8 | 10 | 11 | 13 | 17 | 21 | 25 | 30 |
| 2.25% | 2 | 3 | 5 | 6 | 8 | 9 | 11 | 12 | 16 | 19 | 23 | 28 |
| 2.375% | 2 | 3 | 4 | 6 | 7 | 9 | 10 | 12 | 15 | 18 | 22 | 26 |
| 2.5% | 2 | 3 | 4 | 5 | 7 | 8 | 10 | 11 | 14 | 17 | 20 | 24 |
| 2.625% | 2 | 3 | 4 | 5 | 7 | 8 | 9 | 10 | 13 | 16 | 19 | 22 |
| 2.75% | 2 | 3 | 4 | 5 | 6 | 7 | 9 | 10 | 13 | 15 | 18 | 21 |
| 2.875% | 2 | 3 | 4 | 5 | 6 | 7 | 8 | 9 | 12 | 15 | 17 | 20 |
| 3% | 2 | 3 | 4 | 5 | 6 | 7 | 8 | 9 | 11 | 14 | 16 | 19 |
| 3.125% | 1 | 2 | 3 | 4 | 5 | 7 | 8 | 9 | 11 | 13 | 16 | 18 |
| 3.25% | 1 | 2 | 3 | 4 | 5 | 6 | 7 | 8 | 10 | 13 | 15 | 17 |
| 3.375% | 1 | 2 | 3 | 4 | 5 | 6 | 7 | 8 | 10 | 12 | 14 | 17 |
| 3.5% | 1 | 2 | 3 | 4 | 5 | 6 | 7 | 8 | 10 | 12 | 14 | 16 |
| 3.625% | 1 | 2 | 3 | 4 | 5 | 6 | 7 | 7 | 9 | 11 | 13 | 15 |
| 3.75% | 1 | 2 | 3 | 4 | 5 | 5 | 6 | 7 | 9 | 11 | 13 | 15 |
| 3.875% | 1 | 2 | 3 | 4 | 4 | 5 | 6 | 7 | 9 | 11 | 12 | 14 |
| 4% | 1 | 2 | 3 | 4 | 4 | 5 | 6 | 7 | 8 | 10 | 12 | 14 |

# Refinance Break-Even Tables

## Break-Even Periods (in Months)

Term Left on Current Loan: 120 months
Term on New Loan: 15 years
Points: 1.00%

Income Tax Bracket: Pre-Tax
Points and Costs: Financed

### Other Closing Costs as a Percent of Loan Amount

| Interest Rate Reduction | .25% | .5% | .75% | 1.00% | 1.25% | 1.50% | 1.75% | 2.00% | 2.50% | 3.00% | 3.50% | 4.00% |
|---|---|---|---|---|---|---|---|---|---|---|---|---|
| 0.125% | None | None | None | None | None | None | None | None | None | None | None | None |
| 0.25% | None | None | None | None | None | None | None | None | None | None | None | None |
| 0.375% | None | None | None | None | None | None | None | None | None | None | None | None |
| 0.5% | None | None | None | None | None | None | None | None | None | None | None | None |
| 0.625% | None | None | None | None | None | None | None | None | None | None | None | None |
| 0.75% | 39 | None | None | None | None | None | None | None | None | None | None | None |
| 0.875% | 24 | 34 | None | None | None | None | None | None | None | None | None | None |
| 1% | 20 | 25 | 32 | 45 | None | None | None | None | None | None | None | None |
| 1.125% | 17 | 21 | 26 | 32 | 40 | None | None | None | None | None | None | None |
| 1.25% | 14 | 18 | 22 | 26 | 31 | 37 | 46 | None | None | None | None | None |
| 1.375% | 13 | 16 | 19 | 22 | 26 | 31 | 36 | 42 | None | None | None | None |
| 1.5% | 12 | 14 | 17 | 20 | 23 | 27 | 30 | 35 | 46 | None | None | None |
| 1.625% | 11 | 13 | 15 | 18 | 21 | 24 | 27 | 30 | 38 | 49 | None | None |
| 1.75% | 10 | 12 | 14 | 16 | 19 | 21 | 24 | 27 | 33 | 41 | 52 | None |
| 1.875% | 9 | 11 | 13 | 15 | 17 | 19 | 22 | 24 | 30 | 36 | 44 | 54 |
| 2% | 9 | 10 | 12 | 14 | 16 | 18 | 20 | 22 | 27 | 33 | 39 | 46 |
| 2.125% | 8 | 10 | 11 | 13 | 15 | 17 | 19 | 21 | 25 | 30 | 35 | 41 |
| 2.25% | 8 | 9 | 11 | 12 | 14 | 16 | 17 | 19 | 23 | 27 | 32 | 37 |
| 2.375% | 7 | 9 | 10 | 12 | 13 | 15 | 16 | 18 | 22 | 25 | 30 | 34 |
| 2.5% | 7 | 8 | 10 | 11 | 12 | 14 | 15 | 17 | 20 | 24 | 27 | 32 |
| 2.625% | 6 | 8 | 9 | 10 | 12 | 13 | 15 | 16 | 19 | 22 | 26 | 29 |
| 2.75% | 6 | 7 | 9 | 10 | 11 | 12 | 14 | 15 | 18 | 21 | 24 | 28 |
| 2.875% | 6 | 7 | 8 | 9 | 11 | 12 | 13 | 14 | 17 | 20 | 23 | 26 |
| 3% | 6 | 7 | 8 | 9 | 10 | 11 | 13 | 14 | 16 | 19 | 22 | 25 |
| 3.125% | 5 | 7 | 8 | 9 | 10 | 11 | 12 | 13 | 16 | 18 | 21 | 23 |
| 3.25% | 5 | 6 | 7 | 8 | 9 | 10 | 12 | 13 | 15 | 17 | 20 | 22 |
| 3.375% | 5 | 6 | 7 | 8 | 9 | 10 | 11 | 12 | 14 | 17 | 19 | 21 |
| 3.5% | 5 | 6 | 7 | 8 | 9 | 10 | 11 | 12 | 14 | 16 | 18 | 20 |
| 3.625% | 5 | 6 | 7 | 7 | 8 | 9 | 10 | 11 | 13 | 15 | 17 | 20 |
| 3.75% | 5 | 5 | 6 | 7 | 8 | 9 | 10 | 11 | 13 | 15 | 17 | 19 |
| 3.875% | 4 | 5 | 6 | 7 | 8 | 9 | 10 | 10 | 12 | 14 | 16 | 18 |
| 4% | 4 | 5 | 6 | 7 | 8 | 8 | 9 | 10 | 12 | 14 | 16 | 17 |

## Break-Even Periods (in Months)

Term Left on Current Loan: 120 months
Term on New Loan: 15 years
Points: 2.00%

Income Tax Bracket: Pre-Tax
Points and Costs: Financed

### Other Closing Costs as a Percent of Loan Amount

| Interest Rate Reduction | .25% | .5% | .75% | 1.00% | 1.25% | 1.50% | 1.75% | 2.00% | 2.50% | 3.00% | 3.50% | 4.00% |
|---|---|---|---|---|---|---|---|---|---|---|---|---|
| 0.125% | None | None | None | None | None | None | None | None | None | None | None | None |
| 0.25% | None | None | None | None | None | None | None | None | None | None | None | None |
| 0.375% | None | None | None | None | None | None | None | None | None | None | None | None |
| 0.5% | None | None | None | None | None | None | None | None | None | None | None | None |
| 0.625% | None | None | None | None | None | None | None | None | None | None | None | None |
| 0.75% | None | None | None | None | None | None | None | None | None | None | None | None |
| 0.875% | None | None | None | None | None | None | None | None | None | None | None | None |
| 1% | None | None | None | None | None | None | None | None | None | None | None | None |
| 1.125% | 40 | None | None | None | None | None | None | None | None | None | None | None |
| 1.25% | 31 | 37 | 46 | None | None | None | None | None | None | None | None | None |
| 1.375% | 26 | 31 | 36 | 42 | 51 | None | None | None | None | None | None | None |
| 1.5% | 23 | 27 | 30 | 35 | 40 | 46 | 54 | None | None | None | None | None |
| 1.625% | 21 | 24 | 27 | 30 | 34 | 38 | 43 | 49 | None | None | None | None |
| 1.75% | 19 | 21 | 24 | 27 | 30 | 33 | 37 | 41 | 51 | None | None | None |
| 1.875% | 17 | 20 | 22 | 24 | 27 | 30 | 33 | 36 | 44 | 54 | 76 | None |
| 2% | 16 | 18 | 20 | 22 | 25 | 27 | 30 | 32 | 38 | 46 | 55 | 72 |
| 2.125% | 15 | 17 | 19 | 21 | 23 | 25 | 27 | 30 | 35 | 41 | 48 | 57 |
| 2.25% | 14 | 16 | 17 | 19 | 21 | 23 | 25 | 27 | 32 | 37 | 43 | 49 |
| 2.375% | 13 | 15 | 16 | 18 | 20 | 22 | 23 | 25 | 29 | 34 | 39 | 44 |
| 2.5% | 12 | 14 | 15 | 17 | 19 | 20 | 22 | 24 | 27 | 31 | 36 | 41 |
| 2.625% | 12 | 13 | 15 | 16 | 18 | 19 | 21 | 22 | 26 | 29 | 33 | 37 |
| 2.75% | 11 | 12 | 14 | 15 | 17 | 18 | 19 | 21 | 24 | 27 | 31 | 35 |
| 2.875% | 11 | 12 | 13 | 14 | 16 | 17 | 18 | 20 | 23 | 26 | 29 | 33 |
| 3% | 10 | 11 | 13 | 14 | 15 | 16 | 18 | 19 | 22 | 25 | 28 | 31 |
| 3.125% | 10 | 11 | 12 | 13 | 14 | 16 | 17 | 18 | 21 | 23 | 26 | 29 |
| 3.25% | 9 | 10 | 12 | 13 | 14 | 15 | 16 | 17 | 20 | 22 | 25 | 28 |
| 3.375% | 9 | 10 | 11 | 12 | 13 | 14 | 15 | 16 | 19 | 21 | 24 | 26 |
| 3.5% | 9 | 10 | 11 | 12 | 13 | 14 | 15 | 16 | 18 | 20 | 23 | 25 |
| 3.625% | 8 | 9 | 10 | 11 | 12 | 13 | 14 | 15 | 17 | 19 | 22 | 24 |
| 3.75% | 8 | 9 | 10 | 11 | 12 | 13 | 14 | 15 | 17 | 19 | 21 | 23 |
| 3.875% | 8 | 9 | 10 | 10 | 11 | 12 | 13 | 14 | 16 | 18 | 20 | 22 |
| 4% | 8 | 8 | 9 | 10 | 11 | 12 | 13 | 14 | 15 | 17 | 19 | 21 |

# Refinance Break-Even Tables

| Break-Even Periods (in Months) | | | | | | | | | | | | |
|---|---|---|---|---|---|---|---|---|---|---|---|---|
| Term Left on Current Loan: 120 months<br>Term on New Loan: 15 years<br>Points: 3.00% | | | | | | Income Tax Bracket: Pre-Tax<br>Points and Costs: Financed | | | | | | |
| Other Closing Costs as a Percent of Loan Amount | | | | | | | | | | | | |
| Interest Rate Reduction | .25% | .5% | .75% | 1.00% | 1.25% | 1.50% | 1.75% | 2.00% | 2.50% | 3.00% | 3.50% | 4.00% |
| 0.125% | None | None | None | None | None | None | None | None | None | None | None | None |
| 0.25% | None | None | None | None | None | None | None | None | None | None | None | None |
| 0.375% | None | None | None | None | None | None | None | None | None | None | None | None |
| 0.5% | None | None | None | None | None | None | None | None | None | None | None | None |
| 0.625% | None | None | None | None | None | None | None | None | None | None | None | None |
| 0.75% | None | None | None | None | None | None | None | None | None | None | None | None |
| 0.875% | None | None | None | None | None | None | None | None | None | None | None | None |
| 1% | None | None | None | None | None | None | None | None | None | None | None | None |
| 1.125% | None | None | None | None | None | None | None | None | None | None | None | None |
| 1.25% | None | None | None | None | None | None | None | None | None | None | None | None |
| 1.375% | 51 | None | None | None | None | None | None | None | None | None | None | None |
| 1.5% | 40 | 46 | 55 | None | None | None | None | None | None | None | None | None |
| 1.625% | 34 | 38 | 43 | 49 | 57 | None | None | None | None | None | None | None |
| 1.75% | 30 | 33 | 37 | 41 | 46 | 52 | 59 | None | None | None | None | None |
| 1.875% | 27 | 30 | 33 | 36 | 40 | 44 | 48 | 54 | 75 | None | None | None |
| 2% | 25 | 27 | 30 | 33 | 35 | 39 | 42 | 46 | 55 | 72 | None | None |
| 2.125% | 23 | 25 | 27 | 30 | 32 | 35 | 38 | 41 | 48 | 56 | 71 | None |
| 2.25% | 21 | 23 | 25 | 27 | 30 | 32 | 34 | 37 | 43 | 49 | 58 | 70 |
| 2.375% | 20 | 22 | 23 | 25 | 27 | 29 | 32 | 34 | 39 | 44 | 51 | 59 |
| 2.5% | 19 | 20 | 22 | 24 | 26 | 27 | 29 | 31 | 36 | 40 | 46 | 52 |
| 2.625% | 18 | 19 | 21 | 22 | 24 | 26 | 27 | 29 | 33 | 37 | 42 | 47 |
| 2.75% | 17 | 18 | 20 | 21 | 23 | 24 | 26 | 27 | 31 | 35 | 39 | 43 |
| 2.875% | 16 | 17 | 19 | 20 | 21 | 23 | 24 | 26 | 29 | 33 | 36 | 40 |
| 3% | 15 | 16 | 18 | 19 | 20 | 22 | 23 | 25 | 28 | 31 | 34 | 38 |
| 3.125% | 14 | 16 | 17 | 18 | 19 | 21 | 22 | 23 | 26 | 29 | 32 | 35 |
| 3.25% | 14 | 15 | 16 | 17 | 18 | 20 | 21 | 22 | 25 | 28 | 30 | 34 |
| 3.375% | 13 | 14 | 15 | 17 | 18 | 19 | 20 | 21 | 24 | 26 | 29 | 32 |
| 3.5% | 13 | 14 | 15 | 16 | 17 | 18 | 19 | 20 | 23 | 25 | 28 | 30 |
| 3.625% | 12 | 13 | 14 | 15 | 16 | 17 | 18 | 19 | 22 | 24 | 26 | 29 |
| 3.75% | 12 | 13 | 14 | 15 | 16 | 17 | 18 | 19 | 21 | 23 | 25 | 28 |
| 3.875% | 11 | 12 | 13 | 14 | 15 | 16 | 17 | 18 | 20 | 22 | 24 | 27 |
| 4% | 11 | 12 | 13 | 14 | 15 | 16 | 16 | 17 | 19 | 21 | 23 | 26 |

## Break-Even Periods (in Months)

Term Left on Current Loan: 120 months
Term on New Loan: 15 years
Points: 0.00%

Income Tax Bracket: 40.00%
Points and Costs: Financed

### Other Closing Costs as a Percent of Loan Amount

| Interest Rate Reduction | .25% | .5% | .75% | 1.00% | 1.25% | 1.50% | 1.75% | 2.00% | 2.50% | 3.00% | 3.50% | 4.00% |
|---|---|---|---|---|---|---|---|---|---|---|---|---|
| 0.125% | None | None | None | None | None | None | None | None | None | None | None | None |
| 0.25% | None | None | None | None | None | None | None | None | None | None | None | None |
| 0.375% | None | None | None | None | None | None | None | None | None | None | None | None |
| 0.5% | 13 | None | None | None | None | None | None | None | None | None | None | None |
| 0.625% | 10 | 24 | None | None | None | None | None | None | None | None | None | None |
| 0.75% | 8 | 17 | 33 | None | None | None | None | None | None | None | None | None |
| 0.875% | 7 | 14 | 23 | 39 | None | None | None | None | None | None | None | None |
| 1% | 6 | 12 | 19 | 28 | 42 | None | None | None | None | None | None | None |
| 1.125% | 5 | 10 | 16 | 23 | 31 | 44 | None | None | None | None | None | None |
| 1.25% | 5 | 9 | 14 | 20 | 26 | 34 | 45 | None | None | None | None | None |
| 1.375% | 4 | 8 | 13 | 17 | 23 | 29 | 36 | 46 | None | None | None | None |
| 1.5% | 4 | 8 | 11 | 16 | 20 | 25 | 31 | 38 | 62 | None | None | None |
| 1.625% | 4 | 7 | 10 | 14 | 18 | 23 | 27 | 33 | 47 | None | None | None |
| 1.75% | 3 | 6 | 10 | 13 | 17 | 21 | 25 | 29 | 40 | 57 | None | None |
| 1.875% | 3 | 6 | 9 | 12 | 15 | 19 | 23 | 27 | 36 | 47 | 68 | None |
| 2% | 3 | 6 | 8 | 11 | 14 | 17 | 21 | 24 | 32 | 42 | 55 | None |
| 2.125% | 3 | 5 | 8 | 11 | 13 | 16 | 19 | 23 | 30 | 38 | 48 | 62 |
| 2.25% | 3 | 5 | 7 | 10 | 13 | 15 | 18 | 21 | 27 | 35 | 43 | 54 |
| 2.375% | 3 | 5 | 7 | 9 | 12 | 14 | 17 | 20 | 26 | 32 | 39 | 48 |
| 2.5% | 3 | 5 | 7 | 9 | 11 | 14 | 16 | 19 | 24 | 30 | 36 | 44 |
| 2.625% | 2 | 4 | 6 | 9 | 11 | 13 | 15 | 18 | 23 | 28 | 34 | 41 |
| 2.75% | 2 | 4 | 6 | 8 | 10 | 12 | 14 | 17 | 21 | 26 | 32 | 38 |
| 2.875% | 2 | 4 | 6 | 8 | 10 | 12 | 14 | 16 | 20 | 25 | 30 | 36 |
| 3% | 2 | 4 | 6 | 7 | 9 | 11 | 13 | 15 | 19 | 24 | 28 | 34 |
| 3.125% | 2 | 4 | 5 | 7 | 9 | 11 | 13 | 14 | 18 | 23 | 27 | 32 |
| 3.25% | 2 | 4 | 5 | 7 | 9 | 10 | 12 | 14 | 18 | 22 | 26 | 30 |
| 3.375% | 2 | 4 | 5 | 7 | 8 | 10 | 12 | 13 | 17 | 21 | 25 | 29 |
| 3.5% | 2 | 3 | 5 | 6 | 8 | 10 | 11 | 13 | 16 | 20 | 24 | 27 |
| 3.625% | 2 | 3 | 5 | 6 | 8 | 9 | 11 | 12 | 16 | 19 | 23 | 26 |
| 3.75% | 2 | 3 | 5 | 6 | 7 | 9 | 10 | 12 | 15 | 18 | 22 | 25 |
| 3.875% | 2 | 3 | 4 | 6 | 7 | 9 | 10 | 12 | 15 | 18 | 21 | 24 |
| 4% | 2 | 3 | 4 | 6 | 7 | 8 | 10 | 11 | 14 | 17 | 20 | 23 |

| Break-Even Periods (in Months) | | | | | | | | | | | | |
|---|---|---|---|---|---|---|---|---|---|---|---|---|
| Term Left on Current Loan: 120 months<br>Term on New Loan: 15 years<br>Points: 1.00% | | | | | | Income Tax Bracket: 40.00%<br>Points and Costs: Financed | | | | | | |
| Other Closing Costs as a Percent of Loan Amount | | | | | | | | | | | | |
| Interest Rate Reduction | .25% | .5% | .75% | 1.00% | 1.25% | 1.50% | 1.75% | 2.00% | 2.50% | 3.00% | 3.50% | 4.00% |
| 0.125% | None | None | None | None | None | None | None | None | None | None | None | None |
| 0.25% | None | None | None | None | None | None | None | None | None | None | None | None |
| 0.375% | None | None | None | None | None | None | None | None | None | None | None | None |
| 0.5% | None | None | None | None | None | None | None | None | None | None | None | None |
| 0.625% | None | None | None | None | None | None | None | None | None | None | None | None |
| 0.75% | None | None | None | None | None | None | None | None | None | None | None | None |
| 0.875% | None | None | None | None | None | None | None | None | None | None | None | None |
| 1% | 42 | None | None | None | None | None | None | None | None | None | None | None |
| 1.125% | 31 | 44 | None | None | None | None | None | None | None | None | None | None |
| 1.25% | 26 | 34 | 45 | None | None | None | None | None | None | None | None | None |
| 1.375% | 23 | 29 | 36 | 46 | None | None | None | None | None | None | None | None |
| 1.5% | 20 | 25 | 31 | 38 | 46 | 61 | None | None | None | None | None | None |
| 1.625% | 18 | 23 | 27 | 33 | 39 | 46 | 57 | None | None | None | None | None |
| 1.75% | 17 | 20 | 25 | 29 | 34 | 40 | 47 | 56 | None | None | None | None |
| 1.875% | 15 | 19 | 22 | 26 | 31 | 35 | 41 | 47 | 66 | None | None | None |
| 2% | 14 | 17 | 21 | 24 | 28 | 32 | 37 | 41 | 54 | None | None | None |
| 2.125% | 13 | 16 | 19 | 22 | 26 | 29 | 33 | 37 | 47 | 61 | None | None |
| 2.25% | 13 | 15 | 18 | 21 | 24 | 27 | 31 | 34 | 43 | 53 | 68 | None |
| 2.375% | 12 | 14 | 17 | 20 | 22 | 25 | 28 | 32 | 39 | 48 | 58 | 75 |
| 2.5% | 11 | 14 | 16 | 18 | 21 | 24 | 27 | 30 | 36 | 43 | 52 | 64 |
| 2.625% | 11 | 13 | 15 | 17 | 20 | 22 | 25 | 28 | 34 | 40 | 48 | 57 |
| 2.75% | 10 | 12 | 14 | 17 | 19 | 21 | 24 | 26 | 32 | 37 | 44 | 52 |
| 2.875% | 10 | 12 | 14 | 16 | 18 | 20 | 22 | 25 | 30 | 35 | 41 | 48 |
| 3% | 9 | 11 | 13 | 15 | 17 | 19 | 21 | 24 | 28 | 33 | 39 | 45 |
| 3.125% | 9 | 11 | 13 | 14 | 16 | 18 | 20 | 22 | 27 | 31 | 36 | 42 |
| 3.25% | 9 | 10 | 12 | 14 | 16 | 17 | 19 | 21 | 25 | 30 | 35 | 40 |
| 3.375% | 8 | 10 | 12 | 13 | 15 | 17 | 19 | 20 | 24 | 28 | 33 | 38 |
| 3.5% | 8 | 10 | 11 | 13 | 14 | 16 | 18 | 20 | 23 | 27 | 31 | 36 |
| 3.625% | 8 | 9 | 11 | 12 | 14 | 15 | 17 | 19 | 22 | 26 | 30 | 34 |
| 3.75% | 7 | 9 | 10 | 12 | 13 | 15 | 17 | 18 | 22 | 25 | 29 | 33 |
| 3.875% | 7 | 9 | 10 | 11 | 13 | 14 | 16 | 18 | 21 | 24 | 28 | 31 |
| 4% | 7 | 8 | 10 | 11 | 12 | 14 | 15 | 17 | 20 | 23 | 27 | 30 |

| Break-Even Periods (in Months) | | | | | | | | | | | |
|---|---|---|---|---|---|---|---|---|---|---|---|

**Term Left on Current Loan: 120 months**
**Term on New Loan: 15 years**
**Points: 2.00%**

**Income Tax Bracket: 40.00%**
**Points and Costs: Financed**

| Other Closing Costs as a Percent of Loan Amount | | | | | | | | | | | | |
|---|---|---|---|---|---|---|---|---|---|---|---|---|
| Interest Rate Reduction | .25% | .5% | .75% | 1.00% | 1.25% | 1.50% | 1.75% | 2.00% | 2.50% | 3.00% | 3.50% | 4.00% |
| 0.125% | None | None | None | None | None | None | None | None | None | None | None | None |
| 0.25% | None | None | None | None | None | None | None | None | None | None | None | None |
| 0.375% | None | None | None | None | None | None | None | None | None | None | None | None |
| 0.5% | None | None | None | None | None | None | None | None | None | None | None | None |
| 0.625% | None | None | None | None | None | None | None | None | None | None | None | None |
| 0.75% | None | None | None | None | None | None | None | None | None | None | None | None |
| 0.875% | None | None | None | None | None | None | None | None | None | None | None | None |
| 1% | None | None | None | None | None | None | None | None | None | None | None | None |
| 1.125% | None | None | None | None | None | None | None | None | None | None | None | None |
| 1.25% | None | None | None | None | None | None | None | None | None | None | None | None |
| 1.375% | None | None | None | None | None | None | None | None | None | None | None | None |
| 1.5% | 46 | 61 | None | None | None | None | None | None | None | None | None | None |
| 1.625% | 39 | 47 | 57 | None | None | None | None | None | None | None | None | None |
| 1.75% | 34 | 40 | 47 | 56 | None | None | None | None | None | None | None | None |
| 1.875% | 31 | 36 | 41 | 47 | 55 | 66 | None | None | None | None | None | None |
| 2% | 28 | 32 | 37 | 41 | 47 | 54 | 62 | None | None | None | None | None |
| 2.125% | 26 | 29 | 33 | 37 | 42 | 47 | 53 | 60 | None | None | None | None |
| 2.25% | 24 | 27 | 31 | 34 | 38 | 43 | 47 | 53 | 67 | None | None | None |
| 2.375% | 23 | 25 | 29 | 32 | 35 | 39 | 43 | 47 | 58 | 74 | None | None |
| 2.5% | 21 | 24 | 27 | 30 | 33 | 36 | 40 | 43 | 52 | 63 | 83 | None |
| 2.625% | 20 | 22 | 25 | 28 | 31 | 34 | 37 | 40 | 47 | 56 | 68 | None |
| 2.75% | 19 | 21 | 24 | 26 | 29 | 32 | 34 | 37 | 44 | 51 | 61 | 73 |
| 2.875% | 18 | 20 | 22 | 25 | 27 | 30 | 32 | 35 | 41 | 48 | 55 | 65 |
| 3% | 17 | 19 | 21 | 24 | 26 | 28 | 31 | 33 | 38 | 44 | 51 | 59 |
| 3.125% | 16 | 18 | 20 | 22 | 25 | 27 | 29 | 31 | 36 | 42 | 48 | 55 |
| 3.25% | 16 | 18 | 19 | 21 | 23 | 25 | 28 | 30 | 34 | 39 | 45 | 51 |
| 3.375% | 15 | 17 | 19 | 20 | 22 | 24 | 26 | 28 | 33 | 37 | 42 | 48 |
| 3.5% | 14 | 16 | 18 | 20 | 21 | 23 | 25 | 27 | 31 | 36 | 40 | 45 |
| 3.625% | 14 | 16 | 17 | 19 | 21 | 22 | 24 | 26 | 30 | 34 | 38 | 43 |
| 3.75% | 13 | 15 | 17 | 18 | 20 | 21 | 23 | 25 | 29 | 32 | 37 | 41 |
| 3.875% | 13 | 14 | 16 | 18 | 19 | 21 | 22 | 24 | 28 | 31 | 35 | 39 |
| 4% | 13 | 14 | 15 | 17 | 18 | 20 | 22 | 23 | 26 | 30 | 34 | 37 |

# Refinance Break-Even Tables

## Break-Even Periods (in Months)

Term Left on Current Loan: 120 months
Term on New Loan: 15 years
Points: 3.00%

Income Tax Bracket: 40.00%
Points and Costs: Financed

### Other Closing Costs as a Percent of Loan Amount

| Interest Rate Reduction | .25% | .5% | .75% | 1.00% | 1.25% | 1.50% | 1.75% | 2.00% | 2.50% | 3.00% | 3.50% | 4.00% |
|---|---|---|---|---|---|---|---|---|---|---|---|---|
| 0.125% | None | None | None | None | None | None | None | None | None | None | None | None |
| 0.25% | None | None | None | None | None | None | None | None | None | None | None | None |
| 0.375% | None | None | None | None | None | None | None | None | None | None | None | None |
| 0.5% | None | None | None | None | None | None | None | None | None | None | None | None |
| 0.625% | None | None | None | None | None | None | None | None | None | None | None | None |
| 0.75% | None | None | None | None | None | None | None | None | None | None | None | None |
| 0.875% | None | None | None | None | None | None | None | None | None | None | None | None |
| 1% | None | None | None | None | None | None | None | None | None | None | None | None |
| 1.125% | None | None | None | None | None | None | None | None | None | None | None | None |
| 1.25% | None | None | None | None | None | None | None | None | None | None | None | None |
| 1.375% | None | None | None | None | None | None | None | None | None | None | None | None |
| 1.5% | None | None | None | None | None | None | None | None | None | None | None | None |
| 1.625% | None | None | None | None | None | None | None | None | None | None | None | None |
| 1.75% | None | None | None | None | None | None | None | None | None | None | None | None |
| 1.875% | 55 | 67 | None | None | None | None | None | None | None | None | None | None |
| 2% | 47 | 54 | 63 | None | None | None | None | None | None | None | None | None |
| 2.125% | 42 | 47 | 53 | 61 | None | None | None | None | None | None | None | None |
| 2.25% | 39 | 43 | 48 | 53 | 72 | 67 | 84 | None | None | None | None | None |
| 2.375% | 35 | 39 | 43 | 48 | 59 | 58 | 65 | 74 | None | None | None | None |
| 2.5% | 33 | 36 | 40 | 43 | 52 | 52 | 57 | 63 | 82 | None | None | None |
| 2.625% | 31 | 34 | 37 | 40 | 48 | 48 | 52 | 56 | 68 | None | None | None |
| 2.75% | 29 | 32 | 35 | 37 | 44 | 44 | 48 | 51 | 61 | 73 | None | None |
| 2.875% | 27 | 30 | 32 | 35 | 41 | 41 | 44 | 48 | 55 | 64 | 77 | None |
| 3% | 26 | 28 | 31 | 33 | 38 | 39 | 41 | 44 | 51 | 59 | 68 | 82 |
| 3.125% | 25 | 27 | 29 | 31 | 36 | 36 | 39 | 42 | 48 | 54 | 62 | 72 |
| 3.25% | 24 | 26 | 28 | 30 | 34 | 34 | 37 | 39 | 45 | 51 | 58 | 66 |
| 3.375% | 23 | 24 | 26 | 28 | 32 | 33 | 35 | 37 | 42 | 48 | 54 | 61 |
| 3.5% | 22 | 23 | 25 | 27 | 31 | 31 | 33 | 36 | 40 | 45 | 51 | 57 |
| 3.625% | 21 | 22 | 24 | 26 | 29 | 30 | 32 | 34 | 38 | 43 | 48 | 53 |
| 3.75% | 20 | 22 | 23 | 25 | 28 | 29 | 31 | 32 | 37 | 41 | 45 | 50 |
| 3.875% | 19 | 21 | 22 | 24 | 27 | 28 | 29 | 31 | 35 | 39 | 43 | 48 |
| 4% | 19 | 20 | 22 | 23 | 26 | 27 | 28 | 30 | 34 | 37 | 41 | 46 |

## Break-Even Periods (in Months)

Term Left on Current Loan: 300 months
Term on New Loan: 15 years
Points: 0.00%

Income Tax Bracket: Pre-Tax
Points and Costs: Financed

### Other Closing Costs as a Percent of Loan Amount

| Interest Rate Reduction | .25% | .5% | .75% | 1.00% | 1.25% | 1.50% | 1.75% | 2.00% | 2.50% | 3.00% | 3.50% | 4.00% |
|---|---|---|---|---|---|---|---|---|---|---|---|---|
| 0.125% | 17 | 28 | 36 | 44 | 51 | 57 | 63 | 68 | 78 | 87 | 96 | 104 |
| 0.25% | 11 | 20 | 28 | 35 | 41 | 47 | 53 | 58 | 68 | 77 | 86 | 94 |
| 0.375% | 8 | 15 | 22 | 28 | 34 | 39 | 45 | 50 | 59 | 68 | 77 | 85 |
| 0.5% | 6 | 12 | 18 | 23 | 28 | 33 | 38 | 43 | 52 | 60 | 69 | 77 |
| 0.625% | 5 | 10 | 15 | 19 | 24 | 28 | 32 | 37 | 45 | 53 | 61 | 69 |
| 0.75% | 5 | 9 | 12 | 16 | 20 | 24 | 28 | 32 | 40 | 47 | 55 | 62 |
| 0.875% | 4 | 7 | 11 | 14 | 18 | 21 | 25 | 28 | 35 | 42 | 49 | 56 |
| 1% | 4 | 7 | 10 | 13 | 16 | 19 | 22 | 25 | 31 | 38 | 44 | 50 |
| 1.125% | 3 | 6 | 9 | 11 | 14 | 17 | 20 | 23 | 28 | 34 | 40 | 46 |
| 1.25% | 3 | 5 | 8 | 10 | 13 | 15 | 18 | 21 | 26 | 31 | 36 | 42 |
| 1.375% | 3 | 5 | 7 | 9 | 12 | 14 | 16 | 19 | 24 | 28 | 33 | 38 |
| 1.5% | 3 | 5 | 7 | 9 | 11 | 13 | 15 | 17 | 22 | 26 | 31 | 35 |
| 1.625% | 2 | 4 | 6 | 8 | 10 | 12 | 14 | 16 | 20 | 24 | 29 | 33 |
| 1.75% | 2 | 4 | 6 | 8 | 9 | 11 | 13 | 15 | 19 | 23 | 27 | 31 |
| 1.875% | 2 | 4 | 5 | 7 | 9 | 10 | 12 | 14 | 17 | 21 | 25 | 29 |
| 2% | 2 | 4 | 5 | 7 | 8 | 10 | 11 | 13 | 16 | 20 | 23 | 27 |
| 2.125% | 2 | 3 | 5 | 6 | 8 | 9 | 11 | 12 | 15 | 19 | 22 | 25 |
| 2.25% | 2 | 3 | 5 | 6 | 7 | 9 | 10 | 12 | 15 | 18 | 21 | 24 |
| 2.375% | 2 | 3 | 4 | 6 | 7 | 8 | 10 | 11 | 14 | 17 | 20 | 23 |
| 2.5% | 2 | 3 | 4 | 5 | 7 | 8 | 9 | 11 | 13 | 16 | 19 | 21 |
| 2.625% | 2 | 3 | 4 | 5 | 6 | 8 | 9 | 10 | 13 | 15 | 18 | 20 |
| 2.75% | 2 | 3 | 4 | 5 | 6 | 7 | 8 | 10 | 12 | 14 | 17 | 19 |
| 2.875% | 2 | 3 | 4 | 5 | 6 | 7 | 8 | 9 | 11 | 14 | 16 | 19 |
| 3% | 2 | 3 | 4 | 5 | 6 | 7 | 8 | 9 | 11 | 13 | 15 | 18 |
| 3.125% | 1 | 2 | 3 | 4 | 5 | 6 | 7 | 8 | 11 | 13 | 15 | 17 |
| 3.25% | 1 | 2 | 3 | 4 | 5 | 6 | 7 | 8 | 10 | 12 | 14 | 16 |
| 3.375% | 1 | 2 | 3 | 4 | 5 | 6 | 7 | 8 | 10 | 12 | 14 | 16 |
| 3.5% | 1 | 2 | 3 | 4 | 5 | 6 | 7 | 8 | 9 | 11 | 13 | 15 |
| 3.625% | 1 | 2 | 3 | 4 | 5 | 6 | 6 | 7 | 9 | 11 | 13 | 15 |
| 3.75% | 1 | 2 | 3 | 4 | 5 | 5 | 6 | 7 | 9 | 11 | 12 | 14 |
| 3.875% | 1 | 2 | 3 | 4 | 4 | 5 | 6 | 7 | 9 | 10 | 12 | 14 |
| 4% | 1 | 2 | 3 | 4 | 4 | 5 | 6 | 7 | 8 | 10 | 12 | 13 |

| Break-Even Periods (in Months) | | | | | | | | | | | |
|---|---|---|---|---|---|---|---|---|---|---|---|

Term Left on Current Loan: 300 months  
Term on New Loan: 15 years  
Points: 1.00%

Income Tax Bracket: Pre-Tax  
Points and Costs: Financed

| Other Closing Costs as a Percent of Loan Amount | | | | | | | | | | | |
|---|---|---|---|---|---|---|---|---|---|---|---|
| Interest Rate Reduction | .25% | .5% | .75% | 1.00% | 1.25% | 1.50% | 1.75% | 2.00% | 2.50% | 3.00% | 3.50% | 4.00% |
| 0.125% | 50 | 57 | 62 | 68 | 73 | 78 | 82 | 87 | 95 | 103 | 111 | 118 |
| 0.25% | 41 | 47 | 53 | 58 | 63 | 68 | 73 | 77 | 86 | 94 | 101 | 109 |
| 0.375% | 34 | 39 | 44 | 50 | 54 | 59 | 64 | 68 | 77 | 85 | 92 | 100 |
| 0.5% | 28 | 33 | 38 | 42 | 47 | 51 | 56 | 60 | 68 | 76 | 84 | 91 |
| 0.625% | 24 | 28 | 32 | 37 | 41 | 45 | 49 | 53 | 61 | 68 | 76 | 83 |
| 0.75% | 20 | 24 | 28 | 32 | 36 | 39 | 43 | 47 | 54 | 61 | 69 | 75 |
| 0.875% | 18 | 21 | 25 | 28 | 32 | 35 | 38 | 42 | 49 | 55 | 62 | 69 |
| 1% | 16 | 19 | 22 | 25 | 28 | 31 | 34 | 38 | 44 | 50 | 56 | 63 |
| 1.125% | 14 | 17 | 20 | 23 | 25 | 28 | 31 | 34 | 40 | 45 | 51 | 57 |
| 1.25% | 13 | 15 | 18 | 20 | 23 | 26 | 28 | 31 | 36 | 42 | 47 | 52 |
| 1.375% | 12 | 14 | 16 | 19 | 21 | 23 | 26 | 28 | 33 | 38 | 43 | 48 |
| 1.5% | 11 | 13 | 15 | 17 | 19 | 22 | 24 | 26 | 31 | 35 | 40 | 45 |
| 1.625% | 10 | 12 | 14 | 16 | 18 | 20 | 22 | 24 | 28 | 33 | 37 | 41 |
| 1.75% | 9 | 11 | 13 | 15 | 17 | 19 | 20 | 22 | 26 | 30 | 34 | 39 |
| 1.875% | 9 | 10 | 12 | 14 | 16 | 17 | 19 | 21 | 25 | 28 | 32 | 36 |
| 2% | 8 | 10 | 11 | 13 | 15 | 16 | 18 | 20 | 23 | 27 | 30 | 34 |
| 2.125% | 8 | 9 | 11 | 12 | 14 | 15 | 17 | 19 | 22 | 25 | 28 | 32 |
| 2.25% | 7 | 9 | 10 | 12 | 13 | 15 | 16 | 17 | 21 | 24 | 27 | 30 |
| 2.375% | 7 | 8 | 10 | 11 | 12 | 14 | 15 | 17 | 19 | 22 | 25 | 28 |
| 2.5% | 7 | 8 | 9 | 10 | 12 | 13 | 14 | 16 | 18 | 21 | 24 | 27 |
| 2.625% | 6 | 8 | 9 | 10 | 11 | 12 | 14 | 15 | 18 | 20 | 23 | 26 |
| 2.75% | 6 | 7 | 8 | 10 | 11 | 12 | 13 | 14 | 17 | 19 | 22 | 24 |
| 2.875% | 6 | 7 | 8 | 9 | 10 | 11 | 13 | 14 | 16 | 18 | 21 | 23 |
| 3% | 6 | 7 | 8 | 9 | 10 | 11 | 12 | 13 | 15 | 18 | 20 | 22 |
| 3.125% | 5 | 6 | 7 | 8 | 9 | 11 | 12 | 13 | 15 | 17 | 19 | 21 |
| 3.25% | 5 | 6 | 7 | 8 | 9 | 10 | 11 | 12 | 14 | 16 | 18 | 21 |
| 3.375% | 5 | 6 | 7 | 8 | 9 | 10 | 11 | 12 | 14 | 16 | 18 | 20 |
| 3.5% | 5 | 6 | 7 | 8 | 8 | 9 | 10 | 11 | 13 | 15 | 17 | 19 |
| 3.625% | 5 | 6 | 6 | 7 | 8 | 9 | 10 | 11 | 13 | 15 | 16 | 18 |
| 3.75% | 5 | 5 | 6 | 7 | 8 | 9 | 10 | 11 | 12 | 14 | 16 | 18 |
| 3.875% | 4 | 5 | 6 | 7 | 8 | 9 | 9 | 10 | 12 | 14 | 15 | 17 |
| 4% | 4 | 5 | 6 | 7 | 7 | 8 | 9 | 10 | 12 | 13 | 15 | 17 |

## Break-Even Periods (in Months)

Term Left on Current Loan: 300 months
Term on New Loan: 15 years
Points: 2.00%

Income Tax Bracket: Pre-Tax
Points and Costs: Financed

### Other Closing Costs as a Percent of Loan Amount

| Interest Rate Reduction | .25% | .5% | .75% | 1.00% | 1.25% | 1.50% | 1.75% | 2.00% | 2.50% | 3.00% | 3.50% | 4.00% |
|---|---|---|---|---|---|---|---|---|---|---|---|---|
| 0.125% | 73 | 78 | 82 | 87 | 91 | 95 | 99 | 103 | 110 | 117 | 124 | 131 |
| 0.25% | 63 | 68 | 73 | 77 | 81 | 86 | 90 | 94 | 101 | 108 | 115 | 122 |
| 0.375% | 55 | 59 | 64 | 68 | 72 | 76 | 81 | 84 | 92 | 99 | 106 | 113 |
| 0.5% | 47 | 51 | 56 | 60 | 64 | 68 | 72 | 76 | 83 | 91 | 98 | 105 |
| 0.625% | 41 | 45 | 49 | 53 | 57 | 61 | 64 | 68 | 76 | 83 | 90 | 96 |
| 0.75% | 36 | 40 | 43 | 47 | 51 | 54 | 58 | 61 | 68 | 75 | 82 | 89 |
| 0.875% | 32 | 35 | 38 | 42 | 45 | 49 | 52 | 55 | 62 | 68 | 75 | 81 |
| 1% | 28 | 31 | 34 | 38 | 41 | 44 | 47 | 50 | 56 | 62 | 68 | 75 |
| 1.125% | 25 | 28 | 31 | 34 | 37 | 40 | 42 | 45 | 51 | 57 | 63 | 69 |
| 1.25% | 23 | 26 | 28 | 31 | 33 | 36 | 39 | 41 | 47 | 52 | 58 | 63 |
| 1.375% | 21 | 23 | 26 | 28 | 31 | 33 | 36 | 38 | 43 | 48 | 53 | 58 |
| 1.5% | 19 | 22 | 24 | 26 | 28 | 30 | 33 | 35 | 40 | 44 | 49 | 54 |
| 1.625% | 18 | 20 | 22 | 24 | 26 | 28 | 30 | 32 | 37 | 41 | 46 | 50 |
| 1.75% | 17 | 19 | 20 | 22 | 24 | 26 | 28 | 30 | 34 | 38 | 43 | 47 |
| 1.875% | 16 | 17 | 19 | 21 | 23 | 25 | 26 | 28 | 32 | 36 | 40 | 44 |
| 2% | 15 | 16 | 18 | 20 | 21 | 23 | 25 | 27 | 30 | 34 | 37 | 41 |
| 2.125% | 14 | 15 | 17 | 19 | 20 | 22 | 23 | 25 | 28 | 32 | 35 | 39 |
| 2.25% | 13 | 15 | 16 | 17 | 19 | 20 | 22 | 24 | 27 | 30 | 33 | 36 |
| 2.375% | 12 | 14 | 15 | 17 | 18 | 19 | 21 | 22 | 25 | 28 | 31 | 35 |
| 2.5% | 12 | 13 | 14 | 16 | 17 | 18 | 20 | 21 | 24 | 27 | 30 | 33 |
| 2.625% | 11 | 12 | 14 | 15 | 16 | 18 | 19 | 20 | 23 | 26 | 28 | 31 |
| 2.75% | 11 | 12 | 13 | 14 | 16 | 17 | 18 | 19 | 22 | 24 | 27 | 30 |
| 2.875% | 10 | 11 | 13 | 14 | 15 | 16 | 17 | 18 | 21 | 23 | 26 | 28 |
| 3% | 10 | 11 | 12 | 13 | 14 | 15 | 16 | 18 | 20 | 22 | 25 | 27 |
| 3.125% | 9 | 11 | 12 | 13 | 14 | 15 | 16 | 17 | 19 | 21 | 24 | 26 |
| 3.25% | 9 | 10 | 11 | 12 | 13 | 14 | 15 | 16 | 18 | 21 | 23 | 25 |
| 3.375% | 9 | 10 | 11 | 12 | 13 | 14 | 15 | 16 | 18 | 20 | 22 | 24 |
| 3.5% | 9 | 9 | 10 | 11 | 12 | 13 | 14 | 15 | 17 | 19 | 21 | 23 |
| 3.625% | 8 | 9 | 10 | 11 | 12 | 13 | 14 | 15 | 16 | 18 | 20 | 22 |
| 3.75% | 8 | 9 | 10 | 11 | 11 | 12 | 13 | 14 | 16 | 18 | 20 | 21 |
| 3.875% | 8 | 9 | 9 | 10 | 11 | 12 | 13 | 14 | 15 | 17 | 19 | 21 |
| 4% | 7 | 8 | 9 | 10 | 11 | 12 | 12 | 13 | 15 | 17 | 18 | 20 |

| Break-Even Periods (in Months) | | | | | | | | | | | | |
|---|---|---|---|---|---|---|---|---|---|---|---|---|
| Term Left on Current Loan: 300 months<br>Term on New Loan: 15 years<br>Points: 3.00% | | | | | | Income Tax Bracket: Pre-Tax<br>Points and Costs: Financed | | | | | | |
| Other Closing Costs as a Percent of Loan Amount | | | | | | | | | | | | |
| Interest Rate Reduction | .25% | .5% | .75% | 1.00% | 1.25% | 1.50% | 1.75% | 2.00% | 2.50% | 3.00% | 3.50% | 4.00% |
| 0.125% | 91 | 95 | 99 | 103 | 107 | 111 | 114 | 117 | 124 | 130 | 136 | 142 |
| 0.25% | 82 | 86 | 90 | 94 | 98 | 101 | 105 | 108 | 115 | 122 | 128 | 134 |
| 0.375% | 73 | 77 | 81 | 85 | 88 | 92 | 96 | 99 | 106 | 113 | 119 | 126 |
| 0.5% | 64 | 68 | 72 | 76 | 80 | 84 | 87 | 91 | 98 | 104 | 111 | 117 |
| 0.625% | 57 | 61 | 65 | 68 | 72 | 76 | 79 | 83 | 89 | 96 | 103 | 109 |
| 0.75% | 51 | 54 | 58 | 61 | 65 | 68 | 72 | 75 | 82 | 88 | 95 | 101 |
| 0.875% | 45 | 49 | 52 | 55 | 59 | 62 | 65 | 68 | 75 | 81 | 87 | 94 |
| 1% | 41 | 44 | 47 | 50 | 53 | 56 | 59 | 62 | 68 | 74 | 80 | 86 |
| 1.125% | 37 | 40 | 43 | 45 | 48 | 51 | 54 | 57 | 63 | 68 | 74 | 80 |
| 1.25% | 34 | 36 | 39 | 42 | 44 | 47 | 50 | 52 | 58 | 63 | 68 | 74 |
| 1.375% | 31 | 33 | 36 | 38 | 41 | 43 | 46 | 48 | 53 | 58 | 63 | 69 |
| 1.5% | 28 | 31 | 33 | 35 | 37 | 40 | 42 | 44 | 49 | 54 | 59 | 64 |
| 1.625% | 26 | 28 | 30 | 33 | 35 | 37 | 39 | 41 | 46 | 50 | 55 | 59 |
| 1.75% | 24 | 26 | 28 | 30 | 32 | 34 | 36 | 38 | 42 | 47 | 51 | 55 |
| 1.875% | 23 | 25 | 26 | 28 | 30 | 32 | 34 | 36 | 40 | 44 | 48 | 52 |
| 2% | 21 | 23 | 25 | 27 | 28 | 30 | 32 | 34 | 37 | 41 | 45 | 49 |
| 2.125% | 20 | 22 | 23 | 25 | 27 | 28 | 30 | 32 | 35 | 39 | 42 | 46 |
| 2.25% | 19 | 21 | 22 | 24 | 25 | 27 | 28 | 30 | 33 | 36 | 40 | 43 |
| 2.375% | 18 | 19 | 21 | 22 | 24 | 25 | 27 | 28 | 31 | 34 | 38 | 41 |
| 2.5% | 17 | 19 | 20 | 21 | 23 | 24 | 25 | 27 | 30 | 33 | 36 | 39 |
| 2.625% | 16 | 18 | 19 | 20 | 22 | 23 | 24 | 26 | 28 | 31 | 34 | 37 |
| 2.75% | 16 | 17 | 18 | 19 | 21 | 22 | 23 | 24 | 27 | 30 | 32 | 35 |
| 2.875% | 15 | 16 | 17 | 18 | 20 | 21 | 22 | 23 | 26 | 28 | 31 | 33 |
| 3% | 14 | 15 | 17 | 18 | 19 | 20 | 21 | 22 | 25 | 27 | 30 | 32 |
| 3.125% | 14 | 15 | 16 | 17 | 18 | 19 | 20 | 21 | 24 | 26 | 28 | 31 |
| 3.25% | 13 | 14 | 15 | 16 | 17 | 18 | 19 | 21 | 23 | 25 | 27 | 29 |
| 3.375% | 13 | 14 | 15 | 16 | 17 | 18 | 19 | 20 | 22 | 24 | 26 | 28 |
| 3.5% | 12 | 13 | 14 | 15 | 16 | 17 | 18 | 19 | 21 | 23 | 25 | 27 |
| 3.625% | 12 | 13 | 14 | 15 | 16 | 16 | 17 | 18 | 20 | 22 | 24 | 26 |
| 3.75% | 11 | 12 | 13 | 14 | 15 | 16 | 17 | 18 | 20 | 21 | 23 | 25 |
| 3.875% | 11 | 12 | 13 | 14 | 14 | 15 | 16 | 17 | 19 | 21 | 23 | 24 |
| 4% | 11 | 12 | 12 | 13 | 14 | 15 | 16 | 17 | 18 | 20 | 22 | 24 |

## Break-Even Periods (in Months)

Term Left on Current Loan: 300 months      Income Tax Bracket: 40.00%
Term on New Loan: 15 years      Points and Costs: Financed
Points: 0.00%

### Other Closing Costs as a Percent of Loan Amount

| Interest Rate Reduction | .25% | .5% | .75% | 1.00% | 1.25% | 1.50% | 1.75% | 2.00% | 2.50% | 3.00% | 3.50% | 4.00% |
|---|---|---|---|---|---|---|---|---|---|---|---|---|
| 0.125% | 24 | 37 | 48 | 57 | 65 | 73 | 79 | 86 | 97 | 108 | 118 | 126 |
| 0.25% | 17 | 29 | 39 | 48 | 56 | 63 | 70 | 77 | 89 | 99 | 109 | 118 |
| 0.375% | 13 | 23 | 32 | 40 | 48 | 55 | 62 | 68 | 80 | 91 | 101 | 110 |
| 0.5% | 10 | 19 | 27 | 34 | 41 | 48 | 55 | 61 | 72 | 83 | 93 | 102 |
| 0.625% | 8 | 16 | 23 | 30 | 36 | 42 | 48 | 54 | 65 | 76 | 85 | 95 |
| 0.75% | 7 | 13 | 20 | 26 | 32 | 37 | 43 | 48 | 59 | 69 | 78 | 88 |
| 0.875% | 6 | 12 | 17 | 23 | 28 | 33 | 38 | 43 | 53 | 63 | 72 | 81 |
| 1% | 5 | 10 | 15 | 20 | 25 | 30 | 35 | 39 | 48 | 58 | 66 | 75 |
| 1.125% | 5 | 9 | 14 | 18 | 23 | 27 | 31 | 36 | 44 | 53 | 61 | 69 |
| 1.25% | 5 | 9 | 13 | 17 | 21 | 25 | 29 | 33 | 41 | 49 | 56 | 64 |
| 1.375% | 4 | 8 | 12 | 15 | 19 | 23 | 26 | 30 | 37 | 45 | 52 | 60 |
| 1.5% | 4 | 7 | 11 | 14 | 17 | 21 | 24 | 28 | 35 | 42 | 49 | 56 |
| 1.625% | 4 | 7 | 10 | 13 | 16 | 19 | 23 | 26 | 32 | 39 | 45 | 52 |
| 1.75% | 3 | 6 | 9 | 12 | 15 | 18 | 21 | 24 | 30 | 36 | 43 | 49 |
| 1.875% | 3 | 6 | 9 | 11 | 14 | 17 | 20 | 23 | 28 | 34 | 40 | 46 |
| 2% | 3 | 6 | 8 | 11 | 13 | 16 | 19 | 21 | 27 | 32 | 38 | 43 |
| 2.125% | 3 | 5 | 8 | 10 | 13 | 15 | 18 | 20 | 25 | 30 | 36 | 41 |
| 2.25% | 3 | 5 | 7 | 10 | 12 | 14 | 17 | 19 | 24 | 29 | 34 | 39 |
| 2.375% | 3 | 5 | 7 | 9 | 11 | 13 | 16 | 18 | 23 | 27 | 32 | 37 |
| 2.5% | 3 | 5 | 7 | 9 | 11 | 13 | 15 | 17 | 21 | 26 | 30 | 35 |
| 2.625% | 2 | 4 | 6 | 8 | 10 | 12 | 14 | 16 | 20 | 25 | 29 | 33 |
| 2.75% | 2 | 4 | 6 | 8 | 10 | 12 | 14 | 16 | 20 | 24 | 28 | 32 |
| 2.875% | 2 | 4 | 6 | 8 | 9 | 11 | 13 | 15 | 19 | 23 | 26 | 30 |
| 3% | 2 | 4 | 6 | 7 | 9 | 11 | 13 | 14 | 18 | 22 | 25 | 29 |
| 3.125% | 2 | 4 | 5 | 7 | 9 | 10 | 12 | 14 | 17 | 21 | 24 | 28 |
| 3.25% | 2 | 4 | 5 | 7 | 8 | 10 | 12 | 13 | 17 | 20 | 23 | 27 |
| 3.375% | 2 | 3 | 5 | 7 | 8 | 10 | 11 | 13 | 16 | 19 | 23 | 26 |
| 3.5% | 2 | 3 | 5 | 6 | 8 | 9 | 11 | 12 | 15 | 19 | 22 | 25 |
| 3.625% | 2 | 3 | 5 | 6 | 8 | 9 | 10 | 12 | 15 | 18 | 21 | 24 |
| 3.75% | 2 | 3 | 5 | 6 | 7 | 9 | 10 | 12 | 14 | 17 | 20 | 23 |
| 3.875% | 2 | 3 | 4 | 6 | 7 | 8 | 10 | 11 | 14 | 17 | 20 | 23 |
| 4% | 2 | 3 | 4 | 6 | 7 | 8 | 10 | 11 | 14 | 16 | 19 | 22 |

# Refinance Break-Even Tables

| Break-Even Periods (in Months) | | | | | | | | | | | | |
|---|---|---|---|---|---|---|---|---|---|---|---|---|

Term Left on Current Loan: 300 months      Income Tax Bracket: 40.00%
Term on New Loan: 15 years      Points and Costs: Financed
Points: 1.00%

| Interest Rate Reduction | Other Closing Costs as a Percent of Loan Amount | | | | | | | | | | | |
|---|---|---|---|---|---|---|---|---|---|---|---|---|
| | .25% | .5% | .75% | 1.00% | 1.25% | 1.50% | 1.75% | 2.00% | 2.50% | 3.00% | 3.50% | 4.00% |
| 0.125% | 65 | 73 | 79 | 86 | 92 | 97 | 102 | 108 | 117 | 126 | 134 | 142 |
| 0.25% | 56 | 63 | 70 | 76 | 82 | 88 | 94 | 99 | 109 | 118 | 126 | 134 |
| 0.375% | 48 | 55 | 62 | 68 | 74 | 80 | 85 | 90 | 100 | 110 | 118 | 127 |
| 0.5% | 41 | 48 | 54 | 60 | 66 | 72 | 77 | 83 | 92 | 102 | 111 | 119 |
| 0.625% | 36 | 42 | 48 | 54 | 59 | 65 | 70 | 75 | 85 | 94 | 103 | 112 |
| 0.75% | 32 | 37 | 43 | 48 | 53 | 59 | 64 | 68 | 78 | 87 | 96 | 104 |
| 0.875% | 28 | 33 | 38 | 43 | 48 | 53 | 58 | 62 | 72 | 81 | 89 | 97 |
| 1% | 25 | 30 | 34 | 39 | 44 | 48 | 53 | 57 | 66 | 74 | 83 | 91 |
| 1.125% | 23 | 27 | 31 | 36 | 40 | 44 | 48 | 52 | 61 | 69 | 77 | 85 |
| 1.25% | 21 | 25 | 29 | 32 | 36 | 40 | 44 | 48 | 56 | 64 | 72 | 79 |
| 1.375% | 19 | 23 | 26 | 30 | 34 | 37 | 41 | 45 | 52 | 59 | 67 | 74 |
| 1.5% | 17 | 21 | 24 | 28 | 31 | 35 | 38 | 41 | 48 | 55 | 62 | 69 |
| 1.625% | 16 | 19 | 22 | 26 | 29 | 32 | 35 | 39 | 45 | 52 | 58 | 65 |
| 1.75% | 15 | 18 | 21 | 24 | 27 | 30 | 33 | 36 | 42 | 48 | 55 | 61 |
| 1.875% | 14 | 17 | 20 | 22 | 25 | 28 | 31 | 34 | 40 | 46 | 51 | 57 |
| 2% | 13 | 16 | 18 | 21 | 24 | 26 | 29 | 32 | 37 | 43 | 49 | 54 |
| 2.125% | 13 | 15 | 17 | 20 | 22 | 25 | 28 | 30 | 35 | 41 | 46 | 51 |
| 2.25% | 12 | 14 | 17 | 19 | 21 | 24 | 26 | 28 | 33 | 38 | 43 | 49 |
| 2.375% | 11 | 13 | 16 | 18 | 20 | 22 | 25 | 27 | 32 | 36 | 41 | 46 |
| 2.5% | 11 | 13 | 15 | 17 | 19 | 21 | 24 | 26 | 30 | 35 | 39 | 44 |
| 2.625% | 10 | 12 | 14 | 16 | 18 | 20 | 22 | 24 | 29 | 33 | 37 | 42 |
| 2.75% | 10 | 12 | 14 | 16 | 17 | 19 | 21 | 23 | 27 | 32 | 36 | 40 |
| 2.875% | 9 | 11 | 13 | 15 | 17 | 19 | 20 | 22 | 26 | 30 | 34 | 38 |
| 3% | 9 | 11 | 12 | 14 | 16 | 18 | 20 | 21 | 25 | 29 | 33 | 37 |
| 3.125% | 9 | 10 | 12 | 14 | 15 | 17 | 19 | 21 | 24 | 28 | 31 | 35 |
| 3.25% | 8 | 10 | 12 | 13 | 15 | 16 | 18 | 20 | 23 | 27 | 30 | 34 |
| 3.375% | 8 | 10 | 11 | 13 | 14 | 16 | 17 | 19 | 22 | 26 | 29 | 33 |
| 3.5% | 8 | 9 | 11 | 12 | 14 | 15 | 17 | 18 | 22 | 25 | 28 | 31 |
| 3.625% | 8 | 9 | 10 | 12 | 13 | 15 | 16 | 18 | 21 | 24 | 27 | 30 |
| 3.75% | 7 | 9 | 10 | 11 | 13 | 14 | 16 | 17 | 20 | 23 | 26 | 29 |
| 3.875% | 7 | 8 | 10 | 11 | 12 | 14 | 15 | 17 | 20 | 22 | 25 | 28 |
| 4% | 7 | 8 | 9 | 11 | 12 | 13 | 15 | 16 | 19 | 22 | 25 | 27 |

| Break-Even Periods (in Months) | | | | | | | | | | | |
|---|---|---|---|---|---|---|---|---|---|---|---|

Term Left on Current Loan: 300 months      Income Tax Bracket: 40.00%
Term on New Loan: 15 years      Points and Costs: Financed
Points: 2.00%

| Other Closing Costs as a Percent of Loan Amount | | | | | | | | | | | |
|---|---|---|---|---|---|---|---|---|---|---|---|
| Interest Rate Reduction | .25% | .5% | .75% | 1.00% | 1.25% | 1.50% | 1.75% | 2.00% | 2.50% | 3.00% | 3.50% | 4.00% |
| 0.125% | 92 | 97 | 102 | 108 | 112 | 117 | 121 | 126 | 134 | 142 | 149 | 156 |
| 0.25% | 83 | 88 | 94 | 99 | 104 | 109 | 113 | 118 | 126 | 134 | 142 | 149 |
| 0.375% | 74 | 80 | 85 | 90 | 95 | 100 | 105 | 110 | 118 | 126 | 134 | 142 |
| 0.5% | 66 | 72 | 77 | 83 | 88 | 92 | 97 | 102 | 110 | 119 | 127 | 134 |
| 0.625% | 60 | 65 | 70 | 75 | 80 | 85 | 90 | 94 | 103 | 111 | 119 | 127 |
| 0.75% | 54 | 59 | 64 | 68 | 73 | 78 | 82 | 87 | 96 | 104 | 112 | 120 |
| 0.875% | 48 | 53 | 58 | 62 | 67 | 72 | 76 | 80 | 89 | 97 | 105 | 113 |
| 1% | 44 | 48 | 53 | 57 | 61 | 66 | 70 | 74 | 83 | 91 | 98 | 106 |
| 1.125% | 40 | 44 | 48 | 52 | 57 | 61 | 65 | 69 | 77 | 84 | 92 | 100 |
| 1.25% | 37 | 40 | 44 | 48 | 52 | 56 | 60 | 64 | 71 | 79 | 86 | 94 |
| 1.375% | 34 | 37 | 41 | 45 | 48 | 52 | 56 | 59 | 66 | 74 | 81 | 88 |
| 1.5% | 31 | 35 | 38 | 41 | 45 | 48 | 52 | 55 | 62 | 69 | 76 | 83 |
| 1.625% | 29 | 32 | 35 | 39 | 42 | 45 | 48 | 52 | 58 | 65 | 71 | 78 |
| 1.75% | 27 | 30 | 33 | 36 | 39 | 42 | 45 | 48 | 55 | 61 | 67 | 73 |
| 1.875% | 25 | 28 | 31 | 34 | 37 | 40 | 42 | 45 | 51 | 57 | 63 | 69 |
| 2% | 24 | 26 | 29 | 32 | 35 | 37 | 40 | 43 | 48 | 54 | 60 | 65 |
| 2.125% | 23 | 25 | 28 | 30 | 33 | 35 | 38 | 40 | 46 | 51 | 56 | 62 |
| 2.25% | 21 | 24 | 26 | 28 | 31 | 33 | 36 | 38 | 43 | 48 | 54 | 59 |
| 2.375% | 20 | 22 | 25 | 27 | 29 | 32 | 34 | 36 | 41 | 46 | 51 | 56 |
| 2.5% | 19 | 21 | 24 | 26 | 28 | 30 | 32 | 35 | 39 | 44 | 48 | 53 |
| 2.625% | 18 | 20 | 22 | 24 | 27 | 29 | 31 | 33 | 37 | 42 | 46 | 51 |
| 2.75% | 18 | 19 | 21 | 23 | 25 | 27 | 29 | 31 | 36 | 40 | 44 | 49 |
| 2.875% | 17 | 19 | 21 | 22 | 24 | 26 | 28 | 30 | 34 | 38 | 42 | 46 |
| 3% | 16 | 18 | 20 | 21 | 23 | 25 | 27 | 29 | 33 | 37 | 41 | 45 |
| 3.125% | 15 | 17 | 19 | 21 | 22 | 24 | 26 | 28 | 31 | 35 | 39 | 43 |
| 3.25% | 15 | 17 | 18 | 20 | 22 | 23 | 25 | 27 | 30 | 34 | 37 | 41 |
| 3.375% | 14 | 16 | 18 | 19 | 21 | 22 | 24 | 26 | 29 | 32 | 36 | 40 |
| 3.5% | 14 | 15 | 17 | 18 | 20 | 22 | 23 | 25 | 28 | 31 | 35 | 38 |
| 3.625% | 13 | 15 | 16 | 18 | 19 | 21 | 22 | 24 | 27 | 30 | 33 | 37 |
| 3.75% | 13 | 14 | 16 | 17 | 19 | 20 | 22 | 23 | 26 | 29 | 32 | 36 |
| 3.875% | 13 | 14 | 15 | 17 | 18 | 19 | 21 | 22 | 25 | 28 | 31 | 34 |
| 4% | 12 | 13 | 15 | 16 | 18 | 19 | 20 | 22 | 24 | 27 | 30 | 33 |

# Refinance Break-Even Tables

## Break-Even Periods (in Months)

Term Left on Current Loan: 300 months  
Term on New Loan: 15 years  
Points: 3.00%

Income Tax Bracket: 40.00%  
Points and Costs: Financed

### Other Closing Costs as a Percent of Loan Amount

| Interest Rate Reduction | .25% | .5% | .75% | 1.00% | 1.25% | 1.50% | 1.75% | 2.00% | 2.50% | 3.00% | 3.50% | 4.00% |
|---|---|---|---|---|---|---|---|---|---|---|---|---|
| 0.125% | 113 | 117 | 122 | 126 | 130 | 134 | 138 | 142 | 149 | 156 | 162 | 168 |
| 0.25% | 104 | 109 | 113 | 118 | 122 | 126 | 130 | 134 | 142 | 149 | 155 | 162 |
| 0.375% | 96 | 101 | 105 | 110 | 114 | 118 | 122 | 126 | 134 | 141 | 148 | 155 |
| 0.5% | 88 | 93 | 97 | 102 | 106 | 111 | 115 | 119 | 127 | 134 | 141 | 148 |
| 0.625% | 80 | 85 | 90 | 94 | 99 | 103 | 107 | 111 | 119 | 127 | 134 | 141 |
| 0.75% | 74 | 78 | 83 | 87 | 91 | 96 | 100 | 104 | 112 | 120 | 127 | 134 |
| 0.875% | 67 | 72 | 76 | 81 | 85 | 89 | 93 | 97 | 105 | 113 | 120 | 128 |
| 1% | 62 | 66 | 70 | 74 | 79 | 83 | 87 | 91 | 98 | 106 | 113 | 121 |
| 1.125% | 57 | 61 | 65 | 69 | 73 | 77 | 81 | 84 | 92 | 100 | 107 | 114 |
| 1.25% | 52 | 56 | 60 | 64 | 68 | 71 | 75 | 79 | 86 | 94 | 101 | 108 |
| 1.375% | 49 | 52 | 56 | 59 | 63 | 67 | 70 | 74 | 81 | 88 | 95 | 102 |
| 1.5% | 45 | 49 | 52 | 55 | 59 | 62 | 66 | 69 | 76 | 83 | 89 | 96 |
| 1.625% | 42 | 45 | 48 | 52 | 55 | 58 | 61 | 65 | 71 | 78 | 84 | 91 |
| 1.75% | 39 | 42 | 45 | 48 | 52 | 55 | 58 | 61 | 67 | 73 | 79 | 86 |
| 1.875% | 37 | 40 | 43 | 46 | 48 | 51 | 54 | 57 | 63 | 69 | 75 | 81 |
| 2% | 35 | 37 | 40 | 43 | 46 | 48 | 51 | 54 | 60 | 65 | 71 | 77 |
| 2.125% | 33 | 35 | 38 | 41 | 43 | 46 | 48 | 51 | 56 | 62 | 67 | 73 |
| 2.25% | 31 | 33 | 36 | 38 | 41 | 43 | 46 | 48 | 54 | 59 | 64 | 69 |
| 2.375% | 29 | 32 | 34 | 36 | 39 | 41 | 44 | 46 | 51 | 56 | 61 | 66 |
| 2.5% | 28 | 30 | 32 | 35 | 37 | 39 | 41 | 44 | 48 | 53 | 58 | 63 |
| 2.625% | 27 | 29 | 31 | 33 | 35 | 37 | 40 | 42 | 46 | 51 | 55 | 60 |
| 2.75% | 26 | 28 | 30 | 32 | 34 | 36 | 38 | 40 | 44 | 48 | 53 | 57 |
| 2.875% | 24 | 26 | 28 | 30 | 32 | 34 | 36 | 38 | 42 | 46 | 51 | 55 |
| 3% | 23 | 25 | 27 | 29 | 31 | 33 | 35 | 37 | 40 | 44 | 48 | 53 |
| 3.125% | 23 | 24 | 26 | 28 | 30 | 31 | 33 | 35 | 39 | 43 | 47 | 50 |
| 3.25% | 22 | 23 | 25 | 27 | 28 | 30 | 32 | 34 | 37 | 41 | 45 | 49 |
| 3.375% | 21 | 22 | 24 | 26 | 27 | 29 | 31 | 32 | 36 | 39 | 43 | 47 |
| 3.5% | 20 | 22 | 23 | 25 | 26 | 28 | 30 | 31 | 35 | 38 | 41 | 45 |
| 3.625% | 19 | 21 | 22 | 24 | 26 | 27 | 29 | 30 | 33 | 37 | 40 | 43 |
| 3.75% | 19 | 20 | 22 | 23 | 25 | 26 | 28 | 29 | 32 | 35 | 39 | 42 |
| 3.875% | 18 | 20 | 21 | 22 | 24 | 25 | 27 | 28 | 31 | 34 | 37 | 41 |
| 4% | 18 | 19 | 20 | 22 | 23 | 25 | 26 | 27 | 30 | 33 | 36 | 39 |

# Refinance Break-Even Tables

| Break-Even Periods (in Months) | | | | | | | | | | | |
|---|---|---|---|---|---|---|---|---|---|---|---|

Term Left on Current Loan: 120 months  
Term on New Loan: 30 years  
Points: 0.00%

Income Tax Bracket: Pre-Tax  
Points and Costs: Financed

| Interest Rate Reduction | Other Closing Costs as a Percent of Loan Amount | | | | | | | | | | | |
|---|---|---|---|---|---|---|---|---|---|---|---|---|
| | .25% | .5% | .75% | 1.00% | 1.25% | 1.50% | 1.75% | 2.00% | 2.50% | 3.00% | 3.50% | 4.00% |
| 0.125% | None | None | None | None | None | None | None | None | None | None | None | None |
| 0.25% | None | None | None | None | None | None | None | None | None | None | None | None |
| 0.375% | None | None | None | None | None | None | None | None | None | None | None | None |
| 0.5% | 8 | None | None | None | None | None | None | None | None | None | None | None |
| 0.625% | 6 | 14 | None | None | None | None | None | None | None | None | None | None |
| 0.75% | 5 | 10 | 19 | None | None | None | None | None | None | None | None | None |
| 0.875% | 4 | 8 | 14 | 22 | None | None | None | None | None | None | None | None |
| 1% | 4 | 7 | 11 | 16 | 24 | None | None | None | None | None | None | None |
| 1.125% | 3 | 6 | 10 | 14 | 18 | 25 | None | None | None | None | None | None |
| 1.25% | 3 | 6 | 9 | 12 | 16 | 20 | 26 | 35 | None | None | None | None |
| 1.375% | 3 | 5 | 8 | 10 | 14 | 17 | 21 | 26 | None | None | None | None |
| 1.5% | 3 | 5 | 7 | 9 | 12 | 15 | 18 | 22 | 32 | None | None | None |
| 1.625% | 2 | 4 | 6 | 9 | 11 | 14 | 16 | 19 | 26 | 37 | None | None |
| 1.75% | 2 | 4 | 6 | 8 | 10 | 12 | 15 | 17 | 23 | 31 | 42 | None |
| 1.875% | 2 | 4 | 6 | 7 | 9 | 11 | 13 | 16 | 21 | 27 | 34 | 46 |
| 2% | 2 | 4 | 5 | 7 | 9 | 11 | 12 | 14 | 19 | 24 | 30 | 38 |
| 2.125% | 2 | 3 | 5 | 6 | 8 | 10 | 12 | 13 | 17 | 22 | 27 | 33 |
| 2.25% | 2 | 3 | 5 | 6 | 8 | 9 | 11 | 13 | 16 | 20 | 25 | 30 |
| 2.375% | 2 | 3 | 4 | 6 | 7 | 9 | 10 | 12 | 15 | 19 | 23 | 27 |
| 2.5% | 2 | 3 | 4 | 6 | 7 | 8 | 10 | 11 | 14 | 18 | 21 | 25 |
| 2.625% | 2 | 3 | 4 | 5 | 7 | 8 | 9 | 11 | 13 | 16 | 20 | 23 |
| 2.75% | 2 | 3 | 4 | 5 | 6 | 7 | 9 | 10 | 13 | 16 | 19 | 22 |
| 2.875% | 2 | 3 | 4 | 5 | 6 | 7 | 8 | 10 | 12 | 15 | 18 | 21 |
| 3% | 2 | 3 | 4 | 5 | 6 | 7 | 8 | 9 | 12 | 14 | 17 | 19 |
| 3.125% | 1 | 2 | 3 | 4 | 6 | 7 | 8 | 9 | 11 | 13 | 16 | 19 |
| 3.25% | 1 | 2 | 3 | 4 | 5 | 6 | 7 | 8 | 11 | 13 | 15 | 18 |
| 3.375% | 1 | 2 | 3 | 4 | 5 | 6 | 7 | 8 | 10 | 12 | 15 | 17 |
| 3.5% | 1 | 2 | 3 | 4 | 5 | 6 | 7 | 8 | 10 | 12 | 14 | 16 |
| 3.625% | 1 | 2 | 3 | 4 | 5 | 6 | 7 | 8 | 9 | 11 | 13 | 16 |
| 3.75% | 1 | 2 | 3 | 4 | 5 | 5 | 6 | 7 | 9 | 11 | 13 | 15 |
| 3.875% | 1 | 2 | 3 | 4 | 4 | 5 | 6 | 7 | 9 | 11 | 12 | 14 |
| 4% | 1 | 2 | 3 | 4 | 4 | 5 | 6 | 7 | 8 | 10 | 12 | 14 |

## Refinance Break-Even Tables

| Break-Even Periods (in Months) | | | | | | | | | | | | |
|---|---|---|---|---|---|---|---|---|---|---|---|---|
| Term Left on Current Loan: 120 months<br>Term on New Loan: 30 years<br>Points: 1.00% | | | | | | Income Tax Bracket: Pre-Tax<br>Points and Costs: Financed | | | | | | |
| Other Closing Costs as a Percent of Loan Amount | | | | | | | | | | | | |
| Interest Rate Reduction | .25% | .5% | .75% | 1.00% | 1.25% | 1.50% | 1.75% | 2.00% | 2.50% | 3.00% | 3.50% | 4.00% |
| 0.125% | None | None | None | None | None | None | None | None | None | None | None | None |
| 0.25% | None | None | None | None | None | None | None | None | None | None | None | None |
| 0.375% | None | None | None | None | None | None | None | None | None | None | None | None |
| 0.5% | None | None | None | None | None | None | None | None | None | None | None | None |
| 0.625% | None | None | None | None | None | None | None | None | None | None | None | None |
| 0.75% | None | None | None | None | None | None | None | None | None | None | None | None |
| 0.875% | None | None | None | None | None | None | None | None | None | None | None | None |
| 1% | 24 | None | None | None | None | None | None | None | None | None | None | None |
| 1.125% | 18 | 25 | None | None | None | None | None | None | None | None | None | None |
| 1.25% | 15 | 20 | 25 | 34 | None | None | None | None | None | None | None | None |
| 1.375% | 14 | 17 | 21 | 26 | 32 | None | None | None | None | None | None | None |
| 1.5% | 12 | 15 | 18 | 22 | 26 | 31 | 39 | None | None | None | None | None |
| 1.625% | 11 | 13 | 16 | 19 | 22 | 26 | 31 | 36 | None | None | None | None |
| 1.75% | 10 | 12 | 15 | 17 | 20 | 23 | 26 | 30 | 41 | None | None | None |
| 1.875% | 9 | 11 | 13 | 16 | 18 | 21 | 23 | 26 | 34 | 45 | None | None |
| 2% | 9 | 10 | 12 | 14 | 17 | 19 | 21 | 24 | 30 | 37 | 48 | None |
| 2.125% | 8 | 10 | 12 | 13 | 15 | 17 | 19 | 22 | 27 | 32 | 40 | 51 |
| 2.25% | 8 | 9 | 11 | 13 | 14 | 16 | 18 | 20 | 24 | 29 | 35 | 42 |
| 2.375% | 7 | 9 | 10 | 12 | 13 | 15 | 17 | 19 | 22 | 27 | 32 | 37 |
| 2.5% | 7 | 8 | 10 | 11 | 13 | 14 | 16 | 17 | 21 | 25 | 29 | 34 |
| 2.625% | 7 | 8 | 9 | 10 | 12 | 13 | 15 | 16 | 20 | 23 | 27 | 31 |
| 2.75% | 6 | 7 | 9 | 10 | 11 | 13 | 14 | 15 | 18 | 22 | 25 | 29 |
| 2.875% | 6 | 7 | 8 | 10 | 11 | 12 | 13 | 15 | 17 | 20 | 24 | 27 |
| 3% | 6 | 7 | 8 | 9 | 10 | 11 | 13 | 14 | 17 | 19 | 22 | 25 |
| 3.125% | 5 | 7 | 8 | 9 | 10 | 11 | 12 | 13 | 16 | 18 | 21 | 24 |
| 3.25% | 5 | 6 | 7 | 8 | 9 | 11 | 12 | 13 | 15 | 17 | 20 | 23 |
| 3.375% | 5 | 6 | 7 | 8 | 9 | 10 | 11 | 12 | 14 | 17 | 19 | 22 |
| 3.5% | 5 | 6 | 7 | 8 | 9 | 10 | 11 | 12 | 14 | 16 | 18 | 21 |
| 3.625% | 5 | 6 | 7 | 7 | 8 | 9 | 10 | 11 | 13 | 15 | 18 | 20 |
| 3.75% | 5 | 5 | 6 | 7 | 8 | 9 | 10 | 11 | 13 | 15 | 17 | 19 |
| 3.875% | 4 | 5 | 6 | 7 | 8 | 9 | 10 | 11 | 12 | 14 | 16 | 18 |
| 4% | 4 | 5 | 6 | 7 | 8 | 8 | 9 | 10 | 12 | 14 | 16 | 18 |

| Break-Even Periods (in Months) | | | | | | | | | | | |
|---|---|---|---|---|---|---|---|---|---|---|---|

Term Left on Current Loan: 120 months  
Term on New Loan: 30 years  
Points: 2.00%

Income Tax Bracket: Pre-Tax  
Points and Costs: Financed

| Other Closing Costs as a Percent of Loan Amount | | | | | | | | | | | |
|---|---|---|---|---|---|---|---|---|---|---|---|
| Interest Rate Reduction | .25% | .5% | .75% | 1.00% | 1.25% | 1.50% | 1.75% | 2.00% | 2.50% | 3.00% | 3.50% | 4.00% |
| 0.125% | None | None | None | None | None | None | None | None | None | None | None | None |
| 0.25% | None | None | None | None | None | None | None | None | None | None | None | None |
| 0.375% | None | None | None | None | None | None | None | None | None | None | None | None |
| 0.5% | None | None | None | None | None | None | None | None | None | None | None | None |
| 0.625% | None | None | None | None | None | None | None | None | None | None | None | None |
| 0.75% | None | None | None | None | None | None | None | None | None | None | None | None |
| 0.875% | None | None | None | None | None | None | None | None | None | None | None | None |
| 1% | None | None | None | None | None | None | None | None | None | None | None | None |
| 1.125% | None | None | None | None | None | None | None | None | None | None | None | None |
| 1.25% | None | None | None | None | None | None | None | None | None | None | None | None |
| 1.375% | 33 | None | None | None | None | None | None | None | None | None | None | None |
| 1.5% | 26 | 31 | 39 | None | None | None | None | None | None | None | None | None |
| 1.625% | 23 | 26 | 31 | 36 | 46 | None | None | None | None | None | None | None |
| 1.75% | 20 | 23 | 26 | 30 | 35 | 41 | 54 | None | None | None | None | None |
| 1.875% | 18 | 21 | 23 | 26 | 30 | 34 | 38 | 45 | None | None | None | None |
| 2% | 17 | 19 | 21 | 24 | 27 | 30 | 33 | 37 | 48 | None | None | None |
| 2.125% | 15 | 17 | 19 | 22 | 24 | 27 | 29 | 32 | 40 | 50 | None | None |
| 2.25% | 14 | 16 | 18 | 20 | 22 | 24 | 27 | 29 | 35 | 42 | 52 | None |
| 2.375% | 13 | 15 | 17 | 19 | 20 | 22 | 24 | 27 | 31 | 37 | 44 | 53 |
| 2.5% | 13 | 14 | 16 | 17 | 19 | 21 | 23 | 25 | 29 | 34 | 39 | 46 |
| 2.625% | 12 | 13 | 15 | 16 | 18 | 20 | 21 | 23 | 27 | 31 | 35 | 41 |
| 2.75% | 11 | 13 | 14 | 15 | 17 | 18 | 20 | 22 | 25 | 29 | 33 | 37 |
| 2.875% | 11 | 12 | 13 | 15 | 16 | 17 | 19 | 20 | 23 | 27 | 30 | 34 |
| 3% | 10 | 11 | 13 | 14 | 15 | 17 | 18 | 19 | 22 | 25 | 29 | 32 |
| 3.125% | 10 | 11 | 12 | 13 | 15 | 16 | 17 | 18 | 21 | 24 | 27 | 30 |
| 3.25% | 9 | 11 | 12 | 13 | 14 | 15 | 16 | 17 | 20 | 23 | 25 | 28 |
| 3.375% | 9 | 10 | 11 | 12 | 13 | 14 | 16 | 17 | 19 | 22 | 24 | 27 |
| 3.5% | 9 | 10 | 11 | 12 | 13 | 14 | 15 | 16 | 18 | 21 | 23 | 26 |
| 3.625% | 8 | 9 | 10 | 11 | 12 | 13 | 14 | 15 | 17 | 20 | 22 | 24 |
| 3.75% | 8 | 9 | 10 | 11 | 12 | 13 | 14 | 15 | 17 | 19 | 21 | 23 |
| 3.875% | 8 | 9 | 10 | 11 | 11 | 12 | 13 | 14 | 16 | 18 | 20 | 22 |
| 4% | 8 | 8 | 9 | 10 | 11 | 12 | 13 | 14 | 16 | 17 | 19 | 22 |

# Refinance Break-Even Tables

| Break-Even Periods (in Months) | | | | | | | | | | | |
|---|---|---|---|---|---|---|---|---|---|---|---|

Term Left on Current Loan: 120 months          Income Tax Bracket: Pre-Tax
Term on New Loan: 30 years                      Points and Costs: Financed
Points: 3.00%

| Other Closing Costs as a Percent of Loan Amount | | | | | | | | | | | |
|---|---|---|---|---|---|---|---|---|---|---|---|
| Interest Rate Reduction | .25% | .5% | .75% | 1.00% | 1.25% | 1.50% | 1.75% | 2.00% | 2.50% | 3.00% | 3.50% | 4.00% |
|---|---|---|---|---|---|---|---|---|---|---|---|---|
| 0.125% | None | None | None | None | None | None | None | None | None | None | None | None |
| 0.25% | None | None | None | None | None | None | None | None | None | None | None | None |
| 0.375% | None | None | None | None | None | None | None | None | None | None | None | None |
| 0.5% | None | None | None | None | None | None | None | None | None | None | None | None |
| 0.625% | None | None | None | None | None | None | None | None | None | None | None | None |
| 0.75% | None | None | None | None | None | None | None | None | None | None | None | None |
| 0.875% | None | None | None | None | None | None | None | None | None | None | None | None |
| 1% | None | None | None | None | None | None | None | None | None | None | None | None |
| 1.125% | None | None | None | None | None | None | None | None | None | None | None | None |
| 1.25% | None | None | None | None | None | None | None | None | None | None | None | None |
| 1.375% | None | None | None | None | None | None | None | None | None | None | None | None |
| 1.5% | None | None | None | None | None | None | None | None | None | None | None | None |
| 1.625% | 47 | None | None | None | None | None | None | None | None | None | None | None |
| 1.75% | 35 | 41 | None | None | None | None | None | None | None | None | None | None |
| 1.875% | 30 | 34 | 39 | 45 | None | None | None | None | None | None | None | None |
| 2% | 27 | 30 | 33 | 37 | 42 | 48 | None | None | None | None | None | None |
| 2.125% | 24 | 27 | 29 | 32 | 36 | 40 | 44 | 50 | None | None | None | None |
| 2.25% | 22 | 24 | 27 | 29 | 32 | 35 | 38 | 42 | 52 | None | None | None |
| 2.375% | 21 | 23 | 25 | 27 | 29 | 32 | 34 | 37 | 44 | 53 | None | None |
| 2.5% | 19 | 21 | 23 | 25 | 27 | 29 | 31 | 34 | 39 | 45 | 54 | None |
| 2.625% | 18 | 20 | 21 | 23 | 25 | 27 | 29 | 31 | 35 | 41 | 47 | 55 |
| 2.75% | 17 | 19 | 20 | 22 | 23 | 25 | 27 | 29 | 33 | 37 | 42 | 48 |
| 2.875% | 16 | 18 | 19 | 20 | 22 | 23 | 25 | 27 | 30 | 34 | 39 | 44 |
| 3% | 15 | 17 | 18 | 19 | 21 | 22 | 24 | 25 | 28 | 32 | 36 | 40 |
| 3.125% | 15 | 16 | 17 | 18 | 20 | 21 | 22 | 24 | 27 | 30 | 33 | 37 |
| 3.25% | 14 | 15 | 16 | 17 | 19 | 20 | 21 | 23 | 25 | 28 | 31 | 35 |
| 3.375% | 13 | 14 | 16 | 17 | 18 | 19 | 20 | 22 | 24 | 27 | 30 | 33 |
| 3.5% | 13 | 14 | 15 | 16 | 17 | 18 | 19 | 21 | 23 | 26 | 28 | 31 |
| 3.625% | 12 | 13 | 14 | 15 | 16 | 17 | 19 | 20 | 22 | 24 | 27 | 29 |
| 3.75% | 12 | 13 | 14 | 15 | 16 | 17 | 18 | 19 | 21 | 23 | 26 | 28 |
| 3.875% | 11 | 12 | 13 | 14 | 15 | 16 | 17 | 18 | 20 | 22 | 25 | 27 |
| 4% | 11 | 12 | 13 | 14 | 15 | 16 | 17 | 17 | 19 | 21 | 24 | 26 |

## Break-Even Periods (in Months)

Term Left on Current Loan: 120 months
Term on New Loan: 30 years
Points: 0.00%

Income Tax Bracket: 40.00%
Points and Costs: Financed

### Other Closing Costs as a Percent of Loan Amount

| Interest Rate Reduction | .25% | .5% | .75% | 1.00% | 1.25% | 1.50% | 1.75% | 2.00% | 2.50% | 3.00% | 3.50% | 4.00% |
|---|---|---|---|---|---|---|---|---|---|---|---|---|
| 0.125% | None | None | None | None | None | None | None | None | None | None | None | None |
| 0.25% | None | None | None | None | None | None | None | None | None | None | None | None |
| 0.375% | None | None | None | None | None | None | None | None | None | None | None | None |
| 0.5% | None | None | None | None | None | None | None | None | None | None | None | None |
| 0.625% | 11 | None | None | None | None | None | None | None | None | None | None | None |
| 0.75% | 8 | 23 | None | None | None | None | None | None | None | None | None | None |
| 0.875% | 7 | 15 | None | None | None | None | None | None | None | None | None | None |
| 1% | 6 | 13 | 22 | None | None | None | None | None | None | None | None | None |
| 1.125% | 5 | 11 | 18 | 28 | None | None | None | None | None | None | None | None |
| 1.25% | 5 | 9 | 15 | 22 | 34 | None | None | None | None | None | None | None |
| 1.375% | 4 | 8 | 13 | 19 | 26 | 37 | None | None | None | None | None | None |
| 1.5% | 4 | 8 | 12 | 17 | 22 | 29 | 40 | None | None | None | None | None |
| 1.625% | 4 | 7 | 11 | 15 | 19 | 25 | 31 | 41 | None | None | None | None |
| 1.75% | 3 | 7 | 10 | 14 | 18 | 22 | 27 | 33 | None | None | None | None |
| 1.875% | 3 | 6 | 9 | 12 | 16 | 20 | 24 | 29 | 43 | None | None | None |
| 2% | 3 | 6 | 9 | 12 | 15 | 18 | 22 | 26 | 36 | 56 | None | None |
| 2.125% | 3 | 5 | 8 | 11 | 14 | 17 | 20 | 24 | 32 | 44 | None | None |
| 2.25% | 3 | 5 | 8 | 10 | 13 | 16 | 19 | 22 | 29 | 38 | 52 | None |
| 2.375% | 3 | 5 | 7 | 10 | 12 | 15 | 17 | 20 | 27 | 35 | 44 | 61 |
| 2.5% | 3 | 5 | 7 | 9 | 11 | 14 | 16 | 19 | 25 | 32 | 40 | 50 |
| 2.625% | 2 | 4 | 6 | 9 | 11 | 13 | 15 | 18 | 23 | 29 | 36 | 45 |
| 2.75% | 2 | 4 | 6 | 8 | 10 | 12 | 15 | 17 | 22 | 27 | 34 | 41 |
| 2.875% | 2 | 4 | 6 | 8 | 10 | 12 | 14 | 16 | 21 | 26 | 31 | 38 |
| 3% | 2 | 4 | 6 | 7 | 9 | 11 | 13 | 15 | 20 | 24 | 29 | 35 |
| 3.125% | 2 | 4 | 5 | 7 | 9 | 11 | 13 | 15 | 19 | 23 | 28 | 33 |
| 3.25% | 2 | 4 | 5 | 7 | 9 | 10 | 12 | 14 | 18 | 22 | 26 | 31 |
| 3.375% | 2 | 4 | 5 | 7 | 8 | 10 | 12 | 13 | 17 | 21 | 25 | 29 |
| 3.5% | 2 | 3 | 5 | 6 | 8 | 10 | 11 | 13 | 16 | 20 | 24 | 28 |
| 3.625% | 2 | 3 | 5 | 6 | 8 | 9 | 11 | 12 | 16 | 19 | 23 | 27 |
| 3.75% | 2 | 3 | 5 | 6 | 7 | 9 | 10 | 12 | 15 | 18 | 22 | 26 |
| 3.875% | 2 | 3 | 4 | 6 | 7 | 9 | 10 | 12 | 15 | 18 | 21 | 25 |
| 4% | 2 | 3 | 4 | 6 | 7 | 8 | 10 | 11 | 14 | 17 | 20 | 24 |

| Break-Even Periods (in Months) | | | | | | | | | | | |
|---|---|---|---|---|---|---|---|---|---|---|---|

Term Left on Current Loan: 120 months
Term on New Loan: 30 years
Points: 1.00%

Income Tax Bracket: 40.00%
Points and Costs: Financed

| Interest Rate Reduction | Other Closing Costs as a Percent of Loan Amount | | | | | | | | | | | |
|---|---|---|---|---|---|---|---|---|---|---|---|---|
| | .25% | .5% | .75% | 1.00% | 1.25% | 1.50% | 1.75% | 2.00% | 2.50% | 3.00% | 3.50% | 4.00% |
| 0.125% | None | None | None | None | None | None | None | None | None | None | None | None |
| 0.25% | None | None | None | None | None | None | None | None | None | None | None | None |
| 0.375% | None | None | None | None | None | None | None | None | None | None | None | None |
| 0.5% | None | None | None | None | None | None | None | None | None | None | None | None |
| 0.625% | None | None | None | None | None | None | None | None | None | None | None | None |
| 0.75% | None | None | None | None | None | None | None | None | None | None | None | None |
| 0.875% | None | None | None | None | None | None | None | None | None | None | None | None |
| 1% | None | None | None | None | None | None | None | None | None | None | None | None |
| 1.125% | None | None | None | None | None | None | None | None | None | None | None | None |
| 1.25% | 33 | None | None | None | None | None | None | None | None | None | None | None |
| 1.375% | 26 | 37 | None | None | None | None | None | None | None | None | None | None |
| 1.5% | 22 | 29 | 39 | None | None | None | None | None | None | None | None | None |
| 1.625% | 19 | 25 | 31 | 41 | None | None | None | None | None | None | None | None |
| 1.75% | 17 | 22 | 27 | 33 | 42 | None | None | None | None | None | None | None |
| 1.875% | 16 | 20 | 24 | 29 | 35 | 42 | None | None | None | None | None | None |
| 2% | 15 | 18 | 22 | 26 | 31 | 36 | 43 | 54 | None | None | None | None |
| 2.125% | 14 | 17 | 20 | 24 | 28 | 32 | 37 | 43 | None | None | None | None |
| 2.25% | 13 | 16 | 19 | 22 | 25 | 29 | 33 | 38 | 51 | None | None | None |
| 2.375% | 12 | 15 | 17 | 20 | 23 | 27 | 30 | 34 | 44 | 59 | None | None |
| 2.5% | 11 | 14 | 16 | 19 | 22 | 25 | 28 | 31 | 39 | 50 | 70 | None |
| 2.625% | 11 | 13 | 15 | 18 | 20 | 23 | 26 | 29 | 36 | 44 | 55 | None |
| 2.75% | 10 | 12 | 15 | 17 | 19 | 22 | 24 | 27 | 33 | 40 | 49 | 61 |
| 2.875% | 10 | 12 | 14 | 16 | 18 | 21 | 23 | 26 | 31 | 37 | 44 | 53 |
| 3% | 9 | 11 | 13 | 15 | 17 | 20 | 22 | 24 | 29 | 35 | 41 | 48 |
| 3.125% | 9 | 11 | 13 | 15 | 17 | 19 | 21 | 23 | 28 | 33 | 38 | 45 |
| 3.25% | 9 | 10 | 12 | 14 | 16 | 18 | 20 | 22 | 26 | 31 | 36 | 42 |
| 3.375% | 8 | 10 | 12 | 13 | 15 | 17 | 19 | 21 | 25 | 29 | 34 | 39 |
| 3.5% | 8 | 10 | 11 | 13 | 15 | 16 | 18 | 20 | 24 | 28 | 32 | 37 |
| 3.625% | 8 | 9 | 11 | 12 | 14 | 16 | 17 | 19 | 23 | 27 | 31 | 35 |
| 3.75% | 7 | 9 | 10 | 12 | 13 | 15 | 17 | 18 | 22 | 25 | 29 | 33 |
| 3.875% | 7 | 9 | 10 | 11 | 13 | 15 | 16 | 18 | 21 | 24 | 28 | 32 |
| 4% | 7 | 8 | 10 | 11 | 13 | 14 | 15 | 17 | 20 | 23 | 27 | 30 |

| Break-Even Periods (in Months) | | | | | | | | | | | |
|---|---|---|---|---|---|---|---|---|---|---|---|
| Term Left on Current Loan: 120 months<br>Term on New Loan: 30 years<br>Points: 2.00% | | | | | | Income Tax Bracket: 40.00%<br>Points and Costs: Financed | | | | | |
| Other Closing Costs as a Percent of Loan Amount | | | | | | | | | | | |

| Interest Rate Reduction | .25% | .5% | .75% | 1.00% | 1.25% | 1.50% | 1.75% | 2.00% | 2.50% | 3.00% | 3.50% | 4.00% |
|---|---|---|---|---|---|---|---|---|---|---|---|---|
| 0.125% | None | None | None | None | None | None | None | None | None | None | None | None |
| 0.25% | None | None | None | None | None | None | None | None | None | None | None | None |
| 0.375% | None | None | None | None | None | None | None | None | None | None | None | None |
| 0.5% | None | None | None | None | None | None | None | None | None | None | None | None |
| 0.625% | None | None | None | None | None | None | None | None | None | None | None | None |
| 0.75% | None | None | None | None | None | None | None | None | None | None | None | None |
| 0.875% | None | None | None | None | None | None | None | None | None | None | None | None |
| 1% | None | None | None | None | None | None | None | None | None | None | None | None |
| 1.125% | None | None | None | None | None | None | None | None | None | None | None | None |
| 1.25% | None | None | None | None | None | None | None | None | None | None | None | None |
| 1.375% | None | None | None | None | None | None | None | None | None | None | None | None |
| 1.5% | None | None | None | None | None | None | None | None | None | None | None | None |
| 1.625% | None | None | None | None | None | None | None | None | None | None | None | None |
| 1.75% | 42 | None | None | None | None | None | None | None | None | None | None | None |
| 1.875% | 35 | 43 | None | None | None | None | None | None | None | None | None | None |
| 2% | 31 | 36 | 43 | 54 | None | None | None | None | None | None | None | None |
| 2.125% | 28 | 32 | 37 | 43 | 52 | None | None | None | None | None | None | None |
| 2.25% | 25 | 29 | 33 | 38 | 44 | 51 | 64 | None | None | None | None | None |
| 2.375% | 23 | 27 | 30 | 34 | 39 | 44 | 50 | 59 | None | None | None | None |
| 2.5% | 22 | 25 | 28 | 31 | 35 | 39 | 44 | 49 | 69 | None | None | None |
| 2.625% | 21 | 23 | 26 | 29 | 32 | 36 | 40 | 44 | 55 | None | None | None |
| 2.75% | 19 | 22 | 24 | 27 | 30 | 33 | 36 | 40 | 49 | 60 | None | None |
| 2.875% | 18 | 21 | 23 | 26 | 28 | 31 | 34 | 37 | 44 | 53 | 66 | None |
| 3% | 17 | 20 | 22 | 24 | 27 | 29 | 32 | 35 | 41 | 48 | 57 | 71 |
| 3.125% | 17 | 19 | 21 | 23 | 25 | 27 | 30 | 32 | 38 | 44 | 52 | 61 |
| 3.25% | 16 | 18 | 20 | 22 | 24 | 26 | 28 | 31 | 36 | 41 | 48 | 55 |
| 3.375% | 15 | 17 | 19 | 21 | 23 | 25 | 27 | 29 | 34 | 39 | 44 | 51 |
| 3.5% | 15 | 16 | 18 | 20 | 22 | 24 | 26 | 28 | 32 | 37 | 42 | 47 |
| 3.625% | 14 | 16 | 17 | 19 | 21 | 23 | 25 | 26 | 30 | 35 | 39 | 45 |
| 3.75% | 14 | 15 | 17 | 18 | 20 | 22 | 23 | 25 | 29 | 33 | 37 | 42 |
| 3.875% | 13 | 15 | 16 | 18 | 19 | 21 | 23 | 24 | 28 | 32 | 36 | 40 |
| 4% | 13 | 14 | 16 | 17 | 19 | 20 | 22 | 23 | 27 | 30 | 34 | 38 |

| Break-Even Periods (in Months) | | | | | | | | | | | |
|---|---|---|---|---|---|---|---|---|---|---|---|
| Term Left on Current Loan: 120 months | | | | | | Income Tax Bracket: 40.00% | | | | | |
| Term on New Loan: 30 years | | | | | | Points and Costs: Financed | | | | | |
| Points: 3.00% | | | | | | | | | | | |

| Other Closing Costs as a Percent of Loan Amount | | | | | | | | | | | | |
|---|---|---|---|---|---|---|---|---|---|---|---|---|
| Interest Rate Reduction | .25% | .5% | .75% | 1.00% | 1.25% | 1.50% | 1.75% | 2.00% | 2.50% | 3.00% | 3.50% | 4.00% |
| 0.125% | None | None | None | None | None | None | None | None | None | None | None | None |
| 0.25% | None | None | None | None | None | None | None | None | None | None | None | None |
| 0.375% | None | None | None | None | None | None | None | None | None | None | None | None |
| 0.5% | None | None | None | None | None | None | None | None | None | None | None | None |
| 0.625% | None | None | None | None | None | None | None | None | None | None | None | None |
| 0.75% | None | None | None | None | None | None | None | None | None | None | None | None |
| 0.875% | None | None | None | None | None | None | None | None | None | None | None | None |
| 1% | None | None | None | None | None | None | None | None | None | None | None | None |
| 1.125% | None | None | None | None | None | None | None | None | None | None | None | None |
| 1.25% | None | None | None | None | None | None | None | None | None | None | None | None |
| 1.375% | None | None | None | None | None | None | None | None | None | None | None | None |
| 1.5% | None | None | None | None | None | None | None | None | None | None | None | None |
| 1.625% | None | None | None | None | None | None | None | None | None | None | None | None |
| 1.75% | None | None | None | None | None | None | None | None | None | None | None | None |
| 1.875% | None | None | None | None | None | None | None | None | None | None | None | None |
| 2% | None | None | None | None | None | None | None | None | None | None | None | None |
| 2.125% | 53 | None | None | None | None | None | None | None | None | None | None | None |
| 2.25% | 44 | 51 | 66 | None | None | None | None | None | None | None | None | None |
| 2.375% | 39 | 44 | 50 | 59 | None | None | None | None | None | None | None | None |
| 2.5% | 35 | 39 | 44 | 50 | 57 | 69 | None | None | None | None | None | None |
| 2.625% | 33 | 36 | 40 | 44 | 49 | 55 | 63 | None | None | None | None | None |
| 2.75% | 30 | 33 | 37 | 40 | 44 | 49 | 54 | 60 | None | None | None | None |
| 2.875% | 28 | 31 | 34 | 37 | 41 | 44 | 48 | 53 | 65 | None | None | None |
| 3% | 27 | 29 | 32 | 35 | 38 | 41 | 44 | 48 | 57 | 70 | None | None |
| 3.125% | 25 | 28 | 30 | 33 | 35 | 38 | 41 | 44 | 52 | 61 | 75 | None |
| 3.25% | 24 | 26 | 28 | 31 | 33 | 36 | 38 | 41 | 48 | 55 | 64 | 80 |
| 3.375% | 23 | 25 | 27 | 29 | 31 | 34 | 36 | 39 | 44 | 51 | 58 | 68 |
| 3.5% | 22 | 24 | 26 | 28 | 30 | 32 | 34 | 37 | 42 | 47 | 54 | 61 |
| 3.625% | 21 | 23 | 25 | 27 | 28 | 31 | 33 | 35 | 39 | 44 | 50 | 56 |
| 3.75% | 20 | 22 | 24 | 25 | 27 | 29 | 31 | 33 | 37 | 42 | 47 | 53 |
| 3.875% | 19 | 21 | 23 | 24 | 26 | 28 | 30 | 32 | 36 | 40 | 45 | 50 |
| 4% | 19 | 20 | 22 | 23 | 25 | 27 | 29 | 30 | 34 | 38 | 42 | 47 |

# Refinance Break-Even Tables

| Break-Even Periods (in Months) | | | | | | | | | | | |
|---|---|---|---|---|---|---|---|---|---|---|---|

Term Left on Current Loan: 300 months  Income Tax Bracket: Pre-Tax
Term on New Loan: 30 years  Points and Costs: Financed
Points: 0.00%

| Other Closing Costs as a Percent of Loan Amount | | | | | | | | | | | |
|---|---|---|---|---|---|---|---|---|---|---|---|
| Interest Rate Reduction | .25% | .5% | .75% | 1.00% | 1.25% | 1.50% | 1.75% | 2.00% | 2.50% | 3.00% | 3.50% | 4.00% |
| 0.125% | None | None | None | None | None | None | None | None | None | None | None | None |
| 0.25% | 14 | 33 | None | None | None | None | None | None | None | None | None | None |
| 0.375% | 9 | 19 | 31 | 46 | 67 | None | None | None | None | None | None | None |
| 0.5% | 7 | 14 | 21 | 30 | 40 | 51 | 66 | 86 | None | None | None | None |
| 0.625% | 5 | 11 | 16 | 23 | 29 | 37 | 45 | 54 | 78 | 126 | None | None |
| 0.75% | 5 | 9 | 14 | 18 | 24 | 29 | 35 | 41 | 56 | 75 | 100 | None |
| 0.875% | 4 | 8 | 11 | 16 | 20 | 24 | 29 | 34 | 45 | 58 | 73 | 91 |
| 1% | 4 | 7 | 10 | 13 | 17 | 21 | 25 | 29 | 38 | 47 | 58 | 71 |
| 1.125% | 3 | 6 | 9 | 12 | 15 | 18 | 22 | 25 | 32 | 40 | 49 | 59 |
| 1.25% | 3 | 5 | 8 | 11 | 13 | 16 | 19 | 22 | 29 | 35 | 43 | 51 |
| 1.375% | 3 | 5 | 7 | 10 | 12 | 15 | 17 | 20 | 26 | 32 | 38 | 45 |
| 1.5% | 3 | 5 | 7 | 9 | 11 | 13 | 16 | 18 | 23 | 28 | 34 | 40 |
| 1.625% | 2 | 4 | 6 | 8 | 10 | 12 | 14 | 17 | 21 | 26 | 31 | 36 |
| 1.75% | 2 | 4 | 6 | 8 | 10 | 11 | 13 | 15 | 20 | 24 | 28 | 33 |
| 1.875% | 2 | 4 | 5 | 7 | 9 | 11 | 12 | 14 | 18 | 22 | 26 | 31 |
| 2% | 2 | 4 | 5 | 7 | 8 | 10 | 12 | 13 | 17 | 21 | 24 | 28 |
| 2.125% | 2 | 3 | 5 | 6 | 8 | 9 | 11 | 13 | 16 | 19 | 23 | 26 |
| 2.25% | 2 | 3 | 5 | 6 | 7 | 9 | 10 | 12 | 15 | 18 | 21 | 25 |
| 2.375% | 2 | 3 | 4 | 6 | 7 | 8 | 10 | 11 | 14 | 17 | 20 | 23 |
| 2.5% | 2 | 3 | 4 | 5 | 7 | 8 | 9 | 11 | 13 | 16 | 19 | 22 |
| 2.625% | 2 | 3 | 4 | 5 | 6 | 8 | 9 | 10 | 13 | 15 | 18 | 21 |
| 2.75% | 2 | 3 | 4 | 5 | 6 | 7 | 8 | 10 | 12 | 15 | 17 | 20 |
| 2.875% | 2 | 3 | 4 | 5 | 6 | 7 | 8 | 9 | 12 | 14 | 16 | 19 |
| 3% | 2 | 3 | 4 | 5 | 6 | 7 | 8 | 9 | 11 | 13 | 16 | 18 |
| 3.125% | 1 | 2 | 3 | 4 | 5 | 6 | 7 | 9 | 11 | 13 | 15 | 17 |
| 3.25% | 1 | 2 | 3 | 4 | 5 | 6 | 7 | 8 | 10 | 12 | 14 | 17 |
| 3.375% | 1 | 2 | 3 | 4 | 5 | 6 | 7 | 8 | 10 | 12 | 14 | 16 |
| 3.5% | 1 | 2 | 3 | 4 | 5 | 6 | 7 | 8 | 10 | 11 | 13 | 15 |
| 3.625% | 1 | 2 | 3 | 4 | 5 | 6 | 6 | 7 | 9 | 11 | 13 | 15 |
| 3.75% | 1 | 2 | 3 | 4 | 5 | 5 | 6 | 7 | 9 | 11 | 12 | 14 |
| 3.875% | 1 | 2 | 3 | 4 | 4 | 5 | 6 | 7 | 9 | 10 | 12 | 14 |
| 4% | 1 | 2 | 3 | 4 | 4 | 5 | 6 | 7 | 8 | 10 | 12 | 13 |

| Break-Even Periods (in Months) | | | | | | | | | | | |
|---|---|---|---|---|---|---|---|---|---|---|---|

Term Left on Current Loan: 300 months  
Term on New Loan: 30 years  
Points: 1.00%

Income Tax Bracket: Pre-Tax  
Points and Costs: Financed

| Other Closing Costs as a Percent of Loan Amount | | | | | | | | | | | |
|---|---|---|---|---|---|---|---|---|---|---|---|
| Interest Rate Reduction | .25% | .5% | .75% | 1.00% | 1.25% | 1.50% | 1.75% | 2.00% | 2.50% | 3.00% | 3.50% | 4.00% |
| 0.125% | None | None | None | None | None | None | None | None | None | None | None | None |
| 0.25% | None | None | None | None | None | None | None | None | None | None | None | None |
| 0.375% | 67 | None | None | None | None | None | None | None | None | None | None | None |
| 0.5% | 40 | 51 | 65 | 85 | None | None | None | None | None | None | None | None |
| 0.625% | 29 | 37 | 45 | 54 | 65 | 77 | 94 | 122 | None | None | None | None |
| 0.75% | 24 | 29 | 35 | 41 | 48 | 56 | 64 | 74 | 99 | None | None | None |
| 0.875% | 20 | 24 | 29 | 34 | 39 | 45 | 50 | 57 | 72 | 90 | 115 | None |
| 1% | 17 | 21 | 25 | 29 | 33 | 37 | 42 | 47 | 58 | 70 | 85 | 103 |
| 1.125% | 15 | 18 | 21 | 25 | 28 | 32 | 36 | 40 | 49 | 59 | 69 | 82 |
| 1.25% | 13 | 16 | 19 | 22 | 25 | 28 | 32 | 35 | 42 | 50 | 59 | 69 |
| 1.375% | 12 | 15 | 17 | 20 | 23 | 25 | 28 | 31 | 38 | 44 | 52 | 59 |
| 1.5% | 11 | 13 | 16 | 18 | 20 | 23 | 26 | 28 | 34 | 40 | 46 | 53 |
| 1.625% | 10 | 12 | 14 | 17 | 19 | 21 | 23 | 26 | 31 | 36 | 41 | 47 |
| 1.75% | 9 | 11 | 13 | 15 | 17 | 19 | 22 | 24 | 28 | 33 | 38 | 43 |
| 1.875% | 9 | 11 | 12 | 14 | 16 | 18 | 20 | 22 | 26 | 30 | 35 | 39 |
| 2% | 8 | 10 | 12 | 13 | 15 | 17 | 19 | 20 | 24 | 28 | 32 | 36 |
| 2.125% | 8 | 9 | 11 | 13 | 14 | 16 | 17 | 19 | 23 | 26 | 30 | 34 |
| 2.25% | 7 | 9 | 10 | 12 | 13 | 15 | 16 | 18 | 21 | 25 | 28 | 32 |
| 2.375% | 7 | 8 | 10 | 11 | 13 | 14 | 15 | 17 | 20 | 23 | 26 | 30 |
| 2.5% | 7 | 8 | 9 | 11 | 12 | 13 | 15 | 16 | 19 | 22 | 25 | 28 |
| 2.625% | 6 | 8 | 9 | 10 | 11 | 13 | 14 | 15 | 18 | 21 | 24 | 26 |
| 2.75% | 6 | 7 | 8 | 10 | 11 | 12 | 13 | 15 | 17 | 20 | 22 | 25 |
| 2.875% | 6 | 7 | 8 | 9 | 10 | 12 | 13 | 14 | 16 | 19 | 21 | 24 |
| 3% | 6 | 7 | 8 | 9 | 10 | 11 | 12 | 13 | 16 | 18 | 20 | 23 |
| 3.125% | 5 | 6 | 7 | 8 | 10 | 11 | 12 | 13 | 15 | 17 | 19 | 22 |
| 3.25% | 5 | 6 | 7 | 8 | 9 | 10 | 11 | 12 | 14 | 16 | 19 | 21 |
| 3.375% | 5 | 6 | 7 | 8 | 9 | 10 | 11 | 12 | 14 | 16 | 18 | 20 |
| 3.5% | 5 | 6 | 7 | 8 | 9 | 9 | 10 | 11 | 13 | 15 | 17 | 19 |
| 3.625% | 5 | 6 | 6 | 7 | 8 | 9 | 10 | 11 | 13 | 15 | 17 | 19 |
| 3.75% | 5 | 5 | 6 | 7 | 8 | 9 | 10 | 11 | 12 | 14 | 16 | 18 |
| 3.875% | 4 | 5 | 6 | 7 | 8 | 9 | 9 | 10 | 12 | 14 | 15 | 17 |
| 4% | 4 | 5 | 6 | 7 | 7 | 8 | 9 | 10 | 12 | 13 | 15 | 17 |

## Break-Even Periods (in Months)

Term Left on Current Loan: 300 months
Term on New Loan: 30 years
Points: 2.00%

Income Tax Bracket: Pre-Tax
Points and Costs: Financed

### Other Closing Costs as a Percent of Loan Amount

| Interest Rate Reduction | .25% | .5% | .75% | 1.00% | 1.25% | 1.50% | 1.75% | 2.00% | 2.50% | 3.00% | 3.50% | 4.00% |
|---|---|---|---|---|---|---|---|---|---|---|---|---|
| 0.125% | None | None | None | None | None | None | None | None | None | None | None | None |
| 0.25% | None | None | None | None | None | None | None | None | None | None | None | None |
| 0.375% | None | None | None | None | None | None | None | None | None | None | None | None |
| 0.5% | None | None | None | None | None | None | None | None | None | None | None | None |
| 0.625% | 65 | 78 | 94 | 122 | None | None | None | None | None | None | None | None |
| 0.75% | 48 | 56 | 64 | 74 | 85 | 98 | 116 | None | None | None | None | None |
| 0.875% | 39 | 45 | 51 | 57 | 64 | 72 | 80 | 90 | 114 | None | None | None |
| 1% | 33 | 37 | 42 | 47 | 52 | 58 | 64 | 70 | 85 | 102 | 127 | None |
| 1.125% | 29 | 32 | 36 | 40 | 44 | 49 | 53 | 58 | 69 | 81 | 95 | 113 |
| 1.25% | 25 | 28 | 32 | 35 | 39 | 42 | 46 | 50 | 59 | 68 | 79 | 91 |
| 1.375% | 23 | 25 | 28 | 31 | 34 | 38 | 41 | 44 | 51 | 59 | 68 | 77 |
| 1.5% | 21 | 23 | 26 | 28 | 31 | 34 | 37 | 40 | 46 | 52 | 59 | 67 |
| 1.625% | 19 | 21 | 23 | 26 | 28 | 31 | 33 | 36 | 41 | 47 | 53 | 60 |
| 1.75% | 17 | 19 | 22 | 24 | 26 | 28 | 30 | 33 | 38 | 43 | 48 | 54 |
| 1.875% | 16 | 18 | 20 | 22 | 24 | 26 | 28 | 30 | 35 | 39 | 44 | 49 |
| 2% | 15 | 17 | 19 | 20 | 22 | 24 | 26 | 28 | 32 | 36 | 41 | 45 |
| 2.125% | 14 | 16 | 17 | 19 | 21 | 23 | 24 | 26 | 30 | 34 | 38 | 42 |
| 2.25% | 13 | 15 | 16 | 18 | 20 | 21 | 23 | 24 | 28 | 31 | 35 | 39 |
| 2.375% | 13 | 14 | 15 | 17 | 18 | 20 | 21 | 23 | 26 | 30 | 33 | 37 |
| 2.5% | 12 | 13 | 15 | 16 | 17 | 19 | 20 | 22 | 25 | 28 | 31 | 34 |
| 2.625% | 11 | 13 | 14 | 15 | 17 | 18 | 19 | 21 | 23 | 26 | 29 | 32 |
| 2.75% | 11 | 12 | 13 | 15 | 16 | 17 | 18 | 20 | 22 | 25 | 28 | 31 |
| 2.875% | 10 | 12 | 13 | 14 | 15 | 16 | 17 | 19 | 21 | 24 | 26 | 29 |
| 3% | 10 | 11 | 12 | 13 | 14 | 16 | 17 | 18 | 20 | 23 | 25 | 28 |
| 3.125% | 10 | 11 | 12 | 13 | 14 | 15 | 16 | 17 | 19 | 22 | 24 | 27 |
| 3.25% | 9 | 10 | 11 | 12 | 13 | 14 | 15 | 16 | 19 | 21 | 23 | 25 |
| 3.375% | 9 | 10 | 11 | 12 | 13 | 14 | 15 | 16 | 18 | 20 | 22 | 24 |
| 3.5% | 9 | 9 | 10 | 11 | 12 | 13 | 14 | 15 | 17 | 19 | 21 | 23 |
| 3.625% | 8 | 9 | 10 | 11 | 12 | 13 | 14 | 15 | 17 | 18 | 20 | 23 |
| 3.75% | 8 | 9 | 10 | 11 | 11 | 12 | 13 | 14 | 16 | 18 | 20 | 22 |
| 3.875% | 8 | 9 | 9 | 10 | 11 | 12 | 13 | 14 | 15 | 17 | 19 | 21 |
| 4% | 7 | 8 | 9 | 10 | 11 | 12 | 12 | 13 | 15 | 17 | 18 | 20 |

# Refinance Break-Even Tables

| Break-Even Periods (in Months) | | | | | | | | | | | |
|---|---|---|---|---|---|---|---|---|---|---|---|

Term Left on Current Loan: 300 months  
Term on New Loan: 30 years  
Points: 3.00%

Income Tax Bracket: Pre-Tax  
Points and Costs: Financed

| Other Closing Costs as a Percent of Loan Amount | | | | | | | | | | | |
|---|---|---|---|---|---|---|---|---|---|---|---|
| Interest Rate Reduction | .25% | .5% | .75% | 1.00% | 1.25% | 1.50% | 1.75% | 2.00% | 2.50% | 3.00% | 3.50% | 4.00% |
| 0.125% | None | None | None | None | None | None | None | None | None | None | None | None |
| 0.25% | None | None | None | None | None | None | None | None | None | None | None | None |
| 0.375% | None | None | None | None | None | None | None | None | None | None | None | None |
| 0.5% | None | None | None | None | None | None | None | None | None | None | None | None |
| 0.625% | None | None | None | None | None | None | None | None | None | None | None | None |
| 0.75% | 86 | 99 | 117 | None | None | None | None | None | None | None | None | None |
| 0.875% | 64 | 72 | 80 | 90 | 101 | 115 | 133 | None | None | None | None | None |
| 1% | 53 | 58 | 64 | 70 | 77 | 85 | 93 | 102 | 126 | None | None | None |
| 1.125% | 45 | 49 | 54 | 59 | 64 | 69 | 75 | 81 | 95 | 112 | 135 | 182 |
| 1.25% | 39 | 43 | 46 | 50 | 55 | 59 | 63 | 68 | 79 | 90 | 104 | 120 |
| 1.375% | 35 | 38 | 41 | 44 | 48 | 51 | 55 | 59 | 67 | 77 | 87 | 98 |
| 1.5% | 31 | 34 | 37 | 40 | 43 | 46 | 49 | 52 | 59 | 67 | 75 | 84 |
| 1.625% | 28 | 31 | 33 | 36 | 39 | 41 | 44 | 47 | 53 | 60 | 66 | 74 |
| 1.75% | 26 | 28 | 31 | 33 | 35 | 38 | 40 | 43 | 48 | 54 | 60 | 66 |
| 1.875% | 24 | 26 | 28 | 30 | 32 | 35 | 37 | 39 | 44 | 49 | 54 | 60 |
| 2% | 22 | 24 | 26 | 28 | 30 | 32 | 34 | 36 | 41 | 45 | 50 | 55 |
| 2.125% | 21 | 23 | 24 | 26 | 28 | 30 | 32 | 34 | 38 | 42 | 46 | 51 |
| 2.25% | 20 | 21 | 23 | 25 | 26 | 28 | 30 | 31 | 35 | 39 | 43 | 47 |
| 2.375% | 19 | 20 | 22 | 23 | 25 | 26 | 28 | 30 | 33 | 36 | 40 | 44 |
| 2.5% | 18 | 19 | 20 | 22 | 23 | 25 | 26 | 28 | 31 | 34 | 38 | 41 |
| 2.625% | 17 | 18 | 19 | 21 | 22 | 24 | 25 | 26 | 29 | 32 | 36 | 39 |
| 2.75% | 16 | 17 | 18 | 20 | 21 | 22 | 24 | 25 | 28 | 31 | 34 | 37 |
| 2.875% | 15 | 16 | 18 | 19 | 20 | 21 | 23 | 24 | 26 | 29 | 32 | 35 |
| 3% | 14 | 16 | 17 | 18 | 19 | 20 | 22 | 23 | 25 | 28 | 30 | 33 |
| 3.125% | 14 | 15 | 16 | 17 | 18 | 19 | 21 | 22 | 24 | 27 | 29 | 32 |
| 3.25% | 13 | 14 | 15 | 16 | 18 | 19 | 20 | 21 | 23 | 25 | 28 | 30 |
| 3.375% | 13 | 14 | 15 | 16 | 17 | 18 | 19 | 20 | 22 | 24 | 27 | 29 |
| 3.5% | 12 | 13 | 14 | 15 | 16 | 17 | 18 | 19 | 21 | 23 | 25 | 28 |
| 3.625% | 12 | 13 | 14 | 15 | 16 | 17 | 18 | 18 | 20 | 22 | 25 | 27 |
| 3.75% | 12 | 12 | 13 | 14 | 15 | 16 | 17 | 18 | 20 | 22 | 24 | 26 |
| 3.875% | 11 | 12 | 13 | 14 | 15 | 15 | 16 | 17 | 19 | 21 | 23 | 25 |
| 4% | 11 | 12 | 12 | 13 | 14 | 15 | 16 | 17 | 18 | 20 | 22 | 24 |

| Break-Even Periods (in Months) | | | | | | | | | | | |
|---|---|---|---|---|---|---|---|---|---|---|---|
| Term Left on Current Loan: 300 months<br>Term on New Loan: 30 years<br>Points: 0.00% | | | | | | Income Tax Bracket: 40.00%<br>Points and Costs: Financed | | | | | |
| Other Closing Costs as a Percent of Loan Amount | | | | | | | | | | | |
| Interest Rate Reduction | .25% | .5% | .75% | 1.00% | 1.25% | 1.50% | 1.75% | 2.00% | 2.50% | 3.00% | 3.50% | 4.00% |
|---|---|---|---|---|---|---|---|---|---|---|---|---|
| 0.125% | None | None | None | None | None | None | None | None | None | None | None | None |
| 0.25% | 24 | 79 | None | None | None | None | None | None | None | None | None | None |
| 0.375% | 15 | 33 | 57 | None | None | None | None | None | None | None | None | None |
| 0.5% | 11 | 23 | 37 | 53 | 74 | 112 | None | None | None | None | None | None |
| 0.625% | 9 | 18 | 28 | 39 | 51 | 66 | 84 | 109 | None | None | None | None |
| 0.75% | 7 | 15 | 22 | 31 | 40 | 50 | 61 | 74 | 108 | None | None | None |
| 0.875% | 6 | 13 | 19 | 26 | 33 | 41 | 49 | 59 | 80 | 108 | 162 | None |
| 1% | 6 | 11 | 16 | 22 | 28 | 35 | 42 | 49 | 65 | 84 | 108 | 142 |
| 1.125% | 5 | 10 | 15 | 20 | 25 | 30 | 36 | 42 | 55 | 70 | 87 | 107 |
| 1.25% | 5 | 9 | 13 | 18 | 22 | 27 | 32 | 37 | 48 | 61 | 74 | 90 |
| 1.375% | 4 | 8 | 12 | 16 | 20 | 24 | 29 | 33 | 43 | 54 | 65 | 77 |
| 1.5% | 4 | 7 | 11 | 15 | 18 | 22 | 26 | 30 | 39 | 48 | 58 | 69 |
| 1.625% | 4 | 7 | 10 | 13 | 17 | 20 | 24 | 28 | 35 | 44 | 52 | 62 |
| 1.75% | 3 | 6 | 9 | 12 | 16 | 19 | 22 | 26 | 33 | 40 | 48 | 56 |
| 1.875% | 3 | 6 | 9 | 12 | 15 | 18 | 21 | 24 | 30 | 37 | 44 | 51 |
| 2% | 3 | 6 | 8 | 11 | 14 | 16 | 19 | 22 | 28 | 34 | 41 | 48 |
| 2.125% | 3 | 5 | 8 | 10 | 13 | 15 | 18 | 21 | 26 | 32 | 38 | 44 |
| 2.25% | 3 | 5 | 7 | 10 | 12 | 15 | 17 | 20 | 25 | 30 | 36 | 41 |
| 2.375% | 3 | 5 | 7 | 9 | 11 | 14 | 16 | 18 | 23 | 28 | 34 | 39 |
| 2.5% | 3 | 5 | 7 | 9 | 11 | 13 | 15 | 17 | 22 | 27 | 32 | 37 |
| 2.625% | 2 | 4 | 6 | 8 | 10 | 12 | 15 | 17 | 21 | 25 | 30 | 35 |
| 2.75% | 2 | 4 | 6 | 8 | 10 | 12 | 14 | 16 | 20 | 24 | 29 | 33 |
| 2.875% | 2 | 4 | 6 | 8 | 9 | 11 | 13 | 15 | 19 | 23 | 27 | 31 |
| 3% | 2 | 4 | 6 | 7 | 9 | 11 | 13 | 15 | 18 | 22 | 26 | 30 |
| 3.125% | 2 | 4 | 5 | 7 | 9 | 10 | 12 | 14 | 17 | 21 | 25 | 29 |
| 3.25% | 2 | 4 | 5 | 7 | 8 | 10 | 12 | 13 | 17 | 20 | 24 | 28 |
| 3.375% | 2 | 3 | 5 | 7 | 8 | 10 | 11 | 13 | 16 | 19 | 23 | 26 |
| 3.5% | 2 | 3 | 5 | 6 | 8 | 9 | 11 | 12 | 16 | 19 | 22 | 25 |
| 3.625% | 2 | 3 | 5 | 6 | 8 | 9 | 10 | 12 | 15 | 18 | 21 | 24 |
| 3.75% | 2 | 3 | 5 | 6 | 7 | 9 | 10 | 12 | 14 | 17 | 21 | 24 |
| 3.875% | 2 | 3 | 4 | 6 | 7 | 8 | 10 | 11 | 14 | 17 | 20 | 23 |
| 4% | 2 | 3 | 4 | 6 | 7 | 8 | 10 | 11 | 14 | 16 | 19 | 22 |

| Break-Even Periods (in Months) | | | | | | | | | | | |
|---|---|---|---|---|---|---|---|---|---|---|---|
| Term Left on Current Loan: 300 months<br>Term on New Loan: 30 years<br>Points: 1.00% | | | | | | Income Tax Bracket: 40.00%<br>Points and Costs: Financed | | | | | |
| Other Closing Costs as a Percent of Loan Amount | | | | | | | | | | | |

| Interest Rate Reduction | .25% | .5% | .75% | 1.00% | 1.25% | 1.50% | 1.75% | 2.00% | 2.50% | 3.00% | 3.50% | 4.00% |
|---|---|---|---|---|---|---|---|---|---|---|---|---|
| 0.125% | None | None | None | None | None | None | None | None | None | None | None | None |
| 0.25% | None | None | None | None | None | None | None | None | None | None | None | None |
| 0.375% | None | None | None | None | None | None | None | None | None | None | None | None |
| 0.5% | 74 | 111 | None | None | None | None | None | None | None | None | None | None |
| 0.625% | 51 | 65 | 83 | 108 | None | None | None | None | None | None | None | None |
| 0.75% | 40 | 50 | 61 | 74 | 88 | 107 | 135 | None | None | None | None | None |
| 0.875% | 33 | 41 | 49 | 58 | 68 | 79 | 92 | 106 | 156 | None | None | None |
| 1% | 28 | 35 | 42 | 49 | 56 | 65 | 73 | 83 | 106 | 139 | None | None |
| 1.125% | 25 | 30 | 36 | 42 | 48 | 55 | 62 | 69 | 86 | 106 | 132 | 177 |
| 1.25% | 22 | 27 | 32 | 37 | 42 | 48 | 54 | 60 | 73 | 89 | 106 | 127 |
| 1.375% | 20 | 24 | 29 | 33 | 38 | 43 | 48 | 53 | 64 | 77 | 90 | 106 |
| 1.5% | 18 | 22 | 26 | 30 | 34 | 39 | 43 | 48 | 57 | 68 | 79 | 92 |
| 1.625% | 17 | 20 | 24 | 28 | 31 | 35 | 39 | 43 | 52 | 61 | 71 | 82 |
| 1.75% | 16 | 19 | 22 | 25 | 29 | 32 | 36 | 40 | 47 | 56 | 64 | 74 |
| 1.875% | 14 | 17 | 20 | 24 | 27 | 30 | 33 | 37 | 44 | 51 | 59 | 67 |
| 2% | 14 | 16 | 19 | 22 | 25 | 28 | 31 | 34 | 40 | 47 | 54 | 62 |
| 2.125% | 13 | 15 | 18 | 21 | 23 | 26 | 29 | 32 | 38 | 44 | 50 | 57 |
| 2.25% | 12 | 14 | 17 | 19 | 22 | 25 | 27 | 30 | 35 | 41 | 47 | 53 |
| 2.375% | 11 | 14 | 16 | 18 | 21 | 23 | 26 | 28 | 33 | 39 | 44 | 50 |
| 2.5% | 11 | 13 | 15 | 17 | 20 | 22 | 24 | 27 | 31 | 36 | 42 | 47 |
| 2.625% | 10 | 12 | 14 | 17 | 19 | 21 | 23 | 25 | 30 | 34 | 39 | 44 |
| 2.75% | 10 | 12 | 14 | 16 | 18 | 20 | 22 | 24 | 28 | 33 | 37 | 42 |
| 2.875% | 9 | 11 | 13 | 15 | 17 | 19 | 21 | 23 | 27 | 31 | 35 | 40 |
| 3% | 9 | 11 | 13 | 14 | 16 | 18 | 20 | 22 | 26 | 30 | 34 | 38 |
| 3.125% | 9 | 10 | 12 | 14 | 16 | 17 | 19 | 21 | 25 | 28 | 32 | 36 |
| 3.25% | 8 | 10 | 12 | 13 | 15 | 17 | 18 | 20 | 24 | 27 | 31 | 35 |
| 3.375% | 8 | 10 | 11 | 13 | 14 | 16 | 18 | 19 | 23 | 26 | 30 | 33 |
| 3.5% | 8 | 9 | 11 | 12 | 14 | 15 | 17 | 19 | 22 | 25 | 29 | 32 |
| 3.625% | 8 | 9 | 10 | 12 | 13 | 15 | 16 | 18 | 21 | 24 | 28 | 31 |
| 3.75% | 7 | 9 | 10 | 12 | 13 | 14 | 16 | 17 | 20 | 23 | 27 | 30 |
| 3.875% | 7 | 8 | 10 | 11 | 13 | 14 | 15 | 17 | 20 | 23 | 26 | 29 |
| 4% | 7 | 8 | 9 | 11 | 12 | 14 | 15 | 16 | 19 | 22 | 25 | 28 |

| Break-Even Periods (in Months) | | | | | | | | | | | |
|---|---|---|---|---|---|---|---|---|---|---|---|
| Term Left on Current Loan: 300 months<br>Term on New Loan: 30 years<br>Points: 2.00% | | | | | | Income Tax Bracket: 40.00%<br>Points and Costs: Finance | | | | | |
| Other Closing Costs as a Percent of Loan Amount | | | | | | | | | | | |
| Interest Rate Reduction | .25% | .5% | .75% | 1.00% | 1.25% | 1.50% | 1.75% | 2.00% | 2.50% | 3.00% | 3.50% | 4.00% |
|---|---|---|---|---|---|---|---|---|---|---|---|---|
| 0.125% | None | None | None | None | None | None | None | None | None | None | None | None |
| 0.25% | None | None | None | None | None | None | None | None | None | None | None | None |
| 0.375% | None | None | None | None | None | None | None | None | None | None | None | None |
| 0.5% | None | None | None | None | None | None | None | None | None | None | None | None |
| 0.625% | None | None | None | None | None | None | None | None | None | None | None | None |
| 0.75% | 89 | 107 | 136 | None | None | None | None | None | None | None | None | None |
| 0.875% | 68 | 79 | 92 | 106 | 125 | 155 | None | None | None | None | None | None |
| 1% | 57 | 65 | 74 | 83 | 94 | 106 | 120 | 138 | None | None | None | None |
| 1.125% | 49 | 55 | 62 | 69 | 77 | 86 | 95 | 106 | 131 | 174 | None | None |
| 1.25% | 43 | 48 | 54 | 60 | 67 | 73 | 81 | 88 | 105 | 126 | 155 | None |
| 1.375% | 38 | 43 | 48 | 53 | 59 | 64 | 70 | 76 | 90 | 105 | 123 | 146 |
| 1.5% | 34 | 39 | 43 | 48 | 52 | 57 | 62 | 68 | 79 | 91 | 105 | 121 |
| 1.625% | 31 | 35 | 39 | 43 | 47 | 52 | 56 | 61 | 71 | 81 | 93 | 105 |
| 1.75% | 29 | 32 | 36 | 40 | 43 | 47 | 51 | 55 | 64 | 73 | 83 | 94 |
| 1.875% | 27 | 30 | 33 | 37 | 40 | 44 | 47 | 51 | 59 | 67 | 75 | 85 |
| 2% | 25 | 28 | 31 | 34 | 37 | 40 | 44 | 47 | 54 | 61 | 69 | 77 |
| 2.125% | 23 | 26 | 29 | 32 | 35 | 38 | 41 | 44 | 50 | 57 | 64 | 71 |
| 2.25% | 22 | 25 | 27 | 30 | 33 | 35 | 38 | 41 | 47 | 53 | 59 | 66 |
| 2.375% | 21 | 23 | 26 | 28 | 31 | 33 | 36 | 39 | 44 | 50 | 56 | 62 |
| 2.5% | 20 | 22 | 24 | 27 | 29 | 31 | 34 | 36 | 41 | 47 | 52 | 58 |
| 2.625% | 19 | 21 | 23 | 25 | 27 | 30 | 32 | 34 | 39 | 44 | 49 | 55 |
| 2.75% | 18 | 20 | 22 | 24 | 26 | 28 | 30 | 33 | 37 | 42 | 47 | 52 |
| 2.875% | 17 | 19 | 21 | 23 | 25 | 27 | 29 | 31 | 35 | 40 | 44 | 49 |
| 3% | 16 | 18 | 20 | 22 | 24 | 26 | 28 | 30 | 34 | 38 | 42 | 47 |
| 3.125% | 16 | 17 | 19 | 21 | 23 | 25 | 26 | 28 | 32 | 36 | 40 | 44 |
| 3.25% | 15 | 17 | 18 | 20 | 22 | 24 | 25 | 27 | 31 | 35 | 39 | 42 |
| 3.375% | 14 | 16 | 18 | 19 | 21 | 23 | 24 | 26 | 30 | 33 | 37 | 41 |
| 3.5% | 14 | 15 | 17 | 19 | 20 | 22 | 23 | 25 | 28 | 32 | 35 | 39 |
| 3.625% | 13 | 15 | 16 | 18 | 20 | 21 | 23 | 24 | 27 | 31 | 34 | 38 |
| 3.75% | 13 | 14 | 16 | 17 | 19 | 20 | 22 | 23 | 26 | 30 | 33 | 36 |
| 3.875% | 13 | 14 | 15 | 17 | 18 | 20 | 21 | 23 | 26 | 29 | 32 | 35 |
| 4% | 12 | 14 | 15 | 16 | 18 | 19 | 20 | 22 | 25 | 28 | 31 | 34 |

| Break-Even Periods (in Months) | | | | | | | | | | | | |
|---|---|---|---|---|---|---|---|---|---|---|---|---|
| Term Left on Current Loan: 300 months<br>Term on New Loan: 30 years<br>Points: 3.00% | | | | | | | Income Tax Bracket: 40.00%<br>Points and Costs: Financed | | | | | |
| Other Closing Costs as a Percent of Loan Amount | | | | | | | | | | | | |
| Interest Rate Reduction | .25% | .5% | .75% | 1.00% | 1.25% | 1.50% | 1.75% | 2.00% | 2.50% | 3.00% | 3.50% | 4.00% |
| 0.125% | None | None | None | None | None | None | None | None | None | None | None | None |
| 0.25% | None | None | None | None | None | None | None | None | None | None | None | None |
| 0.375% | None | None | None | None | None | None | None | None | None | None | None | None |
| 0.5% | None | None | None | None | None | None | None | None | None | None | None | None |
| 0.625% | None | None | None | None | None | None | None | None | None | None | None | None |
| 0.75% | None | None | None | None | None | None | None | None | None | None | None | None |
| 0.875% | 127 | 158 | None | None | None | None | None | None | None | None | None | None |
| 1% | 95 | 107 | 121 | 139 | 169 | None | None | None | None | None | None | None |
| 1.125% | 78 | 87 | 96 | 106 | 118 | 131 | 148 | 174 | None | None | None | None |
| 1.25% | 67 | 74 | 81 | 89 | 97 | 106 | 115 | 126 | 155 | None | None | None |
| 1.375% | 59 | 65 | 70 | 77 | 83 | 90 | 97 | 105 | 123 | 146 | 179 | None |
| 1.5% | 53 | 58 | 63 | 68 | 73 | 79 | 85 | 91 | 105 | 121 | 140 | 164 |
| 1.625% | 48 | 52 | 56 | 61 | 66 | 71 | 76 | 81 | 93 | 105 | 119 | 135 |
| 1.75% | 44 | 48 | 51 | 56 | 60 | 64 | 69 | 73 | 83 | 93 | 105 | 118 |
| 1.875% | 40 | 44 | 47 | 51 | 55 | 59 | 63 | 67 | 75 | 84 | 94 | 105 |
| 2% | 37 | 41 | 44 | 47 | 51 | 54 | 58 | 61 | 69 | 77 | 86 | 95 |
| 2.125% | 35 | 38 | 41 | 44 | 47 | 50 | 54 | 57 | 64 | 71 | 79 | 87 |
| 2.25% | 33 | 35 | 38 | 41 | 44 | 47 | 50 | 53 | 59 | 66 | 73 | 80 |
| 2.375% | 31 | 33 | 36 | 39 | 41 | 44 | 47 | 50 | 56 | 62 | 68 | 75 |
| 2.5% | 29 | 32 | 34 | 36 | 39 | 41 | 44 | 47 | 52 | 58 | 64 | 70 |
| 2.625% | 28 | 30 | 32 | 34 | 37 | 39 | 42 | 44 | 49 | 54 | 60 | 66 |
| 2.75% | 26 | 28 | 31 | 33 | 35 | 37 | 40 | 42 | 47 | 52 | 57 | 62 |
| 2.875% | 25 | 27 | 29 | 31 | 33 | 35 | 38 | 40 | 44 | 49 | 54 | 59 |
| 3% | 24 | 26 | 28 | 30 | 32 | 34 | 36 | 38 | 42 | 46 | 51 | 56 |
| 3.125% | 23 | 25 | 27 | 28 | 30 | 32 | 34 | 36 | 40 | 44 | 49 | 53 |
| 3.25% | 22 | 24 | 25 | 27 | 29 | 31 | 33 | 35 | 38 | 42 | 46 | 51 |
| 3.375% | 21 | 23 | 24 | 26 | 28 | 30 | 31 | 33 | 37 | 41 | 44 | 48 |
| 3.5% | 20 | 22 | 24 | 25 | 27 | 29 | 30 | 32 | 35 | 39 | 43 | 46 |
| 3.625% | 20 | 21 | 23 | 24 | 26 | 27 | 29 | 31 | 34 | 37 | 41 | 45 |
| 3.75% | 19 | 20 | 22 | 23 | 25 | 26 | 28 | 30 | 33 | 36 | 39 | 43 |
| 3.875% | 18 | 20 | 21 | 23 | 24 | 26 | 27 | 29 | 32 | 35 | 38 | 41 |
| 4% | 18 | 19 | 20 | 22 | 23 | 25 | 26 | 28 | 31 | 34 | 37 | 40 |

| Break-Even Periods (in Months) | | | | | | | | | | | |
|---|---|---|---|---|---|---|---|---|---|---|---|

Term Left on Current Loan: 120 months
Term on New Loan: 15 years
Points: 0.00%

Income Tax Bracket: Pre-Tax
Points and Costs: Paid in Cash

| Interest Rate Reduction | Other Closing Costs as a Percent of Loan Amount | | | | | | | | | | | |
|---|---|---|---|---|---|---|---|---|---|---|---|---|
| | .25% | .5% | .75% | 1.00% | 1.25% | 1.50% | 1.75% | 2.00% | 2.50% | 3.00% | 3.50% | 4.00% |
| 0.125% | None | None | None | None | None | None | None | None | None | None | None | None |
| 0.25% | None | None | None | None | None | None | None | None | None | None | None | None |
| 0.375% | 10 | None | None | None | None | None | None | None | None | None | None | None |
| 0.5% | 7 | 16 | None | None | None | None | None | None | None | None | None | None |
| 0.625% | 6 | 11 | 19 | 31 | None | None | None | None | None | None | None | None |
| 0.75% | 5 | 9 | 14 | 21 | 29 | None | None | None | None | None | None | None |
| 0.875% | 4 | 8 | 12 | 16 | 22 | 28 | 37 | None | None | None | None | None |
| 1% | 4 | 7 | 10 | 14 | 18 | 22 | 28 | 34 | None | None | None | None |
| 1.125% | 3 | 6 | 9 | 12 | 15 | 19 | 23 | 27 | 38 | None | None | None |
| 1.25% | 3 | 5 | 8 | 11 | 14 | 17 | 20 | 23 | 31 | 41 | None | None |
| 1.375% | 3 | 5 | 7 | 10 | 12 | 15 | 18 | 21 | 27 | 34 | 44 | 60 |
| 1.5% | 3 | 5 | 7 | 9 | 11 | 14 | 16 | 18 | 24 | 30 | 37 | 45 |
| 1.625% | 2 | 4 | 6 | 8 | 10 | 12 | 15 | 17 | 22 | 27 | 32 | 39 |
| 1.75% | 2 | 4 | 6 | 8 | 9 | 11 | 13 | 15 | 20 | 24 | 29 | 35 |
| 1.875% | 2 | 4 | 5 | 7 | 9 | 11 | 12 | 14 | 18 | 22 | 27 | 31 |
| 2% | 2 | 4 | 5 | 7 | 8 | 10 | 12 | 13 | 17 | 21 | 24 | 29 |
| 2.125% | 2 | 3 | 5 | 6 | 8 | 9 | 11 | 12 | 16 | 19 | 23 | 26 |
| 2.25% | 2 | 3 | 5 | 6 | 7 | 9 | 10 | 12 | 15 | 18 | 21 | 25 |
| 2.375% | 2 | 3 | 4 | 6 | 7 | 8 | 10 | 11 | 14 | 17 | 20 | 23 |
| 2.5% | 2 | 3 | 4 | 5 | 7 | 8 | 9 | 11 | 13 | 16 | 19 | 22 |
| 2.625% | 2 | 3 | 4 | 5 | 6 | 8 | 9 | 10 | 13 | 15 | 18 | 21 |
| 2.75% | 2 | 3 | 4 | 5 | 6 | 7 | 8 | 10 | 12 | 14 | 17 | 20 |
| 2.875% | 2 | 3 | 4 | 5 | 6 | 7 | 8 | 9 | 11 | 14 | 16 | 19 |
| 3% | 2 | 3 | 4 | 5 | 6 | 7 | 8 | 9 | 11 | 13 | 15 | 18 |
| 3.125% | 1 | 2 | 3 | 4 | 5 | 6 | 7 | 8 | 10 | 13 | 15 | 17 |
| 3.25% | 1 | 2 | 3 | 4 | 5 | 6 | 7 | 8 | 10 | 12 | 14 | 16 |
| 3.375% | 1 | 2 | 3 | 4 | 5 | 6 | 7 | 8 | 10 | 12 | 14 | 16 |
| 3.5% | 1 | 2 | 3 | 4 | 5 | 6 | 7 | 8 | 9 | 11 | 13 | 15 |
| 3.625% | 1 | 2 | 3 | 4 | 5 | 6 | 6 | 7 | 9 | 11 | 13 | 14 |
| 3.75% | 1 | 2 | 3 | 4 | 5 | 5 | 6 | 7 | 9 | 10 | 12 | 14 |
| 3.875% | 1 | 2 | 3 | 4 | 4 | 5 | 6 | 7 | 8 | 10 | 12 | 14 |
| 4% | 1 | 2 | 3 | 4 | 4 | 5 | 6 | 7 | 8 | 10 | 11 | 13 |

# Refinance Break-Even Tables

| Break-Even Periods (in Months) | | | | | | | | | | | |
|---|---|---|---|---|---|---|---|---|---|---|---|

Term Left on Current Loan: 120 months    Income Tax Bracket: Pre-Tax
Term on New Loan: 15 years    Points and Costs: Paid in Cash
Points: 1.00%

| Other Closing Costs as a Percent of Loan Amount | | | | | | | | | | | | |
|---|---|---|---|---|---|---|---|---|---|---|---|---|
| Interest Rate Reduction | .25% | .5% | .75% | 1.00% | 1.25% | 1.50% | 1.75% | 2.00% | 2.50% | 3.00% | 3.50% | 4.00% |
| 0.125% | None | None | None | None | None | None | None | None | None | None | None | None |
| 0.25% | None | None | None | None | None | None | None | None | None | None | None | None |
| 0.375% | None | None | None | None | None | None | None | None | None | None | None | None |
| 0.5% | None | None | None | None | None | None | None | None | None | None | None | None |
| 0.625% | None | None | None | None | None | None | None | None | None | None | None | None |
| 0.75% | 29 | None | None | None | None | None | None | None | None | None | None | None |
| 0.875% | 22 | 28 | 37 | None | None | None | None | None | None | None | None | None |
| 1% | 18 | 22 | 28 | 34 | 43 | None | None | None | None | None | None | None |
| 1.125% | 15 | 19 | 23 | 27 | 32 | 38 | 46 | None | None | None | None | None |
| 1.25% | 14 | 17 | 20 | 23 | 27 | 31 | 36 | 41 | None | None | None | None |
| 1.375% | 12 | 15 | 18 | 21 | 24 | 27 | 30 | 34 | 44 | 60 | None | None |
| 1.5% | 11 | 14 | 16 | 18 | 21 | 24 | 27 | 30 | 37 | 45 | 58 | None |
| 1.625% | 10 | 12 | 15 | 17 | 19 | 22 | 24 | 27 | 32 | 39 | 47 | 58 |
| 1.75% | 9 | 11 | 13 | 15 | 18 | 20 | 22 | 24 | 29 | 35 | 41 | 48 |
| 1.875% | 9 | 11 | 12 | 14 | 16 | 18 | 20 | 22 | 27 | 31 | 36 | 42 |
| 2% | 8 | 10 | 12 | 13 | 15 | 17 | 19 | 21 | 24 | 29 | 33 | 38 |
| 2.125% | 8 | 9 | 11 | 12 | 14 | 16 | 17 | 19 | 23 | 26 | 30 | 35 |
| 2.25% | 7 | 9 | 10 | 12 | 13 | 15 | 16 | 18 | 21 | 25 | 28 | 32 |
| 2.375% | 7 | 8 | 10 | 11 | 13 | 14 | 15 | 17 | 20 | 23 | 26 | 30 |
| 2.5% | 7 | 8 | 9 | 11 | 12 | 13 | 15 | 16 | 19 | 22 | 25 | 28 |
| 2.625% | 6 | 8 | 9 | 10 | 11 | 13 | 14 | 15 | 18 | 21 | 23 | 26 |
| 2.75% | 6 | 7 | 8 | 10 | 11 | 12 | 13 | 14 | 17 | 20 | 22 | 25 |
| 2.875% | 6 | 7 | 8 | 9 | 10 | 11 | 13 | 14 | 16 | 19 | 21 | 24 |
| 3% | 6 | 7 | 8 | 9 | 10 | 11 | 12 | 13 | 15 | 18 | 20 | 23 |
| 3.125% | 5 | 6 | 7 | 8 | 9 | 10 | 12 | 13 | 15 | 17 | 19 | 22 |
| 3.25% | 5 | 6 | 7 | 8 | 9 | 10 | 11 | 12 | 14 | 16 | 18 | 21 |
| 3.375% | 5 | 6 | 7 | 8 | 9 | 10 | 11 | 12 | 14 | 16 | 18 | 20 |
| 3.5% | 5 | 6 | 7 | 8 | 8 | 9 | 10 | 11 | 13 | 15 | 17 | 19 |
| 3.625% | 5 | 6 | 6 | 7 | 8 | 9 | 10 | 11 | 13 | 14 | 16 | 18 |
| 3.75% | 5 | 5 | 6 | 7 | 8 | 9 | 10 | 10 | 12 | 14 | 16 | 18 |
| 3.875% | 4 | 5 | 6 | 7 | 8 | 8 | 9 | 10 | 12 | 14 | 15 | 17 |
| 4% | 4 | 5 | 6 | 7 | 7 | 8 | 9 | 10 | 11 | 13 | 15 | 16 |

# Refinance Break-Even Tables

## Break-Even Periods (in Months)

Term Left on Current Loan: 120 months　　　　Income Tax Bracket: Pre-Tax
Term on New Loan: 15 years　　　　　　　　　Points and Costs: Paid in Cash
Points: 2.00%

### Other Closing Costs as a Percent of Loan Amount

| Interest Rate Reduction | .25% | .5% | .75% | 1.00% | 1.25% | 1.50% | 1.75% | 2.00% | 2.50% | 3.00% | 3.50% | 4.00% |
|---|---|---|---|---|---|---|---|---|---|---|---|---|
| 0.125% | None | None | None | None | None | None | None | None | None | None | None | None |
| 0.25% | None | None | None | None | None | None | None | None | None | None | None | None |
| 0.375% | None | None | None | None | None | None | None | None | None | None | None | None |
| 0.5% | None | None | None | None | None | None | None | None | None | None | None | None |
| 0.625% | None | None | None | None | None | None | None | None | None | None | None | None |
| 0.75% | None | None | None | None | None | None | None | None | None | None | None | None |
| 0.875% | None | None | None | None | None | None | None | None | None | None | None | None |
| 1% | 43 | None | None | None | None | None | None | None | None | None | None | None |
| 1.125% | 32 | 38 | 46 | None | None | None | None | None | None | None | None | None |
| 1.25% | 27 | 31 | 36 | 41 | 49 | None | None | None | None | None | None | None |
| 1.375% | 24 | 27 | 30 | 34 | 39 | 44 | 50 | 60 | None | None | None | None |
| 1.5% | 21 | 24 | 27 | 30 | 33 | 37 | 41 | 45 | 58 | None | None | None |
| 1.625% | 19 | 22 | 24 | 27 | 29 | 32 | 36 | 39 | 47 | 58 | None | None |
| 1.75% | 18 | 20 | 22 | 24 | 27 | 29 | 32 | 35 | 41 | 48 | 57 | 77 |
| 1.875% | 16 | 18 | 20 | 22 | 24 | 27 | 29 | 31 | 36 | 42 | 49 | 57 |
| 2% | 15 | 17 | 19 | 21 | 22 | 24 | 27 | 29 | 33 | 38 | 43 | 49 |
| 2.125% | 14 | 16 | 17 | 19 | 21 | 23 | 25 | 26 | 30 | 35 | 39 | 44 |
| 2.25% | 13 | 15 | 16 | 18 | 20 | 21 | 23 | 25 | 28 | 32 | 36 | 40 |
| 2.375% | 13 | 14 | 15 | 17 | 18 | 20 | 22 | 23 | 26 | 30 | 34 | 37 |
| 2.5% | 12 | 13 | 15 | 16 | 17 | 19 | 20 | 22 | 25 | 28 | 31 | 35 |
| 2.625% | 11 | 13 | 14 | 15 | 16 | 18 | 19 | 21 | 23 | 26 | 29 | 33 |
| 2.75% | 11 | 12 | 13 | 14 | 16 | 17 | 18 | 20 | 22 | 25 | 28 | 31 |
| 2.875% | 10 | 11 | 13 | 14 | 15 | 16 | 17 | 19 | 21 | 24 | 26 | 29 |
| 3% | 10 | 11 | 12 | 13 | 14 | 15 | 17 | 18 | 20 | 23 | 25 | 28 |
| 3.125% | 9 | 10 | 12 | 13 | 14 | 15 | 16 | 17 | 19 | 22 | 24 | 26 |
| 3.25% | 9 | 10 | 11 | 12 | 13 | 14 | 15 | 16 | 18 | 21 | 23 | 25 |
| 3.375% | 9 | 10 | 11 | 12 | 13 | 14 | 15 | 16 | 18 | 20 | 22 | 24 |
| 3.5% | 8 | 9 | 10 | 11 | 12 | 13 | 14 | 15 | 17 | 19 | 21 | 23 |
| 3.625% | 8 | 9 | 10 | 11 | 12 | 13 | 14 | 14 | 16 | 18 | 20 | 22 |
| 3.75% | 8 | 9 | 10 | 10 | 11 | 12 | 13 | 14 | 16 | 18 | 20 | 21 |
| 3.875% | 8 | 8 | 9 | 10 | 11 | 12 | 13 | 14 | 15 | 17 | 19 | 21 |
| 4% | 7 | 8 | 9 | 10 | 11 | 11 | 12 | 13 | 15 | 16 | 18 | 20 |

# Refinance Break-Even Tables

| Break-Even Periods (in Months) | | | | | | | | | | | |
|---|---|---|---|---|---|---|---|---|---|---|---|

Term Left on Current Loan: 120 months      Income Tax Bracket: Pre-Tax
Term on New Loan: 15 years      Points and Costs: Paid in Cash
Points: 3.00%

| Other Closing Costs as a Percent of Loan Amount | | | | | | | | | | | |
|---|---|---|---|---|---|---|---|---|---|---|---|
| Interest Rate Reduction | .25% | .5% | .75% | 1.00% | 1.25% | 1.50% | 1.75% | 2.00% | 2.50% | 3.00% | 3.50% | 4.00% |
| 0.125% | None | None | None | None | None | None | None | None | None | None | None | None |
| 0.25% | None | None | None | None | None | None | None | None | None | None | None | None |
| 0.375% | None | None | None | None | None | None | None | None | None | None | None | None |
| 0.5% | None | None | None | None | None | None | None | None | None | None | None | None |
| 0.625% | None | None | None | None | None | None | None | None | None | None | None | None |
| 0.75% | None | None | None | None | None | None | None | None | None | None | None | None |
| 0.875% | None | None | None | None | None | None | None | None | None | None | None | None |
| 1% | None | None | None | None | None | None | None | None | None | None | None | None |
| 1.125% | None | None | None | None | None | None | None | None | None | None | None | None |
| 1.25% | 49 | None | None | None | None | None | None | None | None | None | None | None |
| 1.375% | 39 | 44 | 50 | 60 | None | None | None | None | None | None | None | None |
| 1.5% | 33 | 37 | 41 | 45 | 51 | 58 | None | None | None | None | None | None |
| 1.625% | 29 | 32 | 36 | 39 | 43 | 47 | 52 | 58 | None | None | None | None |
| 1.75% | 27 | 29 | 32 | 35 | 38 | 41 | 44 | 48 | 57 | 77 | None | None |
| 1.875% | 24 | 27 | 29 | 31 | 34 | 36 | 39 | 42 | 49 | 57 | 69 | None |
| 2% | 22 | 24 | 27 | 29 | 31 | 33 | 35 | 38 | 43 | 49 | 57 | 66 |
| 2.125% | 21 | 23 | 25 | 26 | 28 | 30 | 33 | 35 | 39 | 44 | 50 | 57 |
| 2.25% | 20 | 21 | 23 | 25 | 26 | 28 | 30 | 32 | 36 | 40 | 45 | 50 |
| 2.375% | 18 | 20 | 22 | 23 | 25 | 26 | 28 | 30 | 34 | 37 | 42 | 46 |
| 2.5% | 17 | 19 | 20 | 22 | 23 | 25 | 26 | 28 | 31 | 35 | 39 | 42 |
| 2.625% | 16 | 18 | 19 | 21 | 22 | 23 | 25 | 26 | 29 | 33 | 36 | 40 |
| 2.75% | 16 | 17 | 18 | 20 | 21 | 22 | 24 | 25 | 28 | 31 | 34 | 37 |
| 2.875% | 15 | 16 | 17 | 19 | 20 | 21 | 22 | 24 | 26 | 29 | 32 | 35 |
| 3% | 14 | 15 | 17 | 18 | 19 | 20 | 21 | 23 | 25 | 28 | 30 | 33 |
| 3.125% | 14 | 15 | 16 | 17 | 18 | 19 | 20 | 22 | 24 | 26 | 29 | 31 |
| 3.25% | 13 | 14 | 15 | 16 | 17 | 18 | 20 | 21 | 23 | 25 | 28 | 30 |
| 3.375% | 13 | 14 | 15 | 16 | 17 | 18 | 19 | 20 | 22 | 24 | 26 | 29 |
| 3.5% | 12 | 13 | 14 | 15 | 16 | 17 | 18 | 19 | 21 | 23 | 25 | 27 |
| 3.625% | 12 | 13 | 14 | 14 | 15 | 16 | 17 | 18 | 20 | 22 | 24 | 26 |
| 3.75% | 11 | 12 | 13 | 14 | 15 | 16 | 17 | 18 | 20 | 21 | 23 | 25 |
| 3.875% | 11 | 12 | 13 | 14 | 14 | 15 | 16 | 17 | 19 | 21 | 23 | 24 |
| 4% | 11 | 11 | 12 | 13 | 14 | 15 | 16 | 16 | 18 | 20 | 22 | 24 |

# Refinance Break-Even Tables

## Break-Even Periods (in Months)

Term Left on Current Loan: 120 months  
Term on New Loan: 15 years  
Points: 0.00%

Income Tax Bracket: 40.00%  
Points and Costs: Paid in Cash

### Other Closing Costs as a Percent of Loan Amount

| Interest Rate Reduction | .25% | .5% | .75% | 1.00% | 1.25% | 1.50% | 1.75% | 2.00% | 2.50% | 3.00% | 3.50% | 4.00% |
|---|---|---|---|---|---|---|---|---|---|---|---|---|
| 0.125% | None | None | None | None | None | None | None | None | None | None | None | None |
| 0.25% | None | None | None | None | None | None | None | None | None | None | None | None |
| 0.375% | None | None | None | None | None | None | None | None | None | None | None | None |
| 0.5% | 12 | None | None | None | None | None | None | None | None | None | None | None |
| 0.625% | 9 | 22 | None | None | None | None | None | None | None | None | None | None |
| 0.75% | 8 | 16 | 29 | None | None | None | None | None | None | None | None | None |
| 0.875% | 6 | 13 | 22 | 33 | None | None | None | None | None | None | None | None |
| 1% | 6 | 11 | 18 | 26 | 36 | None | None | None | None | None | None | None |
| 1.125% | 5 | 10 | 15 | 21 | 29 | 37 | 53 | None | None | None | None | None |
| 1.25% | 5 | 9 | 14 | 19 | 24 | 31 | 39 | 50 | None | None | None | None |
| 1.375% | 4 | 8 | 12 | 17 | 21 | 27 | 33 | 40 | None | None | None | None |
| 1.5% | 4 | 7 | 11 | 15 | 19 | 24 | 29 | 34 | 48 | None | None | None |
| 1.625% | 4 | 7 | 10 | 14 | 17 | 21 | 26 | 30 | 41 | 56 | None | None |
| 1.75% | 3 | 6 | 9 | 13 | 16 | 20 | 23 | 27 | 36 | 47 | 63 | None |
| 1.875% | 3 | 6 | 9 | 12 | 15 | 18 | 21 | 25 | 32 | 41 | 52 | 71 |
| 2% | 3 | 6 | 8 | 11 | 14 | 17 | 20 | 23 | 30 | 37 | 46 | 58 |
| 2.125% | 3 | 5 | 8 | 10 | 13 | 16 | 18 | 21 | 27 | 34 | 42 | 51 |
| 2.25% | 3 | 5 | 7 | 10 | 12 | 15 | 17 | 20 | 26 | 32 | 38 | 46 |
| 2.375% | 3 | 5 | 7 | 9 | 12 | 14 | 16 | 19 | 24 | 30 | 36 | 42 |
| 2.5% | 3 | 5 | 7 | 9 | 11 | 13 | 15 | 18 | 23 | 28 | 33 | 39 |
| 2.625% | 2 | 4 | 6 | 8 | 10 | 13 | 15 | 17 | 21 | 26 | 31 | 37 |
| 2.75% | 2 | 4 | 6 | 8 | 10 | 12 | 14 | 16 | 20 | 25 | 29 | 34 |
| 2.875% | 2 | 4 | 6 | 8 | 9 | 11 | 13 | 15 | 19 | 23 | 28 | 33 |
| 3% | 2 | 4 | 6 | 7 | 9 | 11 | 13 | 15 | 18 | 22 | 27 | 31 |
| 3.125% | 2 | 4 | 5 | 7 | 9 | 10 | 12 | 14 | 18 | 21 | 25 | 29 |
| 3.25% | 2 | 4 | 5 | 7 | 8 | 10 | 12 | 13 | 17 | 20 | 24 | 28 |
| 3.375% | 2 | 3 | 5 | 7 | 8 | 10 | 11 | 13 | 16 | 20 | 23 | 27 |
| 3.5% | 2 | 3 | 5 | 6 | 8 | 9 | 11 | 12 | 16 | 19 | 22 | 26 |
| 3.625% | 2 | 3 | 5 | 6 | 8 | 9 | 10 | 12 | 15 | 18 | 21 | 25 |
| 3.75% | 2 | 3 | 5 | 6 | 7 | 9 | 10 | 12 | 15 | 18 | 21 | 24 |
| 3.875% | 2 | 3 | 4 | 6 | 7 | 8 | 10 | 11 | 14 | 17 | 20 | 23 |
| 4% | 2 | 3 | 4 | 6 | 7 | 8 | 10 | 11 | 14 | 16 | 19 | 22 |

| Break-Even Periods (in Months) | | | | | | | | | | | |
|---|---|---|---|---|---|---|---|---|---|---|---|
| Term Left on Current Loan: 120 months | | | | | | Income Tax Bracket: 40.00% | | | | | |
| Term on New Loan: 15 years | | | | | | Points and Costs: Paid in Cash | | | | | |
| Points: 1.00% | | | | | | | | | | | |

| Other Closing Costs as a Percent of Loan Amount | | | | | | | | | | | |
|---|---|---|---|---|---|---|---|---|---|---|---|
| Interest Rate Reduction | .25% | .5% | .75% | 1.00% | 1.25% | 1.50% | 1.75% | 2.00% | 2.50% | 3.00% | 3.50% | 4.00% |
| 0.125% | None | None | None | None | None | None | None | None | None | None | None | None |
| 0.25% | None | None | None | None | None | None | None | None | None | None | None | None |
| 0.375% | None | None | None | None | None | None | None | None | None | None | None | None |
| 0.5% | None | None | None | None | None | None | None | None | None | None | None | None |
| 0.625% | None | None | None | None | None | None | None | None | None | None | None | None |
| 0.75% | 40 | None | None | None | None | None | None | None | None | None | None | None |
| 0.875% | 26 | 42 | None | None | None | None | None | None | None | None | None | None |
| 1% | 21 | 30 | 43 | None | None | None | None | None | None | None | None | None |
| 1.125% | 18 | 24 | 32 | 43 | None | None | None | None | None | None | None | None |
| 1.25% | 16 | 21 | 27 | 34 | 43 | 62 | None | None | None | None | None | None |
| 1.375% | 14 | 19 | 24 | 29 | 36 | 43 | 55 | None | None | None | None | None |
| 1.5% | 13 | 17 | 21 | 26 | 31 | 37 | 43 | 52 | None | None | None | None |
| 1.625% | 12 | 15 | 19 | 23 | 28 | 32 | 37 | 43 | 61 | None | None | None |
| 1.75% | 11 | 14 | 18 | 21 | 25 | 29 | 33 | 38 | 50 | 71 | None | None |
| 1.875% | 10 | 13 | 16 | 19 | 23 | 26 | 30 | 34 | 44 | 56 | None | None |
| 2% | 9 | 12 | 15 | 18 | 21 | 24 | 28 | 31 | 39 | 49 | 61 | None |
| 2.125% | 9 | 11 | 14 | 17 | 20 | 23 | 26 | 29 | 36 | 44 | 53 | 66 |
| 2.25% | 8 | 11 | 13 | 16 | 18 | 21 | 24 | 27 | 33 | 40 | 48 | 57 |
| 2.375% | 8 | 10 | 13 | 15 | 17 | 20 | 22 | 25 | 31 | 37 | 44 | 52 |
| 2.5% | 8 | 10 | 12 | 14 | 16 | 19 | 21 | 24 | 29 | 35 | 41 | 47 |
| 2.625% | 7 | 9 | 11 | 13 | 16 | 18 | 20 | 22 | 27 | 32 | 38 | 44 |
| 2.75% | 7 | 9 | 11 | 13 | 15 | 17 | 19 | 21 | 26 | 31 | 36 | 41 |
| 2.875% | 7 | 8 | 10 | 12 | 14 | 16 | 18 | 20 | 24 | 29 | 34 | 39 |
| 3% | 6 | 8 | 10 | 12 | 14 | 15 | 17 | 19 | 23 | 27 | 32 | 37 |
| 3.125% | 6 | 8 | 9 | 11 | 13 | 15 | 17 | 18 | 22 | 26 | 30 | 35 |
| 3.25% | 6 | 7 | 9 | 11 | 12 | 14 | 16 | 18 | 21 | 25 | 29 | 33 |
| 3.375% | 6 | 7 | 9 | 10 | 12 | 14 | 15 | 17 | 20 | 24 | 28 | 31 |
| 3.5% | 5 | 7 | 8 | 10 | 12 | 13 | 15 | 16 | 20 | 23 | 27 | 30 |
| 3.625% | 5 | 7 | 8 | 10 | 11 | 13 | 14 | 16 | 19 | 22 | 25 | 29 |
| 3.75% | 5 | 6 | 8 | 9 | 11 | 12 | 14 | 15 | 18 | 21 | 24 | 28 |
| 3.875% | 5 | 6 | 8 | 9 | 10 | 12 | 13 | 15 | 18 | 21 | 24 | 27 |
| 4% | 5 | 6 | 7 | 9 | 10 | 11 | 13 | 14 | 17 | 20 | 23 | 26 |

| Break-Even Periods (in Months) | | | | | | | | | | | | |
|---|---|---|---|---|---|---|---|---|---|---|---|---|

Term Left on Current Loan: 120 months       Income Tax Bracket: 40.00%
Term on New Loan: 15 years       Points and Costs: Paid in Cash
Points: 2.00%

| Interest Rate Reduction | Other Closing Costs as a Percent of Loan Amount | | | | | | | | | | | |
|---|---|---|---|---|---|---|---|---|---|---|---|---|
| | .25% | .5% | .75% | 1.00% | 1.25% | 1.50% | 1.75% | 2.00% | 2.50% | 3.00% | 3.50% | 4.00% |
| 0.125% | None | None | None | None | None | None | None | None | None | None | None | None |
| 0.25% | None | None | None | None | None | None | None | None | None | None | None | None |
| 0.375% | None | None | None | None | None | None | None | None | None | None | None | None |
| 0.5% | None | None | None | None | None | None | None | None | None | None | None | None |
| 0.625% | None | None | None | None | None | None | None | None | None | None | None | None |
| 0.75% | None | None | None | None | None | None | None | None | None | None | None | None |
| 0.875% | None | None | None | None | None | None | None | None | None | None | None | None |
| 1% | None | None | None | None | None | None | None | None | None | None | None | None |
| 1.125% | 36 | 51 | None | None | None | None | None | None | None | None | None | None |
| 1.25% | 30 | 38 | 49 | None | None | None | None | None | None | None | None | None |
| 1.375% | 26 | 32 | 39 | 48 | None | None | None | None | None | None | None | None |
| 1.5% | 23 | 28 | 33 | 40 | 47 | 58 | None | None | None | None | None | None |
| 1.625% | 21 | 25 | 30 | 35 | 40 | 47 | 55 | 71 | None | None | None | None |
| 1.75% | 19 | 23 | 27 | 31 | 35 | 41 | 46 | 53 | None | None | None | None |
| 1.875% | 18 | 21 | 24 | 28 | 32 | 36 | 41 | 46 | 59 | None | None | None |
| 2% | 16 | 19 | 23 | 26 | 29 | 33 | 37 | 41 | 51 | 65 | None | None |
| 2.125% | 15 | 18 | 21 | 24 | 27 | 30 | 34 | 38 | 46 | 56 | 71 | None |
| 2.25% | 14 | 17 | 20 | 22 | 25 | 28 | 31 | 35 | 42 | 50 | 60 | 76 |
| 2.375% | 14 | 16 | 18 | 21 | 24 | 26 | 29 | 32 | 38 | 46 | 54 | 64 |
| 2.5% | 13 | 15 | 17 | 20 | 22 | 25 | 27 | 30 | 36 | 42 | 49 | 57 |
| 2.625% | 12 | 14 | 16 | 19 | 21 | 23 | 26 | 28 | 34 | 39 | 45 | 52 |
| 2.75% | 12 | 14 | 16 | 18 | 20 | 22 | 24 | 27 | 32 | 37 | 42 | 49 |
| 2.875% | 11 | 13 | 15 | 17 | 19 | 21 | 23 | 25 | 30 | 35 | 40 | 45 |
| 3% | 11 | 12 | 14 | 16 | 18 | 20 | 22 | 24 | 28 | 33 | 38 | 43 |
| 3.125% | 10 | 12 | 14 | 15 | 17 | 19 | 21 | 23 | 27 | 31 | 36 | 40 |
| 3.25% | 10 | 11 | 13 | 15 | 17 | 18 | 20 | 22 | 26 | 30 | 34 | 38 |
| 3.375% | 9 | 11 | 13 | 14 | 16 | 18 | 19 | 21 | 25 | 28 | 32 | 36 |
| 3.5% | 9 | 11 | 12 | 14 | 15 | 17 | 19 | 20 | 24 | 27 | 31 | 35 |
| 3.625% | 9 | 10 | 12 | 13 | 15 | 16 | 18 | 20 | 23 | 26 | 30 | 33 |
| 3.75% | 8 | 10 | 11 | 13 | 14 | 16 | 17 | 19 | 22 | 25 | 29 | 32 |
| 3.875% | 8 | 10 | 11 | 12 | 14 | 15 | 17 | 18 | 21 | 24 | 27 | 31 |
| 4% | 8 | 9 | 11 | 12 | 13 | 15 | 16 | 18 | 20 | 23 | 27 | 30 |

| Break-Even Periods (in Months) | | | | | | | | | | | |
|---|---|---|---|---|---|---|---|---|---|---|---|

Term Left on Current Loan: 120 months  Income Tax Bracket: 40.00%
Term on New Loan: 15 years  Points and Costs: Paid in Cash
Points: 3.00%

| Interest Rate Reduction | Other Closing Costs as a Percent of Loan Amount | | | | | | | | | | | |
|---|---|---|---|---|---|---|---|---|---|---|---|---|
| | .25% | .5% | .75% | 1.00% | 1.25% | 1.50% | 1.75% | 2.00% | 2.50% | 3.00% | 3.50% | 4.00% |
| 0.125% | None | None | None | None | None | None | None | None | None | None | None | None |
| 0.25% | None | None | None | None | None | None | None | None | None | None | None | None |
| 0.375% | None | None | None | None | None | None | None | None | None | None | None | None |
| 0.5% | None | None | None | None | None | None | None | None | None | None | None | None |
| 0.625% | None | None | None | None | None | None | None | None | None | None | None | None |
| 0.75% | None | None | None | None | None | None | None | None | None | None | None | None |
| 0.875% | None | None | None | None | None | None | None | None | None | None | None | None |
| 1% | None | None | None | None | None | None | None | None | None | None | None | None |
| 1.125% | None | None | None | None | None | None | None | None | None | None | None | None |
| 1.25% | 60 | None | None | None | None | None | None | None | None | None | None | None |
| 1.375% | 43 | 54 | None | None | None | None | None | None | None | None | None | None |
| 1.5% | 36 | 43 | 52 | 71 | None | None | None | None | None | None | None | None |
| 1.625% | 32 | 37 | 43 | 50 | 60 | None | None | None | None | None | None | None |
| 1.75% | 29 | 33 | 38 | 43 | 49 | 57 | 70 | None | None | None | None | None |
| 1.875% | 26 | 30 | 34 | 38 | 43 | 49 | 55 | 64 | None | None | None | None |
| 2% | 24 | 27 | 31 | 35 | 39 | 43 | 48 | 54 | 70 | None | None | None |
| 2.125% | 22 | 25 | 29 | 32 | 35 | 39 | 43 | 48 | 59 | 77 | None | None |
| 2.25% | 21 | 24 | 27 | 30 | 33 | 36 | 40 | 43 | 52 | 63 | 84 | None |
| 2.375% | 20 | 22 | 25 | 28 | 31 | 34 | 37 | 40 | 47 | 56 | 67 | None |
| 2.5% | 18 | 21 | 23 | 26 | 29 | 31 | 34 | 37 | 44 | 51 | 59 | 71 |
| 2.625% | 17 | 20 | 22 | 24 | 27 | 29 | 32 | 35 | 41 | 47 | 54 | 63 |
| 2.75% | 17 | 19 | 21 | 23 | 25 | 28 | 30 | 33 | 38 | 44 | 50 | 57 |
| 2.875% | 16 | 18 | 20 | 22 | 24 | 26 | 29 | 31 | 36 | 41 | 47 | 53 |
| 3% | 15 | 17 | 19 | 21 | 23 | 25 | 27 | 29 | 34 | 39 | 44 | 49 |
| 3.125% | 14 | 16 | 18 | 20 | 22 | 24 | 26 | 28 | 32 | 37 | 41 | 47 |
| 3.25% | 14 | 16 | 17 | 19 | 21 | 23 | 25 | 27 | 31 | 35 | 39 | 44 |
| 3.375% | 13 | 15 | 17 | 18 | 20 | 22 | 24 | 26 | 29 | 33 | 37 | 42 |
| 3.5% | 13 | 14 | 16 | 18 | 19 | 21 | 23 | 25 | 28 | 32 | 36 | 40 |
| 3.625% | 12 | 14 | 15 | 17 | 19 | 20 | 22 | 24 | 27 | 31 | 34 | 38 |
| 3.75% | 12 | 13 | 15 | 16 | 18 | 20 | 21 | 23 | 26 | 29 | 33 | 36 |
| 3.875% | 12 | 13 | 14 | 16 | 17 | 19 | 20 | 22 | 25 | 28 | 32 | 35 |
| 4% | 11 | 13 | 14 | 15 | 17 | 18 | 20 | 21 | 24 | 27 | 30 | 34 |

# Refinance Break-Even Tables

| Break-Even Periods (in Months) | | | | | | | | | | | |
|---|---|---|---|---|---|---|---|---|---|---|---|
| Term Left on Current Loan: 300 months<br>Term on New Loan: 15 years<br>Points: 0.00% | | | | | | Income Tax Bracket: Pre-Tax<br>Points and Costs: Paid in Cash | | | | | |
| Other Closing Costs as a Percent of Loan Amount | | | | | | | | | | | |
| Interest Rate Reduction | .25% | .5% | .75% | 1.00% | 1.25% | 1.50% | 1.75% | 2.00% | 2.50% | 3.00% | 3.50% | 4.00% |
| 0.125% | 16 | 26 | 33 | 40 | 46 | 51 | 55 | 60 | 68 | 75 | 82 | 88 |
| 0.25% | 11 | 19 | 26 | 32 | 37 | 42 | 47 | 51 | 59 | 66 | 73 | 79 |
| 0.375% | 8 | 15 | 20 | 26 | 31 | 35 | 40 | 44 | 51 | 59 | 65 | 71 |
| 0.5% | 6 | 12 | 17 | 21 | 26 | 30 | 34 | 38 | 45 | 52 | 58 | 64 |
| 0.625% | 5 | 10 | 14 | 18 | 22 | 26 | 29 | 33 | 40 | 46 | 52 | 58 |
| 0.75% | 4 | 8 | 12 | 16 | 19 | 22 | 26 | 29 | 35 | 41 | 47 | 52 |
| 0.875% | 4 | 7 | 10 | 14 | 17 | 20 | 23 | 26 | 31 | 37 | 42 | 47 |
| 1% | 3 | 6 | 9 | 12 | 15 | 18 | 20 | 23 | 28 | 33 | 38 | 43 |
| 1.125% | 3 | 6 | 8 | 11 | 13 | 16 | 18 | 21 | 26 | 30 | 35 | 40 |
| 1.25% | 3 | 5 | 8 | 10 | 12 | 15 | 17 | 19 | 24 | 28 | 32 | 36 |
| 1.375% | 3 | 5 | 7 | 9 | 11 | 13 | 15 | 18 | 22 | 26 | 30 | 34 |
| 1.5% | 3 | 4 | 6 | 8 | 10 | 12 | 14 | 16 | 20 | 24 | 28 | 31 |
| 1.625% | 2 | 4 | 6 | 8 | 10 | 11 | 13 | 15 | 19 | 22 | 26 | 29 |
| 1.75% | 2 | 4 | 6 | 7 | 9 | 11 | 12 | 14 | 17 | 21 | 24 | 27 |
| 1.875% | 2 | 4 | 5 | 7 | 8 | 10 | 12 | 13 | 16 | 20 | 23 | 26 |
| 2% | 2 | 4 | 5 | 6 | 8 | 9 | 11 | 12 | 15 | 18 | 21 | 24 |
| 2.125% | 2 | 3 | 5 | 6 | 8 | 9 | 10 | 12 | 15 | 17 | 20 | 23 |
| 2.25% | 2 | 3 | 5 | 6 | 7 | 9 | 10 | 11 | 14 | 16 | 19 | 22 |
| 2.375% | 2 | 3 | 4 | 6 | 7 | 8 | 9 | 11 | 13 | 16 | 18 | 21 |
| 2.5% | 2 | 3 | 4 | 5 | 7 | 8 | 9 | 10 | 13 | 15 | 17 | 20 |
| 2.625% | 2 | 3 | 4 | 5 | 6 | 7 | 9 | 10 | 12 | 14 | 17 | 19 |
| 2.75% | 2 | 3 | 4 | 5 | 6 | 7 | 8 | 9 | 11 | 14 | 16 | 18 |
| 2.875% | 2 | 3 | 4 | 5 | 6 | 7 | 8 | 9 | 11 | 13 | 15 | 17 |
| 3% | 2 | 3 | 4 | 5 | 6 | 7 | 8 | 9 | 11 | 13 | 15 | 17 |
| 3.125% | 1 | 2 | 3 | 4 | 5 | 6 | 7 | 8 | 10 | 12 | 14 | 16 |
| 3.25% | 1 | 2 | 3 | 4 | 5 | 6 | 7 | 8 | 10 | 12 | 14 | 15 |
| 3.375% | 1 | 2 | 3 | 4 | 5 | 6 | 7 | 8 | 9 | 11 | 13 | 15 |
| 3.5% | 1 | 2 | 3 | 4 | 5 | 6 | 7 | 7 | 9 | 11 | 13 | 14 |
| 3.625% | 1 | 2 | 3 | 4 | 5 | 5 | 6 | 7 | 9 | 11 | 12 | 14 |
| 3.75% | 1 | 2 | 3 | 4 | 5 | 5 | 6 | 7 | 9 | 10 | 12 | 13 |
| 3.875% | 1 | 2 | 3 | 4 | 4 | 5 | 6 | 7 | 8 | 10 | 11 | 13 |
| 4% | 1 | 2 | 3 | 4 | 4 | 5 | 6 | 7 | 8 | 10 | 11 | 13 |

# Refinance Break-Even Tables

## Break-Even Periods (in Months)

Term Left on Current Loan: 300 months  
Term on New Loan: 15 years  
Points: 1.00%

Income Tax Bracket: Pre-Tax  
Points and Costs: Paid in Cash

### Other Closing Costs as a Percent of Loan Amount

| Interest Rate Reduction | .25% | .5% | .75% | 1.00% | 1.25% | 1.50% | 1.75% | 2.00% | 2.50% | 3.00% | 3.50% | 4.00% |
|---|---|---|---|---|---|---|---|---|---|---|---|---|
| 0.125% | 46 | 51 | 55 | 60 | 64 | 68 | 72 | 75 | 82 | 88 | 94 | 99 |
| 0.25% | 37 | 42 | 47 | 51 | 55 | 59 | 63 | 66 | 73 | 79 | 85 | 91 |
| 0.375% | 31 | 35 | 40 | 44 | 48 | 51 | 55 | 59 | 65 | 71 | 77 | 83 |
| 0.5% | 26 | 30 | 34 | 38 | 41 | 45 | 48 | 52 | 58 | 64 | 70 | 75 |
| 0.625% | 22 | 26 | 29 | 33 | 36 | 40 | 43 | 46 | 52 | 58 | 63 | 69 |
| 0.75% | 19 | 22 | 26 | 29 | 32 | 35 | 38 | 41 | 47 | 52 | 57 | 63 |
| 0.875% | 17 | 20 | 23 | 26 | 29 | 31 | 34 | 37 | 42 | 47 | 52 | 57 |
| 1% | 15 | 18 | 20 | 23 | 26 | 28 | 31 | 33 | 38 | 43 | 48 | 53 |
| 1.125% | 13 | 16 | 18 | 21 | 23 | 26 | 28 | 30 | 35 | 40 | 44 | 48 |
| 1.25% | 12 | 15 | 17 | 19 | 21 | 24 | 26 | 28 | 32 | 36 | 41 | 45 |
| 1.375% | 11 | 13 | 15 | 18 | 20 | 22 | 24 | 26 | 30 | 34 | 38 | 42 |
| 1.5% | 10 | 12 | 14 | 16 | 18 | 20 | 22 | 24 | 28 | 31 | 35 | 39 |
| 1.625% | 10 | 11 | 13 | 15 | 17 | 19 | 20 | 22 | 26 | 29 | 33 | 36 |
| 1.75% | 9 | 11 | 12 | 14 | 16 | 17 | 19 | 21 | 24 | 27 | 31 | 34 |
| 1.875% | 8 | 10 | 12 | 13 | 15 | 16 | 18 | 20 | 23 | 26 | 29 | 32 |
| 2% | 8 | 9 | 11 | 12 | 14 | 15 | 17 | 18 | 21 | 24 | 27 | 30 |
| 2.125% | 8 | 9 | 10 | 12 | 13 | 15 | 16 | 17 | 20 | 23 | 26 | 29 |
| 2.25% | 7 | 9 | 10 | 11 | 13 | 14 | 15 | 16 | 19 | 22 | 24 | 27 |
| 2.375% | 7 | 8 | 9 | 11 | 12 | 13 | 14 | 16 | 18 | 21 | 23 | 26 |
| 2.5% | 7 | 8 | 9 | 10 | 11 | 13 | 14 | 15 | 17 | 20 | 22 | 25 |
| 2.625% | 6 | 7 | 9 | 10 | 11 | 12 | 13 | 14 | 17 | 19 | 21 | 24 |
| 2.75% | 6 | 7 | 8 | 9 | 10 | 11 | 13 | 14 | 16 | 18 | 20 | 23 |
| 2.875% | 6 | 7 | 8 | 9 | 10 | 11 | 12 | 13 | 15 | 17 | 19 | 22 |
| 3% | 6 | 7 | 8 | 9 | 10 | 11 | 12 | 13 | 15 | 17 | 19 | 21 |
| 3.125% | 5 | 6 | 7 | 8 | 9 | 10 | 11 | 12 | 14 | 16 | 18 | 20 |
| 3.25% | 5 | 6 | 7 | 8 | 9 | 10 | 11 | 12 | 14 | 15 | 17 | 19 |
| 3.375% | 5 | 6 | 7 | 8 | 9 | 9 | 10 | 11 | 13 | 15 | 17 | 19 |
| 3.5% | 5 | 6 | 7 | 7 | 8 | 9 | 10 | 11 | 13 | 14 | 16 | 18 |
| 3.625% | 5 | 5 | 6 | 7 | 8 | 9 | 10 | 11 | 12 | 14 | 16 | 17 |
| 3.75% | 5 | 5 | 6 | 7 | 8 | 9 | 9 | 10 | 12 | 13 | 15 | 17 |
| 3.875% | 4 | 5 | 6 | 7 | 8 | 8 | 9 | 10 | 11 | 13 | 15 | 16 |
| 4% | 4 | 5 | 6 | 7 | 7 | 8 | 9 | 10 | 11 | 13 | 14 | 16 |

## Break-Even Periods (in Months)

Term Left on Current Loan: 300 months  
Term on New Loan: 15 years  
Points: 2.00%

Income Tax Bracket: Pre-Tax  
Points and Costs: Paid in Cash

### Other Closing Costs as a Percent of Loan Amount

| Interest Rate Reduction | .25% | .5% | .75% | 1.00% | 1.25% | 1.50% | 1.75% | 2.00% | 2.50% | 3.00% | 3.50% | 4.00% |
|---|---|---|---|---|---|---|---|---|---|---|---|---|
| 0.125% | 64 | 68 | 72 | 75 | 78 | 82 | 85 | 88 | 94 | 99 | 104 | 109 |
| 0.25% | 55 | 59 | 63 | 66 | 70 | 73 | 76 | 79 | 85 | 91 | 96 | 101 |
| 0.375% | 48 | 51 | 55 | 59 | 62 | 65 | 68 | 71 | 77 | 83 | 88 | 93 |
| 0.5% | 41 | 45 | 48 | 52 | 55 | 58 | 61 | 64 | 70 | 75 | 80 | 85 |
| 0.625% | 36 | 40 | 43 | 46 | 49 | 52 | 55 | 58 | 63 | 69 | 74 | 79 |
| 0.75% | 32 | 35 | 38 | 41 | 44 | 47 | 49 | 52 | 57 | 63 | 67 | 72 |
| 0.875% | 29 | 31 | 34 | 37 | 40 | 42 | 45 | 47 | 52 | 57 | 62 | 67 |
| 1% | 26 | 28 | 31 | 33 | 36 | 38 | 41 | 43 | 48 | 53 | 57 | 61 |
| 1.125% | 23 | 26 | 28 | 30 | 33 | 35 | 37 | 40 | 44 | 48 | 53 | 57 |
| 1.25% | 21 | 24 | 26 | 28 | 30 | 32 | 34 | 36 | 41 | 45 | 49 | 53 |
| 1.375% | 20 | 22 | 24 | 26 | 28 | 30 | 32 | 34 | 38 | 42 | 45 | 49 |
| 1.5% | 18 | 20 | 22 | 24 | 26 | 28 | 29 | 31 | 35 | 39 | 42 | 46 |
| 1.625% | 17 | 19 | 20 | 22 | 24 | 26 | 28 | 29 | 33 | 36 | 40 | 43 |
| 1.75% | 16 | 17 | 19 | 21 | 22 | 24 | 26 | 27 | 31 | 34 | 37 | 40 |
| 1.875% | 15 | 16 | 18 | 20 | 21 | 23 | 24 | 26 | 29 | 32 | 35 | 38 |
| 2% | 14 | 15 | 17 | 18 | 20 | 21 | 23 | 24 | 27 | 30 | 33 | 36 |
| 2.125% | 13 | 15 | 16 | 17 | 19 | 20 | 22 | 23 | 26 | 29 | 31 | 34 |
| 2.25% | 13 | 14 | 15 | 16 | 18 | 19 | 20 | 22 | 24 | 27 | 30 | 32 |
| 2.375% | 12 | 13 | 14 | 16 | 17 | 18 | 19 | 21 | 23 | 26 | 28 | 31 |
| 2.5% | 11 | 13 | 14 | 15 | 16 | 17 | 19 | 20 | 22 | 25 | 27 | 29 |
| 2.625% | 11 | 12 | 13 | 14 | 15 | 17 | 18 | 19 | 21 | 24 | 26 | 28 |
| 2.75% | 10 | 11 | 13 | 14 | 15 | 16 | 17 | 18 | 20 | 23 | 25 | 27 |
| 2.875% | 10 | 11 | 12 | 13 | 14 | 15 | 16 | 17 | 19 | 22 | 24 | 26 |
| 3% | 10 | 11 | 12 | 13 | 14 | 15 | 16 | 17 | 19 | 21 | 23 | 25 |
| 3.125% | 9 | 10 | 11 | 12 | 13 | 14 | 15 | 16 | 18 | 20 | 22 | 24 |
| 3.25% | 9 | 10 | 11 | 12 | 13 | 14 | 14 | 15 | 17 | 19 | 21 | 23 |
| 3.375% | 9 | 9 | 10 | 11 | 12 | 13 | 14 | 15 | 17 | 19 | 20 | 22 |
| 3.5% | 8 | 9 | 10 | 11 | 12 | 13 | 14 | 14 | 16 | 18 | 20 | 21 |
| 3.625% | 8 | 9 | 10 | 11 | 11 | 12 | 13 | 14 | 16 | 17 | 19 | 21 |
| 3.75% | 8 | 9 | 9 | 10 | 11 | 12 | 13 | 13 | 15 | 17 | 18 | 20 |
| 3.875% | 8 | 8 | 9 | 10 | 11 | 11 | 12 | 13 | 15 | 16 | 18 | 19 |
| 4% | 7 | 8 | 9 | 10 | 10 | 11 | 12 | 13 | 14 | 16 | 17 | 19 |

## Break-Even Periods (in Months)

Term Left on Current Loan: 300 months
Term on New Loan: 15 years
Points: 3.00%

Income Tax Bracket: Pre-Tax
Points and Costs: Paid in Cash

### Other Closing Costs as a Percent of Loan Amount

| Interest Rate Reduction | .25% | .5% | .75% | 1.00% | 1.25% | 1.50% | 1.75% | 2.00% | 2.50% | 3.00% | 3.50% | 4.00% |
|---|---|---|---|---|---|---|---|---|---|---|---|---|
| 0.125% | 78 | 82 | 85 | 88 | 91 | 94 | 96 | 99 | 104 | 109 | 114 | 118 |
| 0.25% | 70 | 73 | 76 | 79 | 82 | 85 | 88 | 91 | 96 | 101 | 106 | 110 |
| 0.375% | 62 | 65 | 68 | 71 | 74 | 77 | 80 | 83 | 88 | 93 | 98 | 102 |
| 0.5% | 55 | 58 | 61 | 64 | 67 | 70 | 73 | 75 | 80 | 85 | 90 | 95 |
| 0.625% | 49 | 52 | 55 | 58 | 61 | 63 | 66 | 69 | 74 | 79 | 83 | 88 |
| 0.75% | 44 | 47 | 49 | 52 | 55 | 57 | 60 | 63 | 67 | 72 | 77 | 81 |
| 0.875% | 40 | 42 | 45 | 47 | 50 | 52 | 55 | 57 | 62 | 67 | 71 | 75 |
| 1% | 36 | 38 | 41 | 43 | 46 | 48 | 50 | 53 | 57 | 61 | 66 | 70 |
| 1.125% | 33 | 35 | 37 | 40 | 42 | 44 | 46 | 48 | 53 | 57 | 61 | 65 |
| 1.25% | 30 | 32 | 34 | 36 | 39 | 41 | 43 | 45 | 49 | 53 | 57 | 61 |
| 1.375% | 28 | 30 | 32 | 34 | 36 | 38 | 40 | 42 | 45 | 49 | 53 | 57 |
| 1.5% | 26 | 28 | 29 | 31 | 33 | 35 | 37 | 39 | 42 | 46 | 49 | 53 |
| 1.625% | 24 | 26 | 28 | 29 | 31 | 33 | 34 | 36 | 40 | 43 | 46 | 50 |
| 1.75% | 22 | 24 | 26 | 27 | 29 | 31 | 32 | 34 | 37 | 40 | 44 | 47 |
| 1.875% | 21 | 23 | 24 | 26 | 27 | 29 | 30 | 32 | 35 | 38 | 41 | 44 |
| 2% | 20 | 21 | 23 | 24 | 26 | 27 | 29 | 30 | 33 | 36 | 39 | 42 |
| 2.125% | 19 | 20 | 22 | 23 | 24 | 26 | 27 | 29 | 31 | 34 | 37 | 40 |
| 2.25% | 18 | 19 | 20 | 22 | 23 | 24 | 26 | 27 | 30 | 32 | 35 | 38 |
| 2.375% | 17 | 18 | 19 | 21 | 22 | 23 | 25 | 26 | 28 | 31 | 33 | 36 |
| 2.5% | 16 | 17 | 19 | 20 | 21 | 22 | 23 | 25 | 27 | 29 | 32 | 34 |
| 2.625% | 15 | 17 | 18 | 19 | 20 | 21 | 22 | 24 | 26 | 28 | 30 | 33 |
| 2.75% | 15 | 16 | 17 | 18 | 19 | 20 | 21 | 23 | 25 | 27 | 29 | 31 |
| 2.875% | 14 | 15 | 16 | 17 | 18 | 19 | 21 | 22 | 24 | 26 | 28 | 30 |
| 3% | 14 | 15 | 16 | 17 | 18 | 19 | 20 | 21 | 23 | 25 | 27 | 29 |
| 3.125% | 13 | 14 | 15 | 16 | 17 | 18 | 19 | 20 | 22 | 24 | 26 | 28 |
| 3.25% | 13 | 14 | 14 | 15 | 16 | 17 | 18 | 19 | 21 | 23 | 25 | 27 |
| 3.375% | 12 | 13 | 14 | 15 | 16 | 17 | 18 | 19 | 20 | 22 | 24 | 26 |
| 3.5% | 12 | 13 | 14 | 14 | 15 | 16 | 17 | 18 | 20 | 21 | 23 | 25 |
| 3.625% | 11 | 12 | 13 | 14 | 15 | 16 | 16 | 17 | 19 | 21 | 22 | 24 |
| 3.75% | 11 | 12 | 13 | 13 | 14 | 15 | 16 | 17 | 18 | 20 | 22 | 23 |
| 3.875% | 11 | 11 | 12 | 13 | 14 | 15 | 15 | 16 | 18 | 19 | 21 | 23 |
| 4% | 10 | 11 | 12 | 13 | 13 | 14 | 15 | 16 | 17 | 19 | 20 | 22 |

# Refinance Break-Even Tables

| Break-Even Periods (in Months) | | | | | | | | | | | |
|---|---|---|---|---|---|---|---|---|---|---|---|

Term Left on Current Loan: 300 months      Income Tax Bracket: 40.00%
Term on New Loan: 15 years      Points and Costs: Paid in Cash
Points: 0.00%

| Other Closing Costs as a Percent of Loan Amount | | | | | | | | | | | |
|---|---|---|---|---|---|---|---|---|---|---|---|
| Interest Rate Reduction | .25% | .5% | .75% | 1.00% | 1.25% | 1.50% | 1.75% | 2.00% | 2.50% | 3.00% | 3.50% | 4.00% |
| 0.125% | 23 | 35 | 45 | 53 | 60 | 67 | 73 | 78 | 88 | 97 | 105 | 112 |
| 0.25% | 16 | 28 | 37 | 45 | 52 | 58 | 64 | 70 | 80 | 89 | 97 | 104 |
| 0.375% | 12 | 22 | 30 | 38 | 45 | 51 | 57 | 62 | 72 | 81 | 89 | 97 |
| 0.5% | 10 | 18 | 26 | 32 | 39 | 44 | 50 | 55 | 65 | 74 | 82 | 90 |
| 0.625% | 8 | 15 | 22 | 28 | 34 | 39 | 44 | 49 | 59 | 67 | 75 | 83 |
| 0.75% | 7 | 13 | 19 | 24 | 30 | 35 | 40 | 44 | 53 | 61 | 69 | 77 |
| 0.875% | 6 | 11 | 17 | 22 | 26 | 31 | 36 | 40 | 48 | 56 | 64 | 71 |
| 1% | 5 | 10 | 15 | 19 | 24 | 28 | 32 | 36 | 44 | 52 | 59 | 66 |
| 1.125% | 5 | 9 | 13 | 18 | 22 | 26 | 29 | 33 | 41 | 48 | 55 | 61 |
| 1.25% | 4 | 8 | 12 | 16 | 20 | 23 | 27 | 30 | 37 | 44 | 51 | 57 |
| 1.375% | 4 | 8 | 11 | 15 | 18 | 22 | 25 | 28 | 35 | 41 | 47 | 53 |
| 1.5% | 4 | 7 | 10 | 14 | 17 | 20 | 23 | 26 | 32 | 38 | 44 | 50 |
| 1.625% | 4 | 7 | 10 | 13 | 16 | 19 | 21 | 24 | 30 | 36 | 41 | 47 |
| 1.75% | 3 | 6 | 9 | 12 | 15 | 17 | 20 | 23 | 28 | 34 | 39 | 44 |
| 1.875% | 3 | 6 | 8 | 11 | 14 | 16 | 19 | 21 | 27 | 32 | 37 | 42 |
| 2% | 3 | 5 | 8 | 10 | 13 | 15 | 18 | 20 | 25 | 30 | 35 | 39 |
| 2.125% | 3 | 5 | 8 | 10 | 12 | 15 | 17 | 19 | 24 | 28 | 33 | 37 |
| 2.25% | 3 | 5 | 7 | 9 | 12 | 14 | 16 | 18 | 23 | 27 | 31 | 36 |
| 2.375% | 3 | 5 | 7 | 9 | 11 | 13 | 15 | 17 | 21 | 26 | 30 | 34 |
| 2.5% | 3 | 5 | 6 | 8 | 10 | 12 | 14 | 16 | 20 | 24 | 28 | 32 |
| 2.625% | 2 | 4 | 6 | 8 | 10 | 12 | 14 | 16 | 20 | 23 | 27 | 31 |
| 2.75% | 2 | 4 | 6 | 8 | 10 | 11 | 13 | 15 | 19 | 22 | 26 | 30 |
| 2.875% | 2 | 4 | 6 | 7 | 9 | 11 | 13 | 14 | 18 | 21 | 25 | 28 |
| 3% | 2 | 4 | 6 | 7 | 9 | 11 | 12 | 14 | 17 | 21 | 24 | 27 |
| 3.125% | 2 | 4 | 5 | 7 | 9 | 10 | 12 | 13 | 17 | 20 | 23 | 26 |
| 3.25% | 2 | 4 | 5 | 7 | 8 | 10 | 11 | 13 | 16 | 19 | 22 | 25 |
| 3.375% | 2 | 3 | 5 | 6 | 8 | 9 | 11 | 12 | 15 | 18 | 21 | 24 |
| 3.5% | 2 | 3 | 5 | 6 | 8 | 9 | 11 | 12 | 15 | 18 | 21 | 24 |
| 3.625% | 2 | 3 | 5 | 6 | 7 | 9 | 10 | 12 | 14 | 17 | 20 | 23 |
| 3.75% | 2 | 3 | 5 | 6 | 7 | 9 | 10 | 11 | 14 | 17 | 19 | 22 |
| 3.875% | 2 | 3 | 4 | 6 | 7 | 8 | 10 | 11 | 14 | 16 | 19 | 21 |
| 4% | 2 | 3 | 4 | 6 | 7 | 8 | 9 | 11 | 13 | 16 | 18 | 21 |

# Refinance Break-Even Tables

| Break-Even Periods (in Months) | | | | | | | | | | | |
|---|---|---|---|---|---|---|---|---|---|---|---|

Term Left on Current Loan: 300 months          Income Tax Bracket: 40.00%
Term on New Loan: 15 years                     Points and Costs: Paid in Cash
Points: 1.00%

| Other Closing Costs as a Percent of Loan Amount | | | | | | | | | | | |
|---|---|---|---|---|---|---|---|---|---|---|---|
| Interest Rate Reduction | .25% | .5% | .75% | 1.00% | 1.25% | 1.50% | 1.75% | 2.00% | 2.50% | 3.00% | 3.50% | 4.00% |
| 0.125% | 49 | 57 | 64 | 70 | 75 | 81 | 86 | 90 | 99 | 107 | 114 | 121 |
| 0.25% | 41 | 48 | 55 | 61 | 67 | 72 | 77 | 82 | 91 | 99 | 106 | 113 |
| 0.375% | 34 | 41 | 48 | 54 | 59 | 64 | 69 | 74 | 83 | 91 | 99 | 106 |
| 0.5% | 29 | 35 | 41 | 47 | 52 | 58 | 62 | 67 | 76 | 84 | 92 | 99 |
| 0.625% | 25 | 31 | 36 | 42 | 47 | 52 | 56 | 61 | 69 | 77 | 85 | 92 |
| 0.75% | 21 | 27 | 32 | 37 | 42 | 46 | 51 | 55 | 63 | 71 | 79 | 86 |
| 0.875% | 19 | 24 | 29 | 33 | 38 | 42 | 46 | 50 | 58 | 66 | 73 | 80 |
| 1% | 17 | 21 | 26 | 30 | 34 | 38 | 42 | 46 | 53 | 61 | 68 | 74 |
| 1.125% | 15 | 19 | 23 | 27 | 31 | 35 | 39 | 42 | 49 | 56 | 63 | 69 |
| 1.25% | 14 | 18 | 21 | 25 | 29 | 32 | 36 | 39 | 46 | 52 | 59 | 65 |
| 1.375% | 13 | 16 | 20 | 23 | 26 | 30 | 33 | 36 | 42 | 49 | 55 | 61 |
| 1.5% | 12 | 15 | 18 | 21 | 24 | 27 | 31 | 34 | 40 | 45 | 51 | 57 |
| 1.625% | 11 | 14 | 17 | 20 | 23 | 26 | 29 | 31 | 37 | 43 | 48 | 54 |
| 1.75% | 10 | 13 | 16 | 19 | 21 | 24 | 27 | 29 | 35 | 40 | 45 | 50 |
| 1.875% | 10 | 12 | 15 | 17 | 20 | 23 | 25 | 28 | 33 | 38 | 43 | 48 |
| 2% | 9 | 11 | 14 | 16 | 19 | 21 | 24 | 26 | 31 | 36 | 40 | 45 |
| 2.125% | 9 | 11 | 13 | 16 | 18 | 20 | 22 | 25 | 29 | 34 | 38 | 43 |
| 2.25% | 8 | 10 | 12 | 15 | 17 | 19 | 21 | 23 | 28 | 32 | 37 | 41 |
| 2.375% | 8 | 10 | 12 | 14 | 16 | 18 | 20 | 22 | 26 | 31 | 35 | 39 |
| 2.5% | 7 | 9 | 11 | 13 | 15 | 17 | 19 | 21 | 25 | 29 | 33 | 37 |
| 2.625% | 7 | 9 | 11 | 13 | 15 | 17 | 18 | 20 | 24 | 28 | 32 | 36 |
| 2.75% | 7 | 9 | 10 | 12 | 14 | 16 | 18 | 19 | 23 | 27 | 30 | 34 |
| 2.875% | 6 | 8 | 10 | 12 | 13 | 15 | 17 | 19 | 22 | 26 | 29 | 33 |
| 3% | 6 | 8 | 10 | 11 | 13 | 15 | 16 | 18 | 21 | 25 | 28 | 31 |
| 3.125% | 6 | 8 | 9 | 11 | 12 | 14 | 16 | 17 | 21 | 24 | 27 | 30 |
| 3.25% | 6 | 7 | 9 | 10 | 12 | 14 | 15 | 17 | 20 | 23 | 26 | 29 |
| 3.375% | 6 | 7 | 9 | 10 | 12 | 13 | 15 | 16 | 19 | 22 | 25 | 28 |
| 3.5% | 5 | 7 | 8 | 10 | 11 | 13 | 14 | 16 | 18 | 21 | 24 | 27 |
| 3.625% | 5 | 7 | 8 | 9 | 11 | 12 | 14 | 15 | 18 | 21 | 23 | 26 |
| 3.75% | 5 | 6 | 8 | 9 | 10 | 12 | 13 | 15 | 17 | 20 | 23 | 25 |
| 3.875% | 5 | 6 | 8 | 9 | 10 | 11 | 13 | 14 | 17 | 19 | 22 | 25 |
| 4% | 5 | 6 | 7 | 9 | 10 | 11 | 12 | 14 | 16 | 19 | 21 | 24 |

| Break-Even Periods (in Months) | | | | | | | | | | | |
|---|---|---|---|---|---|---|---|---|---|---|---|
| Term Left on Current Loan: 300 months<br>Term on New Loan: 15 years<br>Points: 2.00% | | | | | | Income Tax Bracket: 40.00%<br>Points and Costs: Paid in Cash | | | | | |
| Other Closing Costs as a Percent of Loan Amount | | | | | | | | | | | |
| Interest Rate Reduction | .25% | .5% | .75% | 1.00% | 1.25% | 1.50% | 1.75% | 2.00% | 2.50% | 3.00% | 3.50% | 4.00% |
|---|---|---|---|---|---|---|---|---|---|---|---|---|
| 0.125% | 67 | 73 | 78 | 83 | 88 | 93 | 97 | 101 | 109 | 116 | 123 | 129 |
| 0.25% | 58 | 64 | 69 | 75 | 80 | 84 | 89 | 93 | 101 | 108 | 115 | 121 |
| 0.375% | 50 | 56 | 62 | 67 | 72 | 76 | 81 | 85 | 93 | 101 | 108 | 114 |
| 0.5% | 44 | 50 | 55 | 60 | 65 | 69 | 74 | 78 | 86 | 93 | 100 | 107 |
| 0.625% | 39 | 44 | 49 | 54 | 58 | 63 | 67 | 71 | 79 | 87 | 94 | 100 |
| 0.75% | 34 | 39 | 44 | 48 | 53 | 57 | 61 | 65 | 73 | 80 | 87 | 94 |
| 0.875% | 31 | 35 | 40 | 44 | 48 | 52 | 56 | 60 | 67 | 74 | 81 | 88 |
| 1% | 28 | 32 | 36 | 40 | 44 | 48 | 51 | 55 | 62 | 69 | 76 | 82 |
| 1.125% | 25 | 29 | 33 | 37 | 40 | 44 | 47 | 51 | 58 | 64 | 71 | 77 |
| 1.25% | 23 | 27 | 30 | 34 | 37 | 40 | 44 | 47 | 54 | 60 | 66 | 72 |
| 1.375% | 21 | 24 | 28 | 31 | 34 | 38 | 41 | 44 | 50 | 56 | 62 | 68 |
| 1.5% | 19 | 23 | 26 | 29 | 32 | 35 | 38 | 41 | 47 | 53 | 58 | 64 |
| 1.625% | 18 | 21 | 24 | 27 | 30 | 33 | 35 | 38 | 44 | 49 | 55 | 60 |
| 1.75% | 17 | 20 | 22 | 25 | 28 | 31 | 33 | 36 | 41 | 46 | 52 | 57 |
| 1.875% | 16 | 19 | 21 | 24 | 26 | 29 | 31 | 34 | 39 | 44 | 49 | 54 |
| 2% | 15 | 17 | 20 | 22 | 25 | 27 | 30 | 32 | 37 | 42 | 46 | 51 |
| 2.125% | 14 | 16 | 19 | 21 | 23 | 26 | 28 | 30 | 35 | 39 | 44 | 48 |
| 2.25% | 13 | 16 | 18 | 20 | 22 | 24 | 27 | 29 | 33 | 37 | 42 | 46 |
| 2.375% | 13 | 15 | 17 | 19 | 21 | 23 | 25 | 27 | 32 | 36 | 40 | 44 |
| 2.5% | 12 | 14 | 16 | 18 | 20 | 22 | 24 | 26 | 30 | 34 | 38 | 42 |
| 2.625% | 12 | 14 | 15 | 17 | 19 | 21 | 23 | 25 | 29 | 33 | 36 | 40 |
| 2.75% | 11 | 13 | 15 | 17 | 18 | 20 | 22 | 24 | 28 | 31 | 35 | 39 |
| 2.875% | 11 | 12 | 14 | 16 | 18 | 19 | 21 | 23 | 26 | 30 | 34 | 37 |
| 3% | 10 | 12 | 14 | 15 | 17 | 19 | 20 | 22 | 25 | 29 | 32 | 36 |
| 3.125% | 10 | 11 | 13 | 15 | 16 | 18 | 20 | 21 | 24 | 28 | 31 | 34 |
| 3.25% | 9 | 11 | 13 | 14 | 16 | 17 | 19 | 20 | 24 | 27 | 30 | 33 |
| 3.375% | 9 | 11 | 12 | 14 | 15 | 17 | 18 | 20 | 23 | 26 | 29 | 32 |
| 3.5% | 9 | 10 | 12 | 13 | 15 | 16 | 18 | 19 | 22 | 25 | 28 | 31 |
| 3.625% | 9 | 10 | 11 | 13 | 14 | 16 | 17 | 18 | 21 | 24 | 27 | 30 |
| 3.75% | 8 | 10 | 11 | 12 | 14 | 15 | 16 | 18 | 21 | 23 | 26 | 29 |
| 3.875% | 8 | 9 | 11 | 12 | 13 | 15 | 16 | 17 | 20 | 23 | 25 | 28 |
| 4% | 8 | 9 | 10 | 12 | 13 | 14 | 15 | 17 | 19 | 22 | 25 | 27 |

# Refinance Break-Even Tables

| Break-Even Periods (in Months) | | | | | | | | | | | |
|---|---|---|---|---|---|---|---|---|---|---|---|
| Term Left on Current Loan: 300 months<br>Term on New Loan: 15 years<br>Points: 3.00% | | | | | | Income Tax Bracket: 40.00%<br>Points and Costs: Paid in Cash | | | | | |
| Other Closing Costs as a Percent of Loan Amount | | | | | | | | | | | |
| Interest Rate Reduction | .25% | .5% | .75% | 1.00% | 1.25% | 1.50% | 1.75% | 2.00% | 2.50% | 3.00% | 3.50% | 4.00% |
|---|---|---|---|---|---|---|---|---|---|---|---|---|
| 0.125% | 81 | 86 | 90 | 95 | 99 | 103 | 107 | 111 | 118 | 124 | 130 | 136 |
| 0.25% | 72 | 77 | 82 | 86 | 91 | 95 | 99 | 103 | 110 | 117 | 123 | 129 |
| 0.375% | 64 | 69 | 74 | 79 | 83 | 87 | 91 | 95 | 102 | 109 | 116 | 122 |
| 0.5% | 57 | 62 | 67 | 71 | 76 | 80 | 84 | 88 | 95 | 102 | 109 | 115 |
| 0.625% | 51 | 56 | 61 | 65 | 69 | 73 | 77 | 81 | 88 | 95 | 102 | 108 |
| 0.75% | 46 | 51 | 55 | 59 | 63 | 67 | 71 | 75 | 82 | 89 | 96 | 102 |
| 0.875% | 42 | 46 | 50 | 54 | 58 | 62 | 65 | 69 | 76 | 83 | 89 | 96 |
| 1% | 38 | 42 | 46 | 49 | 53 | 57 | 60 | 64 | 71 | 77 | 84 | 90 |
| 1.125% | 34 | 38 | 42 | 46 | 49 | 53 | 56 | 59 | 66 | 72 | 78 | 84 |
| 1.25% | 32 | 35 | 39 | 42 | 45 | 49 | 52 | 55 | 61 | 68 | 74 | 79 |
| 1.375% | 29 | 33 | 36 | 39 | 42 | 45 | 48 | 51 | 57 | 63 | 69 | 75 |
| 1.5% | 27 | 30 | 33 | 36 | 39 | 42 | 45 | 48 | 54 | 60 | 65 | 71 |
| 1.625% | 25 | 28 | 31 | 34 | 37 | 40 | 42 | 45 | 51 | 56 | 61 | 67 |
| 1.75% | 24 | 26 | 29 | 32 | 35 | 37 | 40 | 42 | 48 | 53 | 58 | 63 |
| 1.875% | 22 | 25 | 27 | 30 | 32 | 35 | 38 | 40 | 45 | 50 | 55 | 60 |
| 2% | 21 | 23 | 26 | 28 | 31 | 33 | 35 | 38 | 43 | 47 | 52 | 57 |
| 2.125% | 20 | 22 | 24 | 27 | 29 | 31 | 34 | 36 | 40 | 45 | 49 | 54 |
| 2.25% | 19 | 21 | 23 | 25 | 28 | 30 | 32 | 34 | 38 | 43 | 47 | 51 |
| 2.375% | 18 | 20 | 22 | 24 | 26 | 28 | 30 | 32 | 37 | 41 | 45 | 49 |
| 2.5% | 17 | 19 | 21 | 23 | 25 | 27 | 29 | 31 | 35 | 39 | 43 | 47 |
| 2.625% | 16 | 18 | 20 | 22 | 24 | 26 | 28 | 30 | 33 | 37 | 41 | 45 |
| 2.75% | 16 | 17 | 19 | 21 | 23 | 25 | 27 | 28 | 32 | 36 | 39 | 43 |
| 2.875% | 15 | 17 | 18 | 20 | 22 | 24 | 25 | 27 | 31 | 34 | 38 | 41 |
| 3% | 14 | 16 | 18 | 19 | 21 | 23 | 24 | 26 | 30 | 33 | 36 | 40 |
| 3.125% | 14 | 15 | 17 | 19 | 20 | 22 | 24 | 25 | 28 | 32 | 35 | 38 |
| 3.25% | 13 | 15 | 16 | 18 | 20 | 21 | 23 | 24 | 27 | 31 | 34 | 37 |
| 3.375% | 13 | 14 | 16 | 17 | 19 | 20 | 22 | 23 | 26 | 30 | 33 | 36 |
| 3.5% | 12 | 14 | 15 | 17 | 18 | 20 | 21 | 23 | 26 | 29 | 31 | 34 |
| 3.625% | 12 | 13 | 15 | 16 | 18 | 19 | 20 | 22 | 25 | 28 | 30 | 33 |
| 3.75% | 12 | 13 | 14 | 16 | 17 | 18 | 20 | 21 | 24 | 27 | 29 | 32 |
| 3.875% | 11 | 13 | 14 | 15 | 17 | 18 | 19 | 21 | 23 | 26 | 29 | 31 |
| 4% | 11 | 12 | 13 | 15 | 16 | 17 | 19 | 20 | 22 | 25 | 28 | 30 |

# Refinance Break-Even Tables

| Break-Even Periods (in Months) |
|---|

| Term Left on Current Loan: 120 months | Income Tax Bracket: Pre-Tax |
|---|---|
| Term on New Loan: 30 years | Points and Costs: Paid in Cash |
| Points: 0.00% | |

| Other Closing Costs as a Percent of Loan Amount | | | | | | | | | | | |
|---|---|---|---|---|---|---|---|---|---|---|---|
| Interest Rate Reduction | .25% | .5% | .75% | 1.00% | 1.25% | 1.50% | 1.75% | 2.00% | 2.50% | 3.00% | 3.50% | 4.00% |
| 0.125% | None | None | None | None | None | None | None | None | None | None | None | None |
| 0.25% | None | None | None | None | None | None | None | None | None | None | None | None |
| 0.375% | None | None | None | None | None | None | None | None | None | None | None | None |
| 0.5% | 8 | None | None | None | None | None | None | None | None | None | None | None |
| 0.625% | 6 | 13 | None | None | None | None | None | None | None | None | None | None |
| 0.75% | 5 | 10 | 17 | None | None | None | None | None | None | None | None | None |
| 0.875% | 4 | 8 | 13 | 19 | None | None | None | None | None | None | None | None |
| 1% | 4 | 7 | 11 | 15 | 21 | 30 | None | None | None | None | None | None |
| 1.125% | 3 | 6 | 9 | 13 | 17 | 22 | 28 | None | None | None | None | None |
| 1.25% | 3 | 6 | 8 | 11 | 15 | 18 | 22 | 27 | None | None | None | None |
| 1.375% | 3 | 5 | 7 | 10 | 13 | 16 | 19 | 23 | 32 | None | None | None |
| 1.5% | 3 | 5 | 7 | 9 | 12 | 14 | 17 | 20 | 27 | 36 | None | None |
| 1.625% | 2 | 4 | 6 | 8 | 11 | 13 | 15 | 18 | 23 | 30 | 39 | None |
| 1.75% | 2 | 4 | 6 | 8 | 10 | 12 | 14 | 16 | 21 | 26 | 33 | 42 |
| 1.875% | 2 | 4 | 5 | 7 | 9 | 11 | 13 | 15 | 19 | 24 | 29 | 35 |
| 2% | 2 | 4 | 5 | 7 | 8 | 10 | 12 | 14 | 17 | 22 | 26 | 31 |
| 2.125% | 2 | 3 | 5 | 6 | 8 | 9 | 11 | 13 | 16 | 20 | 24 | 28 |
| 2.25% | 2 | 3 | 5 | 6 | 7 | 9 | 10 | 12 | 15 | 19 | 22 | 26 |
| 2.375% | 2 | 3 | 4 | 6 | 7 | 8 | 10 | 11 | 14 | 17 | 21 | 24 |
| 2.5% | 2 | 3 | 4 | 5 | 7 | 8 | 9 | 11 | 13 | 16 | 19 | 23 |
| 2.625% | 2 | 3 | 4 | 5 | 6 | 8 | 9 | 10 | 13 | 15 | 18 | 21 |
| 2.75% | 2 | 3 | 4 | 5 | 6 | 7 | 8 | 10 | 12 | 15 | 17 | 20 |
| 2.875% | 2 | 3 | 4 | 5 | 6 | 7 | 8 | 9 | 12 | 14 | 16 | 19 |
| 3% | 2 | 3 | 4 | 5 | 6 | 7 | 8 | 9 | 11 | 13 | 16 | 18 |
| 3.125% | 1 | 2 | 3 | 4 | 5 | 6 | 7 | 8 | 11 | 13 | 15 | 17 |
| 3.25% | 1 | 2 | 3 | 4 | 5 | 6 | 7 | 8 | 10 | 12 | 14 | 16 |
| 3.375% | 1 | 2 | 3 | 4 | 5 | 6 | 7 | 8 | 10 | 12 | 14 | 16 |
| 3.5% | 1 | 2 | 3 | 4 | 5 | 6 | 7 | 8 | 9 | 11 | 13 | 15 |
| 3.625% | 1 | 2 | 3 | 4 | 5 | 6 | 6 | 7 | 9 | 11 | 13 | 15 |
| 3.75% | 1 | 2 | 3 | 4 | 5 | 5 | 6 | 7 | 9 | 11 | 12 | 14 |
| 3.875% | 1 | 2 | 3 | 4 | 4 | 5 | 6 | 7 | 8 | 10 | 12 | 14 |
| 4% | 1 | 2 | 3 | 4 | 4 | 5 | 6 | 7 | 8 | 10 | 11 | 13 |

# Refinance Break-Even Tables

## Break-Even Periods (in Months)

Term Left on Current Loan: 120 months  
Term on New Loan: 30 years  
Points: 1.00%

Income Tax Bracket: Pre-Tax  
Points and Costs: Paid in Cash

### Other Closing Costs as a Percent of Loan Amount

| Interest Rate Reduction | .25% | .5% | .75% | 1.00% | 1.25% | 1.50% | 1.75% | 2.00% | 2.50% | 3.00% | 3.50% | 4.00% |
|---|---|---|---|---|---|---|---|---|---|---|---|---|
| 0.125% | None | None | None | None | None | None | None | None | None | None | None | None |
| 0.25% | None | None | None | None | None | None | None | None | None | None | None | None |
| 0.375% | None | None | None | None | None | None | None | None | None | None | None | None |
| 0.5% | None | None | None | None | None | None | None | None | None | None | None | None |
| 0.625% | None | None | None | None | None | None | None | None | None | None | None | None |
| 0.75% | None | None | None | None | None | None | None | None | None | None | None | None |
| 0.875% | None | None | None | None | None | None | None | None | None | None | None | None |
| 1% | 21 | 30 | None | None | None | None | None | None | None | None | None | None |
| 1.125% | 17 | 22 | 28 | None | None | None | None | None | None | None | None | None |
| 1.25% | 15 | 18 | 22 | 27 | 35 | None | None | None | None | None | None | None |
| 1.375% | 13 | 16 | 19 | 23 | 27 | 32 | 40 | None | None | None | None | None |
| 1.5% | 12 | 14 | 17 | 20 | 23 | 27 | 31 | 36 | None | None | None | None |
| 1.625% | 11 | 13 | 15 | 18 | 20 | 23 | 26 | 30 | 39 | None | None | None |
| 1.75% | 10 | 12 | 14 | 16 | 18 | 21 | 24 | 26 | 33 | 42 | None | None |
| 1.875% | 9 | 11 | 13 | 15 | 17 | 19 | 21 | 24 | 29 | 35 | 43 | 61 |
| 2% | 8 | 10 | 12 | 14 | 16 | 17 | 20 | 22 | 26 | 31 | 37 | 45 |
| 2.125% | 8 | 9 | 11 | 13 | 14 | 16 | 18 | 20 | 24 | 28 | 33 | 39 |
| 2.25% | 7 | 9 | 10 | 12 | 14 | 15 | 17 | 19 | 22 | 26 | 30 | 35 |
| 2.375% | 7 | 8 | 10 | 11 | 13 | 14 | 16 | 17 | 21 | 24 | 28 | 32 |
| 2.5% | 7 | 8 | 9 | 11 | 12 | 13 | 15 | 16 | 19 | 23 | 26 | 29 |
| 2.625% | 6 | 8 | 9 | 10 | 11 | 13 | 14 | 15 | 18 | 21 | 24 | 27 |
| 2.75% | 6 | 7 | 8 | 10 | 11 | 12 | 13 | 15 | 17 | 20 | 23 | 26 |
| 2.875% | 6 | 7 | 8 | 9 | 10 | 12 | 13 | 14 | 16 | 19 | 22 | 24 |
| 3% | 6 | 7 | 8 | 9 | 10 | 11 | 12 | 13 | 16 | 18 | 21 | 23 |
| 3.125% | 5 | 6 | 7 | 8 | 10 | 11 | 12 | 13 | 15 | 17 | 20 | 22 |
| 3.25% | 5 | 6 | 7 | 8 | 9 | 10 | 11 | 12 | 14 | 16 | 19 | 21 |
| 3.375% | 5 | 6 | 7 | 8 | 9 | 10 | 11 | 12 | 14 | 16 | 18 | 20 |
| 3.5% | 5 | 6 | 7 | 8 | 8 | 9 | 10 | 11 | 13 | 15 | 17 | 19 |
| 3.625% | 5 | 6 | 6 | 7 | 8 | 9 | 10 | 11 | 13 | 15 | 17 | 18 |
| 3.75% | 5 | 5 | 6 | 7 | 8 | 9 | 10 | 11 | 12 | 14 | 16 | 18 |
| 3.875% | 4 | 5 | 6 | 7 | 8 | 8 | 9 | 10 | 12 | 14 | 15 | 17 |
| 4% | 4 | 5 | 6 | 7 | 7 | 8 | 9 | 10 | 11 | 13 | 15 | 17 |

| Break-Even Periods (in Months) | | | | | | | | | | | |
|---|---|---|---|---|---|---|---|---|---|---|---|

Term Left on Current Loan: 120 months  
Term on New Loan: 30 years  
Points: 2.00%

Income Tax Bracket: Pre-Tax  
Points and Costs: Paid in Cash

| Other Closing Costs as a Percent of Loan Amount | | | | | | | | | | | |
|---|---|---|---|---|---|---|---|---|---|---|---|
| Interest Rate Reduction | .25% | .5% | .75% | 1.00% | 1.25% | 1.50% | 1.75% | 2.00% | 2.50% | 3.00% | 3.50% | 4.00% |
| 0.125% | None | None | None | None | None | None | None | None | None | None | None | None |
| 0.25% | None | None | None | None | None | None | None | None | None | None | None | None |
| 0.375% | None | None | None | None | None | None | None | None | None | None | None | None |
| 0.5% | None | None | None | None | None | None | None | None | None | None | None | None |
| 0.625% | None | None | None | None | None | None | None | None | None | None | None | None |
| 0.75% | None | None | None | None | None | None | None | None | None | None | None | None |
| 0.875% | None | None | None | None | None | None | None | None | None | None | None | None |
| 1% | None | None | None | None | None | None | None | None | None | None | None | None |
| 1.125% | None | None | None | None | None | None | None | None | None | None | None | None |
| 1.25% | 35 | None | None | None | None | None | None | None | None | None | None | None |
| 1.375% | 27 | 32 | 40 | None | None | None | None | None | None | None | None | None |
| 1.5% | 23 | 27 | 31 | 36 | 44 | None | None | None | None | None | None | None |
| 1.625% | 20 | 23 | 26 | 30 | 34 | 39 | 47 | None | None | None | None | None |
| 1.75% | 18 | 21 | 24 | 26 | 29 | 33 | 37 | 42 | None | None | None | None |
| 1.875% | 17 | 19 | 21 | 24 | 26 | 29 | 32 | 35 | 43 | 61 | None | None |
| 2% | 16 | 17 | 20 | 22 | 24 | 26 | 29 | 31 | 37 | 45 | 57 | None |
| 2.125% | 14 | 16 | 18 | 20 | 22 | 24 | 26 | 28 | 33 | 39 | 46 | 55 |
| 2.25% | 14 | 15 | 17 | 19 | 20 | 22 | 24 | 26 | 30 | 35 | 40 | 46 |
| 2.375% | 13 | 14 | 16 | 17 | 19 | 21 | 22 | 24 | 28 | 32 | 36 | 41 |
| 2.5% | 12 | 13 | 15 | 16 | 18 | 19 | 21 | 23 | 26 | 29 | 33 | 37 |
| 2.625% | 11 | 13 | 14 | 15 | 17 | 18 | 20 | 21 | 24 | 27 | 31 | 35 |
| 2.75% | 11 | 12 | 13 | 15 | 16 | 17 | 19 | 20 | 23 | 26 | 29 | 32 |
| 2.875% | 10 | 12 | 13 | 14 | 15 | 16 | 18 | 19 | 22 | 24 | 27 | 30 |
| 3% | 10 | 11 | 12 | 13 | 14 | 16 | 17 | 18 | 21 | 23 | 26 | 29 |
| 3.125% | 10 | 11 | 12 | 13 | 14 | 15 | 16 | 17 | 20 | 22 | 24 | 27 |
| 3.25% | 9 | 10 | 11 | 12 | 13 | 14 | 15 | 16 | 19 | 21 | 23 | 26 |
| 3.375% | 9 | 10 | 11 | 12 | 13 | 14 | 15 | 16 | 18 | 20 | 22 | 25 |
| 3.5% | 8 | 9 | 10 | 11 | 12 | 13 | 14 | 15 | 17 | 19 | 21 | 23 |
| 3.625% | 8 | 9 | 10 | 11 | 12 | 13 | 14 | 15 | 17 | 18 | 20 | 23 |
| 3.75% | 8 | 9 | 10 | 11 | 11 | 12 | 13 | 14 | 16 | 18 | 20 | 22 |
| 3.875% | 8 | 8 | 9 | 10 | 11 | 12 | 13 | 14 | 15 | 17 | 19 | 21 |
| 4% | 7 | 8 | 9 | 10 | 11 | 11 | 12 | 13 | 15 | 17 | 18 | 20 |

# Refinance Break-Even Tables

## Break-Even Periods (in Months)

Term Left on Current Loan: 120 months
Term on New Loan: 30 years
Points: 3.00%

Income Tax Bracket: Pre-Tax
Points and Costs: Paid in Cash

### Other Closing Costs as a Percent of Loan Amount

| Interest Rate Reduction | .25% | .5% | .75% | 1.00% | 1.25% | 1.50% | 1.75% | 2.00% | 2.50% | 3.00% | 3.50% | 4.00% |
|---|---|---|---|---|---|---|---|---|---|---|---|---|
| 0.125% | None | None | None | None | None | None | None | None | None | None | None | None |
| 0.25% | None | None | None | None | None | None | None | None | None | None | None | None |
| 0.375% | None | None | None | None | None | None | None | None | None | None | None | None |
| 0.5% | None | None | None | None | None | None | None | None | None | None | None | None |
| 0.625% | None | None | None | None | None | None | None | None | None | None | None | None |
| 0.75% | None | None | None | None | None | None | None | None | None | None | None | None |
| 0.875% | None | None | None | None | None | None | None | None | None | None | None | None |
| 1% | None | None | None | None | None | None | None | None | None | None | None | None |
| 1.125% | None | None | None | None | None | None | None | None | None | None | None | None |
| 1.25% | None | None | None | None | None | None | None | None | None | None | None | None |
| 1.375% | None | None | None | None | None | None | None | None | None | None | None | None |
| 1.5% | 44 | None | None | None | None | None | None | None | None | None | None | None |
| 1.625% | 34 | 39 | 47 | None | None | None | None | None | None | None | None | None |
| 1.75% | 29 | 33 | 37 | 42 | 48 | None | None | None | None | None | None | None |
| 1.875% | 26 | 29 | 32 | 35 | 39 | 43 | 49 | 61 | None | None | None | None |
| 2% | 24 | 26 | 29 | 31 | 34 | 37 | 41 | 45 | 57 | None | None | None |
| 2.125% | 22 | 24 | 26 | 28 | 31 | 33 | 36 | 39 | 46 | 55 | None | None |
| 2.25% | 20 | 22 | 24 | 26 | 28 | 30 | 32 | 35 | 40 | 46 | 55 | None |
| 2.375% | 19 | 21 | 22 | 24 | 26 | 28 | 30 | 32 | 36 | 41 | 47 | 54 |
| 2.5% | 18 | 19 | 21 | 23 | 24 | 26 | 28 | 29 | 33 | 37 | 42 | 47 |
| 2.625% | 17 | 18 | 20 | 21 | 23 | 24 | 26 | 27 | 31 | 35 | 39 | 43 |
| 2.75% | 16 | 17 | 19 | 20 | 21 | 23 | 24 | 26 | 29 | 32 | 36 | 39 |
| 2.875% | 15 | 16 | 18 | 19 | 20 | 22 | 23 | 24 | 27 | 30 | 33 | 37 |
| 3% | 14 | 16 | 17 | 18 | 19 | 21 | 22 | 23 | 26 | 29 | 31 | 34 |
| 3.125% | 14 | 15 | 16 | 17 | 18 | 20 | 21 | 22 | 24 | 27 | 30 | 32 |
| 3.25% | 13 | 14 | 15 | 16 | 18 | 19 | 20 | 21 | 23 | 26 | 28 | 31 |
| 3.375% | 13 | 14 | 15 | 16 | 17 | 18 | 19 | 20 | 22 | 25 | 27 | 29 |
| 3.5% | 12 | 13 | 14 | 15 | 16 | 17 | 18 | 19 | 21 | 23 | 26 | 28 |
| 3.625% | 12 | 13 | 14 | 15 | 16 | 17 | 17 | 18 | 20 | 23 | 25 | 27 |
| 3.75% | 11 | 12 | 13 | 14 | 15 | 16 | 17 | 18 | 20 | 22 | 24 | 26 |
| 3.875% | 11 | 12 | 13 | 14 | 14 | 15 | 16 | 17 | 19 | 21 | 23 | 25 |
| 4% | 11 | 11 | 12 | 13 | 14 | 15 | 16 | 17 | 18 | 20 | 22 | 24 |

# Refinance Break-Even Tables

| Break-Even Periods (in Months) | | |
|---|---|---|
| Term Left on Current Loan: 120 months<br>Term on New Loan: 30 years<br>Points: 0.00% | | Income Tax Bracket: 40.00%<br>Points and Costs: Paid in Cash |

| Other Closing Costs as a Percent of Loan Amount | | | | | | | | | | | |
|---|---|---|---|---|---|---|---|---|---|---|---|
| Interest Rate Reduction | .25% | .5% | .75% | 1.00% | 1.25% | 1.50% | 1.75% | 2.00% | 2.50% | 3.00% | 3.50% | 4.00% |
| 0.125% | None | None | None | None | None | None | None | None | None | None | None | None |
| 0.25% | None | None | None | None | None | None | None | None | None | None | None | None |
| 0.375% | None | None | None | None | None | None | None | None | None | None | None | None |
| 0.5% | 18 | None | None | None | None | None | None | None | None | None | None | None |
| 0.625% | 10 | None | None | None | None | None | None | None | None | None | None | None |
| 0.75% | 8 | 20 | None | None | None | None | None | None | None | None | None | None |
| 0.875% | 7 | 15 | None | None | None | None | None | None | None | None | None | None |
| 1% | 6 | 12 | 21 | None | None | None | None | None | None | None | None | None |
| 1.125% | 5 | 10 | 17 | 25 | None | None | None | None | None | None | None | None |
| 1.25% | 5 | 9 | 14 | 21 | 29 | None | None | None | None | None | None | None |
| 1.375% | 4 | 8 | 13 | 18 | 24 | 32 | None | None | None | None | None | None |
| 1.5% | 4 | 8 | 11 | 16 | 21 | 26 | 34 | 47 | None | None | None | None |
| 1.625% | 4 | 7 | 10 | 14 | 18 | 23 | 28 | 35 | None | None | None | None |
| 1.75% | 3 | 6 | 10 | 13 | 17 | 21 | 25 | 30 | 44 | None | None | None |
| 1.875% | 3 | 6 | 9 | 12 | 15 | 19 | 23 | 27 | 37 | 55 | None | None |
| 2% | 3 | 6 | 8 | 11 | 14 | 17 | 21 | 24 | 33 | 43 | None | None |
| 2.125% | 3 | 5 | 8 | 11 | 13 | 16 | 19 | 22 | 29 | 38 | 50 | None |
| 2.25% | 3 | 5 | 7 | 10 | 12 | 15 | 18 | 21 | 27 | 34 | 43 | 56 |
| 2.375% | 3 | 5 | 7 | 9 | 12 | 14 | 17 | 19 | 25 | 31 | 39 | 48 |
| 2.5% | 3 | 5 | 7 | 9 | 11 | 13 | 16 | 18 | 23 | 29 | 35 | 43 |
| 2.625% | 2 | 4 | 6 | 8 | 11 | 13 | 15 | 17 | 22 | 27 | 33 | 39 |
| 2.75% | 2 | 4 | 6 | 8 | 10 | 12 | 14 | 16 | 21 | 26 | 31 | 36 |
| 2.875% | 2 | 4 | 6 | 8 | 10 | 12 | 13 | 15 | 20 | 24 | 29 | 34 |
| 3% | 2 | 4 | 6 | 7 | 9 | 11 | 13 | 15 | 19 | 23 | 27 | 32 |
| 3.125% | 2 | 4 | 5 | 7 | 9 | 11 | 12 | 14 | 18 | 22 | 26 | 30 |
| 3.25% | 2 | 4 | 5 | 7 | 8 | 10 | 12 | 14 | 17 | 21 | 25 | 29 |
| 3.375% | 2 | 3 | 5 | 7 | 8 | 10 | 11 | 13 | 16 | 20 | 24 | 27 |
| 3.5% | 2 | 3 | 5 | 6 | 8 | 9 | 11 | 13 | 16 | 19 | 23 | 26 |
| 3.625% | 2 | 3 | 5 | 6 | 8 | 9 | 11 | 12 | 15 | 18 | 22 | 25 |
| 3.75% | 2 | 3 | 5 | 6 | 7 | 9 | 10 | 12 | 15 | 18 | 21 | 24 |
| 3.875% | 2 | 3 | 4 | 6 | 7 | 8 | 10 | 11 | 14 | 17 | 20 | 23 |
| 4% | 2 | 3 | 4 | 6 | 7 | 8 | 10 | 11 | 14 | 16 | 19 | 22 |

## Break-Even Periods (in Months)

Term Left on Current Loan: 120 months  
Term on New Loan: 30 years  
Points: 1.00%

Income Tax Bracket: 40.00%  
Points and Costs: Paid in Cash

### Other Closing Costs as a Percent of Loan Amount

| Interest Rate Reduction | .25% | .5% | .75% | 1.00% | 1.25% | 1.50% | 1.75% | 2.00% | 2.50% | 3.00% | 3.50% | 4.00% |
|---|---|---|---|---|---|---|---|---|---|---|---|---|
| 0.125% | None | None | None | None | None | None | None | None | None | None | None | None |
| 0.25% | None | None | None | None | None | None | None | None | None | None | None | None |
| 0.375% | None | None | None | None | None | None | None | None | None | None | None | None |
| 0.5% | None | None | None | None | None | None | None | None | None | None | None | None |
| 0.625% | None | None | None | None | None | None | None | None | None | None | None | None |
| 0.75% | None | None | None | None | None | None | None | None | None | None | None | None |
| 0.875% | None | None | None | None | None | None | None | None | None | None | None | None |
| 1% | 26 | None | None | None | None | None | None | None | None | None | None | None |
| 1.125% | 20 | 31 | None | None | None | None | None | None | None | None | None | None |
| 1.25% | 17 | 24 | 35 | None | None | None | None | None | None | None | None | None |
| 1.375% | 15 | 20 | 27 | 37 | None | None | None | None | None | None | None | None |
| 1.5% | 13 | 18 | 23 | 29 | 38 | None | None | None | None | None | None | None |
| 1.625% | 12 | 16 | 20 | 25 | 31 | 39 | None | None | None | None | None | None |
| 1.75% | 11 | 15 | 18 | 23 | 27 | 33 | 39 | 50 | None | None | None | None |
| 1.875% | 10 | 13 | 17 | 20 | 24 | 29 | 34 | 40 | None | None | None | None |
| 2% | 10 | 12 | 16 | 19 | 22 | 26 | 30 | 35 | 47 | None | None | None |
| 2.125% | 9 | 12 | 14 | 17 | 21 | 24 | 27 | 31 | 40 | 54 | None | None |
| 2.25% | 8 | 11 | 14 | 16 | 19 | 22 | 25 | 29 | 36 | 46 | 61 | None |
| 2.375% | 8 | 10 | 13 | 15 | 18 | 21 | 23 | 26 | 33 | 41 | 50 | 69 |
| 2.5% | 8 | 10 | 12 | 14 | 17 | 19 | 22 | 25 | 30 | 37 | 45 | 55 |
| 2.625% | 7 | 9 | 11 | 14 | 16 | 18 | 21 | 23 | 28 | 34 | 41 | 49 |
| 2.75% | 7 | 9 | 11 | 13 | 15 | 17 | 19 | 22 | 27 | 32 | 38 | 44 |
| 2.875% | 7 | 8 | 10 | 12 | 14 | 16 | 18 | 21 | 25 | 30 | 35 | 41 |
| 3% | 6 | 8 | 10 | 12 | 14 | 16 | 18 | 20 | 24 | 28 | 33 | 38 |
| 3.125% | 6 | 8 | 10 | 11 | 13 | 15 | 17 | 19 | 23 | 27 | 31 | 36 |
| 3.25% | 6 | 7 | 9 | 11 | 13 | 14 | 16 | 18 | 22 | 26 | 30 | 34 |
| 3.375% | 6 | 7 | 9 | 10 | 12 | 14 | 15 | 17 | 21 | 24 | 28 | 32 |
| 3.5% | 5 | 7 | 8 | 10 | 12 | 13 | 15 | 16 | 20 | 23 | 27 | 31 |
| 3.625% | 5 | 7 | 8 | 10 | 11 | 13 | 14 | 16 | 19 | 22 | 26 | 29 |
| 3.75% | 5 | 7 | 8 | 9 | 11 | 12 | 14 | 15 | 18 | 22 | 25 | 28 |
| 3.875% | 5 | 6 | 8 | 9 | 10 | 12 | 13 | 15 | 18 | 21 | 24 | 27 |
| 4% | 5 | 6 | 7 | 9 | 10 | 11 | 13 | 14 | 17 | 20 | 23 | 26 |

| Break-Even Periods (in Months) | | | | | | | | | | | |
|---|---|---|---|---|---|---|---|---|---|---|---|

Term Left on Current Loan: 120 months  
Term on New Loan: 30 years  
Points: 2.00%

Income Tax Bracket: 40.00%  
Points and Costs: Paid in Cash

| Other Closing Costs as a Percent of Loan Amount | | | | | | | | | | | |
|---|---|---|---|---|---|---|---|---|---|---|---|
| Interest Rate Reduction | .25% | .5% | .75% | 1.00% | 1.25% | 1.50% | 1.75% | 2.00% | 2.50% | 3.00% | 3.50% | 4.00% |
| 0.125% | None | None | None | None | None | None | None | None | None | None | None | None |
| 0.25% | None | None | None | None | None | None | None | None | None | None | None | None |
| 0.375% | None | None | None | None | None | None | None | None | None | None | None | None |
| 0.5% | None | None | None | None | None | None | None | None | None | None | None | None |
| 0.625% | None | None | None | None | None | None | None | None | None | None | None | None |
| 0.75% | None | None | None | None | None | None | None | None | None | None | None | None |
| 0.875% | None | None | None | None | None | None | None | None | None | None | None | None |
| 1% | None | None | None | None | None | None | None | None | None | None | None | None |
| 1.125% | None | None | None | None | None | None | None | None | None | None | None | None |
| 1.25% | None | None | None | None | None | None | None | None | None | None | None | None |
| 1.375% | 31 | None | None | None | None | None | None | None | None | None | None | None |
| 1.5% | 26 | 33 | 45 | None | None | None | None | None | None | None | None | None |
| 1.625% | 22 | 28 | 34 | 44 | None | None | None | None | None | None | None | None |
| 1.75% | 20 | 25 | 30 | 35 | 44 | None | None | None | None | None | None | None |
| 1.875% | 18 | 22 | 26 | 31 | 36 | 43 | 54 | None | None | None | None | None |
| 2% | 17 | 20 | 24 | 28 | 32 | 37 | 43 | 51 | None | None | None | None |
| 2.125% | 16 | 19 | 22 | 25 | 29 | 33 | 38 | 43 | 60 | None | None | None |
| 2.25% | 15 | 17 | 20 | 23 | 27 | 30 | 34 | 38 | 48 | None | None | None |
| 2.375% | 14 | 16 | 19 | 22 | 25 | 28 | 31 | 35 | 43 | 53 | None | None |
| 2.5% | 13 | 15 | 18 | 20 | 23 | 26 | 29 | 32 | 39 | 47 | 58 | None |
| 2.625% | 12 | 15 | 17 | 19 | 22 | 24 | 27 | 30 | 36 | 43 | 51 | 62 |
| 2.75% | 12 | 14 | 16 | 18 | 20 | 23 | 25 | 28 | 33 | 39 | 46 | 54 |
| 2.875% | 11 | 13 | 15 | 17 | 19 | 22 | 24 | 26 | 31 | 37 | 42 | 49 |
| 3% | 11 | 13 | 14 | 16 | 18 | 20 | 23 | 25 | 29 | 34 | 40 | 46 |
| 3.125% | 10 | 12 | 14 | 16 | 18 | 20 | 22 | 24 | 28 | 32 | 37 | 42 |
| 3.25% | 10 | 12 | 13 | 15 | 17 | 19 | 21 | 22 | 26 | 31 | 35 | 40 |
| 3.375% | 9 | 11 | 13 | 14 | 16 | 18 | 20 | 21 | 25 | 29 | 33 | 38 |
| 3.5% | 9 | 11 | 12 | 14 | 15 | 17 | 19 | 21 | 24 | 28 | 32 | 36 |
| 3.625% | 9 | 10 | 12 | 13 | 15 | 16 | 18 | 20 | 23 | 27 | 30 | 34 |
| 3.75% | 9 | 10 | 11 | 13 | 14 | 16 | 17 | 19 | 22 | 26 | 29 | 33 |
| 3.875% | 8 | 10 | 11 | 12 | 14 | 15 | 17 | 18 | 21 | 25 | 28 | 31 |
| 4% | 8 | 9 | 11 | 12 | 13 | 15 | 16 | 18 | 21 | 24 | 27 | 30 |

| Break-Even Periods (in Months) | | | | | | | | | | | |
|---|---|---|---|---|---|---|---|---|---|---|---|
| Term Left on Current Loan: 120 months<br>Term on New Loan: 30 years<br>Points: 3.00% | | | | | | Income Tax Bracket: 40.00%<br>Points and Costs: Paid in Cash | | | | | |
| Other Closing Costs as a Percent of Loan Amount | | | | | | | | | | | |
| Interest Rate Reduction | .25% | .5% | .75% | 1.00% | 1.25% | 1.50% | 1.75% | 2.00% | 2.50% | 3.00% | 3.50% | 4.00% |

| Interest Rate Reduction | .25% | .5% | .75% | 1.00% | 1.25% | 1.50% | 1.75% | 2.00% | 2.50% | 3.00% | 3.50% | 4.00% |
|---|---|---|---|---|---|---|---|---|---|---|---|---|
| 0.125% | None | None | None | None | None | None | None | None | None | None | None | None |
| 0.25% | None | None | None | None | None | None | None | None | None | None | None | None |
| 0.375% | None | None | None | None | None | None | None | None | None | None | None | None |
| 0.5% | None | None | None | None | None | None | None | None | None | None | None | None |
| 0.625% | None | None | None | None | None | None | None | None | None | None | None | None |
| 0.75% | None | None | None | None | None | None | None | None | None | None | None | None |
| 0.875% | None | None | None | None | None | None | None | None | None | None | None | None |
| 1% | None | None | None | None | None | None | None | None | None | None | None | None |
| 1.125% | None | None | None | None | None | None | None | None | None | None | None | None |
| 1.25% | None | None | None | None | None | None | None | None | None | None | None | None |
| 1.375% | None | None | None | None | None | None | None | None | None | None | None | None |
| 1.5% | None | None | None | None | None | None | None | None | None | None | None | None |
| 1.625% | 38 | None | None | None | None | None | None | None | None | None | None | None |
| 1.75% | 32 | 39 | 49 | None | None | None | None | None | None | None | None | None |
| 1.875% | 28 | 33 | 39 | 47 | None | None | None | None | None | None | None | None |
| 2% | 26 | 30 | 34 | 40 | 46 | 57 | None | None | None | None | None | None |
| 2.125% | 23 | 27 | 31 | 35 | 40 | 46 | 53 | None | None | None | None | None |
| 2.25% | 22 | 25 | 28 | 32 | 36 | 40 | 45 | 51 | None | None | None | None |
| 2.375% | 20 | 23 | 26 | 29 | 33 | 36 | 40 | 45 | 57 | None | None | None |
| 2.5% | 19 | 22 | 24 | 27 | 30 | 33 | 37 | 40 | 49 | 62 | None | None |
| 2.625% | 18 | 20 | 23 | 25 | 28 | 31 | 34 | 37 | 44 | 53 | 67 | None |
| 2.75% | 17 | 19 | 21 | 24 | 26 | 29 | 32 | 34 | 41 | 48 | 57 | 71 |
| 2.875% | 16 | 18 | 20 | 23 | 25 | 27 | 30 | 32 | 38 | 44 | 51 | 60 |
| 3% | 15 | 17 | 19 | 21 | 24 | 26 | 28 | 30 | 35 | 41 | 47 | 54 |
| 3.125% | 15 | 16 | 18 | 20 | 22 | 24 | 27 | 29 | 33 | 38 | 44 | 50 |
| 3.25% | 14 | 16 | 18 | 19 | 21 | 23 | 25 | 27 | 32 | 36 | 41 | 46 |
| 3.375% | 13 | 15 | 17 | 19 | 20 | 22 | 24 | 26 | 30 | 34 | 39 | 44 |
| 3.5% | 13 | 15 | 16 | 18 | 20 | 21 | 23 | 25 | 29 | 33 | 37 | 41 |
| 3.625% | 12 | 14 | 16 | 17 | 19 | 20 | 22 | 24 | 27 | 31 | 35 | 39 |
| 3.75% | 12 | 14 | 15 | 17 | 18 | 20 | 21 | 23 | 26 | 30 | 33 | 37 |
| 3.875% | 12 | 13 | 14 | 16 | 17 | 19 | 21 | 22 | 25 | 29 | 32 | 36 |
| 4% | 11 | 13 | 14 | 15 | 17 | 18 | 20 | 21 | 24 | 27 | 31 | 34 |

# Refinance Break-Even Tables

| Break-Even Periods (in Months) | | | | | | | | | | | | |
|---|---|---|---|---|---|---|---|---|---|---|---|---|

Term Left on Current Loan: 300 months  
Term on New Loan: 30 years  
Points: 0.00%

Income Tax Bracket: Pre-Tax  
Points and Costs: Paid in Cash

| Other Closing Costs as a Percent of Loan Amount | | | | | | | | | | | | |
|---|---|---|---|---|---|---|---|---|---|---|---|---|
| Interest Rate Reduction | .25% | .5% | .75% | 1.00% | 1.25% | 1.50% | 1.75% | 2.00% | 2.50% | 3.00% | 3.50% | 4.00% |
| 0.125% | 36 | None | None | None | None | None | None | None | None | None | None | None |
| 0.25% | 13 | 28 | 48 | None | None | None | None | None | None | None | None | None |
| 0.375% | 9 | 18 | 27 | 37 | 49 | 63 | 81 | None | None | None | None | None |
| 0.5% | 7 | 13 | 20 | 26 | 34 | 41 | 50 | 59 | 80 | 111 | None | None |
| 0.625% | 5 | 10 | 15 | 21 | 26 | 32 | 38 | 44 | 57 | 71 | 88 | 109 |
| 0.75% | 5 | 9 | 13 | 17 | 21 | 26 | 31 | 35 | 45 | 56 | 67 | 79 |
| 0.875% | 4 | 7 | 11 | 15 | 18 | 22 | 26 | 30 | 38 | 46 | 55 | 64 |
| 1% | 4 | 7 | 10 | 13 | 16 | 19 | 22 | 26 | 32 | 39 | 47 | 54 |
| 1.125% | 3 | 6 | 9 | 11 | 14 | 17 | 20 | 23 | 29 | 35 | 41 | 47 |
| 1.25% | 3 | 5 | 8 | 10 | 13 | 15 | 18 | 20 | 26 | 31 | 36 | 42 |
| 1.375% | 3 | 5 | 7 | 9 | 12 | 14 | 16 | 18 | 23 | 28 | 33 | 38 |
| 1.5% | 3 | 5 | 7 | 9 | 11 | 13 | 15 | 17 | 21 | 26 | 30 | 34 |
| 1.625% | 2 | 4 | 6 | 8 | 10 | 12 | 14 | 16 | 20 | 23 | 28 | 32 |
| 1.75% | 2 | 4 | 6 | 7 | 9 | 11 | 13 | 15 | 18 | 22 | 25 | 29 |
| 1.875% | 2 | 4 | 5 | 7 | 9 | 10 | 12 | 14 | 17 | 20 | 24 | 27 |
| 2% | 2 | 4 | 5 | 7 | 8 | 10 | 11 | 13 | 16 | 19 | 22 | 25 |
| 2.125% | 2 | 3 | 5 | 6 | 8 | 9 | 11 | 12 | 15 | 18 | 21 | 24 |
| 2.25% | 2 | 3 | 5 | 6 | 7 | 9 | 10 | 11 | 14 | 17 | 20 | 23 |
| 2.375% | 2 | 3 | 4 | 6 | 7 | 8 | 9 | 11 | 13 | 16 | 19 | 21 |
| 2.5% | 2 | 3 | 4 | 5 | 7 | 8 | 9 | 10 | 13 | 15 | 18 | 20 |
| 2.625% | 2 | 3 | 4 | 5 | 6 | 7 | 9 | 10 | 12 | 14 | 17 | 19 |
| 2.75% | 2 | 3 | 4 | 5 | 6 | 7 | 8 | 9 | 12 | 14 | 16 | 18 |
| 2.875% | 2 | 3 | 4 | 5 | 6 | 7 | 8 | 9 | 11 | 13 | 15 | 18 |
| 3% | 2 | 3 | 4 | 5 | 6 | 7 | 8 | 9 | 11 | 13 | 15 | 17 |
| 3.125% | 1 | 2 | 3 | 4 | 5 | 6 | 7 | 8 | 10 | 12 | 14 | 16 |
| 3.25% | 1 | 2 | 3 | 4 | 5 | 6 | 7 | 8 | 10 | 12 | 14 | 16 |
| 3.375% | 1 | 2 | 3 | 4 | 5 | 6 | 7 | 8 | 10 | 11 | 13 | 15 |
| 3.5% | 1 | 2 | 3 | 4 | 5 | 6 | 7 | 7 | 9 | 11 | 13 | 14 |
| 3.625% | 1 | 2 | 3 | 4 | 5 | 6 | 6 | 7 | 9 | 11 | 12 | 14 |
| 3.75% | 1 | 2 | 3 | 4 | 5 | 5 | 6 | 7 | 9 | 10 | 12 | 14 |
| 3.875% | 1 | 2 | 3 | 4 | 4 | 5 | 6 | 7 | 8 | 10 | 12 | 13 |
| 4% | 1 | 2 | 3 | 4 | 4 | 5 | 6 | 7 | 8 | 10 | 11 | 13 |

# Refinance Break-Even Tables

## Break-Even Periods (in Months)

Term Left on Current Loan: 300 months  
Term on New Loan: 30 years  
Points: 1.00%

Income Tax Bracket: Pre-Tax  
Points and Costs: Paid in Cash

### Other Closing Costs as a Percent of Loan Amount

| Interest Rate Reduction | .25% | .5% | .75% | 1.00% | 1.25% | 1.50% | 1.75% | 2.00% | 2.50% | 3.00% | 3.50% | 4.00% |
|---|---|---|---|---|---|---|---|---|---|---|---|---|
| 0.125% | None | None | None | None | None | None | None | None | None | None | None | None |
| 0.25% | None | None | None | None | None | None | None | None | None | None | None | None |
| 0.375% | 49 | 63 | 81 | None | None | None | None | None | None | None | None | None |
| 0.5% | 34 | 41 | 50 | 59 | 69 | 80 | 93 | 111 | None | None | None | None |
| 0.625% | 26 | 32 | 38 | 44 | 50 | 57 | 64 | 71 | 88 | 109 | 147 | None |
| 0.75% | 21 | 26 | 31 | 35 | 40 | 45 | 50 | 56 | 67 | 79 | 93 | 109 |
| 0.875% | 18 | 22 | 26 | 30 | 34 | 38 | 42 | 46 | 55 | 64 | 74 | 84 |
| 1% | 16 | 19 | 22 | 26 | 29 | 32 | 36 | 39 | 47 | 54 | 62 | 70 |
| 1.125% | 14 | 17 | 20 | 23 | 26 | 29 | 32 | 35 | 41 | 47 | 54 | 61 |
| 1.25% | 13 | 15 | 18 | 20 | 23 | 26 | 28 | 31 | 36 | 42 | 48 | 53 |
| 1.375% | 12 | 14 | 16 | 18 | 21 | 23 | 26 | 28 | 33 | 38 | 43 | 48 |
| 1.5% | 11 | 13 | 15 | 17 | 19 | 21 | 23 | 26 | 30 | 34 | 39 | 44 |
| 1.625% | 10 | 12 | 14 | 16 | 18 | 20 | 22 | 23 | 28 | 32 | 36 | 40 |
| 1.75% | 9 | 11 | 13 | 15 | 16 | 18 | 20 | 22 | 25 | 29 | 33 | 37 |
| 1.875% | 9 | 10 | 12 | 14 | 15 | 17 | 19 | 20 | 24 | 27 | 31 | 34 |
| 2% | 8 | 10 | 11 | 13 | 14 | 16 | 17 | 19 | 22 | 25 | 29 | 32 |
| 2.125% | 8 | 9 | 11 | 12 | 13 | 15 | 16 | 18 | 21 | 24 | 27 | 30 |
| 2.25% | 7 | 9 | 10 | 11 | 13 | 14 | 15 | 17 | 20 | 23 | 25 | 28 |
| 2.375% | 7 | 8 | 9 | 11 | 12 | 13 | 15 | 16 | 19 | 21 | 24 | 27 |
| 2.5% | 7 | 8 | 9 | 10 | 11 | 13 | 14 | 15 | 18 | 20 | 23 | 25 |
| 2.625% | 6 | 7 | 9 | 10 | 11 | 12 | 13 | 14 | 17 | 19 | 22 | 24 |
| 2.75% | 6 | 7 | 8 | 9 | 10 | 12 | 13 | 14 | 16 | 18 | 21 | 23 |
| 2.875% | 6 | 7 | 8 | 9 | 10 | 11 | 12 | 13 | 15 | 18 | 20 | 22 |
| 3% | 6 | 7 | 8 | 9 | 10 | 11 | 12 | 13 | 15 | 17 | 19 | 21 |
| 3.125% | 5 | 6 | 7 | 8 | 9 | 10 | 11 | 12 | 14 | 16 | 18 | 20 |
| 3.25% | 5 | 6 | 7 | 8 | 9 | 10 | 11 | 12 | 14 | 16 | 18 | 19 |
| 3.375% | 5 | 6 | 7 | 8 | 9 | 10 | 10 | 11 | 13 | 15 | 17 | 19 |
| 3.5% | 5 | 6 | 7 | 7 | 8 | 9 | 10 | 11 | 13 | 14 | 16 | 18 |
| 3.625% | 5 | 6 | 6 | 7 | 8 | 9 | 10 | 11 | 12 | 14 | 16 | 17 |
| 3.75% | 5 | 5 | 6 | 7 | 8 | 9 | 9 | 10 | 12 | 14 | 15 | 17 |
| 3.875% | 4 | 5 | 6 | 7 | 8 | 8 | 9 | 10 | 12 | 13 | 15 | 16 |
| 4% | 4 | 5 | 6 | 7 | 7 | 8 | 9 | 10 | 11 | 13 | 14 | 16 |

# Refinance Break-Even Tables

| | | | | | | | | | | | | |
|---|---|---|---|---|---|---|---|---|---|---|---|---|
| **Break-Even Periods (n Months)** | | | | | | | | | | | | |

Term Left on Current Loan: 300 months  
Term on New Loan: 30 years  
Points: 2.00%

Income Tax Bracket: Pre-Tax  
Points and Costs: Paid in Cash

| Interest Rate Reduction | Other Closing Costs as a Percent of Loan Amount | | | | | | | | | | | |
|---|---|---|---|---|---|---|---|---|---|---|---|---|
| | .25% | .5% | .75% | 1.00% | 1.25% | 1.50% | 1.75% | 2.00% | 2.50% | 3.00% | 3.50% | 4.00% |
| 0.125% | None | None | None | None | None | None | None | None | None | None | None | None |
| 0.25% | None | None | None | None | None | None | None | None | None | None | None | None |
| 0.375% | None | None | None | None | None | None | None | None | None | None | None | None |
| 0.5% | 69 | 80 | 93 | 111 | None | None | None | None | None | None | None | None |
| 0.625% | 50 | 57 | 64 | 71 | 79 | 88 | 98 | 109 | 147 | None | None | None |
| 0.75% | 40 | 45 | 50 | 56 | 61 | 67 | 73 | 79 | 93 | 109 | 129 | 165 |
| 0.875% | 34 | 38 | 42 | 46 | 50 | 55 | 59 | 64 | 74 | 84 | 96 | 108 |
| 1% | 29 | 32 | 36 | 39 | 43 | 47 | 50 | 54 | 62 | 70 | 79 | 88 |
| 1.125% | 26 | 29 | 32 | 35 | 38 | 41 | 44 | 47 | 54 | 61 | 68 | 75 |
| 1.25% | 23 | 26 | 28 | 31 | 34 | 36 | 39 | 42 | 48 | 53 | 60 | 66 |
| 1.375% | 21 | 23 | 26 | 28 | 30 | 33 | 35 | 38 | 43 | 48 | 53 | 59 |
| 1.5% | 19 | 21 | 23 | 26 | 28 | 30 | 32 | 34 | 39 | 44 | 48 | 53 |
| 1.625% | 18 | 20 | 22 | 23 | 25 | 28 | 30 | 32 | 36 | 40 | 44 | 48 |
| 1.75% | 16 | 18 | 20 | 22 | 24 | 25 | 27 | 29 | 33 | 37 | 41 | 45 |
| 1.875% | 15 | 17 | 19 | 20 | 22 | 24 | 25 | 27 | 31 | 34 | 38 | 41 |
| 2% | 14 | 16 | 17 | 19 | 21 | 22 | 24 | 25 | 29 | 32 | 35 | 39 |
| 2.125% | 13 | 15 | 16 | 18 | 19 | 21 | 22 | 24 | 27 | 30 | 33 | 36 |
| 2.25% | 13 | 14 | 15 | 17 | 18 | 20 | 21 | 23 | 25 | 28 | 31 | 34 |
| 2.375% | 12 | 13 | 15 | 16 | 17 | 19 | 20 | 21 | 24 | 27 | 29 | 32 |
| 2.5% | 11 | 13 | 14 | 15 | 16 | 18 | 19 | 20 | 23 | 25 | 28 | 31 |
| 2.625% | 11 | 12 | 13 | 14 | 16 | 17 | 18 | 19 | 22 | 24 | 27 | 29 |
| 2.75% | 10 | 12 | 13 | 14 | 15 | 16 | 17 | 18 | 21 | 23 | 25 | 28 |
| 2.875% | 10 | 11 | 12 | 13 | 14 | 15 | 17 | 18 | 20 | 22 | 24 | 26 |
| 3% | 10 | 11 | 12 | 13 | 14 | 15 | 16 | 17 | 19 | 21 | 23 | 25 |
| 3.125% | 9 | 10 | 11 | 12 | 13 | 14 | 15 | 16 | 18 | 20 | 22 | 24 |
| 3.25% | 9 | 10 | 11 | 12 | 13 | 14 | 15 | 16 | 18 | 19 | 21 | 23 |
| 3.375% | 9 | 10 | 10 | 11 | 12 | 13 | 14 | 15 | 17 | 19 | 21 | 23 |
| 3.5% | 8 | 9 | 10 | 11 | 12 | 13 | 14 | 14 | 16 | 18 | 20 | 22 |
| 3.625% | 8 | 9 | 10 | 11 | 11 | 12 | 13 | 14 | 16 | 17 | 19 | 21 |
| 3.75% | 8 | 9 | 9 | 10 | 11 | 12 | 13 | 14 | 15 | 17 | 19 | 20 |
| 3.875% | 8 | 8 | 9 | 10 | 11 | 12 | 12 | 13 | 15 | 16 | 18 | 20 |
| 4% | 7 | 8 | 9 | 10 | 10 | 11 | 12 | 13 | 14 | 16 | 17 | 19 |

| Break-Even Periods (in Months) | | | | | | | | | | | |
|---|---|---|---|---|---|---|---|---|---|---|---|

Term Left on Current Loan: 300 months      Income Tax Bracket: Pre-Tax
Term on New Loan: 30 years      Points and Costs: Paid in Cash
Points: 3.00%

| Other Closing Costs as a Percent of Loan Amount | | | | | | | | | | | |
|---|---|---|---|---|---|---|---|---|---|---|---|
| Interest Rate Reduction | .25% | .5% | .75% | 1.00% | 1.25% | 1.50% | 1.75% | 2.00% | 2.50% | 3.00% | 3.50% | 4.00% |
| 0.125% | None | None | None | None | None | None | None | None | None | None | None | None |
| 0.25% | None | None | None | None | None | None | None | None | None | None | None | None |
| 0.375% | None | None | None | None | None | None | None | None | None | None | None | None |
| 0.5% | None | None | None | None | None | None | None | None | None | None | None | None |
| 0.625% | 79 | 88 | 98 | 109 | 124 | 147 | None | None | None | None | None | None |
| 0.75% | 61 | 67 | 73 | 79 | 86 | 93 | 100 | 109 | 129 | 165 | None | None |
| 0.875% | 50 | 55 | 59 | 64 | 69 | 74 | 79 | 84 | 96 | 108 | 123 | 142 |
| 1% | 43 | 47 | 50 | 54 | 58 | 62 | 66 | 70 | 79 | 88 | 98 | 108 |
| 1.125% | 38 | 41 | 44 | 47 | 50 | 54 | 57 | 61 | 68 | 75 | 83 | 91 |
| 1.25% | 34 | 36 | 39 | 42 | 45 | 48 | 51 | 53 | 60 | 66 | 72 | 79 |
| 1.375% | 30 | 33 | 35 | 38 | 40 | 43 | 45 | 48 | 53 | 59 | 64 | 70 |
| 1.5% | 28 | 30 | 32 | 34 | 37 | 39 | 41 | 44 | 48 | 53 | 58 | 63 |
| 1.625% | 25 | 28 | 30 | 32 | 34 | 36 | 38 | 40 | 44 | 48 | 53 | 57 |
| 1.75% | 24 | 25 | 27 | 29 | 31 | 33 | 35 | 37 | 41 | 45 | 49 | 53 |
| 1.875% | 22 | 24 | 25 | 27 | 29 | 31 | 32 | 34 | 38 | 41 | 45 | 49 |
| 2% | 21 | 22 | 24 | 25 | 27 | 29 | 30 | 32 | 35 | 39 | 42 | 46 |
| 2.125% | 19 | 21 | 22 | 24 | 25 | 27 | 28 | 30 | 33 | 36 | 39 | 43 |
| 2.25% | 18 | 20 | 21 | 23 | 24 | 25 | 27 | 28 | 31 | 34 | 37 | 40 |
| 2.375% | 17 | 19 | 20 | 21 | 23 | 24 | 25 | 27 | 29 | 32 | 35 | 38 |
| 2.5% | 16 | 18 | 19 | 20 | 22 | 23 | 24 | 25 | 28 | 31 | 33 | 36 |
| 2.625% | 16 | 17 | 18 | 19 | 20 | 22 | 23 | 24 | 27 | 29 | 32 | 34 |
| 2.75% | 15 | 16 | 17 | 18 | 20 | 21 | 22 | 23 | 25 | 28 | 30 | 32 |
| 2.875% | 14 | 15 | 17 | 18 | 19 | 20 | 21 | 22 | 24 | 26 | 29 | 31 |
| 3% | 14 | 15 | 16 | 17 | 18 | 19 | 20 | 21 | 23 | 25 | 28 | 30 |
| 3.125% | 13 | 14 | 15 | 16 | 17 | 18 | 19 | 20 | 22 | 24 | 26 | 28 |
| 3.25% | 13 | 14 | 15 | 16 | 17 | 18 | 18 | 19 | 21 | 23 | 25 | 27 |
| 3.375% | 12 | 13 | 14 | 15 | 16 | 17 | 18 | 19 | 21 | 23 | 24 | 26 |
| 3.5% | 12 | 13 | 14 | 14 | 15 | 16 | 17 | 18 | 20 | 22 | 24 | 25 |
| 3.625% | 11 | 12 | 13 | 14 | 15 | 16 | 17 | 17 | 19 | 21 | 23 | 24 |
| 3.75% | 11 | 12 | 13 | 14 | 14 | 15 | 16 | 17 | 19 | 20 | 22 | 24 |
| 3.875% | 11 | 12 | 12 | 13 | 14 | 15 | 16 | 16 | 18 | 20 | 21 | 23 |
| 4% | 10 | 11 | 12 | 13 | 13 | 14 | 15 | 16 | 17 | 19 | 21 | 22 |

# Refinance Break-Even Tables

| Break-Even Periods (in Months) | | | | | | | | | | | |
|---|---|---|---|---|---|---|---|---|---|---|---|
| Term Left on Current Loan: 300 months<br>Term on New Loan: 30 years<br>Points: 0.00% | | | | | | Income Tax Bracket: 40.00%<br>Points and Costs: Paid in Cash | | | | | |
| Other Closing Costs as a Percent of Loan Amount | | | | | | | | | | | |

| Interest<br>Rate<br>Reduction | .25% | .5% | .75% | 1.00% | 1.25% | 1.50% | 1.75% | 2.00% | 2.50% | 3.00% | 3.50% | 4.00% |
|---|---|---|---|---|---|---|---|---|---|---|---|---|
| 0.125% | None | None | None | None | None | None | None | None | None | None | None | None |
| 0.25% | 23 | 55 | None | None | None | None | None | None | None | None | None | None |
| 0.375% | 14 | 30 | 48 | 72 | None | None | None | None | None | None | None | None |
| 0.5% | 11 | 22 | 33 | 46 | 60 | 77 | 99 | None | None | None | None | None |
| 0.625% | 9 | 17 | 26 | 35 | 45 | 56 | 67 | 79 | 111 | None | None | None |
| 0.75% | 7 | 14 | 21 | 29 | 36 | 44 | 53 | 61 | 81 | 104 | 135 | None |
| 0.875% | 6 | 12 | 18 | 24 | 31 | 37 | 44 | 51 | 65 | 82 | 100 | 121 |
| 1% | 6 | 11 | 16 | 21 | 27 | 32 | 38 | 44 | 56 | 68 | 82 | 97 |
| 1.125% | 5 | 10 | 14 | 19 | 24 | 28 | 33 | 38 | 49 | 59 | 71 | 83 |
| 1.25% | 5 | 9 | 13 | 17 | 21 | 25 | 30 | 34 | 43 | 52 | 62 | 72 |
| 1.375% | 4 | 8 | 12 | 15 | 19 | 23 | 27 | 31 | 39 | 47 | 56 | 65 |
| 1.5% | 4 | 7 | 11 | 14 | 18 | 21 | 25 | 28 | 35 | 43 | 51 | 58 |
| 1.625% | 4 | 7 | 10 | 13 | 16 | 19 | 23 | 26 | 33 | 39 | 46 | 53 |
| 1.75% | 3 | 6 | 9 | 12 | 15 | 18 | 21 | 24 | 30 | 36 | 43 | 49 |
| 1.875% | 3 | 6 | 9 | 11 | 14 | 17 | 20 | 22 | 28 | 34 | 40 | 46 |
| 2% | 3 | 6 | 8 | 11 | 13 | 16 | 18 | 21 | 26 | 32 | 37 | 43 |
| 2.125% | 3 | 5 | 8 | 10 | 12 | 15 | 17 | 20 | 25 | 30 | 35 | 40 |
| 2.25% | 3 | 5 | 7 | 9 | 12 | 14 | 16 | 19 | 23 | 28 | 33 | 38 |
| 2.375% | 3 | 5 | 7 | 9 | 11 | 13 | 15 | 18 | 22 | 27 | 31 | 36 |
| 2.5% | 3 | 5 | 7 | 9 | 11 | 13 | 15 | 17 | 21 | 25 | 29 | 34 |
| 2.625% | 2 | 4 | 6 | 8 | 10 | 12 | 14 | 16 | 20 | 24 | 28 | 32 |
| 2.75% | 2 | 4 | 6 | 8 | 10 | 12 | 13 | 15 | 19 | 23 | 27 | 31 |
| 2.875% | 2 | 4 | 6 | 8 | 9 | 11 | 13 | 15 | 18 | 22 | 26 | 29 |
| 3% | 2 | 4 | 6 | 7 | 9 | 11 | 12 | 14 | 17 | 21 | 24 | 28 |
| 3.125% | 2 | 4 | 5 | 7 | 9 | 10 | 12 | 13 | 17 | 20 | 23 | 27 |
| 3.25% | 2 | 4 | 5 | 7 | 8 | 10 | 11 | 13 | 16 | 19 | 23 | 26 |
| 3.375% | 2 | 3 | 5 | 6 | 8 | 9 | 11 | 13 | 16 | 19 | 22 | 25 |
| 3.5% | 2 | 3 | 5 | 6 | 8 | 9 | 11 | 12 | 15 | 18 | 21 | 24 |
| 3.625% | 2 | 3 | 5 | 6 | 7 | 9 | 10 | 12 | 14 | 17 | 20 | 23 |
| 3.75% | 2 | 3 | 5 | 6 | 7 | 9 | 10 | 11 | 14 | 17 | 20 | 22 |
| 3.875% | 2 | 3 | 4 | 6 | 7 | 8 | 10 | 11 | 14 | 16 | 19 | 22 |
| 4% | 2 | 3 | 4 | 6 | 7 | 8 | 9 | 11 | 13 | 16 | 18 | 21 |

# Refinance Break-Even Tables

| **Break-Even Periods (in Months)** |
|:---|

Term Left on Current Loan: 300 months      Income Tax Bracket: 40.00%
Term on New Loan: 30 years      Points and Costs: Paid in Cash
Points: 1.00%

| Interest Rate Reduction | Other Closing Costs as a Percent of Loan Amount | | | | | | | | | | | |
|---|---|---|---|---|---|---|---|---|---|---|---|---|
|  | .25% | .5% | .75% | 1.00% | 1.25% | 1.50% | 1.75% | 2.00% | 2.50% | 3.00% | 3.50% | 4.00% |
| 0.125% | None | None | None | None | None | None | None | None | None | None | None | None |
| 0.25% | None | None | None | None | None | None | None | None | None | None | None | None |
| 0.375% | 59 | 90 | None | None | None | None | None | None | None | None | None | None |
| 0.5% | 39 | 53 | 68 | 87 | 116 | None | None | None | None | None | None | None |
| 0.625% | 30 | 40 | 50 | 61 | 73 | 87 | 103 | 124 | None | None | None | None |
| 0.75% | 25 | 32 | 40 | 48 | 57 | 66 | 76 | 86 | 111 | 149 | None | None |
| 0.875% | 21 | 27 | 34 | 40 | 47 | 54 | 62 | 69 | 86 | 105 | 128 | 164 |
| 1% | 18 | 24 | 29 | 35 | 40 | 46 | 52 | 59 | 72 | 86 | 101 | 119 |
| 1.125% | 16 | 21 | 26 | 31 | 35 | 41 | 46 | 51 | 62 | 74 | 86 | 99 |
| 1.25% | 14 | 19 | 23 | 27 | 32 | 36 | 41 | 45 | 55 | 65 | 75 | 86 |
| 1.375% | 13 | 17 | 21 | 25 | 29 | 33 | 37 | 41 | 49 | 58 | 67 | 76 |
| 1.5% | 12 | 16 | 19 | 23 | 26 | 30 | 33 | 37 | 45 | 52 | 60 | 68 |
| 1.625% | 11 | 14 | 18 | 21 | 24 | 27 | 31 | 34 | 41 | 48 | 55 | 62 |
| 1.75% | 10 | 13 | 16 | 19 | 22 | 25 | 28 | 32 | 38 | 44 | 51 | 57 |
| 1.875% | 10 | 12 | 15 | 18 | 21 | 24 | 26 | 29 | 35 | 41 | 47 | 53 |
| 2% | 9 | 12 | 14 | 17 | 19 | 22 | 25 | 27 | 33 | 38 | 44 | 50 |
| 2.125% | 9 | 11 | 13 | 16 | 18 | 21 | 23 | 26 | 31 | 36 | 41 | 46 |
| 2.25% | 8 | 10 | 13 | 15 | 17 | 20 | 22 | 24 | 29 | 34 | 39 | 44 |
| 2.375% | 8 | 10 | 12 | 14 | 16 | 19 | 21 | 23 | 28 | 32 | 37 | 41 |
| 2.5% | 7 | 9 | 11 | 14 | 16 | 18 | 20 | 22 | 26 | 30 | 35 | 39 |
| 2.625% | 7 | 9 | 11 | 13 | 15 | 17 | 19 | 21 | 25 | 29 | 33 | 37 |
| 2.75% | 7 | 9 | 10 | 12 | 14 | 16 | 18 | 20 | 24 | 28 | 31 | 35 |
| 2.875% | 6 | 8 | 10 | 12 | 14 | 15 | 17 | 19 | 23 | 26 | 30 | 34 |
| 3% | 6 | 8 | 10 | 11 | 13 | 15 | 16 | 18 | 22 | 25 | 29 | 32 |
| 3.125% | 6 | 8 | 9 | 11 | 13 | 14 | 16 | 17 | 21 | 24 | 28 | 31 |
| 3.25% | 6 | 7 | 9 | 10 | 12 | 14 | 15 | 17 | 20 | 23 | 27 | 30 |
| 3.375% | 6 | 7 | 9 | 10 | 12 | 13 | 15 | 16 | 19 | 22 | 26 | 29 |
| 3.5% | 5 | 7 | 8 | 10 | 11 | 13 | 14 | 16 | 19 | 22 | 25 | 28 |
| 3.625% | 5 | 7 | 8 | 9 | 11 | 12 | 14 | 15 | 18 | 21 | 24 | 27 |
| 3.75% | 5 | 6 | 8 | 9 | 10 | 12 | 13 | 15 | 17 | 20 | 23 | 26 |
| 3.875% | 5 | 6 | 8 | 9 | 10 | 11 | 13 | 14 | 17 | 20 | 22 | 25 |
| 4% | 5 | 6 | 7 | 9 | 10 | 11 | 12 | 14 | 16 | 19 | 22 | 24 |

# Refinance Break-Even Tables

| Break-Even Periods (in Months) | | | | | | | | | | | |
|---|---|---|---|---|---|---|---|---|---|---|---|

Term Left on Current Loan: 300 months  Income Tax Bracket: 40.00%
Term on New Loan: 30 years  Points and Costs: Paid in Cash
Points: 2.00%

| Other Closing Costs as a Percent of Loan Amount | | | | | | | | | | | |
|---|---|---|---|---|---|---|---|---|---|---|---|
| Interest Rate Reduction | .25% | .5% | .75% | 1.00% | 1.25% | 1.50% | 1.75% | 2.00% | 2.50% | 3.00% | 3.50% | 4.00% |
| 0.125% | None | None | None | None | None | None | None | None | None | None | None | None |
| 0.25% | None | None | None | None | None | None | None | None | None | None | None | None |
| 0.375% | None | None | None | None | None | None | None | None | None | None | None | None |
| 0.5% | 77 | 100 | None | None | None | None | None | None | None | None | None | None |
| 0.625% | 55 | 67 | 80 | 95 | 113 | 143 | None | None | None | None | None | None |
| 0.75% | 44 | 52 | 61 | 71 | 81 | 92 | 105 | 119 | None | None | None | None |
| 0.875% | 37 | 43 | 50 | 58 | 65 | 73 | 82 | 91 | 111 | 136 | None | None |
| 1% | 32 | 37 | 43 | 49 | 55 | 62 | 68 | 75 | 90 | 106 | 125 | 148 |
| 1.125% | 28 | 33 | 38 | 43 | 48 | 54 | 59 | 65 | 77 | 89 | 103 | 118 |
| 1.25% | 25 | 29 | 34 | 38 | 43 | 47 | 52 | 57 | 67 | 78 | 89 | 100 |
| 1.375% | 22 | 26 | 30 | 34 | 39 | 43 | 47 | 51 | 60 | 69 | 78 | 88 |
| 1.5% | 21 | 24 | 28 | 31 | 35 | 39 | 43 | 46 | 54 | 62 | 71 | 79 |
| 1.625% | 19 | 22 | 26 | 29 | 32 | 36 | 39 | 43 | 50 | 57 | 64 | 72 |
| 1.75% | 18 | 21 | 24 | 27 | 30 | 33 | 36 | 39 | 46 | 52 | 59 | 66 |
| 1.875% | 16 | 19 | 22 | 25 | 28 | 31 | 34 | 36 | 42 | 48 | 55 | 61 |
| 2% | 15 | 18 | 21 | 23 | 26 | 29 | 31 | 34 | 40 | 45 | 51 | 57 |
| 2.125% | 14 | 17 | 19 | 22 | 24 | 27 | 29 | 32 | 37 | 42 | 48 | 53 |
| 2.25% | 14 | 16 | 18 | 21 | 23 | 25 | 28 | 30 | 35 | 40 | 45 | 50 |
| 2.375% | 13 | 15 | 17 | 20 | 22 | 24 | 26 | 28 | 33 | 38 | 42 | 47 |
| 2.5% | 12 | 14 | 16 | 19 | 21 | 23 | 25 | 27 | 31 | 36 | 40 | 45 |
| 2.625% | 12 | 14 | 16 | 18 | 20 | 22 | 24 | 26 | 30 | 34 | 38 | 42 |
| 2.75% | 11 | 13 | 15 | 17 | 19 | 21 | 23 | 25 | 28 | 32 | 36 | 40 |
| 2.875% | 11 | 13 | 14 | 16 | 18 | 20 | 22 | 23 | 27 | 31 | 35 | 38 |
| 3% | 10 | 12 | 14 | 15 | 17 | 19 | 21 | 22 | 26 | 30 | 33 | 37 |
| 3.125% | 10 | 12 | 13 | 15 | 17 | 18 | 20 | 22 | 25 | 28 | 32 | 35 |
| 3.25% | 10 | 11 | 13 | 14 | 16 | 18 | 19 | 21 | 24 | 27 | 31 | 34 |
| 3.375% | 9 | 11 | 12 | 14 | 15 | 17 | 18 | 20 | 23 | 26 | 29 | 33 |
| 3.5% | 9 | 10 | 12 | 13 | 15 | 16 | 18 | 19 | 22 | 25 | 28 | 31 |
| 3.625% | 9 | 10 | 11 | 13 | 14 | 16 | 17 | 19 | 21 | 24 | 27 | 30 |
| 3.75% | 8 | 10 | 11 | 12 | 14 | 15 | 17 | 18 | 21 | 24 | 26 | 29 |
| 3.875% | 8 | 9 | 11 | 12 | 13 | 15 | 16 | 17 | 20 | 23 | 26 | 28 |
| 4% | 8 | 9 | 10 | 12 | 13 | 14 | 16 | 17 | 19 | 22 | 25 | 27 |

| Break-Even Periods (in Months) | | |
|---|---|---|
| Term Left on Current Loan: 300 months<br>Term on New Loan: 30 years<br>Points: 3.00% | Income Tax Bracket: 40.00%<br>Points and Costs: Paid in Cash | |

| | Other Closing Costs as a Percent of Loan Amount | | | | | | | | | | | |
|---|---|---|---|---|---|---|---|---|---|---|---|---|
| Interest Rate Reduction | .25% | .5% | .75% | 1.00% | 1.25% | 1.50% | 1.75% | 2.00% | 2.50% | 3.00% | 3.50% | 4.00% |
| 0.125% | None | None | None | None | None | None | None | None | None | None | None | None |
| 0.25% | None | None | None | None | None | None | None | None | None | None | None | None |
| 0.375% | None | None | None | None | None | None | None | None | None | None | None | None |
| 0.5% | None | None | None | None | None | None | None | None | None | None | None | None |
| 0.625% | 87 | 104 | 127 | None | None | None | None | None | None | None | None | None |
| 0.75% | 66 | 76 | 87 | 98 | 112 | 129 | 154 | None | None | None | None | None |
| 0.875% | 54 | 61 | 69 | 78 | 86 | 96 | 106 | 117 | 146 | None | None | None |
| 1% | 46 | 52 | 58 | 65 | 72 | 79 | 86 | 94 | 111 | 130 | 156 | None |
| 1.125% | 40 | 45 | 51 | 56 | 62 | 68 | 74 | 80 | 93 | 107 | 122 | 140 |
| 1.25% | 36 | 40 | 45 | 50 | 55 | 59 | 65 | 70 | 80 | 92 | 104 | 117 |
| 1.375% | 32 | 36 | 40 | 45 | 49 | 53 | 58 | 62 | 71 | 81 | 91 | 102 |
| 1.5% | 29 | 33 | 37 | 41 | 44 | 48 | 52 | 56 | 64 | 73 | 81 | 90 |
| 1.625% | 27 | 30 | 34 | 37 | 41 | 44 | 48 | 51 | 59 | 66 | 74 | 82 |
| 1.75% | 25 | 28 | 31 | 34 | 38 | 41 | 44 | 47 | 54 | 61 | 68 | 75 |
| 1.875% | 23 | 26 | 29 | 32 | 35 | 38 | 41 | 44 | 50 | 56 | 63 | 69 |
| 2% | 22 | 24 | 27 | 30 | 33 | 35 | 38 | 41 | 47 | 52 | 58 | 64 |
| 2.125% | 20 | 23 | 25 | 28 | 31 | 33 | 36 | 38 | 44 | 49 | 54 | 60 |
| 2.25% | 19 | 22 | 24 | 26 | 29 | 31 | 34 | 36 | 41 | 46 | 51 | 56 |
| 2.375% | 18 | 21 | 23 | 25 | 27 | 30 | 32 | 34 | 39 | 43 | 48 | 53 |
| 2.5% | 17 | 19 | 22 | 24 | 26 | 28 | 30 | 32 | 37 | 41 | 46 | 50 |
| 2.625% | 17 | 19 | 21 | 23 | 25 | 27 | 29 | 31 | 35 | 39 | 43 | 48 |
| 2.75% | 16 | 18 | 20 | 22 | 23 | 25 | 27 | 29 | 33 | 37 | 41 | 45 |
| 2.875% | 15 | 17 | 19 | 21 | 22 | 24 | 26 | 28 | 32 | 35 | 39 | 43 |
| 3% | 14 | 16 | 18 | 20 | 21 | 23 | 25 | 27 | 30 | 34 | 38 | 41 |
| 3.125% | 14 | 16 | 17 | 19 | 21 | 22 | 24 | 26 | 29 | 33 | 36 | 40 |
| 3.25% | 13 | 15 | 17 | 18 | 20 | 21 | 23 | 25 | 28 | 31 | 35 | 38 |
| 3.375% | 13 | 14 | 16 | 18 | 19 | 21 | 22 | 24 | 27 | 30 | 33 | 36 |
| 3.5% | 12 | 14 | 15 | 17 | 18 | 20 | 21 | 23 | 26 | 29 | 32 | 35 |
| 3.625% | 12 | 13 | 15 | 16 | 18 | 19 | 21 | 22 | 25 | 28 | 31 | 34 |
| 3.75% | 12 | 13 | 14 | 16 | 17 | 19 | 20 | 21 | 24 | 27 | 30 | 33 |
| 3.875% | 11 | 13 | 14 | 15 | 17 | 18 | 19 | 21 | 23 | 26 | 29 | 32 |
| 4% | 11 | 12 | 14 | 15 | 16 | 17 | 19 | 20 | 23 | 25 | 28 | 31 |